PROFITS, DEFICITS AND INSTABILITY

Also by Dimitri B. Papadimitriou

THE POLITICAL ECONOMY OF GREECE

Profits, Deficits and Instability

Dimitri B. Papadimitriou
Professor of Economics
Bard College, Annandale-on-Hudson, New York

Foreword by Paul Sarbanes

St. Martin's Press   New York

First published in the United States of America in 1992

Printed in Hong Kong

ISBN 0–312–06721–6

Library of Congress Cataloging-in-Publication Data
Profits, deficits, and instability/edited by Dimitri B.
Papadimitriou; foreword by Paul Sarbanes.
p.   cm.
Includes index.
ISBN 0–312–06721–6
1. Profit   2. Budget deficits.   3. Business cycles.
I. Papadimitriou, Dimitri B.
HB601.P8855   1992
338.5'42—dc20   91–17392
                                           CIP

For Jerome Levy (1882–1967)

Contents

Part II   Deficits

Part III   Instability

Foreword

In the spirit of the Jerome Levy Economics Institute, I would like to look ahead with you at the emerging economic agenda.

First and foremost, from the Washington perspective, is the budget deficit. On the occasion of the conference on 'Profits and Instability' at the Jerome Levy Economics Institute, Robert Eisner has spoken eloquently over the years about the impact of the budget deficit. Much of what he says needs to be considered very carefully. The fact remains, however, that in the policy arena the budget deficit and the decisions associated constitute an enormous obstacle to policy-making. The Congress is now engaged in a dialogue with the administration on this very question. What confronts the United States is a difficult situation. There is a budget deficit that is broadly perceived to be too high, particularly in a time of roughly 5 per cent unemployment.

The difficulty, simply put, is that the United States has not reached the point of putting together the kind of package that President Reagan was finally brought to consider after the stock-market break in October of 1987. Until that point, you will recall, the administration insisted that the sole approach to reducing the budget deficit lay in further restraint in domestic spending. The Congress rejected this approach because some of these programmes serve essential humanitarian needs and others, like education, research and development or physical infrastructure, represent an investment in the future strength of the USA's national economy. Failure to make the appropriate investments now will weaken the economy tomorrow. Furthermore, in the view of Congress, there are other dimensions that could help address the deficit question, namely, restraint in defence spending and increased revenues.

After the stock-market break, the President agreed to accept a broader framework for agreement, and indeed within three weeks an agreement was reached between the Administration and the Congress on the general outline of the budget and on deficit reduction targets. It included revenue, domestic programmes, and defence. Here, I would use the analogy of a three-legged stool. All the pressure cannot be placed on one leg only; the pressure must be distributed amongst the three. If that is done, there is a good chance of accomplishing something.

Unfortunately, the United States faces today the same stalemate it faced a year ago, and it is difficult at this point to predict how it will be resolved. It is unfortunate that during his campaign, President Bush made an absolute, uncategorical statement about the revenue leg of the stool, so to speak, that he has not disavowed. If we can break this deadlock and put together a balanced programme that moves the deficit steadily downwards year to year, we can also address the urgent question of public investment priorities.

Let me turn now to the international side of the economic agenda, beginning with the unprecedented trade deficit. In the early 1980s the merchandise trade account declined precipitously, in part reflecting an over-valued dollar which took a very heavy toll on the industrial sector in the United States. Since 1985 the value of the dollar has been brought down to more realistic levels, yet despite some improvements the trade deficit remains very high. While progress in reducing the budget deficit would help, it is not the sole factor determining the trade deficit; that relationship is very complex and by no means as direct as some have asserted. If the US is to be competitive in world markets, productivity will inevitably have to rise. This will require important policy changes at home, with a renewed commitment to education, training, civilian research and development, physical infrastructure. This course, however, raises anew the dilemma of seeking additional budget resources at a time when those resources are already severely strained.

What is more, the current account deficit is now in a sharply negative position. Although for years US investment earnings abroad more than compensated for the modest deficit in the USA's merchandise trade account, this is no longer the case. Since 1982 the United States has run a deficit in our current account, and virtually all forecasts show that the current account deficit will persist for a number of years. As a result, the United States has moved into a net-debtor status for the first time since the First World War. At the end of 1987 its net asset position was a negative $370 billion, and for 1988 it is expected to be in the range of $500 billion. It will continue to worsen so long as the current account remains in deficit, and some predict it will reach a trillion dollars before levelling off. Like any debtor nation, the United States will have to service this debt in the years to come.

The US debtor status is different in many important respects from that of other debtor countries; but it has implications not only for economic policy-making but for the political position of the United States in the international arena. Onno Ruding, the Dutch official serving as head of the IMF, summed up the American dilemma in blunt terms: 'The US,' he said, 'will have to tailor monetary and interest rate policy more to external considerations. My American friends are not accustomed to the fact that the United States is a highly indebted country.' These developments mark a sharp departure from historical trends in the US economy since the First World War. They raise urgent questions about the way we have defined our economic agenda since the end of the Second World War; in my view the fundamental assumptions underlying that agenda have shifted, and we have been slow to recognise the change.

US domestic and international economic issues are now inextricably intertwined. It is difficult indeed to address a problem in one arena without recognising its consequences in the other. The world economy is much more integrated now than in the past, and is moving increasingly in that direction. Europe 92, as it is called, is an obvious example. It will have significant consequences for the US but we are only slowly turning our attention to it.

In addition, long-standing international economic relationships have changed. The counterpart to US current account deficits are the large surpluses of such countries as Japan and Germany, Taiwan and South Korea. This phenomenon has no precedent in our experience, yet US policy must be made in the context of these changes.

Let me turn next to two issues very much related to the changed environment in which we find ourselves. One is the issue of Third World debt and how to manage it. The other is an issue which I predict will move increasingly to the front of the American economic and political agenda: the broad question of burden-sharing. In the not-too-distant future, this issue is likely to overshadow much of the Congressional debate on a range of issues.

The Third World debt problem is not new. For nearly a decade it has moved in a vicious cycle of crisis, half-solution, reversal, impasse. It has been clear for some time that austerity regimes have been self-defeating. Debtor countries adopting these programmes have experienced an outflow of scarce capital at a time when new capital resources from abroad have not been forthcoming. Economic growth has not resumed; rather, the result has been economic stagnation and declining standards of living.

Economic hardship gives rise to popular unrest or the loss of confidence in democratic institutions. In many countries, with emerging democratic governments, the challenge arises from demagogues of both the left and the right. The recent events in Venezuela were sobering evidence of that challenge. Venezuela, a nation which for thirty years has sustained a democratic system, has elected a populist leader. Yet as he moved to take some very important and difficult economic steps, the challenge arose right in the streets of his country.

For a number of years, the debt problem, although widely discussed, was not on the national agenda. Instead, it was seen as a problem involving debtor countries in the developing world and creditor banks in the industrial world, to be settled on an *ad hoc* basis. Indeed, in the 1982–8 period 101 debt reschedulings have been negotiated. Yet, the problem remains. The report issued by the Inter-American Dialogue called for a broader range of alternatives, extending to both debt and debt service reduction: 'Creditor countries and banks,' concluded the report, 'increasingly recognize that the economies of Latin America cannot be restructured and primed for growth without substantially higher levels of external capital, that the region's capital requirements cannot be met by new lending alone, and that debt reduction is therefore essential.'

A change in US thinking on this subject is also taking place. Secretary of the Treasury Nicholas Brady made a significant breakthrough in US policy and cast the debt issue in a new light. He noted in part: 'Commercial banks need to work with debtor nations to provide a broader range of alternatives for financial support including greater efforts to achieve both debt and debt service reduction and to provide new lending.' Well, this represents an important juncture in debt policy.

What Secretary Brady has thus far put forward is really more an approach than a detailed plan. With regard to debt policy, to paraphrase Winston Churchill, we are not now at the beginning of the end, or even the end of the beginning, but perhaps this is the beginning of the beginning.

In that sense I welcome the change that is now apparently taking place. As Treasury Secretary Donald Regan was a rigorous proponent of the austerity formula. But this policy was counterproductive, analogous to telling a thirsty person that the solution to his problem is to stop being thirsty. Mr Regan's successor at the Treasury, James Baker, who is now Secretary of State, understood the urgency of moving from austerity to a path of economic growth. To carry forward the thirst metaphor, Secretary Baker placed a glass on the table. Unfortunately, it proved to be empty.

The Brady approach goes a step further, in principle proposing to put water in the glass. But the details remain to be worked out. The critical question now is one of implementation: whether a laudable approach can be transformed into a timely and workable plan.

Finally, let me turn to the question of burden-sharing. Too often, in my view, this issue is seen in narrow terms, specifically as a question of the relative security obligations of NATO members and Japan. The United States spends roughly 6.5 per cent of GNP on defence; Japan spends 1 per cent. The United States thus provides the security umbrella under which Japan and other Pacific rim countries are sheltered. For some the remedy lies in having Japan assume the major responsibility for its own defence. I see it rather differently, and would note the idea is not only controversial among Japan's former enemies but within Japan itself. The solution lies, in my view, in Japan's carrying a larger part of the economic costs of the US security umbrella, since under that umbrella Japan is able to run a very significant trade surplus, currently $50 billion. It is important today to re-examine burden-sharing in the broader context of relative responsibilities in the international economy. The US assumed the central role in the world economy after the Second World War because the US occupied the dominant position in the world economy. It no longer enjoys unquestioned economic hegemony. Although still the world's largest economy, the United States is no longer the world's only economic power. It is long past time to look to other strong economies to make a significant contribution, and the Third World debt issue offers an excellent opportunity for others' participation and indeed the Brady Plan postulates a Japanese contribution. It is important to assure that it be done on a multilateral basis rather than a unilateral so that it does not create an exclusive trade relationship that will only complicate the very problems we are trying to solve.

Let me close by saying that the economic horizon is not so much cloudy as it is hazy. It will take the best efforts of the world of ideas and the world of affairs working together to address the questions I have tried to lay before you. The economic framework in which the United States is operating both at home and abroad must be adjusted to reflect changes in the world economy, because the framework in which it operates is no longer applicable. We need, therefore, to address the budget deficit, and trade deficits, the Third World debt and burden-sharing questions. We need a fundamental reassessment, to create a framework that is feasible and reasonable. Trivial ambitions, as someone remarked earlier, generally produce trivial results.

When Daniel Burnham built Union Station, once the imposing gateway to the nation's capital, he spoke about the psychological significance of form and vision. He believed, as he said, 'Only a grand vision can move men's minds.' I think we face such a challenge today, and know the Jerome Levy Economics Institute will play an important part in our efforts to meet it as the papers in this book reveal.

PAUL SARBANES

Acknowledgements

I would like to express my sincere gratitude to the Board of Governors of the Jerome Levy Economics Institute of Bard College for sponsoring the Conference on 'Profits and Instability' from which this collection of papers is drawn. I am indebted in many ways to the contributors for their promptness and their readiness in carrying out revisions. I want to thank Linda Christensen and Betty Shea for their hard work in preparing this book, Tim Farmiloe, our publishing editor, for his cooperation and Keith Povey's editorial assistance. But as always I must single out my assistant Susan Howard, whose skill, loyalty, devotion and good humour could not be matched by any other individual. I am indeed deeply grateful to her.

DIMITRI B. PAPADIMITRIOU

Notes on the Contributors

A. Asimakopulos was Dow Professor of Political Economy, McGill University until his death in 1990. He taught at MIT, University of Washington, Clare College, of Cambridge University, Monash University and served as managing Editor of the Canadian Journal of Economics from 1968 to 1972. He was a Fellow of the Royal Society of Canada, the author of many books and a contributor to many economic journals. His recent books include *Economic Theory, Welfare and the State* (also published by Macmillan) and *Investment, Employment and Income Distribution*.

John Caskey is Assistant Professor of Economics, Swarthmore College. Dr Caskey has published on macroeconomics and international finance in professional journals. He has been a consultant to World Bank in Angola, 1988 and Visiting Scholar, Federal Reserve Bank of Kansas City.

Richard H. Day is Professor of Economics, University of Southern California. Professor Day has taught at the University of Wisconsin, Madison, and his current research includes dynamic economic models, theory of unstable and chaotic economic systems, and the dynamics of information processes.

Richard DeKaser is Senior Economist for Data Resources, Inc. Mr DeKaser is currently investigating the historical determinants of industry profitability.

David Dollar is Assistant Professor of Economics, University of California-Los Angeles; Economist, The World Bank, 1989. Dr Dollar's areas of research are international diffusion of technology and productivity growth.

Gerard Duménil is a Researcher in Economics at CNRS. Dr Duménil is the author of a number of books and a contributor to many economic journals.

Robert Eisner is Professor of Economics, Northwestern University. He holds graduate degrees from Columbia and Johns Hopkins University. Dr Eisner is a past president of the American Economic Association and the author of many books and articles in economics. His recent books include *How Real is the Federal Debt* and *The Total Incomes System of Accounts*. Both books reflect Dr Eisner's current research interests on adjusted measures of national income and product accounts, budget deficits and debt.

Steven Fazzari is Associate Professor of Economics, Washington University-St Louis. Dr Fazzari's research on the link between finance and investment, the role of the financial system in propagating business cycles and the course of fluctuations in aggregate output and employment has been published in academic journals and conference volumes.

Stanley J. Feldman is Professor of Finance, Graduate School of Business, Bentley College and until recently Executive Vice President and Chief Economist, Data Resources, Inc. Dr Feldman is a contributor to many economic journals and his current research centres on using input–output techniques to quantify the role of technical change in industry and its implications for industry financial performance.

Reiner Franke is Associate Professor in Mathematics and Mathematical Economics and Research Scholar, University of Bremen. Dr Franke's research focuses on asset markets, capacity utilisation and variable productivity growth.

Albert Gailord Hart is Professor of Economics Emeritus, Columbia University. Professor Hart is actively involved in researching issues of fixed investment using *ex-ante* data.

John Hudson is Senior Lecturer in Econometrics, University of Bath. Dr Hudson is the author of many articles and of the book *Unemployment After Keynes*. Dr Hudson's research includes issues of unemployment, inflation, expectations, political business cycles, bankruptcies and general equilibrium models.

Marc Jarsulic is Associate Professor of Economics, University of Notre Dame. He holds a Ph.D from the University of Pennsylvania, has contributed to several economics journals and has edited *Money and Macro Policy*. His latest book is *Effective Demand and Income Distribution*. Dr Jarsulic is a former research fellow of the Jerome Levy Economics Institute.

Charles P. Kindleberger is Ford International Professor of Economics Emeritus, MIT. Dr Kindleberger is an expert on the theory of multinational corporations and a well-known authority on foreign trade. He has written texts on international economics and economic development, and he is the author of numerous books and articles. His most recent book is *The International Economic Order*. Professor Kindleberger is a past president of the American Economic Association, a member of the American Academy for the Advancement of Science and the Board of Advisors of the Jerome Levy Economics Institute.

Richard Kopcke is Vice President and Economist, Federal Reserve Bank of Boston.

Dominique Lévy is a Researcher in Mathematical Economics at CNRS. Dr Lévy is the author of a number of books and a contributor to many economic journals.

Thomas R. Michl is Assistant Professor of Economics, Colgate University. His research interests centre on macroeconomic profitability and technical change.

Hyman P. Minsky is Professor Emeritus of Economics at Washington University, St Louis. Professor Minsky has also taught at Brown University and the University of California, Berkeley. He is the author of *John Maynard Keynes, Can 'It' Happen Again?* and *Stabilizing an Unstable Economy* as well as contributor to many professional journals and the public press. Dr Minsky is a member of the Board of Advisors of the Jerome Levy Economics Institute and a member of the Executive Committee of the Eastern Economic Association.

Dennis C. Mueller is Professor of Economics at the University of Maryland; he is the author of many articles and the books *Profits in the Long-Run*, *The Corporation*, and *The Modern Corporation*. He is past President of the Southern Economic Association, Public Choice Society and the Industrial Organization Society.

Edward J. Nell is Professor of Economics, Graduate Faculty, New School for Social Research. Professor Nell was a Rhodes scholar and has taught at Wesleyan University, the University of East Anglia (UK), McGill University and the University of Bremen (FRG). Professor Nell has written extensively on the subject of economics and his many articles have been included in major economic journals. He is the author of *Rational Economic Man*, *Free Market Conservatism: A Critique of Theory and Practice*, and *Growth, Profits and Property*. His most recent book is *Prosperity and Public Spending*

Dimitri B. Papadimitriou is Executive Vice President and Professor of Economics, Bard College, and Executive Director of the Jerome Levy Economics Institute and the Bard Center. He has been Visiting Scholar, Center for Economic Planning and Research (Athens, Greece) and Wye Fellow, Aspen Institute. Dr Papadimitriou is a member of the Board of Governors of the Jerome Levy Economics Institute and a contributor to economic journals.

Paul Sarbanes is the Democrat US Senator from Maryland; Chairman, Joint Economic Committee; member, Banking, Housing and Urban Affairs and Foreign Relations Committees of the US Senate. Senator Sarbanes was educated at Princeton University, Phil Beta Kappa and Holds the LL.B., cum laude from Harvard Law School. He was a Rhodes scholar, Balliol College, Oxford University and is admitted to practise by Maryland Court of Appeals. Senator Sarbanes was assistant to Walter Heller, Chairman of the Council of Economic Advisers. Senator Sarbanes was elected to the US Senate in 1976 and re-elected in 1982.

Willi Semmler is Associate Professor, Graduate Faculty, New School for Social Research. Dr Semmler is the author of *Competition, Monopoly and Differential Profit Rates*, and *Competition, Instability and Nonlinear Cycles*, and a contributor to economic journals.

Anwar Shaikh is Chairman and Professor of Economics, Graduate Faculty, New School for Social Research. He is a former research fellow of the Jerome Levy Economics Institute of Bard College and in the past he has been a Distinguished Scholar to China under the auspices of the National Academy of Sciences, a research fellow for the Hamburg Institute for Social Science and the Lehrman Institute. He is an associate editor of the *Cambridge Journal of Economics* and is currently working on the nonlinear dynamics of effective demand, growth and cycles.

Tzong-yau Lin is Chief Economist at the Central Bank of China.

Wai-man Tse obtained a PhD from the University of Southern California.

Edward N. Wolff is Professor of Economics, New York University. Professor Wolff served as a research associate at the National Bureau of Economic Research from 1974 to 1977 and is the author of many articles published in books and economic journals. His most recent book was *Growth, Accumulation and Unproductive Activity*.

1 Introduction

Dimitri B. Papadimitriou

The papers in this volume were presented and discussed at the inaugural conference on 'Profits and Instability' of The Jerome Levy Economics Institute of Bard College on 16–18 March 1989. The purpose of the conference was to discuss recent research findings on various aspects of profits, deficits and instability, and the connection of these findings among the three issues themselves and their relevance to economic policy as well. Concerns and worries about the future that focus on the question of whether America is number one situate the problems of profitability, increasing debt and economic stability at centre stage.

Business accounting defines profits as the excess of total revenues over total costs. Alternately, in economic theory profits have been variously defined on the basis of what is being measured and for what purpose, for example as the return to ownership or the return to entrepreneurship, and as national income profits or real profits. The concept of profits, however, should not be reduced simply to matters of measurement alone, but rather to its role within the workings of an economic system. For the determination of profits can provide crucial insights into the interrelations between corporate investment and financing activity, the causes of instability and the secular and cyclical changes in production and employment.

To begin with the beginning, Smith, Ricardo and the other classical economists were primarily concerned with the wealth of nations and as such identified prosperity with the creation of surplus from which the concept of profit emanates. Smith recognised that higher rates of profit are associated with lower levels of capital stock employed and thus with a declining state of the wealth of society (Smith, 1937, book 1, ch. 9). Ricardo, in concert with Smith, asserted that higher profits were related with lower wages, but since in the progress of society and increasing wealth wages will be rising, profits will experience a downward trend (Ricardo, 1986, ch. 4). The Ricardian wage – profit trade-off established the relevance of the labour theory of value, a concept of crucial importance in the Marxian analysis, in determining the general rate of profit, that is, the ratio of surplus to the means of production (Marx, 1967, vol. 3).

Smith, Ricardo and Marx, each in his own way, sought to frame a logically coherent theory of the rate of profit within the classical system of value and distribution, but apparently not satisfactorily to the late-nineteenth-century thinkers. The classical analysis gave way ultimately to a new development of economic theory – the neoclassical theory – which

1

endeavoured to provide the solution for measuring value (outside the muddled thinking on the part of the classics aligned with the labour measure of value) on which a coherent theory of profit might be based (Eatwell, 1982, p. 213). The reconstruction of economic theory was shaped along the lines of a purer framework divorced from the political and ethical elements of classical thought. The need was to be met by the publication of three works, now considered economic classics, of W. S. Jevons, *Theory of Political Economy* (London, 1871), Karl Menger, *Grundsätze der Volkwirtschaftslehre* (Vienna, 1871) and Leon Walras, *Élements d' économie politique* (Lausanne, 1874–7), whose claim to fame was having initiated the so-called marginal revolution and its accompanied notion of general equilibrium. And even though the authors' method and substance of economic analysis were different, their theorising was nevertheless developed on more precise and scientific lines with an emphasis on microeconomic reasoning (Deane, 1989, ch. 7). The new theory concentrated on utility and rational behaviour, competition and efficiency in allocation of given endowments and production functions for optimum returns (profits), thus retreating from macroeconomic questions of stability and wealth accumulation.

By the end of the first quarter of the twentieth century, the neoclassical orthodoxy was much more advanced than the original state of 'Walras's economics' because of the needed attention to the erratic nature of money and inflation and high unemployment; and it was furthermore well grounded in the teaching of economics at university halls. The ethical preoccupations and the inherent uncertainties of the architecture of classical thought were replaced by the exactness of mathematical tools and concepts used to solve wide-ranging economic problems. These were mainly centred on policy issues of the day, for example unemployment, business fluctuations and policies affecting international trade.

But the answers provided, framed within the context of the new theory, were useful to the extent the underlying assumptions were realistic and consistent with the actual economic conditions and events; and moreover were dependent 'on the stability of the economic system [the new economics] was designed to interpret' (Deane, pp. 143–4). The response of the new theory to the problems of an unstable world economy was not satisfactory. The two canons on which it was anchored, that of perfect competition and perfect rationality, did not seem plausible, once imperfect competition and uncertainty were allowed to be brought in and when it was realised that perfect rationality presupposes perfect knowledge of the past and future as well, at the particular moment of choosing amongst a number of actions. Thus the 'Great Theory' of Jevons, Menger, Walras and Marshall was disconcertingly being pushed aside in preference of the theory of employment and output as emerged from the writings of Wicksell, Keynes, Joan Robinson, Hicks and Kalecki and as developed further by Samuelson, Kaldor and many others even to this day (Shackle, 1967, ch. 18).

Keynes's *General Theory of Employment, Interest and Money* (1936) provided a theoretical structure within which the problems of under-employment of capital and labour could be analysed. Macroeconomics began to resurface as the Keynesian management of aggregate demand for which strategic adjustment of government expenditures and tax schemes were prescribed. It was now that the budget deficits of the USA, France and Germany which were financing industrial recovery, were sanctioned; and that internal stability could be easily assured once fluctuations in aggregate demand and supply predictable by the appropriate fiscal policy, would avert their imbalance (Deane, ch. 9).

Not surprisingly, Keynes's macroeconomic prescriptions for a stabilised and prosperous economy were not immune to divergences of opinion as much political as methodological. These were primarily reflected in the conflict of those supporting *laissez-faire* with those of government interven-tion. It was not long before Milton Friedman's restatement of the quantity theory of money was launched as an attack on the core of the *General Theory*, and to initiate the development of monetarism. It was therefore predictable that views about economic policy from the now diverse com-munity of economists together with political arguments would lead to what appears as incomprehensible advice for solutions to contemporary econ-omic problems.

The collection of the papers contained in this book are based on various methodological views, but each in its own way aims to contribute to a better understanding of the current economic problems of declining profits, the explosion of private and public debt and the relationship of the two to economic instability, and in turn to participate significantly in the debate of public policy. A good number of the essays analyse the experi-ences of the 'good' or 'bad old times', not to frame the future in the image of the past, but to understand the particular conditions and arrangements that were important in those times.

The book opens with Hyman Minsky's essay (Chapter 2) in which he outlines the current state of instability in terms of financial relations as these affect financing activities. He specifically refers to the present over-indebtedness and cash payment commitments of firms whose liability structures and low profits lead to an overall macroeconomic financial fragility. Drawing from the Levy–Kalecki–Keynes framework, he force-fully argues for an apt intervention in the form of an effective stabilisation policy that provides inducements to invest and finance investment, control of the government deficit and the trade imbalance, all of which will ensure the stability between realised and expected profits.

In Chapter 3, A. Asimakopulos, also drawing from the Kaleckian frame-work, analyses the determinants of US profits, that is, aggregate retained earnings, as a macroeconomic variable over a thirty-nine year (1950–88) period. He finds that the determinants, namely *gross private domestic investment*, *government deficit*, *net foreign investment* and *personal savings*, affect aggregate retained earnings, the first three positively, the fourth negatively. These results provide an explanation of the significant changes that have occurred in these variables, especially in the 1980s, that are consistent with the structural changes of the US economy.

Both Thomas Michl in Chapter 4 and Stanley Feldman and Richard DeKaser in Chapter 5 focus on the US manufacturing sectors in their analyses on the rate of profit and the changes in the growth of profits respectively. Michl's analysis involves the empirical testing of a modified *wage-rate profit-rate frontier* relation (he uses wage-share profit-rate frontiers), to track the movements in the rate of profit from 1949 to 1987. He distinguishes three moments: first, from 1949 to 1970 in which the declining rate of profit is attributed to the rising wage share, especially during the 1960s; second, the 1970s during which the profit rate is 'squeezed' from the rising costs of raw material, and third, the 1980s during which the low profitability is assumed to be the result of the extensive and costly capital-using, labour-saving implementation of technical change. The essay by Feldman and DeKaser reviews the changes in profits over the period between 1950 and 1983 from an alternate perspective. By utilising a decomposition model, the authors are able to estimate the contributions to the change in profits from the following: sales volume, sales price, input price and factor productivity.

The essay by Dennis Mueller in Chapter 6 is an extension of his previous work (Mueller, 1986) on the *persistence* of profitability across firms. In this essay, Mueller compares the US estimates with those for Canada, West Germany, France, Japan, the UK and Sweden and raises important issues that need to be considered prior to instituting antimonopoly public policies.

Chapter 6 is supplemented, in Chapter 7, by an analysis of profit-rate and wage-rate *convergence* in a number of countries and industries. Edward Wolff and David Dollar present the results of their examination on convergence for twelve manufacturing industries in eight OECD countries over the 1963–83 period. They find considerable variation in profit rates among both countries and industries; and moreover that some tendency toward convergence exists across countries within industry, but none across industries within country. The chapter concludes with comments by Thomas Michl.

In Chapter 8, Albert Hart makes a convincing argument that expected profits rather than realised profits are the motivating factor for fixed investment. In his essay, he presents the results of his analysis of profit and fixed investment expenditures utilising both *ex post* and *ex ante* data.

John Hudson in the last essay (Chapter 9) of Part I, assesses the impact of profitability on the supply side of the economy. He finds that profits perform a crucial role in maintaining supply side equilibrium by encouraging the birth of new firms, as well as ensuring that inefficient firms do not utilise scarce resources. He favours a public policy of training new entrepreneurs to minimise firm bankruptcies which impose costs upon an economy.

The essays in the second part of the book concentrate on the issue of deficit and debt in both the private and public sectors and its effects on profitability and stabilisation of an economy. Charles Kindleberger in Chapter 10 discusses in his historically oriented essay the issue of quality of private debt. The recent unravelling of the 'junk bonds' market bespeaks of the importance of his concern. John Caskey and Steven Fazzari in Chapter 11 support Kindleberger's thesis by estimating the significance of debt and financial distress in macroeconomic stability. Their results show that effects of high indebtedness are 'sufficiently strong to overcome the economy's endogenous stabilising mechanisms' (page 213). They conclude with a number of policy recommendations that merit serious consideration.

Edward Nell considers the issue of corporate investment (Chapter 12), by asking the question: 'Why do corporations pay dividends?' (page 219). The focus of his essay is theoretical, and he answers the question by constructing a model in which corporate pricing behaviour is connected with output and investment decisions, financing options, and dividend payments. The chapter concludes with a thoughtful commentary by Richard Kopcke.

In the last chapter (13) of this part, Robert Eisner restates his more or less 'controversial' position on the necessity to conform government accounting to that practised by business (Eisner, 1986). He concludes that concerns about government deficits and debt may be unjustified, at least for the present time, if we were to properly account for many of the government capital expenditures and the appreciation in value of public assets. Moreover, he suggests that the trade deficit, although it needs to be controlled, is not yet alarming, if we were also to properly account for the appreciated values of our investments abroad.

The contributions in the third part of the book take up the issue of macroeconomic stability mostly at the theoretical level. The model formulations include linear and nonlinear representations of the interactions between the product and financial assets markets. Anwar Shaikh, in Chapter 14, pursues the Harrod-Domar problematic of the 'intractable instability of warranted growth'. He formulates a dynamic model that integrates Kalecki's macrofluctuations with Harrod's endogenous growth. His test for exogenous disturbances, for example an increase in government deficit spending, yields an initial Keynesian 'pumping' effect in output and employment, with a simultaneous Classical 'dampening'effect on the rate of growth of output and employment, with ultimately a state of instability.

The thesis that profitability is a prominent determinant of stability is advanced by G Duménil and D Lévy in Chapter 15. Utilising behavioural assumptions, the authors construct a dynamic model to analyse macro-economic stability. Their empirical analysis of US manufacturing industries for the post Second World War period shows that stability is related to the movements of the rate of profit.

Marc Jarsulic in Chapter 16 integrates the view that declining profitability is a structural determinant of instability with Minsky's financial fragility proposition resulting from over-indebtedness of firms. The macrodynamic model he develops can be used to show that an economy with debt can have stable and unstable regions whose proximity depends on changes in expectational and structural factors such as fixed or variable interest rate and income shares.

The essay by Franke and Semmler in Chapter 17 extends their previous work (Franke and Semmler, 1989) of dynamical macroeconomic models dealing with debt financing of firms, stability and business cycles. In this essay, they consider the role of expectations not in terms of the 'animal spirits' à la Keynes, but endogenously determined. Their model, which can be used to determine stability, is an *IS/LM* type macrodynamic model that explains the turning points of cycles in relation to the interplay of investment decisions and the holding of assets based on the weight of the 'expectations' variable.

The last chapter of the book (18) by Tzong-yao Lin, Wai-man Tse and Richard Day is also concerned with the relation of expectations and stability. The authors, utilising a neoclassical growth model with adaptive expectations, show how various qualitatively distinct kinds of behaviour can occur depending on the parameters of technology time preference, population growth, capital depreciation and the rate of neutral technological progress.

I hope that my attempt to bring out the relevance of the interrelationships between profits, deficits and instability contained in these, at first glance disparate, essays has been successful. But that I must leave to the reader to decide.

References

Deane, Phyllis, *The State and the Economic System: An Introduction to the History of Political Economy* (Oxford: Oxford University Press, 1989).
Eatwell, John, 'Competition', in Ian Bradley and Michael Howard (eds), *Classical and Marxian Political Economy* (New York: St. Martin's Press, 1982).
Eisner, Robert, *How Real is the Federal Deficit?* (New York: The Free Press, 1986).
Franke, R. and W. Semmler, 'Debt Financing of Firms, Stability, and Cycles in a

Macroeconomic Growth Model' in W. Semmler (ed.), *Financial Dynamics and Business Cycles: New Perspectives* (Armonk, New York: M.E. Sharpe, Inc., 1989).

Keynes, J.M., *The General Theory of Employment, Interest, and Money* (New York: Harcourt Brace Jovanovich, reprint 1967).

Marx, Karl, *Capital: A Critique of Political Economy*, vol. 3, *The Process of Capitalist Production as a Whole*, F. Engels (ed.). Reprint (New York: International Publishers, 1967).

Morishima, M., *Walras' Economics* (Cambridge: Cambridge University Press, 1977).

Mueller, Dennis C., *Profits in the Long Run* (Cambridge: Cambridge University Press, 1986).

Ricardo, David, *Principles of Political Economy*, vol. 1, P. Sraffa (ed.) (Cambridge: Cambridge University Press, 1986).

Semmler, Willi, *Financial Dynamics and Business Cycles: New Perspectives* (Armonk, New York: M.E. Sharpe, Inc., 1989).

Shackle, G. L. S., *The Years of High Theory* (Cambridge: Cambridge University Press, 1967).

Smith, Adam, *An Inquiry into the Nature and Causes of the Wealth of Nations*, Edwin Cannan (ed.) (New York: The Modern Library, reprint 1937).

Part I
Profits

2 Profits, Deficits and Instability: A Policy Discussion

Hyman P. Minsky

2.1 INTRODUCTION

Some four score years ago Jerome Levy had the insight that the cyclical behaviour of a capitalist economy depends upon the course of profits through time, and that this course depends upon the structure of what we would now call aggregate demand. In particular Jerome Levy advanced the proposition that in a simple small government capitalist economy, with external trade mostly in balance, total profits equals investment. In the argument that follows upon this insight, investment is shown to be the independent variable and profits the dependent variable. This leads to a simple equation: Profits = Investment.[1] In thinking about economics as he did, Jerome Levy anticipated the economics of Keynes and Kalecki.

However, investment takes place because profits are expected in the future, and in turn these future profits depend upon future investment. A paradoxical proposition results. Investment takes place now because the main actors in investment decisions, entrepreneurial business men and bankers, expect investment to take place in the future.

The simple skeletal profit equals investment relation can readily be expanded to allow for the structure of our sophisticated economy. Complications in the theory that are introduced in order to better mimic the world in which we live establish that in a complex capitalist economy:

Profits = Investment + Government Deficit − The Deficit on International Trade − Savings out of Wages + Consumption out of Profits.[2]

Each element on the right hand side of this profit identity can be replaced by a behavioural equation. This set up can be used to construct a macroeconomic model that first determines aggregate profits and then determines aggregate demand.

Jerome Levy's insight leads to the proposition that the mass of profits are determined by macroeconomic relations, in particular the structure of

11

demands and the availability of financing. Individual profit seeking businesses compete for shares in this aggregate. One aspect of this competition is that firms strive for efficiency in production, another is that firms strive to carve out markets that can be controlled. Each entrepreneur, aided and abetted by his bankers, aims to contain the exposure of his firm to profit eroding competition. This view, that macroeconomic relations determine aggregate profits and that market power and the technical conditions of production determine the distribution of profits among firms, is fundamentally different from the orthodox view which holds that both the mass and the distribution of profits are determined by the technical condition of production and market structure.

Therefore for stabilisation policy to be effective both realised profits and expectations of the future flow of profits need to be stabilised. In a modern economy profit expectations are stabilised by policy measures that operate upon the inducements to invest and the financing of investment, the government deficit, the propensities to consume and the foreign trade balance. If the economy's structural relations, such as the government's commitments to spend, the tax code and the size of government make the government deficit move quickly and strongly in the opposite direction from investment, then both realised and expected profits will be stabilised. Once rational bankers and business men learn from experience that actual profits do not fall when private investment declines they will modify their preferred portfolios to take advantage of the stability of profits.

By focusing on investment, the financing of investment, and the financing of positions in capital assets, a profit-oriented analysis of capitalist economies leads to an emphasis upon the proximate institutions with which business men interact as they seek financing. The structure of financial institutions and the instruments used in financing activity are important determinants of what happens. The flows of payments from debtors to fulfil financial contracts and the flows of funds from financial institutions to investing units are important in determining the path of the economy.

In our economy at every date liability structures priorly commit a portion of gross profits to the validation of debts even as contracts are negotiated which commit future profits to the payment of interest, dividends and the repayment of principle. The flow of such contract fulfilment payments to financial intermediaries, money managers and ultimate owners of financial instruments is a principle source of the funds that are available to acquire newly issued financial instruments. A shortfall of contract fulfilment payments implies that the market for new contracts to finance investment and positions in both newly produced and inherited capital will be adversely affected.

A comprehensive or systemic shortfall of profits below what had been anticipated or 'expected' when financial engagements were undertaken diminishes the flow of new financing for investment. This will tend to lower investment and lower gross profits. As the repercussions from an initial shortfall of cash to validate debts impinge upon financial institutions available financing decreases. This can lead to further subsequent shortfalls in cash available to validate debts. The financing circuit – the flow of funds from gross business profits to the validation of debts to the supply of funds for investment financing – implies that a potential for a debt deflation, such as took place between 1929 and 1933, exists in the normal processes of a capitalist economy (Fisher, 1933; Minsky, 1982; Caskey and Fazzari, 1987).

All economies with sophisticated financial institutions have developed formal or informal institutions that intervene to try to contain or abort debt deflations. These institutions are the central banks. In the United States the central bank includes not only the Federal Reserve System but also the various deposit insurance organisations.

The stock-market crashes of October 1987 and 1989, the debacle of the savings and loan associations and the FSLIC, the continuing problem of Latin American debts, and the unravelling of the junk bond market show that aborting or containing potential debt deflations is a serious current policy problem. Over the 1980s a dominant determinant of Federal Reserve System actions has been the need to act as a lender of last resort in response to financial trauma.[3]

The perspective on the economy that follows from Jerome Levy's insight emphasises money flows. This ties the size and type of incomes that are generated in production and distribution to the financial realities of the economy. A strong form of orthodox economic theory finds that what happens in financial markets to be of little or no importance in determining what happens in the economy.[4] In sharp contrast the economic theory that begins with the formulations of Levy, Keynes and Kalecki makes financial relations and the financing of activity critical determinants of system behaviour.[5]

2.2 FINANCING

In a modern capitalist economy, investment is always an exchange of money now which is used to pay for the creation of capital assets, for future money that is expected to be forthcoming as the capital assets are employed. Investment therefore depends upon present financing conditions and present views of future profits of the business men and bankers whose negotiations lead to investment financing.

From the perspective of investing units financing conditions are the terms upon which money now can be obtained for a range of contractual and contingent commitments to pay money in the future. The money raised now is presumably committed to the creation of capital assets. Thus the economy can be characterised by a structure of profit expectations and realisations by firms that operate the economy's private capital assets and who need to fulfil contractual payment commitments. Both the economy's capital asset and financing structure link the past, the present and the future.

Keynes's comment to the effect that an outstanding characteristic of the world in which we live is 'A system of borrowing and lending based upon margins of safety' is evident in financial commitments. The margins of safety that are embodied in contracts as they are negotiated reflect the beliefs of both the borrowers and the lenders as to the assurance of expected cash flows. These expectations reflect views about the nature of the economy as well as the rational man's knowledge that experience may falsify expectations. The rational assumption for an economist to make who attempts to deal seriously with investment is that business men and bankers are wise enough to understand that the theory they hold to be true which guides the formation of their expectations, may be false.

The liability structure of a business organisation is a prior commitment of profit flows. Similarly, household debt is a prior commitment of household income, government debt is a prior commitment of tax receipts, and international debts are prior commitments of balance of payments receipts. The complex financial structure of a modern economy rests upon the size and distribution of cash flows that the production of income generates.

2.3   UNCERTAINTY

Keynes introduced the proposition that financing is based upon margins of safety into the discourse. But no one *knows* the future that is relevant for financial decisions. Financial decisions are made on the basis of a future conjured up by borrowers and lenders as the result of negotiations in which information and disinformation are exchanged. The negotiated result reflects views about the prospects of a particular project in the light of the successes and failures of the economy over the recent and more distant pasts. The attitudes of agents toward risk, what economists call risk aversion, is not a genetic trait but rather reflects perspectives on how the economy works which are derived from both the recent and longer-term performance of the economy.

In the current world the formation of expectations that guide investment decisions has to combine:

1. the overall success of leading capitalist economies since the end of the Second World War;
2. the spate of financial trauma over the past twenty years whose extent and effects have been contained; and
3. the knowledge that in the 1930s capitalist economies were failures.

The ruling expectations will differ and therefore the behaviour of the economy will differ if business men and bankers determine their behaviour by using a model that maintains that capitalist economies are normally successful rather than by using a model that maintains that what happened between 1929 and 1933 was a normal though rare event which can happen again if appropriate circumstances reign. Investment and financing can be expected to ride right through a financial crisis if the first view is dominant whereas a financial crisis may have serious repercussions if the second view is dominant. A fundamental uncertainty in an economy where financial disruptions occur from time to time is what model of the economy guides the behaviour of the agents in the economy and what leads agents to switch from one model to another (Friedman and Laibson, 1989).

Agents' uncertainty as to the appropriate model to use in forming expectations is especially marked if a substantial number of years have elapsed since the last financial crisis that was associated with a deep depression. Over the intervening years both legislated and administrated actions and evolutionary developments changed the institutions of the economy. As a result the past has become a less than perfect guide to the behaviour of markets and institutions, especially in a world where central banks exist and are supposed to intervene to contain financial crises. Central banks are supposed to assure that 'It' (a debt deflation) will not occur, but 'Are they able to do so?' becomes a question that guides decisions. In particular what is the model of the economy that guides the actions of the present Central Bankers and under what circumstances will this model change is a relevant question for investing units and portfolio managers.

This fundamental uncertainty means that the margins of safety that units seek to attain will vary. Two types of margins of safety can be distinguished. One is the excess of expected cash flows in over the cash flows committed by the liability structure. The second is the asset structure of portfolios, where money and instruments which are readily marketable at prices that are largely assured provide safety in the form of liquidity. We can expect the desired level of both of these margins to diminish over periods of protracted success, and increase suddenly if events trigger a re-evaluation which increases the (subjectively held) prospect of a serious financial trauma.

If a firm's or its banker's desired margin of safety increases then units are likely to use available cash flows in excess of those needed to fulfil payment commitments to reduce debts. This will tend to decrease investment and when generalised to lower profits.

Simultaneously firms and bankers can try to increase their holdings of monetary or liquid assets. This will tend to lower the market price of shares, ordinary debts and capital assets. As interest rates on new debts increase to meet the rates available from depreciated inherited assets,

investment and therefore profits will tend to decrease. The reactions to a
shortfall of profits in a world characterised by uncertainty as to the correct
model of the economy to use in drawing inferences about how the economy
will behave may well make things worse not better (Caskey and Fazzari,
1987).

2.4 WHAT IS GOING ON NOW?

Irving Fisher published 'The Debt Deflation Theory of Great Depressions'
in 1933, soon after the Great Contraction that began in 1929 reached its
climax. Fisher identified a nine link process of debt deflation, which had as
an initial condition 'a state of over-indebtedness'. The over-indebtedness,
which Fisher never really explained, led to failures to fulfil commitments
on inherited debts, contractions in new debt, and declines in what we now
call Gross National Product, prices, wages, employment and profits. The
reactions by households, businesses and financial institutions, each attempting to do the best they could for themselves in the existing situation,
only made the situation worse. A debt deflation demonstrates that markets
are not always self-equilibrating within the time-frame relevant to human
life (Minsky, 1982).

Over the period 1929–33 current dollar GNP fell by roughly 50 per cent.
Over this period government did not decrease so that government as a
percent of GNP increased from 3 to 6 per cent. We know that humanitarian rather than economic impulses led the Roosevelt administration to
further increase the size of government. The recovery of 1933–6 took place
as profits revived under the stimulus of increased government deficits and a
revival of investment.

Were it not for the size of the government and lender of last resort
interventions the USA would have experienced a close approximation to a
debt deflation and a serious depression several times during the past twenty
years. Even with the size of government, the refinancing of the FSLIC by
the government, and the support that banks and other financial institutions
receive from the FDIC and the Federal Reserve, the current situation may
get out of control. This is so because of the smaller weight that the United
States now has in the world economy, the way the dollar has been
compromised by fiscal deficits and the questionable willingness and ability
of the now more important Europe and Japan to act as the sustainers of
global profits.

The 1980s began as an euphoric period for the banking and financial
community in the United States. The tax and spending policies of the
Reagan administration created a fiscal policy posture that was equivalent
to a war. The massive increase in the government's debt and the deteriora-

tion in the balance of trade are evidence for the war economics reading of the 1980s.

The exception to a war economy reading of the Reagan years is to be found in the labour market; Johnny did not go marching off to war. As a result the prolonged expansion and economic euphoria took place without creating a tight labour market (Kindleberger, 1978). The weakening of unions during the 1980s by government being unfriendly, protracted unemployment and product competition from imports meant that the expansion of the 1980s took place with a decrease in the rate of increase of money wages; an euphoric expansion took place even as the rate of inflation decreased. The wage and cartel driven inflation of the 1970s was replaced by a more modest inflation that was driven by profits and interest rates. The rentier was resuscitated in the 1980s.

It took 42 months for the Great Contraction of 1929–33 to reduce the economy to the chaotic conditions that ruled in the winter of 1933. Given the defences against an unconstrained debt deflation that were put in place in the aftermath of the great depression and which are still in place we would expect that a contraction would both take longer and not be as deep as that of the 1930s. We may be in a debt deflation and not know it.

2.5 APT AND INEPT INTERVENTION

The trajectory that an economy follows through time depends upon the interactions between endogenous dynamics, that would determine a not necessarily satisfactory path of the economy through time, and constraints and interventions which make up a structure of regulation which contains the economy to what are expected to be tolerable or satisfactory outcomes. It follows that over the longer run the satisfactory performance of a capitalist economy depends upon the aptness of the structure of regulation. Because profit-seeking agents learn how a regulatory structure operates and because regulation means that some perceived profit opportunities are not open to exploitation, there are incentives for agents to change their behaviour to evade or avoid the constraints.

This implies that over time the consequences of a structure of intervention changes. Interventions that start out being constructive can be transformed into sources of instability and inefficiency. The debacle of the thrifts and the hapless performance of the FSLIC as it tried to cope with the problems of the 1980s demonstrate that a structure of regulation and intervention that initially was successful can become perverse. The experience with the thrifts and the FSLIC is not an argument for *laissez-faire* but rather an argument that intervention cannot be frozen in time but must adapt as institutional and usage evolution takes place; successful capitalism requires both a structure of regulation and a sophisticated awareness of the way profit seeking drives the evolution of structures and behaviour.

The FSLIC debacle can serve as a model for the pitfalls that the regulation of financial institutions face if the regulators are not aware of how the incentive structure is affected by regulation. Initially, in what I call the Jimmy Stewart days, savings and loan associations were real estate financing institutions which operated within a restricted geographical area.[6] The great contraction played havoc with real estate values and the ability of households to fulfil mortgage commitments. Even though the typical mortgage was of relatively short duration, many savings and loan associations found themselves in a liquidity bind and with questionable net worths. Widespread runs and suspensions of payments occurred.

A major objective of the New Deal was to create an economy in which home ownership was widespread. Mortgage and deposit insurance were initiated to further this objective. Deposit insurance was not a free good. The premium structure imposed costs but more importantly the deposit insurance organisation had the right to examine and guide the behaviour of insured institutions. Examination and constraints upon behaviour were part of the deposit insurance deal. Savings and loan associations remained simple institutions with local home mortgages as their primary asset and pass-book savings as their main liability; a simple-minded management, such as that provided by the Jimmy Stewart character in the aforementioned film, would do.

Deposit insurance overcame depositor aversion created by the experience of 1929–33. With deposit insurance and bank examination in place there were three levels of protection for deposits:

1. Cash flows of the insured organisation, due to fund income supplemented by fee income, exceeded funding costs;
2. Equity of the deposit institutions; and
3. Deposit insurance.

The deposit insurance fund was protected against claims by the positive cash flows of the insured institutions and their positive net worth. The Home Loan Banks were put in place to provide liquidity, to enable S&Ls to acquire funds when they had a cash drain. The Home Loan Banks also provided channels by which funds in excess of what a local community could provide were available in rapidly growing regions. With mortgage insurance, deposit insurance and the provision of liquidity by the Home Loan Banks it was believed that the standard home loan mortgage could be safely transformed into a long-term, fixed interest rate, and fully amortised instrument for which the monthly payments for modest homes were in line with what a worker earned (Hart, 1938).

The flaw in this set-up was that the S&Ls were funding long-term fixed interest rate mortgages with short-term funds. The rates on the mortgages in portfolio set an implicit ceiling to the deposit rates and the cost of services that the S&Ls could meet. The institutional structure put in place in the 1930s assumed that interest rates would not escalate rapidly, for example, that accelerating inflation would not be a major nor a lasting problem, and that alternative assets to savings deposits that paid market interest rates which included inflation premiums would not be available for 'small' depositors.

The Volcker era, 1979–86, saw high and rapidly escalating interest rates and the development of new instruments which offered risk averse investors presumably safe returns. These developments forced the savings banks to meet the market. The result stripped the savings banks of their surplus cash flows and equity. The only protection remaining for depositors was the protection afforded by deposit insurance. Given the evaporation of the protections that positive cash flows and institutional equity provided for the deposit insurance fund, supervision of the thrift institutions should have tightened. Instead an ideology of deregulation ruled the land and the savings institutions were granted the ability to broaden their portfolios by buying corporate debts and by financing land development and construction; they were permitted to move into the high risk part of the financing structure.

As many savings and loan associations had a negative net worth and were experiencing losses, it was possible to buy control of a great deal of funds with a small investment. Business plans to grow out of the current losing situation by acquiring high-yielding short-term construction and land development positions were put forth and accepted by regulatory authorities.

If a banker has a customer whose cash flow is negative and whose net worth is evaporating then the banker's supervision becomes ever more close. Bankers are known to become intrusive in such workout circumstances. Bankers do not give zero or negative net worth customers an unlimited line of credit. In the case of the savings and loan associations even as their cash flows and equity were stripped supervision was relaxed; they were in effect given unlimited lines of credit.

During the 1980s the supervisory oversight of savings institutions became ever more relaxed. The negative net worth organisations took on high interest rate assets and increased their liabilities, presumably guided by a strategy of growing out of the negative net worth situation. One objective was to increase fee incomes and lessen the reliance on fund incomes. Fee incomes are associated with volume. Relaxing loan standards is one way to obtain volume.

This strategy enabled many S&Ls to book large profits on the basis of accrued but not as yet paid income. A slowdown in real estate activity meant that underlying land and development assets yielded no income. No cash was available to pay financing costs. The S&Ls solution was to allow debtors to pay interest by adding to the amount owned. The institutions booked such accruals as income and used them to pay interest and other expenses.

Deposit insurance was never insurance in the sense that there was an actuarially sound assessment of exposure and a fee structure that financed expected losses. Deposit insurance was able to pay for the occasional losses of the 1935–80 period, but as almost all losses were due to fraud or gross incompetence, a bonding operation would have sufficed. Deposit insurance as protection against systemic losses by depositors at banks and thrift institutions was always a pledge of the full faith and credit of the United States (Campbell and Minsky, 1987). Although Congress had asserted the full faith and credit obligation from the beginning of deposit insurance, Congress evaded funding the payoff of deposits in the early part of the 1980s when losses by S&Ls overwhelmed the insurance funds reserves.

The collapse of savings institutions and their deposit insurance fund was undoubtedly due to a combination of ignorance and venality; officials were ignorant of the relevant economics and a risk exposure situation in the zero and negative net worth institutions that constituted an invitation to scoundrels. An initially apt system of intervention evolved into an inept system. Intervention is necessary but has to be done wisely. Policy-makers cannot be guided by a naive theory which does not allow for scoundrels in which unconstrained markets always reach a best result.

The funds provided by Congress to resolve the problem of the thrifts seems certain to fall short of the amount needed to validate outstanding deposits. Further funds will have to be provided. The commitment of the full faith and credit of the United States to the insuring of deposits was made in the 1930s. The question that we now face is how good is the full faith and credit of the United States.

Debts are prior commitments of future incomes. The incomes being committed as Congress authorises the issuance of debts are future tax receipts. But the United States government now has a structural deficit; it is engaged in a variety of Ponzi finance. If the full faith and credit of the government is to have lasting worth then its budget has to be in a structural surplus; for example, the budget will be in surplus whenever the economy is at full employment and there is no special spending such as a war brings forth.

2.6 POLICY

The recent S&L refinancing placed the government's full faith and credit on the line. But the value of the government's full faith and credit depends upon whether the government's revenues are ample; it is the possibility of a positive cash flow to the government that makes government debts valuable and central banks powerful. An in principle balanced budget or surplus when the economy is operating in a normal fashion is needed for both the prevention of inflation and the containing of deep depressions.

The haemorrhaging of United States profits by way of the trade deficit needs to be stopped. The policies of the great asset holding surplus countries, Germany and Japan, can be described as beggaring their neighbour; their prosperity rests upon impoverishing the United States.

A tariff for revenue purposes will improve both deficits. An exclusionary tariff such as Smoot Hawley represented, is not desirable. It is likely that a tariff for revenue purposes will not be sufficient to meet the enlarged deficit that the Savings and Loan refinancing will lead. The usual suspects such as a substantial excise tax on gasoline and a value added tax need to be considered.

Tariffs increase the market power of domestic firms and unions. A strong pro-competition 'anti-trust' policy needs to accompany a tariff. Labour's demand for good jobs at good pay will be at least partially satisfied by the price differential induced by a tariff.

As financial and economic uncertainties become more evident, the policy agenda will turn to the creation of a financial structure that is less subject to excesses of speculation and which supports enterprise.

2.7 CONCLUSION

We may now be closer to the Fisher initial condition for a debt deflation, over-indebtedness, than ever before in the era of big government capitalism that was ushered in by the Second World War. As the S&L crisis, other banking system crises, and the stock-market declines of 1987 and 1989 show, the US experienced events which were capable of triggering a debt deflation. These crises have taken place as the United States clout, to use a good Chicago word, is much diminished. The next time, the United States may not be able to do the job of containing a crisis without the active cooperation of the major exporting economies. It is questionable whether the appropriate international economic cooperation will be forthcoming. In these quite possible circumstances the questions raised and the approach taken by Jerome Levy some eighty years ago – and by Keynes and Kalecki some fifty years ago – will take on a new urgency even as the way of thinking about economics that they developed takes on a greater relevance.

Notes

1. This formation has appeared in the literature as, for example: S. J. and D. A. Levy, *Profits and the Future of American Society* (New York: Harper & Row, 1983); M. Kalecki, 'The Determinants of Profits', in *Selected Essays on the Dynamics of a Capitalist Economy (1933–1970)*, ch. 7 (Cambridge: Cambridge University Press, 1971); H. P. Minsky, 'Finance and Profits', in H. P. Minsky, *Can 'It' Happen Again* (Armonk, NY: M. E. Sharpe, Inc., 1982), and *Stabilizing an Unstable Economy* (New Haven: Yale University Press, 1986).
2. This expanded profit equation can be considered as the equivalent of the $Y = C + I + G \, X - M$ equation that is the base of the econometric forecasting models.
3. This has been documented by R. M. Giordano, *The Federal Reserves Response to the Stock Market Crash* (Goldman Sachs Economic Research Group, New York, 1987).
4. The classic statement is the Modigliani-Miller theorem. F. Modigliani and M. M. Miller, 'The Cost of Capital, Corporation Finance and the Theory of Investment', *American Economic Review*, 48 (June 1958) pp. 261–97.
5. Another way of phrasing the above is that money is neutral in orthodox theory but it is not neutral in the economic theory that is built on a Levy–Kalecki–Keynes framework.
6. The reference is to *It's a Wonderful Life*, a classic film.

References

Campbell, C. and H. P. Minsky, 'How to Get Off the Back of a Tiger' or 'Do Initial Conditions Constrain Deposit Insurance Reform?', in *Merging Commercial and Investment Banking* (Chicago: Federal Reserve Bank of Chicago, 1987).
Caskey, J. and S. Fazzari, 'Aggregate Demand Contractions with Nominal Debt Commitments: Is Wage Flexibility Stabilizing?', *Economic Inquiry*, 25 (1987).
Fisher, I., 'The Debt Deflation Theory of Great Depressions', *Econometrica* (1933).
Friedman, B. and D. Laibson, 'Implications of Extraordinary Movements in Stock Prices', *Brookings Papers on Economic Activity*, vol. 2 (1989) pp. 137–89.
Giordano, R. M., *The Federal Reserves Response to the Stock Market Crash* (New York: Goldman Sachs Economic Research Group, 1987).
Hart, A. G., *Debts and Recovery 1929/1937* (New York: Twentieth Century Fund, 1938).
Kalecki, M., 'The Determinants of Profits', in *Selected Essays on the Dynamics of a Capitalist Economy (1933–1970)* (Cambridge: Cambridge University Press, 1971).
Kindleberger, Charles, *Manias, Panics and Crashes: A History of Financial Crises* (New York: Basic Books, 1978).
Levy, S. J. and D. A., *Profits and the Future of American Society* (New York: Harper & Row, 1983).
Minsky, H., *Can 'It' Happen Again* (Armonk, New York: M. E. Sharpe, Inc., 1982).
Minsky, H., *Stabilizing an Unstable Economy* (New Haven: Yale University Press, 1986).
Minsky, H. P., 'Debt Deflation Processes in Today's Institutional Environment' *Banca Nazionale Del Lavoro Quarterly Review* (December 1982) pp. 375–95.
Modigliani, F. and M. M. Miller, 'The Cost of Capital, Corporation Finance and the Theory of Investment', *American Economic Review*, 48 (June 1958) pp. 261–97.

3 The Determinants of Profits: United States, 1950–88

A. Asimakopulos

3.1 INTRODUCTION

The total profits obtained in an economy in a particular interval of time is a macroeconomic variable, and it can be shown to be determined by the net effects of four other macroeconomic variables. These variables are gross private domestic investment, the government deficit, net foreign investment and personal saving. This approach to the determination of profits can be traced to Kalecki (1954), but there are strong hints of it in the Marxist literature on the realisation of profits. There are encouraging signs that this general approach is gaining wider currency. It has a prominent role in two recent publications, Levy and Levy (1983), and Minsky (1986).

An examination of the determinants of profits in the United States economy in the post-war period shows that there have been substantial changes in the relative importance and even in the nature of the influence of these determinants. There have also been substantial changes in the relative importance of the incomes that can be considered as constituents of profits, where the profits category includes interest and dividend payments. All these changes reflect the significant structural changes that have been occurring in the United States economy. The tracing-out of these changes in the determinants of profits, and in the constituent parts of total profits, can thus be a useful first step in the examination of the structural changes that have occurred in the United States economy over the post-war period.

3.2 PROFITS IN A SIMPLE MODEL OF A CAPITALIST ECONOMY

The two major categories of incomes in capitalist economies are wages and profits. Wages are the payments for all the labour services used in production, while profits are the incomes received for the organisation of production and for the use of capital in production. In simple models of capitalist economies, both rent on land that is an element of production, and interest payments for the loan of capital used in production, are included in profits.

Another distinction between incomes that is useful for our purposes, is the distinction between contractual and residual incomes. Contractual incomes are those that are paid as a result of fixed arrangements. For example, labour of a particular type is hired at some stipulated rate and paid according to hours worked. Interest and rent payments could also be contractual. They depend on the terms at which loans and land are made available to those organising production. But some part of profits (and thus the value for total profits) must always be residual and dependent on the extent to which receipts turn out to exceed costs. There is no one to guarantee the incomes of those who organise production and who make payment commitments to those who provide labour services, loans and land. These incomes of the organisers of production depend, in the final analysis, on how well their ventures into an environment that can never be fully known, turn out. Some capital incomes are also residual, for example the returns obtained for capital provided by the organisers of production, and to capital used by others to buy 'shares' in the enterprise. These incomes depend on the fortunes of the enterprise. Some part of labour incomes might also be residual – for example, some employees in managerial positions might receive bonuses whose values depend on how well the enterprises had fared in a particular period. However, at the level of abstraction of this paper, labour incomes are taken to be contractual, with all the residual elements appearing in the profits category. (Alternatively, the bonuses paid to managers can be seen as part of the disposition of profits.)

For gross profits – in the broadest sense of this term – to be earned in any period, the revenues of a production enterprise (or firm) in that period must be greater than its total payments for labour and materials used in that period. When these total revenues, and total payments, are each aggregated over all firms, with the sum of the latter then being subtracted from the sum of the former in order to obtain total gross profits for the economy, the interfirm transactions for materials used in current production cancel out. It can thus be concluded that in a closed economy, with no government taxes or expenditures, total gross profits are equal to the difference between total revenues (less those arising from the purchases of materials by other firms that use them in current production) and total labour payments. The complete expenditure of current labour incomes on the goods produced by firms can only cover the wage costs of current production, with a positive value for profits dependent on expenditures from non-labour income sources. (If only part of current labour incomes are spent on goods, with the remainder being saved, then 'outside' expenditures must cover this saving out of wage incomes (Sw) before profits can be obtained.) These non-labour sources of expenditures in this simple model could be the various components of profits, wealth, or loans. The expenditures themselves could be on consumption goods (referred to here as capitalists' consumption (Cc)), or on investment goods (I). (Investment goods, in this context, include all the various items of capital equipment, buildings, etc., as well as the net increase in the values of stocks of materials, goods in process, and finished goods that are held by producers.) An equation for the determination of gross profits in this case, can be written as:

$$P = I + Cc - Sw \tag{1}$$

Equation (1) represents a definitional relation; it follows from the definition of profits and the cancellation of some revenues and costs. In spite of this, it can be read, under certain circumstances, as a causal relation that not only shows the values for total profits, but also the causal determinants of these values. If the interval of time used in the analysis is short, so that the current expenditures on the right-hand side of the equation are independent of the current profits on the left-hand side, then equation (1) represents a causal relation. Profits, in this short interval of time, are determined by (and are not just equal to) the sum of investment and capitalist consumption expenditures, minus saving out of wages. Since profits must, by definition, be equal to this combination of these items which are independent of current profits, then it follows that these items can be considered to be the determinants of these profits.[1]

The assertion of a causal relation that goes from right to left in equation (1) is not inconsistent with the recognition that profits are important determinants of capitalists' expenditures, but profits only affect these expenditures after a time-lag. It is the existence of this time-lag that allows for a one-way causal relation from expenditures to profits over a shorter interval of time. If the basic interval of time for the analysis is a quarter of a year, then in that interval capitalists' expenditures are largely independent of current profits, and the requirements for a causal interpretation of equation (1) is satisfied. Capitalists' consumption expenditures can be said to be a function of current and expected future incomes and of wealth. That portion of current incomes made up of interest receipts is largely determined by the terms at which loans were made in the past. This dependence on conditions in earlier periods also holds for current dividend income, since these dividends are largely based on profits in preceding quarters and the long-term dividend policies of firms. It is thus not unreasonable to assume that capitalists' consumption expenditures in a particular quarter of a year are independent of profits in that quarter. Current investment expenditures, which are largely the result of investment decisions made in the past, are also very much influenced by past profits. These profits have influenced expectations of future profitability that have a positive effect on investment decisions, and they provide, directly and indirectly, funds for investment expenditures. The retention of profits by firms provide a direct source of funds for investment spending, but a record of profitability also serves as an indication to lenders that these firms are acceptable risks. It is thus reasonable to assume that investment expenditures in a particular quarter are independent of the receipt of profits in that quarter. The value for workers' saving (with consumers' credit it might even be negative) is also independent of current profits. The requirement for a causal interpretation of equation (1), if the basic interval of time is a quarter of a year, is thus satisfied.

The profits term (P) shown in equation (1) covers the incomes of capitalists – interest (IN) and dividend (D) payments – as well as the gross retained earnings of firms (P'). These interest payments are contractual and, subject to the non-bankruptcy of firms, are independent of the value for profits in a particular quarter. Given the time-lag in the declaration of dividends, and the long-term nature of the dividend policies of firms, dividend payments in a quarter can also be considered 'contractual' as far as the current period is considered. Gross retained earnings are thus the residual incomes for the quarter, with their values being equal to the difference between gross profits and the sum of contractual payments that fall in the profits category. The value for gross retained earnings is the balancing item in the profits equation, given the independent determination (with respect to this quarter's profits) of the values for the other items in equation (1). It is the residual income that is determined by economic conditions in the particular interval of time, and by the enterprises' contractual commitments to capitalists for the period.

When current interest and dividend payments are subtracted from both sides of equation (1), an equation for gross retained earnings is derived.

$$P' = I - (D + IN - Cc) - Sw \tag{2}$$

With capitalists' incomes being the sum of dividend and interest payments (receipts), the term in brackets on the right-hand side of equation (2) is equal to capitalists' saving for the period. This equation can thus be rewritten as

$$P' = I - PS \tag{3}$$

where PS is total personal saving. The necessary equality of the two sides of equation (3) can still be used to provide a causal explanation for current gross retained earnings. Gross investment (a positive effect) and personal saving (a negative effect) are the determinants of current gross retention by firms. A familiar rearrangement of equation (3), with personal saving added to both sides, shows the necessary equality between saving and investment, but this does not eliminate the causal explanation for gross retained earnings provided by this equation if the time interval is short. It is the independently determined values for gross private domestic investment and personal saving that determine the quarterly value for gross retained earnings.

3.3 PROFITS IN AN OPEN ECONOMY WITH GOVERNMENT ACTIVITY

The extension of the simple model of a capitalist economy to allow for international trade and government taxation and expenditure, does not change the basic nature of the profits equation. What this extension does is to increase both the potential sources of 'outside' expenditures that contribute to profits, and the potential sources of 'leakages' that diminish profits. Government expenditures on goods and services produced by firms add to profits, while taxes decrease after-tax profits directly if they are levied on profits, and indirectly if they prevent expenditures on goods that would have taken place out of untaxed wage or capitalists' incomes. Export sales are another source of receipts that add to gross profits, while imports drain away expenditures that could potentially have resulted in higher profits. It is the net effect of the introduction of the government and foreign trade sectors that are relevant in a profits equation. The gross retained earnings of firms (still denoted by P', even though it is now obtained by subtracting profits taxes as well as dividend and interest payments from gross profits for the quarter) can be shown as being determined by the items in equation (4).

$$P' = I + GD + IS - PS \tag{4}$$

where: GD is the government deficit, the difference for all levels of government between total expenditures on goods and services plus transfer payments, and total revenues from all sources of taxation; IS is the economy's surplus on foreign transactions, or its net foreign investment. PS, as in equation (3), stands for personal saving, but the income component of this item is now made up of personal incomes including transfers, less personal taxes. Both consumption and investment expenditures can now be directed to foreign as well as to domestic goods.

The introduction of the government and foreign sectors has not changed the causal interpretation of the profits equation where it refers to a relatively short interval of time. The values for the items on the right-hand side of the equation are largely independent of current retained earnings, and thus they can be taken to be their determinants. (The estimates for government revenues in the national accounts may include estimates of taxes on current profits, so that estimates of the government deficit may not be independent of current profits. This, and possibly other examples of some small feedbacks from estimates of current profits to the values for the items on the right-hand side of equation (4), are not sufficient to alter the conclusion that the main causal direction for that equation is from the right to the left.) These values on the right-hand side of equation (4) cannot be read as showing that a given increase in, say, investment will result in an equal increase in gross retained earnings. This increase in investment, by promoting economic activity, will tend to increase government revenues and to reduce the government deficit. Part of the increase in investment expenditures could be directed to imports, thus reducing the international surplus (net foreign investment), and personal saving might also be affected. The net effect on profits of an increase in investment thus depends on how this increase affects the values of the remaining causal determinants in the particular quarter.

The following example of this interdependence between the determinants of profits also makes clear the importance of the particular historical circumstances in which a change takes place. Consider the net effects on profits of changes in government tax and expenditure programmes that increase the government deficit. If this change occurs in a situation where there is a considerable amount of unemployment, with a history of relatively stable prices and no immediate concerns about inflation, then it probably will result in increased output and employment, with only a modest decrease in the international surplus. A substantial portion of the change in the government deficit will thus be reflected in an increase in gross retained earnings. If, however, the change in budgetary policy occurs in a situation where there is considerable concern about inflation, it might be accompanied by a monetary policy, and bond-market reactions, that result in sharply higher interest rates. This could have an adverse effect on investment, while also leading to an appreciation in the country's exchange rate as funds flow in from other countries to take advantage of high interest rates. The country's international competitive position would be adversely affected by such an appreciation in its exchange rate, with imports being encouraged and exports being discouraged. The net effects on gross retained earnings of this increase in the government deficit might thus be relatively small under these circumstances.

Data for the items in equation (4) are readily available on a quarterly basis from the national accounts estimates for any country. They can be rearranged to show the necessary equality between saving and investment, or to show the necessary equality between net saving in the private sector and the sum of government deficit and net foreign investment. (In the national accounts a statistical discrepancy is introduced in order to ensure this equality, because of errors of estimates that are not necessarily offsetting.) This latter equality is obtained from equation (4) by transferring the personal saving and gross private domestic investment terms to the left-hand side of the equation, as shown in equation (5).

$$P' + PS - I = GD + IS \qquad (5)$$

No causal direction can be inferred between the two sides of equation (5), because of the interdependence of the current values of some of the items on both sides of the equation. The presence of P', an item whose value is determined residually, as part of the gross private sector surplus means that it is this surplus that takes the value required to validate equation (5). For example, a reduction in tax rates that results in a higher government deficit that is not fully offset by a lower value for net foreign investment, means that the gross private sector surplus must be higher. If it is not sufficiently higher because of induced, or independently determined changes in personal saving or investment, then it is higher because of the changed value for gross retained earnings.

From the national accounts estimates it is also possible to obtain data on dividend and net interest payments of businesses, and thus it is possible to trace the changes over time in the relative importance of the three main components of (after-tax) gross profits. There were, as we shall see, substantial changes in the relative importance of these items in the United States economy over the period of our study.

An examination of quarterly data for the United States economy in the post-war interval will also indicate the important changes in the determinants of profits over that interval. The reasons for these changes lie in the decisions made by large numbers of individuals and groups that have affected investment and consumption expenditures; the changes in trade laws, exchange rates and other factors that affect international competitiveness and the trade balance; and the changes in the structures of the government budgets that affect the government deficit. A macroeconomic presentation such as this one can only present an overall view of the net effects of the many changes that are taking place in any economy. It is not a substitute for a detailed examination of the particular changes that result in the net changes picked up by the macroeconomic data.

3.4 THE DETERMINANTS OF UNITED STATES PROFITS, 1950–88

The data for gross retained earnings and their determinants are summarised in Table 3.1 on the basis of the turning points for the National Bureau of Economic Research reference cycles. Seven full cycles, and a long (continuing) expansion, occupy the almost 39-year (154-quarter) period of

Table 3.1 Average values of gross retained earnings and their determinants ($ billion) 1950–88

	P'	I	(% of P')	GD	(% of P')	IS	(% of P')	PS	(% of P')
(Cycle 1: 50:1 → 54:2; Expansion (A): 50:1 → 53:2; Contraction (B): 53:3 → 54:2)									
1.	37.0	55.5	(150.0)	0.3	(0.8)	−0.4	(−1.1)	16.4	(44.3)
A.	36.2	56.5	(156.1)	−2.2	(−6.1)	−0.3	(−0.8)	15.9	(43.9)
B.	39.9	52.1	(130.6)	9.2	(23.1)	−0.5	(−1.3)	18.1	(45.4)
(Cycle 2: 54:3 → 58:2; Expansion (A): 54:3 → 57:3; Contraction (B): 57:4 → 58:2)									
2.	50.1	67.8	(135.3)	−0.2	(−0.4)	2.2	(4.4)	19.9	(39.7)
A.	49.8	69.3	(139.2)	−2.3	(−4.6)	2.3	(4.6)	19.2	(38.6)
B.	51.4	61.6	(119.8)	9.2	(17.9)	2.1	(4.1)	22.5	(43.8)
(Cycle 3: 58:3 → 61:1; Expansion (A): 58:3 → 60:2; Contraction (B): 60:3 → 61:1)									
3.	59.2	76.3	(128.9)	2.3	(3.9)	1.3	(2.2)	22.3	(37.7)
A.	59.1	78.0	(132.0)	2.6	(4.4)	0.1	(0.2)	22.7	(38.4)
B.	59.5	71.8	(120.7)	1.6	(2.7)	4.6	(7.7)	21.2	(35.6)
(Cycle 4: 61:2 → 70:4; Expansion (A): 61:2 → 69:4; Contraction (B): 70:1 → 70:4)									
4.	89.1	117.9	(132.3)	3.1	(3.5)	4.2	(4.7)	36.8	(41.3)
A.	87.1	114.4	(131.3)	2.2	(2.5)	4.1	(4.7)	34.5	(39.6)
B.	106.7	148.8	(139.5)	10.6	(9.9)	4.8	(4.5)	57.7	(54.1)
(Cycle 5: 71:1 → 75:1; Expansion (A): 71:1 → 73:4; Contraction (B): 74:1 → 75:1)									
5.	146.8	213.0	(145.1)	7.8	(5.3)	4.1	(2.8)	78.9	(53.7)
A.	140.5	204.4	(145.5)	5.8	(4.1)	2.4	(1.7)	72.2	(51.4)
B.	162.1	233.7	(144.2)	12.7	(7.8)	8.2	(5.1)	94.9	(58.5)

(Cycle 6: 75:2 → 80:3; Expansion (A): 75:2 → 80:1; Contraction (B): 80:2 → 80:3)

6.	277.0	360.8	(130.3)	22.8	(8.2)	5.8	(2.1)	108.5	(39.2)
A.	270.6	355.4	(131.3)	20.6	(7.6)	4.3	(1.6)	105.8	(39.1)
B.	341.6	415.2	(121.5)	45.3	(13.3)	21.3	(6.2)	134.7	(39.4)

(Cycle 7: 80:4 → 82:4; Expansion (A): 80:4 → 81:3; Contraction (B): 81:4 → 82:4)

7.	392.1	478.6	(122.1)	66.3	(16.9)	5.2	(1.3)	156.1	(39.8)
A.	377.7	503.6	(133.3)	22.8	(6.0)	9.5	(2.5)	154.3	(40.9)
B.	403.6	458.6	(113.6)	101.2	(25.1)	1.7	(0.4)	157.5	(39.0)

Expansion (A) 83:1 → 88:2

8.									
A.	531.2	649.0	(122.2)	119.8	(22.6)	−111.2	(−20.9)	130.1	(24.5)

Note: The sum of the determinants of profits do not add up to *P'* because of statistical discrepancy and the non-zero values in some years for wage accruals less disbursements and net capital grants received by the United States, as well as rounding errors in the calculation of averages.

Source: Table 3.A1 of the appendix to this chapter.

this study. The average values for the items in equation (4) are shown for each cycle as a whole, as well as for each expansion and contraction. The ratios (expressed as percentages) of the average values of each of the determinants to the average values for gross retained earnings are also shown in Table 3.1. They can be used to illustrate the relative changes in the average values of the determinants of profits.

Certain features are common to most of the cycles. The relative import-ance of investment is higher in the expansions than in the contractions, with the only exception being the long expansion of the 1960s where trend growth appears to have dominated the cyclical change. The expected reverse pattern is generally found for the government deficit, with its relative value being higher during contractions than during expansions. There do not appear to be consistent cyclical patterns for the international surplus and for personal saving. Their relative importance has sometimes increased during contractions, while at other times they have increased during expansions. Longer-term changes in the relative importance of the determinants of profits can also be discerned from the data in Table 3.1. Their relative importance is lower at the end of our period of study for both investment and personal saving. The opposite trend is found for the government deficit as a contribution to profits, while the international surplus has ended up being a negative factor.

One way of illustrating these longer-term changes is by comparing the long expansion interval that closes our period with the long expansion in the 1960s. The government budgets in both were in a deficit position, but the ratio of these deficits to gross earnings in the earlier expansion was only about one-tenth the value it attained in the later expansion. The change in the international surplus was even more drastic. It went from a positive contributor to profits to an important negative factor. The ratios of personal saving to profits also show significant differences, with the ratio having a much lower value in the current expansion. Another way of illustrating the important changes that appear to have taken place in the United States economy, is to divide the post-1970 period into two parts that begin and end with the same cyclical phases. The first part begins with the onset of contraction in the first quarter of 1970, and ends with the completion of an expansion phase in the first quarter of 1980. The second begins where the first leaves off, in 1980:2, and ends in the last quarter (1988:2) covered by our period.[2] The average values for re-tained earnings and their determinants over each of these intervals are shown in Table 3.2.

The figures in Table 3.2 confirm the changes that were apparent in the comparison of the 1960s and 1980s expansion periods. The large govern-ment deficits reflect significant changes in the structure of government budgets, while the sharp reversal in the international surplus reflects a deterioration in the economy's international competitiveness. There was

Table 3.2 Average values of gross retained earnings and their determinants ($ billion) 1970:1–1980:1, and 1980:2–1988:2

	P'	I	(% of P')	GD	(% of P')	IS	(% of P')	PS	(% of P')
1970:1–1980:1	203.3	276.2	(135.9)	14.1	(6.9)	4.2	(2.1)	90.0	(44.3)
1980:2–1988:2	481.8	588.3	(122.1)	100.7	(21.9)	–71.5	(–14.8)	137.4	(28.5)

Source: Table 3.A1 of the appendix to this chapter.

Table 3.3   Gross (after-tax) profits and components, 1970:1–1980:1, and 1980:2–1988:2

	P	*P'*	*U*	*D*	*IN*
1970:1–1980:1	322.5	203.3	41.3	33.0	86.2
1980:2–1988:2	856.4	481.8	69.9	77.3	297.3
Percentage increase	165.6	137.0	69.2	134.2	244.9

Source: Table 3.A1 of the appendix to this chapter.

also a substantial decline in the value of personal saving relative to the government deficit and to investment.

No attempt will be made here to explain the reasons for this change. But it can be observed that the tight monetary policy adopted as an anti-inflationary measure in October 1979, and the subsequent bond market reactions to the growing government deficits, led to very high real interest rates. This served both to dampen investment and to increase the international value of the dollar as foreign funds moved into United States securities to take advantage of these high interest rates. Very significant changes thus occurred in relative prices that heavily penalised exports and favoured imports. It took a while for the effects of this change to become apparent in net foreign investment, but with the recovery of the United States economy in 1983 the international surplus moved in a sharply negative direction. The effects of the 1979 monetary policy continued to be felt long after it was abandoned in October 1982 as a result of a market slowdown in United States economic activity and problems with international debts (Friedman, 1988). With the United States recovery leading the world, and the adverse changes in international relative prices, its trade balance fell into a strongly negative position from which it has yet to recover.

Throughout the 39-year period of this study there has been a steady increase in the growth of net interest paid by businesses relative to the other components of gross profits. This trend reflects increases in the rates of interest and in the financing methods used by firms. In Table 3.3 the average values for gross (after-tax) profits (P), and their three major components, gross retained earnings (P'), dividends (D) and net interest (IN), as well as undistributed profits (U), are shown separately for the 1970s and 1980s. An examination of the percentage increases from the average values of the earlier period to the average values of the later period makes clear the marked relative increase in net interest paid by businesses.

3.5 CONCLUSION

Aggregate retained earnings in a quarter of a year are causally determined by gross private domestic investment, the government deficit, the international surplus (or net foreign investment) and personal saving. The first three determinants have a positive effect on these earnings, while the last one has a negative effect. The profits equation can be deduced from the definition of profits, and it also follows from the necessary ex post equality between saving and investment for each interval of time. If this interval of time is relatively short, it can be argued that this definitional relation is a causal one, because of the independence of the current values of the 'determinants' from the current values of retained earnings. This is not to deny the importance of these earnings on, for example, investment, but this influence is felt only after a time-lag greater than a quarter of a year.

An examination of average values for gross retained earnings makes clear the important changes that have taken place in the determinants of profits in the 1980s.

APPENDIX

Table 3.A1   Quarterly values for gross retained earnings and their determinants, United States, 1950–88

	P'	I	GD	IS	PS
1950:1	29.8	44.8	−6.0	−1.0	17.2
2	31.1	51.8	6.1	−1.3	12.5
3	32.3	56.8	15.8	−2.7	6.1
4	34.0	66.9	16.4	−2.5	14.5
1951:1	30.9	62.2	18.3	−1.7	9.6
2	35.5	65.3	7.8	0.3	19.4
3	38.7	59.9	0.2	2.2	19.0
4	38.9	54.6	−2.0	2.7	18.5
1952:1	39.1	55.5	−0.1	3.6	17.6
2	37.8	49.0	−4.4	1.2	15.9
3	37.8	52.5	−7.2	−1.0	19.6
4	40.2	57.0	−3.4	−1.2	16.6
1953:1	40.7	56.5	−5.1	−1.3	16.6
2	39.7	57.7	−5.3	−1.8	19.0
3	39.8	55.7	−5.7	−1.1	18.6
4	37.9	49.7	−12.0	−0.9	19.5
1954:1	40.1	50.9	−11.2	−0.4	18.8
2	41.7	52.0	−7.7	0.4	15.5
3	42.4	54.7	−6.6	0	15.4
4	44.8	58.9	−3.3	1.0	16.2

Continued on page 36

Table 3.A1   Continued

	P'	I	GD	IS	PS
1955:1	47.8	64.8	0.1	0.6	14.0
2	49.2	69.6	3.3	−0.2	15.2
3	49.5	71.3	3.7	0.9	17.2
4	50.3	73.3	5.5	0.5	17.7
1956:1	50.1	72.8	5.6	1.0	19.3
2	50.3	72.2	5.0	2.3	21.1
3	51.5	72.8	4.6	3.1	22.0
4	51.2	72.9	5.5	4.6	23.1
1957:1	53.2	71.9	3.9	5.6	21.9
2	53.5	71.7	1.5	4.9	23.5
3	54.2	73.6	1.5	5.0	23.4
4	53.1	67.1	−3.3	3.7	22.0
1958:1	50.2	59.5	−10.0	1.6	23.1
2	51.0	58.2	−14.2	0.9	22.5
3	53.5	64.1	−14.9	1.2	25.2
4	56.9	72.1	−11.5	0	26.5
1959:1	59.3	76.9	−4.7	−1.4	22.8
2	62.0	84.4	0	−2.0	24.1
3	59.4	78.4	−1.1	−0.5	19.4
4	60.3	81.1	−0.6	−0.8	21.1
1960:1	61.5	88.7	7.9	1.7	22.3
2	59.9	78.1	4.3	2.5	20.1
3	60.3	77.4	1.4	3.7	21.3
4	59.3	68.5	−1.2	4.8	19.7
1961:1	58.9	69.5	−5.1	5.3	22.5
2	62.0	74.7	−5.2	4.0	23.5
3	62.7	81.2	−3.9	3.8	26.5
4	64.2	83.0	−2.9	3.7	26.9
1962:1	68.7	87.9	−5.5	3.0	27.2
2	68.1	88.0	−3.6	4.6	27.0
3	68.9	89.3	−2.7	4.3	26.1
4	71.5	85.4	−3.3	3.4	23.4
1963:1	71.4	88.9	−1.8	3.8	24.1
2	73.0	92.2	2.5	5.3	24.5
3	74.1	95.7	1.8	4.6	23.3
4	74.7	95.8	0.4	6.0	26.8
1964:1	78.7	98.2	−2.1	8.2	27.7
2	78.7	98.7	−6.1	6.8	32.6
3	79.8	100.0	−1.1	7.6	31.0
4	79.8	101.6	0.3	7.4	34.8
1965:1	86.6	114.4	5.6	5.8	30.8
2	87.9	114.0	4.4	7.1	32.7
3	89.0	117.4	−3.8	6.0	38.3
4	91.3	118.8	−4.0	5.9	35.5

Table 3.A1 Continued

	P'	I	GD	IS	PS
1966:1	94.0	128.2	1.0	4.7	33.7
2	94.8	129.1	2.2	3.9	34.6
3	94.8	127.6	−2.1	2.7	35.9
4	98.7	129.6	−6.3	3.9	39.7
1967:1	97.0	125.5	−14.1	4.4	44.5
2	96.7	120.6	−15.6	3.6	43.1
3	98.8	126.5	−14.4	3.2	45.8
4	102.1	130.1	−13.0	2.9	47.2
1968:1	99.4	133.8	−9.6	1.8	45.0
2	103.2	137.4	−12.2	2.3	47.3
3	104.2	136.8	−2.5	1.6	37.8
4	106.2	139.9	0.4	0.9	39.8
1969:1	107.4	151.3	11.4	1.7	33.9
2	107.2	151.8	11.9	0.7	37.8
3	107.6	158.1	8.4	1.5	48.2
4	104.5	151.6	8.0	2.8	48.9
1970:1	102.4	146.2	−2.3	4.8	48.5
2	108.5	148.2	9.9	6.3	58.2
3	108.4	153.5	14.0	4.6	61.7
4	107.5	147.3	20.7	3.5	62.5
1971:1	118.4	166.6	18.2	5.3	64.4
2	121.1	173.4	21.3	1.0	70.3
3	125.7	177.0	20.5	0.6	68.3
4	130.6	172.9	17.8	−1.9	62.4
1972:1	135.4	188.3	7.1	−3.9	58.1
2	143.7	199.1	4.0	−3.8	53.8
3	142.8	205.7	0.7	−2.3	59.6
4	147.5	214.9	1.7	−1.5	73.9
1973:1	152.1	228.0	−7.4	2.8	75.7
2	153.3	237.8	−5.3	5.7	85.2
3	156.5	237.2	−9.4	13.2	90.1
4	158.4	252.3	−9.6	13.6	105.0
1974:1	155.5	238.1	−5.7	8.8	101.8
2	157.0	241.3	2.4	5.2	89.2
3	154.2	238.9	1.3	2.0	92.1
4	163.9	245.1	19.3	5.6	103.6
1975:1	179.8	204.9	46.2	19.3	87.7
2	193.5	204.6	96.0	23.2	126.7
3	206.9	229.5	57.6	20.5	100.7
4	215.6	239.3	60.0	23.4	103.4
1976:1	223.4	264.5	45.7	1.9	99.7
2	223.1	275.8	36.6	1.5	98.6
3	226.4	279.6	38.5	0.7	95.6
4	229.4	290.6	32.7	10.3	89.2

Continued on page 38

Table 3.A1   Continued

	P'	I	GD	IS	PS
1977:1	240.3	311.5	17.6	6.7	76.4
2	262.3	341.4	17.7	1.4	88.9
3	277.2	363.7	20.6	−0.5	101.9
4	275.4	359.6	20.6	−7.8	95.6
1978:1	278.0	379.7	17.3	−8.2	107.6
2	296.3	420.2	−6.6	−2.1	106.6
3	305.5	424.7	−0.6	0.8	110.5
4	315.9	442.7	−8.5	1.8	116.0
1979:1	317.8	446.9	−20.7	6.9	122.8
2	327.2	463.2	−18.6	−0.8	120.3
3	335.5	461.5	−8.1	5.7	117.6
4	330.4	447.8	1.4	−1.5	111.5
1980:1	331.0	461.0	12.1	1.4	127.3
2	340.1	425.0	41.9	13.4	132.9
3	343.0	405.4	48.6	29.2	136.5
4	351.8	456.4	35.5	8.0	150.9
1981:1	378.0	506.9	14.6	17.4	152.2
2	383.7	515.3	14.8	6.0	147.0
3	397.2	535.9	26.2	6.6	167.0
4	405.4	504.0	63.0	12.3	171.6
1982:1	392.6	459.5	76.0	7.3	155.0
2	399.4	467.8	77.7	16.5	161.7
3	409.7	452.2	122.5	−12.3	156.0
4	411.1	409.6	166.8	−15.4	143.1
1983:1	433.9	428.3	149.2	−2.1	139.5
2	453.0	481.3	126.0	−27.7	121.1
3	472.0	519.7	126.2	−46.7	116.4
4	487.4	579.8	112.9	−57.4	145.4
1984:1	491.5	663.0	91.6	−73.9	181.1
2	509.6	664.0	95.8	−91.8	152.8
3	514.2	670.3	110.6	−92.0	165.2
4	522.6	661.8	122.1	−106.1	157.3
1985:1	518.4	639.3	96.3	−87.5	128.7
2	532.4	652.3	146.9	−109.4	167.8
3	554.1	626.7	138.0	−118.9	93.3
4	554.6	654.1	145.9	−141.6	111.7
1986:1	565.6	686.6	131.4	−127.4	136.9
2	557.8	667.8	174.3	−139.8	154.1
3	562.3	653.0	143.5	−149.0	98.8
4	554.3	656.4	128.5	−153.3	96.8
1987:1	549.0	685.5	140.6	−154.8	130.8
2	555.5	698.5	82.6	−158.6	69.5
3	569.6	702.8	85.5	−161.1	72.6
4	570.0	764.9	110.7	−167.8	144.0

Table 3.A1   Continued

	P'	I	GD	IS	PS
1988:1	576.4	763.2	99.2	−151.3	149.9
2	583.3	758.1	77.1	−129.1	127.8

Note: The sum of the determinants of profits do not add up to P' because of statistical discrepancy and the non-zero values in some years for wage accruals less disbursements and net capital grants received by the United States, as well as rounding errors in the calculation of averages.

Sources: 1970 to 1982, *National Income and Product Accounts of the United States, 1929–82, Statistical Tables*;
1983, *Survey of Current Business*, July 1986;
1984, *Survey of Current Business*, July 1987;
1985–7, *Survey of Current Business*, July 1988;
1988, *Survey of Current Business*, October 1988.

Notes

1. Kalecki (1954, pp. 45–7) argued that the profits equation shows a causal relation, with capitalists' investment and consumption determining profits. But the reason given by Kalecki – 'that capitalists may decide to consume and to invest more in a given period than in the preceding one, but they cannot decide to earn more. It is, therefore, their investment and consumption decisions which determine profits, and not vice versa' – is not sufficient for this conclusion. It does not exclude the possibility that these decisions may be a function of current profits, which would make the profits equation one of mutual dependence (cf. Asimakopulos (1987)).
2. This latter interval was called the 'Reagan Years' in Asimakopulos (1989).

References

Asimakopulos, A., 'Kalecki on the Determinants of Profits', in G. Fink, G. Poll and M. Riese (eds), *Economic Theory, Political Power and Social Justice: Festschrift Kazimierz Laski* (Wien: Springer-Verlag 1987) pp. 19–42.

Asimakopulos, A., 'Kalecki and the Determinants of Profits: United States Profits in the Reagan Years', in P. Davidson and J. Kregel (eds), *Macroeconomic Problems and Policies of Income: Distribution, Functional, Personal and International* (Brookfield, VT: Edward Elgar, 1989).

Friedman, B. M., 'Lessons on Monetary Policy from the 1980s', *Journal of Economic Perspectives*, 2 (Summer 1988) pp. 51–72.

Kalecki, M., *Theory of Economic Dynamics* (London: Allen & Unwin, 1954).

Levy, S. J. and D. A. Levy, *Profits and the Future of American Society* (New York: Harper & Row, 1983).

Minsky, H., *Stabilizing an Unstable Economy* (New Haven: Yale University Press, 1986).

4 Why is the Rate of Profit Still So Low?

Thomas R. Michl

The general concept of a wage–profit frontier provides a theoretical framework for studying the issues of technical change and income distribution. It can also be given empirical content as a vehicle for understanding movements in the rate of profit over time. This chapter first links up the more familiar wage–rate profit–rate frontier to the more empirically tractable wage–share profit–rate frontier in the context of a discussion of technical change and the rate of profit. The theory of technical change developed motivates an empirical model of the wage–share profit–rate frontier which is used to analyse movements in the rate of profit in US manufacturing industries from 1949 to 1987. Recent movements since about 1970 provide support for an old thesis that capital-using, labour-saving technical changes can, under some circumstances, reduce the rate of profit.

Because the manufacturing industries enjoy the benefits of declining raw material prices in the 1980s, the rhetorical question that titles this chapter is appropriate. A potential answer that emerges from the chapter is that the manufacturing rate of profit is still low because the output–capital ratio has fallen, ostensibly as the result of capital–using, labour–saving technical changes.

4.1 TECHNICAL CHANGE AND THE RATE OF PROFIT

The possibility that technical change could reduce the rate of profit was first advanced by Marx in an effort to explain what was then widely regarded as a stylised fact, namely that the rate of profit was declining secularly. The essential insights of his explanation, together with modern criticisms of it, are elucidated in a simple heuristic one–sector production model. In addition to its expositional value, this exercise provides a basis for the empirical work to follow.

The theoretical literature on technical change and the rate of profit uses wage–rate profit–rate equations as its expository device. It will be helpful to relate this device to the corresponding wage–share profit–rate equation used in the applied sections of the chapter. First, the price equation for a closed economy with one commodity produced by labour and non-depreciating fixed capital using fixed–coefficient technology is

$$P = a P R + W l \tag{1}$$

where P = Price of output, X
a = Capital per unit of output, K/X
R = Rate of profit
W = Money wage
l = Labour hours per unit of output, L/X.

This equation, and the wage–profit frontiers below, apply to a state of full capacity utilisation. The wage–rate profit–rate equation derived from the price equation is

$$W/P = x - k R \tag{2}$$

where W/P = Real or product wage
x = Output per hour, $1/l$
k = Capital per hour, K/L.

The wage–share profit–rate equation derived similarly is

$$w = 1 - a R \tag{3}$$

where w = Wage share, WL/PX.

Note that both the wage–rate and wage–share equations have the output–capital ratio as their R-axis intercept. The wage–rate equation has output per worker (hour) as its wage–axis intercept, while the wage–share equation has unity as its vertical intercept. An increase in labour productivity, or a labour–saving technical change, sends the wage–rate equation's intercept upward.

Now assume that a capital–using ($a'>a$), labour–saving ($l'<l$) technical change occurs, using primes to denote the new production coefficients. If the new technique lowers unit costs and raises the profit rate for an individual firm at the existing wages and prices, it is said to be viable. Profit maximising firms will adopt such a technique because it raises their private rate of return during the interval in which their rivals have yet to switch over to the new technology; call this their transitional rate of profit. As the new technique disperses through the economy, spread by firms operating under the decision rule of adopting all viable techniques, it will clearly change the technological coefficients in the price, wage–rate, and wage–share equations.

Figure 4.1 shows such a technical change. The solid lines represent the wage–rate or wage–share equation associated with the old technique; dashed lines represent those associated with the new technique. Points labelled *A* on both panels represent the old equilibrium. The new technique is assumed to be viable, which means that the 'pivot point' with the old wage–rate profit–rate line on Figure 4.1(i) lies to the southeast of the old equilibrium at point *A*. The issue is whether such a technical change can lower the rate of profit.

Marx's insight was that a capital–using technical change has costs and benefits in terms of its ultimate impact on the social rate of profit. The cost is that it raises the amount of fixed capital[1] per unit of output. The benefit is that it increases output per worker–hour, and if wages do not rise *pari passu*, reduces the wage share (equivalently, raises the profit share). Marx essentially argued that the costs will tend to outweigh the benefits under some conditions, and technical changes will then depress profitability.

Marx himself writes as if these conditions include a state of constant product or real wages, but this is shown to be wrong by Okishio (1961) and Roemer (1977). An example of the Okishio Theorem, as this finding is now called, is given in the movements from points *A* to points *B* on Figure 4.1(i) and (ii). From the condition that real wages remain constant, start in Figure 4.1(i) and move laterally to point *B*. The new equilibrium profit rate has increased by virtue of the assumption that the technical change is viable. Roemer (1977; 1979) offers a rigorous proof that this will occur in a multi-commodity world under a wide variety of assumptions about technology.

Because the wage–rate and wage–share equations have the same *R*-axis intercept, it is possible to translate points from one to the other simply by dropping down vertically from the wage–rate equation's line in panel (i) to the wage–share equation's line in panel (ii). Thus, point *B* on the new wage–share equation line in panel (ii) corresponds to point *B* on the new wage–rate equation line in panel (i). On the wage–share profit–rate diagram it is quite transparent that the technical change under consideration has reduced the wage share sufficiently to compensate for the increased capital–output ratio. In terms of the simple cost–benefit metaphor, the benefits of an increased profit share have overwhelmed the costs of an increased capital–output ratio.

The second thought experiment in Figure 4.1 illustrates the effect of the same technical change under the assumption that the wage share remains constant. Obviously, in this case, there are no benefits so the costs will dominate and the rate of profit will fall. Since we are holding the wage share constant, begin in panel (ii), and move from point *A* to point *C* laterally. Again, we can translate point *C* into its corresponding point on the wage–rate profit–rate frontier in panel (i) directly above it. In this case product wages have risen proportionally to the increase in output per hour, by the assumption that the wage share remains constant. The result that viable, capital–using, labour–saving technical changes will depress the rate of profit when the wage share is constant[1] is shown for the two–sector case

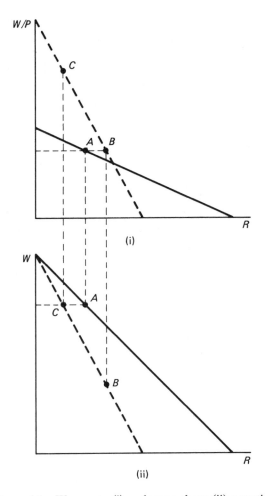

Figure 4.1   Wage rate (i) and wage share (ii) equations

by Roemer (1978) and Laibman (1982). Note that what is involved is the important distinction between the private and social rate of return, for the latter declines even as individual firms seek somewhat myopically to increase the former. While Marx may have erred in the details, the essential insight that technical change can reduce profitability emerges as a possibility that depends on the effects of technical change on product wages.

It is worth considering this point in some detail. The assumption of this comparative equilibrium analysis is that during the traverse, changes occur in the money wage, the price, or both. In the case of constant real wages, one can assume that as technical change disperses, prices and money wages decline proportionately. In the case of a constant wage share, one can assume that as the technical change disperses, prices decline but money wages remain constant. Which path the economy travels along depends on the bargaining position of workers.

In the Okishio case, workers are assumed to be in such a weak bargaining position that they are unable to capture any of the fruits of technical change in the form of a higher real wage rate. In the second case, workers are assumed to be in such a strong bargaining position that they are able to capture all the fruits of technical change, in the sense that their wages rise *pari passu* with productivity. While this logical ordering from technical change to real wages will not appeal to those who require wages to be determined by competitive labour market-clearing conditions, it will appeal to those who work in the classical (Smith–Ricardo–Marx) tradition in which real wages have important historical and institutional determinates.

From the perspective of the causal ordering from technical change to real wages, a natural resolution to the obvious indeterminacy of the effect of technical change on the rate of profit is at hand. Does capital–using labour–saving technical change raise or lower the rate of profit? Clearly, it depends on how much of the productivity dividend is captured by workers through their bargaining position. Returning to Figure 4.1, it is clearly possible for the new equilibrium to lie between *B* and *C* on either of the new wage–profit lines. Whether product wages rise sufficiently to depress profitability cannot be determined on *a priori* grounds.

In this intermediate case,[2] in which product wages rise less than proportionately to the increase in output per worker, technical change has the effect of reducing the wage share, as is evident in panel (ii). Thus, the essential insight of Marx's theory remains valid, namely that it is possible for the costs of the technical change (higher capital–output ratio) to outweigh the benefits (higher profit share). The defining characteristic of this process is the simultaneous decline in the wage share, output–capital ratio, and rate of profit. Some of the evidence presented below can be interpreted as an historical example of this intermediate case.

4.2 THE WAGE–PROFIT FRONTIER

Before proceeding to the evidence, let me clarify the assumptions I make in using the term 'wage–profit frontier' in the remainder of the chapter. If the world conformed to the assumptions of the simple heuristic model just presented, it would be possible in principle to study movements in the wage–share profit–rate equations over time by using readily available descriptive statistics. There are two types of deviation from the model we must consider.

First, there may be a multiplicity of wage–rate profit–rate lines, each representing a different technology, in existence at a point in time. The envelope formed by all the existing wage–rate profit–rate lines constitutes a wage–profit frontier (or factor price frontier) in the strictest sense of the term. In this case, it is difficult to generalise about the corresponding wage–share profit–rate frontier. For instance, with a well-behaved Cobb–Douglas technology (unitary elasticity of substitution), the wage–share profit–rate frontier is horizontal, with an intercept equal to the elasticity of output with respect to labour. With an elasticity of substitution that is not unity, or that varies, or with technology that is ill-behaved from a neo-classical point of view, many other configurations are possible.

In the applied work below, I assume that at a point in time there is only one fixed-coefficient production process constraining the economy. The economy thus moves along the wage–profit lines associated with this technology over short periods of time, and I shall call the wage–share profit–rate line in effect at a point in time the wage–profit frontier. Further, I assume that as new techniques become available and are adopted, the technological constraints and the corresponding wage–profit frontier evolve over time.[3] This strategy is an attempt to translate the foregoing comparative equilibrium analysis into a tractable framework for studying historical data.

A second set of problems includes the following three items, listed with their resolution in this chapter. Even with fixed coefficients, a multi-commodity economy has a nonlinear wage–profit frontier; I use a linear approximation. The economy does not operate at full utilisation all or most of the time; I adjust the profit rate data for capacity utilisation. Actual depreciation rates are not zero; I use a gross accounting rate of return to measure the rate of profit. The manufacturing sector uses intermediate inputs and raw material; I add raw material to the foregoing production model and estimate the wage–profit frontiers for a fixed capital, labour, raw material model.

4.3 A CAPITAL, LABOUR, RAW MATERIAL MODEL

Purchases of raw material from the primary sector amount to about 10 per cent of total manufacturing output, and non-raw material intermediate inputs make up about 50 per cent of total output. The cost shares of these categories appear in columns 2 and 4 of Table 4.1 for years in which the relevant input–output data exist. Most of the non-raw material intermediates are own-inputs, produced within the manufacturing sector. The price of these inputs, relative to a manufacturing output price index, and their share in total output are fairly constant (see columns 4 and 5). This constancy justifies the use of a capital, labour, raw material (KLM) production model.[4] By netting out non-raw material intermediates from total output and by assuming that the prices of these inputs do not move

Table 4.1 Selected cost shares and relative prices shares in total output and relative price indexes

Column	Wages	Raw material share	Relative price of raw material	Non-raw material inter-mediates	Relative price of non-raw material intermediates	Net non-raw material intermediates	
						Wages	Raw material
	(1)	(2)	(3)	(4)	(5)	(6)	(7)
Year							
1949	24.5%	—	111.6	—	95.3	—	—
1958	26.7	10.9%	98.7	52.7%	101.5	56.4%	23.0%
1961	26.9	9.8	91.7	53.7	99.9	58.0%	21.1
1963	26.8	9.0	90.1	53.6	98.5	57.7	19.3
1967	27.2	7.9	88.3	54.3	97.3	59.5	17.2
1972	27.1	8.2	94.5	53.2	95.7	57.9	17.5
1977	23.9	10.2	98.2	53.8	101.1	51.7	22.0
1982	24.5	12.9	100.0	53.0	100.0	52.1	27.4
1987	25.2	—	92.5	—	103.9	—	—

Source: See text and data appendix.

too differently from total output prices, we can transform the wage share data into a form appropriate for the *KLM* model. Columns 6 and 7 show the value of the wage and raw material shares in total output net of non-raw material intermediate goods for input–output years. I adopt the expedient of using the average value of the non-raw material intermediate cost share, from column 4, to generate a time series on total output net of non-raw material intermediates, which I shall refer to in the rest of the chapter as total output.

The share of raw materials in total output follows movements in raw material prices, shown in column 3, quite closely. I assume that the fixed-coefficient for raw material remains constant over the estimating interval from 1949 to 1987. Experiments with alternative assumptions (trends or shifts) were unsuccessful, and the results with this assumption are reasonable.

The price equation and wage-share profit-rate equation for the *KLM* model are

$$P = aPR + Wl + mP_m \tag{4}$$

where P_m = Price of raw materials
             m = Raw material per unit of output

$$w = 1 - mp_m - aR \tag{5}$$

where p_m = Relative price of raw materials.

There are several useful links between this wage-share equation and value-added accounting categories, and these links elucidate how the wage-profit frontier responds to raw material price shocks. The R-intercept is now $(1 - mp_m)/a$, or the ratio of value added to capital stock. The w-intercept is now $(1 - mp_m)$, or the ratio of value added to total output. Thus, a raw material relative price increase shifts the entire wage–profit frontier toward the origin. Higher raw material prices redistribute income from manufacturing back to the primary sector, lower the ratio of value added to total output, and lower the ratio of value added to capital stock. Obviously, raw material price declines have the opposite effects. If we ignored these effects, and generated a wage–profit frontier using value-added categories alone, we would risk conflating technical-change driven movements in the output–capital ratio with raw material price effects.

4.4 CAPACITY UTILISATION ADJUSTMENTS

I adopt the technique of dividing the profit rate and the output–capital ratio by one of several capacity utilisation indexes in order to approximate

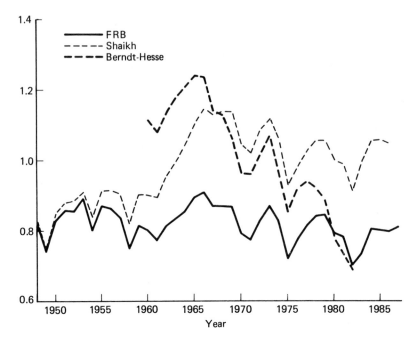

Figure 4.2   Alternative utilisation indexes

Source: See data appendix and text.

the values of these ratios at some hypothetical full capacity level of
production. Clearly some adjustment is necessary since the *KLM* production model applies to such a state of full utilisation, and the manufacturing industries spend much time by any of the indexes described here in a
state of excess capacity. This adjustment effectively shifts a given observation (in wage-share, profit-rate space) to the right for slump years, and to
the left during years of over-utilisation.

Ideally, one wants a technique that mainly fills in the valleys in these two
time series, with the assumption that the peaks represent periods during
which capacity limits are being approached or reached. The existing
indexes of utilisation in manufacturing have differing properties with
respect to this ideal. The Federal Reserve Board Capacity Utilization
Index, for example, is widely criticised by economists for its lack of
theoretical foundation. One implication of the rather *ad hoc* procedures by
which it is constructed is that secular trends in utilisation appear to be
smoothed out of the index, which has a very trendless time profile relative
to other indexes. Figure 4.2 displays three alternative indexes of capacity
utilisation in manufacturing, where this assertion can be verified.

The FRB index suggests that the 1960s is a period of only slightly higher
utilisation by comparison with other periods. Both alternative indexes in

Figure 4.2 suggest the 1960s is a period of rather unusually high utilisation by comparison either with preceding or succeeding periods, as does the Christensen-Jorgenson (1969) index, not shown, which spans 1948–65. For this reason I use a utilisation index constructed by Shaikh (1988) in the figures below. In descriptive statistics and econometric estimates, however, I report results using all three indexes, the FRB index (see data appendix), the Shaikh index (1988), and the Berndt-Hesse index (1986). Important theoretical and practical issues in defining and measuring utilisation remain unresolved, and I return briefly to this issue in the chapter's conclusion.

4.5 ADJUSTED OUTPUT–CAPITAL RATIOS AND PROFIT RATES

Table 4.2 reports average values of the unadjusted and adjusted total output–capital ratio (columns 1 through 4) and gross accounting rate of return (columns 5 through 8) over five-year intervals.

With the exception of the adjusted output–capital ratio derived from the Berndt-Hesse index, there is a clear pattern of secular decline in the output–capital ratios reported here. Based on the theoretical concepts developed earlier, this decline suggests that technical change is capital-using. I exploit the uniformity of this technical change by assuming that the capital–output ratio increases along a linear trend path in the econometric estimates below. There is no theoretical reason to expect this kind of uniformity, but using a time index to model technical change is a well-established procedure in applied work on production functions.

Measuring the rate of profit by a gross accounting rate of return eliminates the need to deal with messy problems of depreciation. The gross accounting rate equals gross operating surplus (profits, net interest, and depreciation) divided by gross capital stock. Thus, no capital consumption adjustments to depreciation are necessary. The non-existence of such adjustments for US manufacturing is the reason the gross rate of return was chosen, with the simplification of the model a serendipitous side-effect. The gross capital stock sums gross fixed stocks (of equipment and structures) and end-of-year inventories. Both the rate of profit and output–capital ratios in Table 4.2 have gross capital stock in the denominator. While including inventories is a departure from the fixed capital notion in the production model described earlier, it has the advantage of yielding a measure of the rate of return that is broadly comparable to other measures used in the literature.

The adjusted rates of return in columns 6 to 8 decline substantially over the entire interval, but the declines are not very uniform. Most of the decline seems to be concentrated in the period from 1965 to 1975. This pattern is consistent with the impression that the US economy underwent a

Table 4.2 Output–capital ratios and profit rates

| | Total output–gross capital ratios | | | | Gross accounting rates of return | | | |
| | Unadjusted | FRB | Adjusted Shaikh | Berndt-Hesse | Unadjusted | FRB | Adjusted Shaikh | Berndt-Hesse |
Column	(1)	(2)	(3)	(4)	(5)	(6)	(7)	(8)
Years								
1951–55	.839	.981	.948	—	17.3%	20.3%	19.6%	—
1956–60	.762	.839	.858	—	14.6	18.0	16.4	—
1961–65	.784	.940	.788	.671	16.4	19.6	16.4	14.0
1966–70	.732	.849	.653	.663	15.1	17.5	13.5	13.6
1971–75	.667	.831	.640	.687	11.8	14.7	11.3	12.2
1976–80	.641	.788	.626	.722	10.7	13.2	10.5	12.0
1981–85	.567	.741	.567	—	9.2	12.0	9.2	—
1986–87	.557	.693	.526	—	10.5	13.1	9.5	—

Notes: Total output is net of non-raw material intermediate inputs. See text and data appendix for further details.

period of profit squeeze during the late 1960s from the upward pressure of product wages, and was subsequently hit by a severe raw material price shock in 1974/5. After 1970 or so, the rate of return remains at very low levels relative to previous years, and at the end of the sample, 1987, the rate of profit is still low. The interesting question is why the rate of return remains at such a low level despite the favourable developments represented by declining raw material prices and the weakness of labour costs during the 1980s.

4.6 ESTIMATES OF THE KLM WAGE–PROFIT FRONTIER

The wage-share profit-rate equation for a *KLM* model is written below as it will be estimated, with the definitions of the terms appropriately sharpened. The equation is

$$w = 1 - m\, p_m - [a\, p_k](t)\, R_g \qquad (6)$$

where w = Wage share in total output net of non-raw material
intermediates
  a = Constant-dollar gross capital–output coefficient
  P_k = Relative price of gross capital stocks[5]
  t = Time index
  R_g = Gross accounting rate of return adjusted for utilisation
  p_m = Relative price index for raw materials
  m = Raw material-output coefficient.

Estimates of this equation appear in Table 4.3, and are explained as follows. Because OLS results showed substantial serial correlation of error terms, the results in Table 4.3 are generated by a Cochrane-Orcutt transformation of the data, with the first-order ϱ shown in the last row of the table. It was also necessary to constrain the intercept of this equation to its theoretical value of unity by making $(1 - w)$ the dependent variable, and suppressing the constant term. The first three estimates differ in their utilisation indexes. Estimate 1 uses the FRB index, estimate 2 uses the Shaikh index, and estimate 3 uses the Berndt-Hesse index. Results are similar across these three estimates, but in figures below, the data and fitted frontiers for estimate 2 are shown. Estimate 4 uses the Shaikh index, but restricts the sample to 1959–87 to check the sensitivity of results to the poorer-quality pre-1958 data on output and relative prices.

The plausibility and fit of these estimates should be evaluated against actual data on adjusted capital–output ratios and raw material cost shares in total output (net non-raw material intermediates) shown above in Tables 4.1 and 4.2. The time index used equals unity in 1948 and increments by

Table 4.3   Estimates of the KLM wage–profit frontier

Estimates Years	(1) 1949–87	(2) 1949–87	(3) 1961–82	(4) 1959–87
Independent variable				
R_g	.344 (2.40)	.309 (2.22)	.642 (2.26)	.202 (1.18)
R_g X Time	.020 (5.47)	.030 (6.02)	.023 (2.15)	.033 (3.61)
p_m	.321 (12.30)	.323 (11.71)	.295 (6.89)	.328 (9.75)
R_2	.641	.638	.680	.672
Durbin-Watson	2.13	2.03	2.08	2.10
ϱ	.596	.490	.434	.481

Notes: Absolute *t*-statistic is in parenthesis. The dependent variable is
100 X (1 − *w*). See text and data appendix for further detail.

one unit each year. The implied beginning of period (1949) adjusted
capital–output ratios from estimates 1 and 2 are 0.384 and 0.369 (or 2.60
and 2.71 when expressed as output–capital ratios). Clearly these estimates
are considerably lower than the range of actual values of the adjusted
capital–output ratios. The implied adjusted capital–output ratio in estimate
3 is 1.03 (or 0.97 expressed as an output–capital ratio), which is also below
actual value ranges. The end-of-period estimates of capital–output ratios
also lie below actual values.

The annual increments in the capital–output ratio in these estimates lie
close to the actual increments in Table 4.2. From 1949 to 1987, the
capital–output ratio formed with the FRB and Shaikh utilisation indexes
rose an average of 0.013 and 0.025, which compare reasonably well to the
coefficients on R_gX Time.[6]

The coefficient on relative raw material prices measures the implied cost
share in total output evaluated at the base year, 1982. Compared to the
actual values given in column 7 of Table 4.2, the estimates in Table 4.3
have the right order of magnitude but are too large.

In general, these discrepancies between actual and implied values may
derive from the fact that we are linearly approximating a segment of the
nonlinear wage–profit frontier of a multi-commodity economic system.
Measurement error in the independent variables may also be creating bias
toward zero in the coefficient estimates.

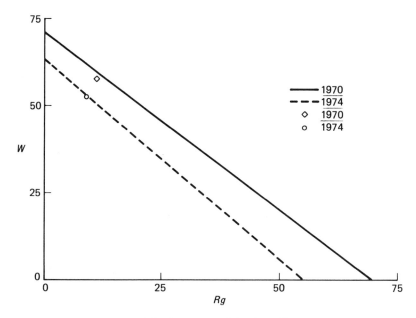

Figure 4.3   Raw material price effects

4.7   THE EVOLUTION OF THE WAGE–PROFIT FRONTIER, 1949–87

Two analytical exercises convey an appreciation of the relationship between actual data and the estimated wage–profit frontiers. First, consider the effects of the raw material price increases of the 1970s, which push the frontier toward the origin. Figure 4.3 presents the wage–profit frontiers predicted by estimate 2 of Table 4.3 for 1970 and 1974 (the year a spike in a broad index of raw material prices occurs), and the actual observations for these two years, marked by a diamond and a circle. This presentation of the data will help put into perspective Figure 4.5 below which shows the whole sample of observations from 1949 to 1987. The whole sample lies in a fairly small 'box' surrounding the observations identified in Figure 4.3 for 1970 and 1974.

In Figure 4.3, one can get some sense of the magnitude of the raw material price shocks, which drive the observations in a southwesterly direction from 1970 to 1974. Raw material price declines, such as occur fairly sharply during the 1980s and fairly gradually over the 1950s and 1960s, have the reverse effect of shifting the wage–profit frontier outward.

A second exercise, presented in Figure 4.4, illustrates the effect of the rising capital–output ratio, which rotates the frontier inward as we

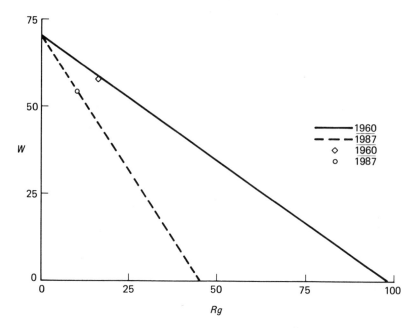

Figure 4.4　Effect of declining output–capital ratio

observed in the theoretical example in Figure 4.1(ii). In Figure 4.4, the estimated frontiers for 1960 and 1987 share roughly the same intercept on the wage-share axis because of the congruence of relative raw material prices in these two years. Thus, the inward rotation is the consequence of the time-dependent rise in the capital–output ratios, without any complications from raw material prices. The actual observations for 1960 and 1987 are shown in Figure 4.4 again as a diamond and a circle.

The southwesterly movement from 1960 to 1987 results from the process of capital-using technical change in the model. In point of fact, the comparison of 1960 to 1987 does not merely reflect a technical-change-driven decline in the rate of profit, for, as we shall see, the late 1960s is a period of profit squeeze, in which rising product wages play a major role in pushing the manufacturing industries up along the wage–profit frontier, in effect. However, after 1970, this pressure from wage costs ceases, and over the interval 1970 to 1981 is replaced by pressure from raw material costs. In the 1980s, as raw material prices decline, the rate of profit remains at a low level, consistent with the thesis that capital-using technical change has caused a decline in the rate of profit.

Thus, a comparison of 1970 to 1987 can be appropriately related to the comparative equilibrium analysis in the first part of the chapter. In the terms of that analysis, the wage share has declined over this interval, but not sufficiently to offset the effect of an increased capital–output ratio on

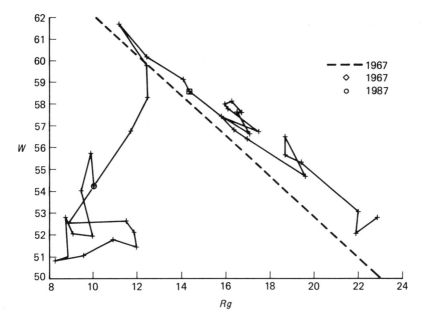

Figure 4.5   Wage share and rate of profit, US manufacturing, 1949–87

the rate of profit. Thus, the pattern of movement is characteristic of the intermediate case described earlier, lying between the two extremes given by a constant wage share and a constant product wage. In this intermediate case, the wage share, profit rate, and output–capital ratio decline simultaneously.

In order to show all this in detail, the origin has been displaced in Figure 4.5 in order to zoom in on the 'box' containing the full sample of observations. The observations, represented by crosses, begin in the southeast corner in 1949 and are connected to facilitate finding any particular year by tracing the path from observation to observation. The observation for 1987 is marked by a circle to help in orientation.

Note that the wage share reaches its zenith in 1970. From 1949 to 1970, one can discern the inverse movements characteristic of motion along a wage–profit frontier. In fact, however, based on the estimates in Table 4.3, the wage–profit frontier is 'twisted' during this period under the combined influence of a declining output–capital ratio (rotates it inward) and slowly declining rate material prices (shifts it outward). This twisting actually pushes the relevant range of the frontier (i.e. the region where the observations lie) outward during the 1960s, so that the profit squeeze of the 1960s takes place across a more favourable wage–profit tradeoff made possible by lower raw material prices.

The estimated wage–profit frontier for 1967 is shown as the dotted straight line in Figure 4.5, and the observation for 1967 is marked off with a square, in order to convey a sense of the approximate position of the frontier during the late 1960s when a profit squeeze from rising wages. This profit squeeze peaks around 1970, after which time raw material price shocks play a prominent role.

We have already highlighted the first bout of raw material price inflation in the early 1970s. From 1978 to 1981 a smaller inward shift of the wage–profit frontier occurs, again driving the observations toward the origin in a southwesterly direction. After 1981 the raw material relative price decline sets in, and by 1987 the relative price index for raw materials reaches 1960s levels. The final observation for 1987 lies in the southwestern region of the figure.

4.8   A SUMMARY OF MOVEMENTS IN THE WAGE–PROFIT FRONTIER

It is now possible to bring together the strands of the discussion and provide a quick summary of movements in the cyclically adjusted rate of profit from 1949 to 1987, as suggested by the estimates. There are three distinct moments. First, from 1949 to 1970, a rising wage share in the 1960s appears to be the driving force behind the fairly large decline in profitability. Of the remaining factors, the benefits of declining raw material prices more than offset the effects of a declining output–capital ratio. Second, during the 1970s, two sharp raw material price spikes drive the wage–profit frontier inward, sending the observations in a southwesterly direction. The repeated profit squeezes, first from wages in the 1960s and then from raw materials in the 1970s, explain why most of the decline in profitability is concentrated in the interval from 1965 to 1975. Third, during the 1980s in the aftermath of the raw material price spikes, the frontier drifts outward as raw material prices decline. As is clear in Figure 4.5, by 1987 the observations lie well within the frontiers that characterised the system before the price shocks. In the estimates developed here, this failure for the observations to return to their position on the figure before the price shocks results from a rising capital–output ratio or ostensibly from the effects of capital-using technical change. One can interpret this movement from 1970 or so to 1987 as evidence for the characteristic pattern suggested by the Marxian theory of technical change: namely, simultaneous decline in the wage share, output–capital ratio, and rate of profit.

4.9   CONCLUDING NOTES

It is wise to end on a cautionary note, both to carefully qualify the results and to provide suggestions for further research. First, the wage-share profit-rate frontiers estimated here represent, in principle, the constraints imposed by full utilisation of industrial capacity. During periods of excess capacity, when the economy moves within its wage-rate and wage-share profit-rate frontiers, very different properties may characterise its behaviour. It would be inappropriate to interpret the results here as describing the actual movements of the manufacturing sector without serious attention to this distinction. The results should be interpreted as describing notional movements along an evolving wage–profit frontier.

Second, conceptual or measurement errors in the capacity utilisation indexes or adjustment techniques could be confusing a technologically driven decline in the output–capital ratio with the effects of a stagnation in demand. To relate this possibility to the first point, a 'stagnationist' interpretation of the economy's position *circa* 1987 could be that it is an illustration of a movement into the region within the wage–profit frontier. In any event, alternative explanations of the low rate of profit in US manufacturing clearly need to address the role of declines in the output–capital ratio.

DATA APPENDIX

Output and Output Deflator

Total output and the output deflator for 1958–87 come from 'Time Series Data for Input–Output Industries', unpublished printout from the Office of Economic Growth of the Bureau of Labour Statistics, provided to me by Valerie Personick. Data cover BLS sector 231, equivalent to SIC 20–39. For 1948–57, these data are extrapolated backwards using shipments (for output) and the Producer Price Index for Finished Goods (for the output deflator), taken from *Economic Report of the President, 1989* (Washington: GPO, 1989) tables B-56 and B-63.

Gross Operating Surplus and Total Compensation

The source for gross operating surplus and total compensation is the unpublished Bureau of Economic Analysis printout of the data underlying table 6.1 of the National Income and Product Accounts, provided to me by Michael Mohr.

Capital Stocks

End-of-year gross capital stocks of equipment and structures are from *Fixed Reproducible Wealth in the United States, 1925–85* (Washington: GPO, 1986) table A7 (at current cost) and table A6 (at constant cost). These data are updated in the *Survey of Current Business*.

End-of-year inventories are from *The National Income and Product Accounts of the United States, 1929–82* (Washington: GPO, 1986) tables 5.10 (at current prices) and 5.11 (at constant prices). These data are updated in the *Survey of Current Business*. I took them from CITIBASE, using fourth-quarter totals to get as close to end-of-year values as possible.

Price Indexes for Intermediate Inputs

The price indexes for raw materials (Producer Price Index for Crude Materials for Further Processing) and non-raw material intermediates (Producer Price Index for Materials and Components for Manufacturing) are from *Economic Report of the President, 1989* (Washington: GPO, 1989) table B-63.

Capacity Utilisation Indexes

The Federal Reserve Board Capacity Utilization Index for Manufacturing is from *Economic Report of the President, 1989* (Washington: GPO, 1989) table B-51. Since the Shaikh index from 'Capital Utilization Rates and the Long-Term Trend of the Rate of Profit in US Manufacturing, 1909–85' (unpublished manuscript, 1988) ends in 1985, it was necessary to 'chain' it to the FRB index to generate an estimate for 1987. I regressed the Shaikh index on time and the FRB index over 1948–85 and forecast out-of-sample to 1987. Then I used the growth from 1985 to 1987 of the predicted value of the Shaikh index from this regression to extrapolate the original series out to 1987. The other index is from Ernst Berndt and Dieter Hesse, 'Measuring and Assessing Capacity Utilisation in the Manufacturing Section of Nine OECD Countries' *European Economic Review* (1986).

Table 4.1

Data for columns 2 and 4 are from the Input–Output Tables of the US economy. For 1958, 1961, 1963, and 1967, I use *Historical Statistics of the US* (Washington: GPO, 1974) Series F668-680. For 1972, I use Philip M. Ritz *et al.*, 'Dollar-Value Tables for the 1972 Input–Output Study', *Survey of Current Business* (April 1979) table 1. For 1977, I use Interindustry Economics Division, 'The Input–Output Structure of the US Economy, 1977', *Survey of Current Business* (May 1984) table 1. For 1982, I use Interindustry Economics Division, 'Annual Input–Output Accounts of the US Economy, 1982', *Survey of Current Business* (April 1988) table 1. Raw materials are the inputs purchased from Input–Output industries 1–10, broadly Agriculture and Mining. Non-raw material inputs are all other purchased inputs, calculated as the residual from total intermediate inputs after raw materials are removed. Both are expressed as percentages of total industry output from the Input–Output accounts.

Notes

1. These two authors make somewhat more complex assumptions about the distribution of income after a technical change, but for economy of presentation it suffices to say that in a one-commodity model, their assumptions translate into a constant wage share.
2. This presentation in terms of two extreme cases and the indeterminate intermediate case owes much to Foley (1986).
3. Obviously, at a point in time all past technologies will be known and will be eligible for adoption, but they will only become viable if product wages decline substantially, an eventuality assumed to be unimportant in the application of the model.
4. An alternative strategy, to estimate a fixed capital, labor, non-raw material

intermediate input, raw material (KLNM) production model, is pursued in Michl (1989). The broad conclusions that emerge from the KLNM model do not conflict with the results presented below. The major difference is that the decline in raw material prices in the 1980s does not increase the w-axis intercept of the wage–profit frontier as much in the KLNM model, apparently because non-raw material intermediate prices remain high.

5. I have written the relative price term into this equation as a reminder that in a multi-commodity model a relative price vector of fixed capital stocks would appear in the wage-share profit-rate equation. Fur further discussion of this point, see Michl (1989).

6. The capital–output ratio adjusted by the Berndt-Hesse index has no trend from 1962 to 1979 and then actually falls by about 10 per cent.

References

Berndt, E. R. and D. Hesse, 'Measuring and Assessing Capacity Utilization in the Manufacturing Sector of Nine OECD Countries', *European Economic Review*, 30, 5 (1986) pp. 961–89.

Christensen, L. R. and D. W. Jorgenson, 'The Measurement of US Real Capital Input, 1929–1967', *Review of Income and Wealth*, 15, 4 (1969) pp. 293–320.

Foley, D. K., *Money, Accumulation, and Crisis* (New York: Harwood Academic Publishers, 1986).

Laibman, D., 'Technical Change, the Real Wage, and the Rate of Exploitation', *Review of Radical Political Economics*, 14, 2 (1982) pp. 95–105.

Michl, T. R., 'Wage–Profit Curves in US Manufacturing', Colgate University Economics Discussion Paper no. 89–07, Hamilton, New York (1989).

Okishio, Nubuo, 'Technical Changes and the Rate of Profit', *Kobe University Economic Review*, 7 (1961) pp. 85–99.

Roemer, John, 'Technical Change and the "Tendency of the Rate of Profit to Fall"', *Journal of Economic Theory*, 16 (1977) pp. 403–24.

Roemer, J., 'The Effect of Technological Change on the Real Wage and Marx's Falling Rate of Profit', *Australian Economic Papers*', (June 1978) pp. 152–66.

Roemer, J., 'Continuing Controversy on the Falling Rate of Profit: Fixed Capital and Other Issues', *Cambridge Journal of Economics*, 3 (1979) pp. 379–98.

Shaikh, Anwar, 'Capital Utilization Rates and the Long-Term Trend of the Rate of Profit in US Manufacturing, 1909–1985', xerox at the New School for Social Research, New York (1988).

5 The Determinants of Profit Growth in the Manufacturing Sectors

Stanley J. Feldman and Richard DeKaser

5.1 INTRODUCTION

The central driving force behind a capitalist economy is the pursuit of profits. Profits provide a critical source of financing for capital expansion which results in future profit growth, and create the basis upon which markets assign values to companies and industries. Economists and financial professionals have shown a renewed interest in the determinants of profit change as the inflation experience of the 1970s indicated that profit levels and growth can be artificially inflated during periods of rapid price change. Inflation induced profit growth is the result of calculating inventory profit on an historical cost basis rather than on a replacement cost basis and under depreciating assets during periods when the replacement cost of capital is rising. In both instances the firm and/or the industry records positive incremental profit change which is only transitory.

In addition to these general inflation induced increases to profit change, there are sector or industry specific pricing impacts where sales price increases disproportionately to increases in factor prices. Feldman and Von Loggrenberg (1981, pp. 47–53) have referred to this effect as price over recovery, and Feldman, in a series of articles (1987, pp. 21–32, and 1986, pp. 21–34), has suggested that price, over recovery induced profit growth is a lower quality profit stream than profit growth that comes from other determinants like productivity and/or volume growth. The reason for this is that price over recovery induced profit growth can be bid away by lower cost foreign producers and/or domestic and foreign suppliers of substitute products or services. Therefore, price induced profit growth at the industry level that is not a function of patent rights and/or trade restrictions is not as sustainable as profit growth resulting from volume and productivity growth. On the other hand, Brown (1986, pp. 37–49) using the *Data Resources Factor Input and Margin Model* has shown that inflation management (essentially the combination of the productivity and price over recovery) contributions have become generally less important since the 1982 recession as a result of cyclical increases in productivity growth and a narrowing of the gap between the growth in sales and factor prices.

While this analysis was insightful, it did not include industry specific capital costs and the only measure of productivity applied to labour. The research presented in this chapter builds on the earliest work of Feldman and subsequent research by Brown by using an inherently richer data set, including measures of multi-factor productivity, and employing a more comprehensive profit decomposition model.

The analysis of the sources of firm profitability, as opposed to industry profitability, has been pursued by the accounting profession. A series of papers (Miller, 1984, pp. 145–53; Brayton, 1985, pp. 54–8; Chaudry, 1982; Ruch, 1982) have argued that firms should not only set profit goals, but should set standards for each determinant of profit growth. In this way, a firm can judge actual performance against what was expected and where performance fell short and develop strategies to reduce or preferably remove the differential. Kendrick (1984) in collaboration with the American Productivity Center in Houston has attempted to relate the vast research findings on the measurement and determinants of productivity growth to measuring and monitoring firm productivity performance.

This chapter builds upon this work. Since most large companies (Fortune 1000) produce in multiple lines of business, company-wide standards need to be developed from those standards established for each line of business or business segment. One approach is to set standards based on how the industries perform. Thus, if a firm operates in the metal and machinery lines of business, the standard for productivity's contribution to profit growth should be the weighted contributions registered in the metal and machinery sectors over the recent past. This approach requires that one calculates not only the productivity contribution to profit growth but the volume and price contributions as well. This chapter extends the work that has been done in industry structural analysis in several important ways. First, it provides a formal derivation for decomposing profit change into its major determinants – productivity, volume and price – over recovery. Second, it applies the decomposition method for the first time to a rich data set developed by the BLS which covers all two digit SIC manufacturing industries. Third, it analyses the characteristics of profit performance of industries as opposed to volume and/or productivity performance. While there is obviously a close relationship between these concepts, industries can and do register solid volume and productivity growth and yet record poor profit growth. Fourth, the chapter focuses on the importance of productivity growth to industry profit growth. Since profits are a nominal concept, it is necessary to convert efficiency gains to increments in profits. During periods of rapidly rising prices, small gains of productivity can give rise to large increases in profits. In order to avoid the illusion that inflation imparts, the productivity contribution is divided into scale and price effects. The scale contribution suggests that if the production base of an industry is increasing, it is very possible that declines in productivity growth can be offset by scale increases so that profit growth due to productivity (in the absence of rising prices) can actually rise over time.

This chapter proceeds by first demonstrating that the change in profits can analytically be divided into contributions due to productivity, volume, sales price and factor or input costs. Succeeding sections analyse how each of the above factors have contributed to profit growth and to what degree they have changed over time. The final section presents the basic conclusions of the analysis and indicates the direction that further research should take.

5.2   THE PROFIT DECOMPOSITION MODEL (PDM)

PDM is obtained by first totally differentiating the basic profit identity, which is shown as equation (1), to obtain equation (2).

$$\pi = PQ - \sum_i p_i q_i \tag{1}$$

$$d\pi = PdQ + QdP - \sum_i p_i dq_i - \sum_i q_i dp_i \tag{2}$$

where P = Sales price
$\quad\quad\quad Q$ = Volume
$\quad\quad\quad p_i$ = Input price
$\quad\quad\quad q_i$ = Input quantity
$\quad\quad\quad \pi$ = Profit

Multiplying (2) by successive terms of one in the form of $Q/Q, P/P, q_i/q_i, p_i/p_i$ and then adding and subtracting the expression for total costs multiplied by the percent change in volume yields equation (3). For small changes in the left-hand side variables equation (3) will yield actual profit change.

$$d\pi = \pi dQ/Q + PQdP/P + \sum_i p_i q_i (dQ/Q - dq_i/q_i) - \sum_i p_i q_i (dp_i/p_i) \tag{3}$$

where $\pi(dQ/Q)$ = Volume contribution

$\quad\quad\quad PQ(dP/P)$ = Sales price contribution

$\quad\quad\quad \sum_i p_i q_i (dQ/Q - dq_i/q_i)$ = Multi-factor productivity contribution

$\quad\quad\quad \sum_i p_i q_i (dp_i/p_i)$ = Input price contribution.

In the real world where discrete data is being used and the changes in data values are large, equation (3) must be amended to include several interaction terms. The result is equation (4) which is the basic PDM result.

$$\Delta\pi = \pi\Delta Q/Q + PQ\Delta P/P + \sum_i p_i q_i(\Delta Q/Q - \Delta q_i/q_i) - \sum_i p_i q_i(\Delta p_i/p_i)$$

$$+ \Delta P \Delta Q - \sum_i \Delta p_i \Delta q_i \tag{4}$$

Dividing equation (4) by last period's profit level yields equation (5) which indicates the percent contribution of each determinant to the growth in profits.

$$\frac{\Delta\pi}{\pi(-1)} = \frac{\pi(\Delta Q/Q)}{\pi(-1)} + \frac{PQ\Delta P/P}{\pi(-1)} + \frac{\sum_i p_i q_i(\Delta Q/Q - \Delta q_i/q_i)}{\pi(-1)}$$

$$- \frac{\sum_i p_i q_i(\Delta p_i/p_i)}{\pi(-1)} + \frac{\Delta P \Delta Q}{\pi(-1)} - \frac{\sum_i \Delta p_i \Delta q_i}{\pi(-1)} \tag{5}$$

The third term of equation (5) can be further decomposed into two additional components: productivity contribution due to scale (the first term of equation (6)) and productivity contribution due to factor prices (the second term of equation (6)).

$$\sum_i p_i q_i(\Delta Q/Q - \Delta q_i/q_i) = \sum_i q_i(\Delta Q/Q) - \Delta q_i/q_i -$$

$$\left[\sum_i p_i q_i(\Delta Q/Q) - \Delta q_i/q_i - (\sum_i q_i \Delta Q/Q - \Delta q_i/q_i) \right] \tag{6}$$

This distinction is made because factor price increases can offset productivity growth declines thus creating the illusion that productivity is making an increasing contribution to profit growth. In other words, smaller efficiency gains are being valued at higher factor prices. This decomposition also indicates that an industry's resource base can be increasing while productivity growth is declining, resulting in real increases in profit growth due to productivity. Thus productivity does not have to increase at an increasing rate for the productivity contribution to profit growth to increase.

Equation (5) was implemented by multiplying the lagged value of profits, revenue, and total cost by their respective rate of change variables and dividing the products by profit lagged one period. Several things should be noted about equation (5). First, the volume contribution to profit growth will tend to be smaller than productivity since an industry's cost base is much larger than its profit level. The same reasoning applies when comparing the sales price to the volume contribution.

Second, how equation (5) is implemented will determine whether it retains its identity status. This will depend on whether the implicit aggregate input prices and quantities grow at the same rate as the weighted average of the growth of individual factor prices and quantities. In any one year there will not be an equivalency, although the differences will be small. However, these small differences translate into larger profit change differences since the PDM requires that growth rates be multiplied by dollar levels. Since we desire to analyse the role of individual factors (rather than the aggregate input) to profit growth, the above aggregation restriction was not imposed. As the empirical work will demonstrate, our approach does not create a serious problem for the analysis.

Third, the interaction terms represent joint price–volume and joint factor price–quantity impacts. These impacts tend to be small and offsetting. Since any rule we develop would be arbitrary and bias the measurement of the pure independent affects, we decided not to decompose the interaction terms. This decision also creates a bias in the reported results since the measured independent effects for volume and price are smaller than they, in fact, are. One would presume that most of this downward bias influences the sales price impact since its independent effect is much larger than the effect of volume. Not decomposing the factor price–quantity interaction term creates a downward bias for factor price and productivity contributions to profit growth. The productivity contribution is additionally biased downward by not fully attributing the volume impact. Again, because these biases are generally small and because the independent impacts capture most of the change in profits, we opted not to arbitrarily decompose the interaction terms and attribute their impacts to any of the pure determinants of profit growth.[1]

5.3   THE SOURCES OF PROFIT GROWTH: SOME THEORETICAL CONSIDERATIONS

Equation (5) indicates that profit growth can come from a number of sources. It also implies that, *ceteris paribus*, sales price, productivity and factor price contributions have the largest impacts on profit growth. The model as currently configured does not value one source of profit growth over another. It merely quantifies what actually happened. However, simple micro theory suggests that the composition of profit does make a difference in terms of its sustainability or long-term growth potential. Industries that obtain more of their profit growth through productivity growth contribution should also register higher growth in profits than industries that are less dependent on productivity. This follows from the fact that productivity enhancing strategies can increase profits and its growth rate without encouraging increased competition. Sales price increases, without any real and/or perceived increase in value, raise profits initially. In the long run, however, such strategies will be vulnerable to lower cost from foreign competition and customer migration toward them. Hence, an industry that increases its profit growth by predominantly raising sales price will have a lower quality (less sustainable and more uncertain) profit stream than an industry where productivity is making an increasing contribution to profit growth.

The composition of profit growth also has direct implications for the valuing of profit streams. Consider the constant dividend growth model put forth by Shapiro and Gordon (1956, pp. 103–10). This model states that the present value of an income stream is equal to next period's dividend, divided by the difference between the discount rate and long-term growth of dividends. If sales price induced profit streams are more difficult to sustain than productivity induced profit streams (and dividend streams as well), then a rational investor will both increase the discount rate and reduce the estimate of long-term dividend growth. These adjustments will combine to reduce the value of the sales price induced profit (dividend) stream relative to the productivity enhanced stream. Hence, profit growth that emanates from productivity contribution is more valuable and industries that are characterised by rising productivity contributions are likely to register higher profit growth and therefore be more highly valued.

The theoretical considerations noted certainly suggest that an industry comparison of the sources of profit growth is a necessary first step prior to broaching the more difficult issues associated with identifying and quantifying the determinants of these contributions to each industry's profit growth and the resulting issues of valuation. It is this task and the accompanying analysis to which we now turn.

5.4 DATA UTILISED IN THE STUDY

The basic data set used in this study was developed by the BLS as part of its ongoing work in studying industry productivity. The basic methodology developed by BLS for constructing its data is clearly presented in 'Trends in Multi-factor Productivity, 1948–81' (Bulletin 2178, September 1983). The data provided by the BLS include price and quantity values for aggregate output of each two-digit manufacturing industry and the manufacturing aggregate. Input prices and input quantities for five categories of inputs for each two-digit industry were also developed. These input categories are labour, materials, capital, energy, and services. For purposes of studying profit change, the original BLS data set was amended. Capital costs in a multi-factor productivity environment include both the costs associated with using the capital in production and the rate of return on that capital. In order to separate the return on capital, or its equivalent, profits before taxes, we developed profit data by industry using the gross product originating data published by the Bureau of Economic Analysis, Department of Commerce. Using this data (which was the data source used by the BLS to develop its capital cost variable), we subtracted corporate and non-corporate profits for each industry from the capital cost variable for each industry as reported by the BLS. This yielded an industry specific capital cost variable that only reflected the dollar costs of each industry using its capital base. A real capital cost quantity was developed by dividing each industry's adjusted capital cost by the industry's rental price of capital as developed and published by the BLS. This rental price variable measures the average unit price that an industry would have to pay if it rented its capital rather than purchased it outright. Therefore, it includes the return to capital of the renting industry as a cost to the industry that uses the capital. Hence, the real capital cost measure developed represents the capital input used in production. The other price and quantity variables were not adjusted and therefore were used as originally published by the BLS.

Using the BLS data, we calculated multi-factor indexes for each industry and the manufacturing aggregate. Our indexes were calculated as the growth in real gross output less the weighted average growth of the real values of the individual inputs. Because of the PDM specification, the factor weights represent the share that a factor is of total cost lagged one period. The weights varied over time to reflect the changing composition of inputs. Using factor share weights based on the average of factor shares for successive periods (a requirement of a Tornqvist index) does not alter any of the results. The capital cost variable was reduced by the value of the dollar return as noted above. Thus, total cost for each industry does not include an industry's return to capital as is the case in all estimates of multi-factor productivity. This does not alter our estimate of multi-factor productivity growth in any significant way and does not alter the conclusion that there has been a productivity growth slowdown. For example, the BLS calculates that multi-factor productivity growth in manufacturing over the 1949 to 1973 and 1973 to 1983 periods were 1.5 per cent and 0.3 per cent respectively. Our estimates are 1.6 per cent for the earlier period and 0.5 per cent for the later period. Similarly, small differences occur at the industry level.

5.5   EMPIRICAL RESULTS

5.5.1   Accuracy of the PDM

In order to demonstrate the degree to which the PDM accurately approximates the actual change in profit, we regressed actual profit change against estimated profit change from the PDM. The results from these regressions

Table 5.1   Relationship between actual and estimated profit change

Sector	Constant coefficient	T-value	Slope coefficient	T-value	D-W	$\bar{R}^2$
Total						
mfg.	.777	4.390	.894	50.33	1.57	.987
SIC 20	.033	3.610	.955	63.87	1.88	.992
21	.017	2.065	.712	14.80	1.64	.869
22	.026	2.073	1.028	28.39	1.16	.961
23	.008	.559	.881	14.39	1.21	.862
24	.133	2.98	.916	20.10	.87	.924
25	.004	1.98	.964	53.27	2.71	.989
26	.036	4.56	.926	62.89	1.39	.992
27	.012	4.32	1.000	124.4	2.15	.988
28	.090	3.66	.912	51.63	1.71	.988
29	.106	2.05	.686	12.43	1.44	.823
30	.048	3.66	.860	23.49	1.21	.943
31	.004	.41	.635	6.81	2.1	.580
32	.063	3.15	.856	24.46	1.26	.948
33	.212	1.36	.454	13.34	1.91	.843
34	.039	2.86	.883	58.90	1.73	.991
35	.101	3.07	.799	46.59	1.77	.985
36	.109	3.55	.873	33.41	1.79	.971
371	.575	1.65	.303	5.79	1.76	.500
38	.025	3.07	.812	45.66	2.42	.984
39	.013	1.91	.791	47.02	2.02	.985

Source: Bureau of the US Census and Data Resources, Inc.

are presented in Table 5.1. In virtually all cases the approximation is very highly correlated with actual profit change. In five of the industries (SICs 21, 23, 31, 33, and 371) the $\bar{R}^2$ is below .95. Of these, only two have relatively low $\bar{R}^2$'s, SICs 31 (Leather and leather products) and 371 (Motor vehicles and motor vehicle equipment). The slope coefficients indicate that variations in the PDM approximation have a slight bias which suggests that a given change in estimated profit change translates to a somewhat lower change in actual profit change. The Durbin-Watson generally indicates the absence of serial correlation (value of 1.7 or more), thus suggesting that the PDM framework captures all the systematic variation in actual profit change. In short, these results suggest that the PDM can be used to evaluate the contribution made by each identified determinant of profit change.

5.5.2   Variability in Profit Growth

To set the stage for the decomposition analysis to follow, it is worthwhile to summarise how the growth rate in profits has changed over time. Table 5.2

shows average annual growth rates in industry profits, the standard deviation and the coefficient of variation over the 1950–83 time frame and three sub-periods. These sub-periods were chosen in part because they coincide with the time frame over which much of the productivity analysis has been done and because they approximately represent phases in the long-term growth path of the post Second World War US economy. The first three columns indicate that average profit growth has been trending lower since the 1950–65 period. For the manufacturing aggregate, profit growth averaged 8.3 per cent over the 1950–65 period, slowed down to 2.6 per cent during the 1966–72 period and rose in the 1973–83 period to 5.7 per cent. While some of this growth improvement could be associated with accelerating inflation over this time frame, one must keep in mind that profits while a nominal measure, can be thought of as a quasi real concept since inflation helps by raising revenue and hinders profit change through rising factor prices. Hence, it is relative prices that matter to profit change and not the overall increase in inflation. Across industries the same general pattern emerges as that for the manufacturing aggregate, with the exception of SIC 35 (Non-electrical machinery), where profit levels declined as domestic producers lost market share in world markets in the latter 1970s and early 1980s, SIC 30 (Rubber and miscellaneous plastic products) and SIC 38 (Instruments).

The variability of profit growth has increased over time as measured by the standard deviation of profit growth. For the manufacturing aggregate absolute variability has increased by six percentage points between the 1973–83 interval and the 1950–65 interval. During the 1966–72 period, variability declined relative to both the latter and former periods and followed the same general pattern as the average profit growth measure. Again, across industries the pattern was similar to that observed for manufacturing, although there were exceptions particularly when comparing the 1966–72 period to the earlier interval. In SIC 20 (Food and kindred products), SIC 24 (Lumber), SIC 32 (Stone clay and glass), SIC 33 (Primary metals), SIC 371 (Autos and auto parts) and SIC 39 (Miscellaneous manufacturing) absolute profit growth variability increased.

Although absolute profit growth variability increased over the 1950–83 period, when one normalises the measure to control for growth in the average a different conclusion emerges. The last four columns of Table 5.2 presents a relative measure of variability – the coefficient of variation. While relative profit growth variability increased for the manufacturing aggregate from the earliest to the latest interval, this does not characterise the industries that make up SIC 2 and SICs 30 and 31. The remaining industries, other than SIC 33 (Primary metals), are capital goods sectors, and the relative variability in their profit growth has increased. Indeed, these increases were more than sufficient to offset the reductions in the relative variability of the non-durable goods industries resulting in the

Table 5.2 Comparison over time of average and variability of profit growth by industry

Sector	1950 to 1983			1950 to 1965			1966 to 1972			1973 to 1983		
	Average % change	Standard deviation	Coefficient of variation	Average % change	Standard deviation	Coefficient of variation	Average % change	Standard deviation	Coefficient of variation	Average % change	Standard deviation	Coefficient of variation
Manufacturing	6.3	23.616	3.750	8.3	22.027	2.650	2.6	17.525	6.843	5.7	28.419	4.947
Food & Kindred Products (20)	5.0	12.454	2.467	3.3	8.074	2.415	2.3	7.882	3.415	9.4	17.633	1.875
Tobacco Products (21)	7.4	9.606	1.299	6.2	7.861	1.259	5.3	6.276	1.188	9.8	12.729	1.294
Textile Mill Products (22)	11.3	48.311	4.279	11.7	43.652	3.718	3.1	17.346	5.533	18.1	64.457	3.559
Apparel (23)	7.7	16.077	2.075	4.8	15.596	3.264	9.7	11.430	1.174	10.8	18.039	1.666
Lumber & Wood (24)	61.6	320.343	5.198	9.4	31.108	3.303	16.2	35.575	2.201	167.2	546.252	3.268
Furniture & Fixtures (25)	8.6	22.696	2.637	9.6	25.671	2.678	9.2	19.485	2.117	9.4	20.857	2.210
Paper & Allied Products (26)	7.8	25.729	3.307	7.9	25.205	3.205	5.0	20.903	4.220	10.5	28.238	2.701
Printing & Publishing (27)	7.1	11.914	1.670	6.3	12.784	2.019	5.0	9.604	1.917	9.7	11.095	1.140
Chemicals & Allied Products (28)	6.8	23.520	3.480	8.8	21.332	2.424	4.1	11.546	2.798	6.5	30.764	4.748
Rubber & Plastics (30)	17.7	52.410	2.955	17.5	57.310	3.279	18.2	44.254	2.434	17.0	47.894	2.812
Leather Products (31)	7.3	26.899	3.660	5.4	20.135	3.741	1.8	21.012	11.633	13.8	35.486	2.580
Stone, Clay & Glass (32)	NC	NC	NC	6.3	19.940	3.160	5.6	26.429	4.758	NC	NC	NC
Primary Metals (33)	NC	NC	NC	12.7	38.465	3.024	14.3	87.209	6.082	NC	NC	NC
Fabricated Metal Products (34)	7.6	22.731	3.008	8.9	24.277	2.720	10.2	22.296	2.183	6.7	21.778	3.243
Non-Electrical Machinery & Computers (35)	3.8	27.514	7.180	9.9	23.907	2.417	4.3	15.334	3.581	-3.8	35.362	-9.296
Electronic Machinery (36)	12.3	39.921	3.238	13.3	31.764	2.381	12.6	34.705	2.757	15.5	53.181	3.430
Automobiles & Trucks (371)	NC	NC	NC	27.1	85.393	3.148	39.1	123.783	3.164	NC	NC	NC
Instruments (38)	10.0	23.910	2.391	16.6	24.737	1.487	13.5	20.905	1.551	1.1	22.856	21.470
Misc. Manufactures (39)	NC	NC	NC	5.4	22.114	4.083	14.6	21.366	1.466	NC	NC	NC

NC denotes non-calculable intervals because of negative profit levels.
Sources: Bureau of Labour Statistics, 'Trends and Multi-Factor Productivity, 1948-81' (Bulletin 2178, September 1983). Data Resources Inc

measured trend increase in the manufacturing aggregate's coefficient of variation.

To summarise, profit growth has declined from the levels achieved during the 1950–65 period but increased during the 1973–83 period relative to the 1966–72 interval. This is true for the manufacturing aggregate and for most of its segments. However, the variability of profit growth, as measured by the coefficient of variation, shows a very much different pattern. This is particularly evident when evaluating the pattern for the individual industries that make up manufacturing. For over half of these sectors, there is less dispersion about its average profit growth during the 1973–83 sub-period than during earlier intervals. This implies that the certainty of achieving specific profit growth levels has been increasing over time. This finding is in contrast to the notion that profit growth has become less predictable. Indeed, when these calculations were extended to include the period from 1984 to 1987 the reduction in relative profit volatility was even more impressive. The coefficient of variation for the manufacturing aggregate over the extended period was 3.17. The average annual growth over this period was 9 per cent with a standard deviation of 28.9 per cent or about unchanged from its value over the 1973–83 interval.

5.5.3   The Determinants of Profit Growth in Industry

Table 5.3 decomposes profit growth into the growth attributable to each determinant for the manufacturing aggregate and its two-digit components for the 1950–83 interval. The results strongly confirm the importance of the productivity contribution to profit growth. Indeed, across all sectors except three (Stone, Primary metals, and Autos) the contribution from productivity growth exceeds the contribution from volume growth. In each of these industries the productivity contribution to profit growth was decidedly negative. The productivity growth contribution is also widely dispersed around the contribution for the manufacturing aggregate with Lumber ranked highest (42 per cent) and Autos ranked the lowest (−34 per cent). Six out of nineteen industries had productivity growth contributions that exceeded the manufacturing average (SICs 20, 22, 23, 24, 30, 36).

The price recovery contribution to profit growth is negative for the manufacturing aggregate and for all industries except for Tobacco products (SIC 21), Printing and Publishing (SIC 27), Stone, clay and glass (SIC 32) and Autos and trucks (SIC 371). The results for tobacco are consistent with empirical research that finds the demand for cigarettes to be quite inelastic with respect to price; a point covered later in some depth. The results for autos are in part a function of the Voluntary Trade Agreement (VTA) which was initiated in 1976 and limited Japanese auto sales to 1.8 million units.This quota was increased to 2.3 million units in 1984. While the

Table 5.3   Contributions to profit growth by industry, 1950 to 1983

Sector	Productivity	Rank	Sales volume	Rank	Price recovery	Rank
Manufacturing	0.147	–	0.033	–	–0.130	
Food & Kindred Products (20) ..	0.152	6	0.024	17	–0.140	15
Tobacco Products (21)..............	0.008	18	0.005	20	0.058	2
Textile Mill Products (22)	0.366	2	0.033	10	–0.332	21
Apparel (23)	0.230	5	0.024	18	–0.168	17
Lumber & Wood (24)	0.417	1	0.026	16	–0.200	18
Furniture & Fixtures (25)	0.145	9	0.033	11	–0.084	11
Paper & Allied Products (26)	0.118	12	0.040	8	–0.094	12
Printing & Publishing (27).........	0.036	17	0.035	9	0.001	4
Chemicals & Allied Products (28)..................................	0.130	10	0.053	5	–0.118	13
Rubber & Plastics (30).............	0.331	4	0.053	4	–0.237	19
Leather Products (31)...............	0.114	13	–0.001	21	–0.069	10
Stone, Clay & Glass (32)..........	–0.274	20	0.026	15	0.117	1
Primary Metals (33)	–0.099	19	0.016	19	–0.016	7
Fabricated Metal Products (34)	0.093	14	0.029	12	–0.049	8
Non-Electrical Machinery & Computers (35)	0.125	11	0.045	7	–0.146	16
Electronic Machinery (36).........	0.335	3	0.059	3	–0.292	20
Automobiles & Trucks (371)	–0.336	21	0.045	6	0.039	3
Instruments (38)	0.145	8	0.062	2	–0.124	14
Misc. Manufactures (39)	0.067	16	0.027	14	–0.065	9

A rank of 1 indicates greatest positive contribution to profit.
Source: Data Resources Inc.

Japanese were not the only exporter to the US, their competitive threat was fundamentally based on low cost rather than quality; a selling feature that became more dominant in the beginning of the 1980s as Japanese labour costs began rising relative to countries like Korea. Thus, by restricting low-cost competition, the VTA allowed domestic producers to raise prices at a rate that exceeded the increase in factor costs. In the case of the printing and publishing sector, price over recovery began during the 1966–72 period and remained positive through the 1973–83 period. It is not clear why this development occurred without specifying a complete model of price over recovery induced profit growth. A similar conclusion must also be reached with regard to stone, clay and glass.

Table 5.4 shows how the contributions to profit growth have changed over three sub-periods. The contribution to profit growth from productivity for the manufacturing aggregate declined by six percentage points between the 1966–72 interval and the 1950–65 period. In the 1973–83 period, the contribution to profit growth rose by four percentage points, from about 10.6 per cent to 14.5 per cent. At the industry level the patterns were very

Table 5.4 Contributions to profit growth by industry over three sub-periods

Sector	Productivity contribution			Sales volume contribution			Net price contribution		
	1950–1965	1966–1972	1973–1983	1950–1965	1966–1972	1973–1983	1950–1965	1966–1972	1973–1983
Manufacturing	0.167	0.106	0.145	0.041	0.038	0.017	-0.135	-0.135	-0.120
Food & Kindred Products (20)	0.176	0.103	0.149	0.027	0.027	0.017	-0.180	-0.126	-0.090
Tobacco Products (21)	0.049	0.115	-0.118	0.011	0.005	-0.003	-0.012	-0.070	0.243
Textile Mill Products (22)	0.335	0.202	0.515	0.036	0.064	0.008	-0.286	-0.281	-0.431
Apparel (23)	0.207	0.359	0.180	0.028	0.023	0.018	-0.143	-0.307	-0.116
Lumber & Wood (24)	0.196	0.152	0.906	0.029	0.057	0.002	-0.174	-0.096	-0.303
Furniture & Fixtures (25)	0.165	0.154	0.110	0.039	0.053	0.012	-0.098	-0.148	-0.022
Paper & Allied Products (26)	0.077	0.166	0.147	0.051	0.041	0.023	-0.063	-0.191	-0.076
Printing & Publishing (27)	0.108	0.004	-0.049	0.042	0.032	0.028	-0.084	0.011	0.119
Chemicals & Allied Products (28)	0.154	0.088	0.122	0.070	0.064	0.020	-0.141	-0.130	-0.078
Rubber & Plastics (30)	0.360	0.299	0.310	0.063	0.079	0.023	-0.249	-0.237	-0.221
Leather Products (31)	0.044	0.108	0.221	0.015	-0.007	-0.020	-0.038	-0.126	-0.077
Stone, Clay & Glass (32)	0.073	0.026	-0.969	0.049	0.026	-0.006	-0.067	-0.013	0.466
Primary Metals (33)	0.072	0.176	-0.522	0.040	0.014	-0.019	-0.019	-0.212	0.113
Fabricated Metal Products (34)	0.124	0.058	0.070	0.050	0.028	0.000	-0.096	-0.042	0.014
Non-Electrical Machinery & Computers (35)	0.088	0.113	0.187	0.049	0.045	0.039	-0.049	-0.143	-0.291
Electronic Machinery (36)	0.324	0.246	0.407	0.073	0.051	0.044	-0.273	-0.269	-0.334
Automobiles and Trucks (371)	0.251	0.586	-1.776	0.063	0.054	0.012	-0.168	-0.426	0.635
Instruments (38)	0.228	0.143	0.026	0.067	0.065	0.053	-0.153	-0.125	-0.083
Misc. Manufactures (39)	0.183	0.217	-0.198	0.040	0.050	-0.007	-0.180	-0.186	0.179

Source: Data Resources Inc.

Table 5.5   Scale contributions to industry profit growth over three sub-periods

	1950–1965	*1966–1972*	*1973–1983*
Manufacturing	.128	.051	.033
SIC 20	.156	.068	.052
SIC 21	.035	.069	−.039
SIC 22	.300	.146	.215
SIC 23	.204	.272	.093
SIC 24	.142	.066	.141
SIC 25	.137	.085	.043
SIC 26	.071	.088	.051
SIC 27	.079	.001	−.011
SIC 28	.118	.046	.025
SIC 30	.327	.186	.072
SIC 31	.080	.068	.113
SIC 32	.057	.006	−.188
SIC 33	.065	.067	−.067
SIC 34	.091	.027	.019
SIC 35	.057	.049	.049
SIC 36	.220	.115	.115
SIC 371	.177	.281	−.361
SIC 38	.183	.066	.013
SIC 39	.149	.122	.045

Source: Data Resources Inc.

different. Comparing the 1966–72 interval with the 1973–83 interval, the contributions from productivity declined in eleven industries and rose in eight industries. Moreover, during this later sub-period, six industries had productivity growth contributions that were larger than their levels during the 1950–65 time frame. These six industries are: SIC 22 (Textile mill products), SIC 24 (Lumber), SIC 26 (Paper), SIC 31 (Leather), SIC 35 (Non-electrical machinery), and SIC 36 (Electrical machinery). However, except for SIC 31, these increased contributions were related to the effect of pricing these efficiency gains at rapid and continually rising prices.

This effect can be seen in Table 5.5 which shows the scale productivity growth contribution (productivity contribution in the absence of factor price inflation) to profit growth. For the manufacturing aggregate the scale contribution is lower in each sub-period from 1950–65 (12.8 per cent) to 1973–83 (3.3 per cent). This trend decline mirrors the documented decline in multi-factor productivity growth. In the sectors noted above that registered rising nominal productivity growth contributions, only one, SIC 31, had a scale contribution during the 1973–83 period that exceeded the value achieved during the earliest period. This was directly related to rising multi-factor productivity growth (0.2 per cent vs. 0.8 per cent). In SIC 24 (Lumber) the scale contribution was about the same in the later sub-period as it was in the earliest period, while in SIC 26 it was slightly less (7.1 per cent in 1950–65 vs. 5.1 per cent in 1973–83). In both industries declines in average productivity growth contributed to the declines in the scale contributions. Similarly, the scale contribution in SIC 35 (Non-electrical machinery which includes computers) was 5.7 per cent in the earlier period versus 4.9 per cent in the later interval. However, productivity growth increased from the earliest sub-period to the latest (0.9 per cent vs. 1.3 per cent). The scale contribution declined because the resource base did not increase enough relative to the low level of productivity in the earlier period. In SIC 36 the decline in the scale contribution is related to the decline in productivity growth that was registered in the later period relative to the earlier time frame (2.6 per cent vs. 1.7 per cent). Hence, the declines registered in these industries were both a function of a slowdown in productivity growth and slower growth in the resource base. These negatives were offset by rising factor prices that allowed these industries to receive more dollars per efficiency gain over time, thus giving the illusion of rising productivity contribution to profit growth.

As shown in Tables 5.4 and 5.5, several industries registered negative productivity growth contributions in both nominal and real terms (scale) in the 1973–83 interval. These industries include SIC 21 (Tobacco), SIC 27 (Printing), SIC 32 (Stone, clay and glass), SIC 33 (Steel) and SIC 371 (Autos and trucks). All of these manufacturing segments experienced reductions in productivity between the sub-intervals. However, not all of the negative contribution can be explained by the decline in productivity. In the auto industry particularly, the real resource base has been showing a lower trend since its 1974 peak while the metal sectors reached a peak in 1980. Likewise, the real resource base in tobacco was no larger in 1983 than it was in 1954. Only in printing and publishing has the real resource base been on a continuously rising uptrend.

Table 5.4 also indicates that the volume contribution to profit growth declined quite substantially between 1950–65 and 1973–83 for the manufacturing aggregate and each of the manufacturing industries as well. Most of the decline took place after the 1965–72 sub-period and is directly related to the rising import growth witnessed across a broad array of US manufacturing sectors. Table 5.6 provides evidence of this effect. Except in SICs 24 and 26, import penetration (constant dollar imports divided by domestic consumption) rose significantly between 1977 and 1981 in the subset of two-digit industries shown. In SICs 24 and 26 import penetration also rose but by less than one percentage point. In short, imports were rising faster than domestic consumption thus restricting growth in domestic output and its contribution to profit growth.

The net price or price over recovery contribution has not dramatically changed in the three time periods. For manufacturing as a whole, price recovery remained negative in each sub-period indicating that US indus-

Table 5.6   The change in import share in several two-digit SIC
manufacturing industries

Industry	Import share: 1977 (constant dollars)	Import share: 1981 (constant dollars)
SIC 22	3.7%	5.1%
SIC 24	9.1%	9.4%
SIC 26	7.3%	7.9%
SIC 31	34.9%	53.7%
SIC 35	6.3%	7.9%
SIC 36	11.5%	16.4%

Sources: Bureau of the US Census
Data Resources Inc.

tries as a group were not completely passing through higher factor costs in the form of higher sales prices. This profile also characterises most two-digit industries over each interval. However, during the 1973–83 interval price recovery became quite positive in several industries. This turnaround occurred in SICs 21, 27, 32, 33, 34, 371 and 39. Except for SIC 34 (Fabricated metals), productivity contributions were decidedly negative in these industries during this time frame. This suggests that these industries had to offset rising factor prices through raising output prices. While productivity offsets were possible, these industries chose not to respond in this way because it was apparently easier and less costly to raise sales prices. This strategy is only viable if the demand elasticities with respect to price are inelastic or if the industry believes that profits can be maximised by giving up market share in return for a higher unit product price. This strategy is associated with differentiating the product and puts firms that pursue this strategy on a different and steeper demand curve than firms that adopt strategies of minimising unit price in an attempt to maximise unit volume. Hence, the market share impact relates to the choice of the demand curve while the price elasticity effect refers to the revenue and profit implications of moving along a demand curve.

Product demands are inelastic with respect to price if there is a limited number of competitors or if switching costs associated with moving to the competitive product are very high. At the industry level (given the level of imports) switching costs are much greater than at the product level, since switching means moving from the product set of one industry to the product set of another industry as opposed to substituting a product of one firm for a very similar product of another firm. The demand elasticity argument directly applies to the tobacco industry while in the other industries it is almost impossible to disentangle the market share from the price elasticity determinant without a complete model of profit growth. As a result we only explored the relationship between tobacco demand and tobacco price since a price recovery model for each industry is well beyond the scope of this chapter.

In order to explore the tobacco price recovery relationship, the following model was estimated using a two-stage approach to control for simultaneity bias. The basic model is given by equation (7):

LOG(REAL TOBACCO OUTPUT) = A + B[LOG(TOBACCO PRICE)] + C[LOG(REAL DISPOSABLE INCOME)] + D[LOG(UNEMPLOYMENT RATE, NON-WHITE)]   (7)

The logic of the equation is straightforward. The demand for tobacco is inversely related to its price and positively related to real income available for spending. The demand for tobacco has also been claimed to be countercyclical by executives of tobacco companies. To test this hypothesis we included the unemployment rate among non-white workers. This was done because the percentage of non-whites who smoke exceeds that for the white working population. The overall unemployment rate was also employed and the results were not nearly as significant. The above model was estimated over the 1966–83 period since this was the time frame over which the tobacco industry was characterised by price over-recovery. The empirical results are shown in Table 5.7 and support the maintained hypothesis. The price elasticity of demand is 0.12 per cent indicating demand is very price inelastic. The demand for tobacco is income inelastic as well with a coefficient of 0.31 per cent. The unemployment rate impact is small and borderline significant. The results also support the hypothesis that the demand has become more inelastic during the 1973–83 period, thus giving rise to the more positive price recovery contribution to profit growth during the latter relative to the former time period. This test was carried out using a standard 'dummy' variable technique and the results also appear in Table 5.7. A two-stage technique was not used since the ordinary least square results were virtually the same as the two-stage results when the earlier equation was estimated. The 'dummy variable' coefficient is positive and significant indicating that tobacco demand is more price inelastic during the 1973–83 period than during the 1966–72 interval.

Short of a complete model that would explain the price recovery turnaround in the auto and steel industries, the history of trade developments certainly suggests that the intent to limit the share of domestic consumption that can be taken by imports supported both industry's ability to raise sales prices more than proportionately to factor prices. This effect has been noted in the auto industry. The experience in the steel industry sheds even more light on the price recovery turnaround. In 1969, a set of voluntary restraint agreements were established which effectively set steel quotas, but they were abandoned in 1971. In 1978, a trigger price mechanism was established which set price standards for foreign steel. If foreign steel was

Table 5.7   Tobacco industry demand equation time period: 1966 to 1983

Equation: LOG[RQ21] = A + B*LOG[QI21] + C*LOG[DPI82] + D*LOG[UN]

Variable name	Coefficient	T-stat.
Constant	−5.085	−8.772
QI21 (Tobacco price)	−.121*	−2.806
DPI82 (Disposable per. income)	.313	3.193
UN (Unemployment, non-white)	.059	1.299
$\bar{R}^2$ = .64		
D–W = 1.34		
SER = .023		
* = Two-stage estimator		

Test for Change in Price Elasticity of Demand

Equation: LOG[RQ21] = A + B*LOG[QI21] + C*D* LOG[QI21] + E*LOG[DPI82] + F*LOG[UN]

Variable name	Coefficient	T-stat.
A	−4.155	−5.506
B	−.119	−2.985
C*D	.008	1.859
D = 0; 1966 to 1972		
D = 1; 1973 to 1983		
E	.187	1.580
F	.055	1.300
$\bar{R}^2$ = .70; D–W = 1.80; SER = .02		

sold below these minima, the transactions were reviewed to determine whether anti-dumping regulations were violated. In 1982 the EEC–US steel trade agreement was established which limited steel imports from the EEC to about 7 per cent of the US market. This type of agreement was folded into the Voluntary Restraint Agreement in 1984 which limited the market share of other steel country exporters. Thus the ability to raise prices more than proportionately to increases in factor costs, in large measure is the result of restricting competition either through setting price floors and/or quantity quotas.

5.5.4   The Productivity Factor Price Nexus

The contribution of factor cost to profit growth can be calculated by multiplying the difference in growth between productivity and factor costs by total costs lagged one period and dividing the result by profits lagged

Table 5.8   Factor cost contribution to profit growth by industry

Sector	All factors	Labour	Capital	Materials	Energy	Services
Manufacturing......................	–0.462	–0.206	–0.042	–0.155	–0.014	–0.045
Food & Kindred Products (20)................................	–0.841	–0.149	–0.062	–0.576	–0.011	–0.043
Tobacco Products (21)..........	–0.267	–0.039	–0.124	–0.083	–0.002	–0.019
Textile Mill Products (22)......	–0.322	–0.123	–0.018	–0.147	–0.012	–0.022
Apparel (23)........................	–0.377	–0.168	–0.009	–0.167	–0.003	–0.029
Lumber & Wood (24)...........	–0.653	–0.269	–0.049	–0.282	–0.017	–0.036
Furniture & Fixtures (25)......	–0.605	–0.226	–0.012	–0.311	–0.007	–0.050
Paper & Allied Products (26)	–0.398	–0.143	–0.030	–0.172	–0.028	–0.025
Printing & Publishing (27).....	–0.412	–0.201	–0.018	–0.130	–0.004	–0.059
Chemicals & Allied Products (28)................................	–0.327	–0.095	–0.032	–0.132	–0.024	–0.045
Rubber & Plastics (30)..........	–0.866	–0.292	–0.057	–0.446	–0.022	–0.050
Leather Products (31)...........	–0.602	–0.284	–0.011	–0.253	–0.007	–0.047
Stone, Clay & Glass (32).......	–0.926	–0.370	–0.080	–0.331	–0.076	–0.069
Primary Metals (33)	–1.176	–0.404	–0.105	–0.537	–0.073	–0.056
Fabricated Metal Products (34)................................	–0.650	–0.246	–0.021	–0.337	–0.009	–0.037
Non-Electrical Machinery & Computers (35)	–0.413	–0.187	–0.022	–0.173	–0.005	–0.026
Electronic Machinery (36)	–0.594	–0.270	–0.034	–0.222	–0.008	–0.060
Automobiles & Trucks (371)	0.242	0.053	0.017	0.160	0.003	0.009
Instruments (38)..................	–0.438	–0.202	–0.020	–0.172	–0.004	–0.039
Misc. Manufactures (39)........	–0.475	–0.176	–0.019	–0.228	–0.006	–0.047

Source: Data Resources Inc.

one period. Table 5.8 presents the results of this calculation for the manufacturing aggregate and each two-digit SIC industry. The results indicate that productivity growth does not offset factor price inflation in any industry or in the manufacturing aggregate. Moreover, this result holds for each individual factor as well, and it indicates that firms and industries have not been successful or have not consciously attempted to fully offset rising factor prices through productivity growth. This is a puzzling result since one would expect, *a priori*, that large and continuous factor price increases would result in significant factor mix changes that keep the factor cost contribution to profit growth much lower than it is. This, of course, gets back to the central question of why productivity growth was not greater particularly in those industries where factor prices were rising sharply. Beyond this, the data raises the issue of why productivity growth of individual factors was not large enough to fully offset the increase in their factor prices. Although not shown, this also characterises various sub-intervals and therefore is not a function of averaging several extreme observations. Unfortunately we can only raise the issue of why productivity offsets did not occur and conclude that this is an interesting territory for further research.

Table 5.9 Industries that have registered the largest increase in costs relative to profits

	Cost contribution (1950–1966)	Cost contribution (1973–1983)	Critical contributing factors
Manufacturing	−.085	−1.087	E,S,M
SIC 20	−.149	−1.874	M
SIC 22	−.126	−1.041	L,M
SIC 24	−.068	−1.623	L,M,E,S
SIC 25	−.175	−1.315	L,M,S
SIC 30	−.173	−2.245	L,M
SIC 32	−.132	−2.288	L,M,E,S,C
SIC 33	−.219	−2.637	L,M (Primary), E,S
SIC 36	−.071	−1.539	L,S,M

L = Labour
M = Materials
S = Services
E = Energy
C = Capital
Source: Data Resources, Inc.

Before concluding this section, we explore which industries registered the largest cost contributions to profit growth over the 1973–83 sub-interval relative to the 1950–65 period and which factors of production were the major contributors. These results are shown in Table 5.9. Labour and materials were the two factors that contributed most to the rising of factor costs in the industries shown. For example, in the primary metals industry, the key determinant of the significant overall cost increase was the rapidly rising cost of materials, excluding energy. While capital costs rose in all industries, it generally was not the primary driving force behind the very large cost contributions that were recorded in the most current interval. Service costs rose rapidly over the 1973–83 period, although these increases began to become significant during the 1966–72 time frame. In addition, increases in service costs made a larger negative contribution to profit growth than rising energy costs in most segments of the manufacturing sector. Since Kendrick (1987, pp. 28–35) has shown that there is a definite downward bias in measures of service sector output, it is more than likely that actual purchases of services are larger and have grown faster than our data set indicates. This would imply that service costs have made a greater negative contribution to profit growth than is indicated in this chapter.

5.6 SUMMARY AND CONCLUSIONS

The central purpose of this chapter is to explore the determinants of profit growth in the manufacturing aggregate and its two-digit components. We approached this task by first showing that industry profit growth can be decomposed into its major determinants: profit growth due to (i) volume growth (volume contribution), (ii) sales price growth (sales price contribution), (iii) input price growth (input price contribution), and (iv) productivity growth (productivity growth contribution). This last determinant of profit growth can be further decomposed into the factor price effect (pricing efficiency gains at higher price levels) and the scale contribution (the productivity contribution which is unrelated to factor price changes). Using a data set constructed by the Bureau of Labour Statistics, we demonstrated the following:

1. The productivity contribution to profit growth increased in the 1973–83 time frame relative to the 1966–72 period for the manufacturing aggregate although the contribution was below the level achieved during the Golden Age of productivity growth (1950 to 1965).
2. This pattern does not characterise the various two-digit segments. During the 1973–83 period six industries (Textile Mill Products, Lumber, Paper, Leather, Non-electrical machinery and Electrical machinery) recorded productivity contributions that exceeded the levels registered during the Golden Age. However, most of the favourable impact was a result of rising factor prices and except for the Leather industry the scale contributions mirrored the down-trend in multi-factor productivity growth. In several industries (notably steel and the autos) the scale contribution declines were both a product of declines in productivity growth and declines in the resource base from peak levels achieved earlier.
3. While the price recovery term is negative for manufacturing and most industries in each of the three sub-periods, it turned decidedly positive in the tobacco, steel and auto sectors during the 1973–83 interval. We demonstrated that in the tobacco industry this finding was consistent with demand being inelastic with respect to price while trade restrictions in steel and autos helped explain some of the turnaround in these industries.
4. The volume contribution declined significantly after 1972 for the manufacturing aggregate and each two-digit industry. We demonstrated that this was associated with the increase in the real import share across a broad array of industries.

Although the analysis presented here is comprehensive, it does suggest, however, areas for further research. While we have quantified the impact of key determinants of profit growth, we have not isolated the key driving variables behind these factors in the context of a complete model of profit growth determination. We are currently developing a model using a decomposition approach that concentrates on the change in the rate of return on capital rather than profit growth and linking this structure to a model of industry valuation. Indeed, it will be this research that will, we believe, extend our current efforts and allow us to better understand the process of profit creation and valuation.

Note

1. The average growth in profits in the manufacturing aggregate attributable to the price–volume interaction and the factor price–quantity interaction terms over the 1950–83 period is 0.5 per cent and 0.9 per cent respectively. These small percentages are representative of the various two-digit segments as well.

References

Brayton, G. E., 'Productivity Measure Aids in Profit Analysis', *Management Accounting* (January 1985) pp. 54–8.

Brown, G., 'The Determinants of Profitability', *Data Resources Interindustry Review* (Spring 1986) pp. 37–49.

Chaudry, A. M., 'Projecting Productivity to the Bottom Line', *Productivity Brief*, no. 18 (Houston: American Productivity Center, 1982).

Feldman, S. J., 'The Quality of Industry Cash Flow and Investment Decision Making', *Data Resources Interindustry Review* (Fall 1986) pp. 21–34.

Feldman, S. J., 'Cash Flow Prospects for US Industry and the Reemergence of US Manufacturing', *Data Resources US Industry Review*, Fourth Quarter (1987) pp. 21–32.

Feldman, S. J. and B. Von Loggrenberg, 'Analyzing the Sources of Sectoral Profitability', *Data Resources Interindustry Review* (Fall 1981) pp. 47–53.

Kendrick, J. W., *Improving Company Productivity Performance* (Baltimore and London: The Johns Hopkins University Press, 1984).

Kendrick, J. W., 'Service Sector Productivity', *Business Economics* (April 1987) pp. 28–35.

Miller, D. M., 'Profitability Equals Productivity Plus Price Recovery', *Harvard Business Review* (May–June 1984) pp. 145–53.

Ruch, W. A., 'Your Key to Planning Profits', *Productivity Brief*, no. 18 (Houston: American Productivity Center, 1982).

Shapiro, E. and M. J. Gordon, 'Capital Equipment Analysis: The Required Rate of Profit', *Management Science* (October 1956) pp. 103–10.

6 The Persistence of Profits

Dennis C. Mueller*

6.1 TWO VIEWS OF COMPETITION

Two views about competition exist. The first sees competition as a process for allocating resources to their optimal uses. The price mechanism is the instrument for achieving this goal, and when it functions properly equilibria emerge with prices equated to marginal social costs of production. When it malfunctions, equilibria exist with some prices above marginal costs, and society suffers a welfare loss from the under-consumption of these goods. Such malfunctions are usually attributed to an insufficient number of buyers or sellers. Monopoly is seen as the antithesis of competition. Thus, under the first view, competition is seen as a process for determining prices and quantities, the allocation of resources for a given set of tastes and technological opportunities. At its zenith, competition produces an equilibrium set of prices which induce a Pareto optimal allocation of the economy's goods and services. Such equilibria are anticipated so long as monopolistic elements are absent.

The other view of competition sees it not as a process for allocating a given stock of resources, but as a process for transforming these resources into new products and production techniques. Competition takes the form not of lower prices for an existing set of products, but of new and improved ideas, and these in turn are the property of the individual(s) who created them, and his/her/their employer. In the first instance, competition for a new product is competition for a newly created monopoly. With time the monopoly disappears as other firms imitate and improve upon the new product. Thus, monopoly is an integral part of a dynamically competitive process. A passing stage in an industry's evolution, whose presence might signify progressive good performance just as readily as poor performance.

When competition is viewed as a dynamic process of new product and process creation, the concept of equilibrium does not play an important role. What is of interest is not the constellation of prices and allocation of resources at a particular point in time, but their movements over time. The perspective is that of a system in flux, of constant disequilibria evolving through time, rather than of a system in a state of equilibrium at a particular point in time.

It is the first view of competition that informs most economic analysis and underlies most model building. And it is the first view of competition that is predominant in the economics classroom. Yet it is arguably the second view that more accurately describes actual competition.

6.2 THE SCHUMPETERIAN PERSPECTIVE

The second representation of the competitive process owes its origin to Joseph Schumpeter (1934, 1950), of course. The salient feature of Schumpeter's description of the capitalist process is its dynamic nature. Iconoclastic entrepreneurs introduce innovations – new products, new production processes, new marketing techniques, new organisational structures – which create temporary monopolistic advantages over their competitors. These transitory monopolies create pockets of profits, which in turn provide the incentive for imitators to step forward and thereby drive these profits back to zero. Thus, the 'process of creative destruction' proceeds; innovation creating monopoly, monopoly creating profits, profits creating imitators until a state of normalcy returns, only to be followed by new innovations and a repeat of the cycle.

This Schumpeterian image of the competitive process often seems to underlie more informal arguments by economists in favour of capitalist institutions over socialist institutions, unregulated markets over regulated markets, or in explanation for why some developed countries out perform others over the long run. Yet the Schumpeterian perspective has had little impact on the development of more formal models of market behaviour. Efforts to move the profession in this direction (Clark, 1961; McNulty, 1968; Kirzner, 1973), although often applauded, do not launch a subsequent stream of research, which develops their initial insights. The Schumpeterian perspective remains just that, a perspective on the nature of competition, rather than a model of the competitive process.

The most important exception to this generalisation is perhaps the evolutionary model of capitalism of Nelson and Winter (1982).[1] Nelson and Winter consciously eschew standard neoclassical models of profit maximising firms operating in competitive markets, and the notion that these markets are in equilibrium. Rather, they trace the evolution of firms and industries over time using simulation techniques. Although these simulations trace out a rich mosaic of a capitalist economy's evolution, a mosaic which does accord well with actual experience in many ways, they do not constitute a formal test of a Schumpeterian or evolutionary model against, say, a neoclassical model. They raise rather than answer the question of how to test a Schumpeterian model of the competitive process.

Such a test would seem to have to consist of at least two elements: first, an examination of the histories of various industries to see whether they follow the innovation–imitation–maturity cycle sketched by Schumpeter, and, second, an examination of the profit histories of firms and industries to see whether the process of dynamic competition does indeed erode abnormal profits over time.

Case study evidence on product and industry life cycles seems to support a Schumpeterian description of an industry's evolution (Gort and Klepper, 1982; and Klepper and Graddy, 1984). Initial innovations are followed by the entry of numerous 'imitators', which in turn leads to a shake-out phase in an industry's evolution, which might be likened to Schumpeter's gale of creative destruction. While this general pattern accords with the Schumpeterian view of industry dynamics, industry life cycles appear to enfold at substantially different speeds, and exceptions do exist (ibid). Moreover, the studies of product life cycles have not investigated the profit performances of the innovating and imitating firms. Indeed, very little is known about the intertemporal patterns of profitability for individual firms and industries in general. This void is filled to some extent by this chapter.

We test two main tenets of the Schumpeterian thesis: (i) that the competitive process does successfully erode positions of excess profits: that is, in the long run all economic rents tend toward zero; and (ii) that the erosion process proceeds quickly. While the first hypothesis can be clearly formulated and tested – rents are either zero or they are not – the second hypothesis is more equivocal. How quick is quick? We shall not actually try to answer this question, but rather present evidence of the speed of adjustment of profits to their long-run equilibrium values.

6.3   INTERTEMPORAL PATTERNS OF PROFITABILITY

Assume that firm i's return on capital in year t, π_{it}, is composed potentially of three components: (i) a competitive return, c, common to all companies; (ii) a permanent rent, r_i, specific to firm i, which could be a premium for risk; and (iii) a short-run rent s_{it} with zero expected value.

$$\pi_{it} = c + r_i + s_{it} \tag{1}$$

For a t sufficiently long s_{it} might be assumed to have mean zero and constant variance over time, and the hypothesis that competition eventually drives all profit rates to a common normal level could be tested simply by comparing mean profit rates across firms to see whether they are significantly different from one another, given their intertemporal variances.

Such a test would require, if t is measured in years, that any short-run rents earned this year are independent of rents earned last year. A more reasonable assumption concerning the s_{it} is that they are intertemporally related, but converge on zero. Let s_{it} be defined by

$$s_{it} = \lambda s_{it-1} + u_{it} \tag{2}$$

where $0 < \lambda < 1$, and the u_{it} are distributed $N(0, \sigma^2)$. Assuming (2) holds in every period it can be used to remove s_{it} from (1) to obtain

$$\pi_{it} = (1 - \lambda)(c + r_i) + \lambda\pi_{it-1} + u_{it} \tag{3}$$

Letting $\hat{\alpha}$ and $\hat{\lambda}_i$ be the estimates from the autoregressive equation

$$\pi_{it} = \hat{\alpha}_i + \hat{\lambda}_i \pi_{it-1} + u_{it} \tag{4}$$

one derives an estimate of the long-run projected profits of firm i, π_{ip}, as

$$\hat{\pi}_{ip} = \frac{\hat{\alpha}_i}{1 - \hat{\lambda}_i} \tag{5}$$

A test of the hypothesis that competition drives all profit rates to a common competitive level would be to test whether the $\hat{\pi}_{ip}$ differ significantly across firms. Were no significant differences found, one would accept the hypothesis that all long-runs rents, r_i, are zero.

Even if one were to accept that hypothesis, however, one might be interested in examining the magnitude of the $\hat{\lambda}_i$s. The bigger $\hat{\lambda}_i$ is, the slower short-run rents erode, and the more a firm's profits constitute a slowly moving average around $c + r_i$. To see the difference between $\hat{\pi}_{ip}$ and $\hat{\lambda}$ more clearly, consider the following two firms. Firm 1 has a very high $\hat{\pi}_{ip}$, but $\hat{\lambda} = 0$; firm 2's $\hat{\pi}_{ip}$ equals the competitive rate of return c, but its $\hat{\lambda}$ is very large, say 0.9. The implications would be that firm 1 earns substantial permanent rents equal to $\pi_{ip} - c$, but that any short-run rents it experiences are expected to disappear within a year. The second firm's short-run rents are highly correlated, however, and induce moving averages of lengthy periodicity. But they cycle around and converge upon the competitive return. In the long run, it is this return toward which 2's dampening cycle is moving.

6.4 EMPIRICAL ESTIMATES: PERSISTENCE OF PROFITS

We test for the existence of persistent differences in profitability using a sample of 551 manufacturing firms drawn from the surveys of the 1000 largest firms in 1950 and 1972 conducted by the FTC.[2] Basically any firm from either of these lists for which there is complete financial data over the 23-year period is included in the sample. The sample includes all companies satisfying this criterion regardless of the extent of their merger activity, and thus includes many firms with radically different product structures in 1972 than they possessed in 1950, a point to which we shall return.

Table 6.1   Summary of results from autoregressive profits' equations
$$\pi_{it} = \hat{a}_i + \hat{\lambda}_i \pi_{it-1} + u_{it}, \; \hat{\pi}_{ip} = \hat{a}_i/(1 - \hat{\lambda}_i)$$
Mean

	Mean	S.E.	Minimum	Maximum
$\hat{\pi}_{ip}$	.002	.017	−.099	.193
λ	.210	−.210	−.262	.935
$\bar{R}^2$	.052		−.062	.855

We define a company's return on capital as its profits net of taxes and gross of interest divided by total assets. We use a net of tax definition of profits on the assumption that the convergence of profits to the competitive return is driven by the exit and entry of other firms, and that this entry and exit responds to after tax profit levels.

While we have modelled the competitive return, c, as if it were a constant, it may vary over time as business cycle factors and long-run trends raise and lower the average performance of firms in the economy. To allow for these common intertemporal patterns, we take each firm's annual profit rate as a deviation from the sample mean for that year. In effect, we assume that the relationship between the competitive return c, and the average return on capital is invariant over time. Later we shall also allow for firm and industry differences in c due to risk.

Table 6.1 summarises the results for the estimations of equation (4) for the 551 firms. Starting with the bottom row we see that the average fit to the autoregressive equation was rather weak, with a mean $\bar{R}^2$ of only .052. Thus, the transitory component of a firm's profit rate would not seem to require more than a year to be eliminated in many cases. A similar conclusion is implied by the figures for $\hat{\lambda}$. On average only 18 per cent of any deviation from last year's sample mean is expected to reoccur this year.[3] The distribution of $\hat{\lambda}$s is obviously positively skewed, however, with the mean $\hat{\lambda}$ pulled down by the negative $\hat{\lambda}$s. Of the latter *none* of the 122 $\hat{\lambda}$s that were negative had a value for $|\hat{\lambda}| > 1.72$ times its standard error (the critical value for a two-tailed, 10 per cent level test). Thus, the $\hat{\lambda}$s for these firms are consistent with the hypothesis that the short-run rents of these firms vary independently over time. Of the $\hat{\lambda}$s greater than zero, on the other hand, 120 exceeded their standard errors by more than a factor of 1.72. This figure is more than four times the 28 one expects under a 5 per cent level, one-tail test, if all $\hat{\lambda}$s are zero, but random factors generate significant coefficients in 5 per cent of the equations. Thus, (4) does describe the pattern of profits over time for a significant fraction of companies.

The fairly low mean value for $\hat{\lambda}$ across the sample combined with almost 80 per cent of the $\hat{\lambda}$s being insignificantly different from zero (5 per cent, one-tail test) draws our attention to the long-run projected returns for the firms.[4] Of these, 274 exceed their standard errors by a factor of more than 1.72, the critical value for a 10 per cent, two-tail test.[5] Thus, almost half of the firms in the sample are projected to earn long-run returns significantly different from the average firm in the sample. Assuming some positive rents exist due to market power, the sample mean should exceed c, however. The relevant question is really, what fraction of firms have profit rates significantly different from c; the competitive return on capital?

We answer this question in two ways. First, note that if all $\hat{\pi}_{ip}$ equal a common c, all will equal one another. The hypothesis that all $\hat{\pi}_{ip}$ converge to a common, competitive c can thus be tested by seeing whether restricting all firms to have the same $\hat{\pi}_{ip}$ results in a significant increase in the sum of squared residuals from the unconstrained estimates. It does. The F-statistic with $(551, 11020)$ degrees of freedom is 2.423 considerably above the critical value of 1.15 for a 1 per cent level significance test.

An alternative way to approach the question, and one which sheds some light on the value of c, employs the following logic. Most firms in a competitive economy should either have returns on capital close to the competitive return, or be converging on it. Thus, the number of $\hat{\pi}_{ip}$s significantly different from c should be less than for any other arbitrarily chosen benchmark return on capital. We thus did a search for c over the range $-.020$ to $+.010$ at $.001$ intervals to find that return from which the minimum number of $\hat{\pi}_{ip}$s were significantly different (10 per cent, two-tailed test). Three values ($-.016$, $-.014$, and $-.012$) all had the minimum number of significantly different $\hat{\pi}_{ip}$s, 259. The intervening numbers, $-.015$ and $-.013$ had 262 and 260 significantly different $\hat{\pi}_{ip}$s respectively. The number of significantly different $\hat{\pi}_{ip}$s rises steadily as one moves away from $-.016$ and $-.012$ in either direction reaching 273 at $-.020$ and 323 at $.010$. Thus, it seems reasonable to conclude, by the logic sketched above, that c falls in the range $-.016$ to $-.012$ with $-.014$ being a good point estimate. The competitive return on capital is then $.014$ below the average, which for the 23-year period 1950–72 was $.076$. The competitive return on capital is thus estimated to be 18 per cent below the average return on capital, an estimate which is quite close to the lower of the two estimates made before, using a totally different logical argument (Mueller, 1986, ch. 2).

If all $\hat{\pi}_{ip}$s equalled c, one would expect 55 $\hat{\pi}_{ip}$s to differ from c by more than 1.72 times these standard errors (the critical value for a 10 per cent level, two-tailed test), assuming a normal distribution around c. The distribution of $\hat{\pi}_{ip}$ around c is not normal, rather it is positively skewed, nevertheless the number of $\hat{\pi}_{ip}$ differing from c by more than 1.72 times these standard errors, 259, seems sufficiently more than 55, to allow us to conclude that there exist a sizeable number of firms with nonzero permanent rents. While short-run rents appear to erode quite quickly for most firms, there exist significant differences in long-run rents across firms.

6.5 THE SIZE OF THE RENTS

Although the results of the previous section reject the hypothesis that the returns on assets of all firms converge on a common competitive return, the qualitative nature of the test conceals the magnitude of the differences in $\hat{\pi}_{ip}$ across firms. How much of the deviation in profit rates observed at any point in time is permanent, how much is transitory? To answer this question, we regress $\hat{\pi}_{ip}$ back onto the deviation of each firm's profit rate from the sample mean averaged over the initial three years of the time period, π_{50}.[6] Equation (1) of Table 6.2 states that over 50 per cent of any deviation from the sample average in those first three years is projected to persist indefinitely.

6.6 AN ADJUSTMENT FOR MERGERS

As noted above, firms from the 1000 largest manufacturing companies' lists of 1950 and 1972 are included in the sample if complete accounting data are available regardless of the extent of their merger activity. Mergers have an averaging effect on corporate profitability, however, which conceals the extent to which a firm's returns in a given line of business persistently differ from the returns of other firms. This averaging effect ensues because firms with below-average returns are more likely to acquire companies with profit rates above their own, while firms with above normal returns are more likely to acquire companies with returns below their own. Thus, mergers should raise the profit rates of below-average profit firms, and lower the rates of above-average profit companies. Moreover, when the acquired company's assets are entered into the acquiring company's books at the acquired firm's purchase price, any long-run rents the acquired firm was earning should be capitalised into the purchase price, and its return on these assets equal the normal return on capital. Thus, the long-run returns of a company are driven toward the normal return in direct proportion to the assets it acquires.

To allow for the averaging effect of mergers, the assets a firm acquired in year t were divided by its assets at the beginning of t, and cumulated over the 23-year sample period. This summation, GAQ, measures the relative growth in the firm's assets for acquisitions. Now assume that r is the fraction of the deviation from the sample mean return observed in 1950–2, which will persist indefinitely. Assume further that all of the acquired assets have an average return equal to the sample mean. The expected return on the assets after mergers, r^*, is then a weighted sum of the return on the initial assets (r), and on the acquired assets (zero), with weights one and GAQ. That is,

Table 6.2 The magnitude of persistent profit rate differences with adjustment for mergers
(Dependent variable = $\hat{\pi}_p$)

Equation	Int.	π_{50}	$\dfrac{\pi_{50}}{1+GAQ}$	$\bar{R}^2$
1	−.0009	.542		.317
	1.25	15.52		
2	−.0009		.691	.334
	1.33		16.15	

Note: *t* values under coefficients.

$$r^* = \frac{r \cdot 1 + GAQ \cdot 0}{1 + GAQ} \tag{6}$$

We can then obtain an estimate of r, the fraction of π_{50} that persists indefinitely, by regressing $\hat{\pi}_p$ on $\pi_{50}/(1 + GAQ)$. The coefficient on this weighted π_{50} variable is the fraction of π_{50} projected to persist indefinitely when GAQ is zero. As GAQ increases the estimated fraction of the initial deviation of a firm's profit rate that persists is driven to zero.

Equation 2 in Table 6.2 presents the results when π_{50} is weighted by $1/(1 + GAQ)$. The coefficient on π_{50} is substantially higher implying a permanent deviation in a company's profit rate from the sample average of 69.1 per cent of that observed in 1950–2. The fit to the data is also improved. Had no mergers taken place between 1950 and 1972, we estimate that 69.1 per cent of the profit differences that existed in 1950–2 would have persisted indefinitely. The averaging effect of mergers conceals to a considerable degree the extent to which profit rate differences across firm lines of business persist.

6.7 A FIRM EFFECTS MODEL OF PROFITABILITY

We have established that there are significant differences in the long-run profit rates of companies. What accounts for these differences?

To explain them, we develop a model, which allows both for firm specific differences in efficiency and product quality, and industry differences in the degree of cooperation among firms. Thus, we employ a model that incorporates both the 'new' and the 'old' learnings regarding market structure and profit performance.

Let i's demand schedule be approximated by the linear function

$$p_i = a_i - bx_i - b\sigma \sum_{j \neq i} x_j \tag{7}$$

where p_i is i's price, x_i output, and σ is an index of product differentiation running from 0 (a pure monopolist) to 1.0 (a homogeneous product). The a_i capture quality differences across firms. The higher a_i, the more buyers are willing to pay for each unit of output due, presumably, to the superior quality they associate with the firm's product. Efficiency differences are represented by firm specific unit costs, c_i. Cooperation among sellers is modelled by assuming that each seller maximises an objective function equal to its profits and a weighted sum of the profits of the other firms in the industry.[7]

$$O_i = \pi_i + \theta \sum_{j \neq i} \pi_j \qquad \pi_i = (p_i - c_i)x_i \tag{8}$$

The weight placed on the other firms' profits parameterises cooperation; $\theta = 1$ implies perfect collusion, $\theta = 0$ Cournot independence, $\theta < 0$ rivalry. Maximising (8) with respect to x_i and a little algebra yields

$$\frac{\pi_i}{S_i} \approx \frac{1}{\eta} \left(\frac{m_i}{\sigma} - m_i \theta + \theta \right) \tag{9}$$

where S_i is i's sales, m_i its market share, and η the industry demand elasticity.

Following in the tradition of the industrial organisation literature we shall assume that the degree of cooperation is dependent on the four firm concentration ratio C_4. No consensus exists as to what the functional form relating θ and C_4 is, so let us assume that whatever the true function form is, it can be approximated by the quadratic.

$$\theta = a + bC_4 + cC_4^2 \tag{10}$$

The product differentiation parameter, σ, must range between 0 and 1. It seems reasonable to assume that the products of an industry with no advertising and inventive activity are homogeneous, and that those for industries with substantial advertising and inventive activity are differentiated. Thus, we seek a functional form for σ which takes on the value one when advertising and inventive activity are zero, and falls as these activities increase in importance. A relatively simple functional form having this property, with ADV being the industry advertising to sales ratio, and PAT industry patents over sales, is

$$\sigma = \frac{d}{d + eADV + fPAT} \tag{11}$$

Table 6.3   Results from firm effect model
($\hat{\pi}_p$ dependent variable, $n = 551$)

Eq.	Int.	m	$(1-m)C_4$	$(1-m)C_4^2$	mADV	mPat	AmC_4	AmC_4^2	$\bar{R}^2$	n
1	−.022	.030	.063	−0.079	.023	.067			.122	551
	2.45	1.52	1.52	1.71	4.79	2.86				
2	−.014	−.005	.058	.010	.041	.060	.014	−.031	.134	551
	1.55	.22	.13	.19	4.45	2.59	2.59	2.99		
3	−.016	−.022	.014		.041	.060	.014	−.030	.136	551
	3.81	.13	1.29		4.49	2.59	2.91	3.45		

Note: t values under coefficients.

Experimentation with more complicated functional forms for (11) did not produce a superior fit to the data.

Substitution from (10) and (11) into (9) yields[8]

$$\frac{\pi_i}{S_i} = \frac{1}{\eta} (a + (1-a)m_i + b(1-m_i)C_4 + c(1-m_i)C_4^2 + \tfrac{d}{e}m_i \, ADV$$

$$+ \tfrac{d}{f}m_i \, PAT) \tag{12}$$

Estimates of (12) using an estimate of the projected profits to sales ratio as dependent variable, and two alternative measures of demand elasticities as right hand side weights led to a performance of the model similar but slightly inferior to that when the projected return on assets $\hat{\pi}_{ip}$ is the dependent variable and all η are assumed equal.[9] We report only the results for these regressions. Variables are defined in the appendix.

Table 6.3, row 1 contains the results from estimating (12). The first two coefficients can be used to solve for a and the assumed constant η. It is reasonable to assume that a from (10) is non-positive, that is, an unconcentrated industry achieves at best a Cournot equilibrium. The estimate of a/η is negative (η is defined to be positive). But when one uses the intercept and the coefficient on m to solve for a and η, the latter takes on a value of over 100. Market share m appears in every term and there would appear to be collinearity among the terms driving the coefficient on m down, and thus exaggerating the size of η. Both the market share-advertising and -patenting terms have positive and significant coefficients. Market share in conjunction with product differentiation is strongly associated with long-run profitability.

The coefficients on the two C_4 terms imply an inverted-U relationship which peaks at a C_4 of .40, less than the sample mean of .45. Cooperation weakens beyond the middle range of concentration values. Above a C_4 of .80 industry behaviour is more rivalrous than at a $C_4 = 0$. These results are

consistent with recent findings indicating a weak relationship if any between concentration and profitability in the presence of market share (note
both t- values are less than 2.0) (Shepherd, 1972, 1975; Gale and Branch,
1982; Ravenscraft, 1983; and Mueller, 1986) and a relationship that runs
counter to the 'old' learning with respect to concentration, collusion and
profitability.

The strong relationship between profitability and the market share
product differentiation variables suggests that the more profitable firms are
those which succeed in differentiating their products in industries in which
product differentiation is important, that is, they are more efficient than
their competitors in utilising the non-price modes of competition.

This strong performance of market share and product differentiation
leads one to question whether the somewhat perverse relationship between
concentration and profitability may also be related to non-price rivalry.
Perhaps cooperation slackens as product differentiation becomes more
important in an industry, and it is this non-price rivalry that is somehow
reflected in equation 1 of Table 6.3. As a rough test of this conjecture, I
multiplied the two concentration terms by industry patent and advertising
intensity. The former had no effect, but the addition of ADV times $(1 -
m)C_4$ and $(1 - m)C_4^2$ (AmC_4 and AmC_4^2 respectively) did raise the R^2
(equation 2). There is obvious multicollinearity among the four terms
involving C_4, which is broken when $(1 - m)C_4^2$ is dropped (equation 3).
Equation 3 suggests a *weak* positive relationship between concentration
and profitability in industries where there is no advertising, and an inverted-U relationship when advertising is present. Moreover, the peak of
the curve shifts leftward as advertising intensity increases approaching a
peak at a C_4 of .23 in highly advertising intensive industries.

To test properly for the interaction between advertising and concentration at the industry level, one must employ a model of behaviour at the
industry level. But the results of this section may help to explain the riddle
in the recent literature regarding the impacts of concentration and market
share on profitability. Neither variable has a strong impact by itself, but
both have a significant relationship in the presence of product differentiation. Successful product differentiation as measured by market share is
associated with high profitability. But high concentration and high product
differentiation may lead to more intense rivalry and lower profitability,
ceteris paribus.

Adjustments to this basic firm effects model to allow for risk, diversification, company size and growth do not fundamentally alter the relationships reported in Table 6.3 (Mueller, 1986). Market share remains
positively associated with long-run profitability in the presence of product
differentiation. Concentration is negatively related, particularly in the
presence of advertising.

6.8 THE RESULTS FROM OTHER COUNTRIES

Table 6.4 presents results from other countries along with those of the United States regarding the persistence of profits. Following Mueller (1986, ch. 2), the samples for each country are broken into six equal-sized sub-samples ordered by the profit levels of the companies in the initial year of the sample period. Thus, for Canada, sub-sample 1 is the 27 companies with the highest profits in 1968, sub-sample 2 the 27 companies with the next highest initial profits, and so on (one sub-sample has only 26 companies).

Consider first the values of $\hat{\lambda}$. With the exception of Sweden, the mean values of $\hat{\lambda}$ in all countries averaged around 0.5 or lower. Read literally, these estimates imply that about 90 per cent of any deviation from a firm's long-run profit rate is eliminated in three years. While this is appreciably faster than econometric estimates from structural models suggest (Geroski and Masson, 1987), there are good reasons to think that these are lower bound estimates. In particular, many accounting practices – like profits taxation – tend to 'smooth' profits data, thereby importing a degree of convergence towards the norm independent of any competitive pressures. Thus, it appears that the competitive process works no faster than three to five years on average in eliminating short-run rents. While not slow, this process can by no means be thought of as instantaneous.

In every country, permanent differences in profitability across firms were observed. The sub-sample of firms with the highest initial profits had highest long-run projected profits in every single country. The sub-sample with lowest initial profits had the lowest projected profits in every country save Sweden and the UK where it was the second lowest initial profit groups that had the lowest projected profits.[10] The correlations between $\hat{\pi}$ and π_0 range from .244 in West Germany to .603 in Sweden. Firms with above (below) normal profits at a given point in time can be expected to earn above (below) normal profits into the indefinite future.

Despite this common pattern of permanent departures from average profits across the countries, important differences exist among countries in the extent to which profits persist permanently. These differences are readily apparent when one compares the fraction of initial profits which are projected to persist indefinitely across the several countries. Table 6.5 gives the ratio of projected initial profits for the highest and lowest initial profit sub-groups. Two clusters of results exist. Canada, France and the United States (1950–72) all have substantial degrees of persistence. If we regard the initial point in time for each study as essentially randomly selected, then for Canada, France and the United States, between 50 and 85 per cent of the differences in profit rates from the average of their highest and lowest profit firms are projected to persist indefinitely. In contrast, for the FRG, Japan, Sweden, and the UK, these percentages range from 15 to 35 per cent.

The Persistence of Profits

Table 6.4 International comparison of the persistence of profits

Country		Canada			Federal Republic of Germany		
Period		1968–82			1961–82		
Number of firms		161			290		
variables		$\hat{\pi}_p$	$\hat{\lambda}$	π_o	$\hat{\pi}_p$	$\hat{\lambda}$	π_o
sub-sample	1	7.912	.341	14.410	.480	.515	4.574
	2	2.669	.295	4.460	.353	.282	1.655
	3	1.833	.208	1.034	.466	.337	.186
	4	− .016	.233	−1.542	.243	.427	− .851
	5	−1.206	.252	−4.885	−.361	.394	−1.768
	6	−10.801	.465	−12.774	−1.138	.398	−3.705
A		76	(47.2)		160	(55.2)	
B		33	(20.5)		53	(18.3)	
C		23	(14.3)		50	(17.2)	
D		83	(51.6)		204	(70.3)	
E		0	(0.0)		0	(0.0)	
F		0			0		
G		0.454			0.244		
H		N.A.			0.736		
Country		France			Japan		
Period		1965–82			1964–82		
Number of firms		450			376		
variables		$\hat{\pi}_p$	$\hat{\lambda}$	π_o	$\hat{\pi}_p$	$\hat{\lambda}$	π_o
sub-sample	1	6.40	.543	8.50	.7369	.6325	3.4095
	2	1.72	.392	2.90	.2824	.4579	1.1582
	3	− .06	.330	− .20	.1476	.4563	.4219
	4	−1.35	.244	−1.50	−.1913	.3917	−.2445
	5	−1.64	.322	−3.30	−.6326	.4447	−1.1735
	6	−3.29	.368	−6.60	−.7571	.4053	−3.5742
A		223	(49.6)		250	(66.5)	
B		N.A.			62	(16.5)	
C		N.A.			56	(14.9)	
D		204	(45.3)		285	(75.8)	
E		5	(0.1)		1	(0.3)	
F		5			1		
G		0.359			0.305		
H		0.789			0.869		

Notes:

A = the number of cases for which $\bar{R}^2 > 0.1$ (in parentheses are percentages)
B = the number of cases for which $\hat{\alpha}$ is significantly positive (10 per cent level two-tailed test) (in parentheses are percentages)
C = the number of cases for which $\hat{\alpha}$ is significantly negative (10 per cent level two-tailed test) (in parentheses are percentages)
D = the number of cases for which $\hat{\lambda}$ is significantly positive (10 per cent level one-tailed test) (in parentheses are percentages)

Country		United Kingdom			United States		
Period		1951–77			1950–72		
Number of firms		243			551		
variables		$\hat{\pi}_p$	$\hat{\lambda}$	π_o	$\hat{\pi}_p$	$\hat{\lambda}$	π_o
sub-sample	1	1.911	.574	9.081	4.6789	.1214	5.4944
	2	.892	.449	3.827	1.5139	.1664	2.0933
	3	.138	.446	1.559	.1721	.2121	.4196
	4	– .577	.457	– .415	–.4646	.2547	–.8739
	5	–1.051	.472	–2.057	–1.6377	.2015	–2.2439
	6	– .666	.548	–4.209	–2.8270	.1419	–4.6637
A		228	(93.8)		117	(21.2)	
B		37	(15.2)		125	(22.7)	
C		37	(15.2)		149	(27.0)	
D		185	(76.1)		152	(27.6)	
E		0	(0.0)		0	(0.0)	
F		1			0		
G		0.339			0.582		
H		N.A.			0.916		
Country		Sweden					
Period		1967–85					
Number of firms		43					
variables		$\hat{\pi}_p$	$\hat{\lambda}$	π_o			
sub-sample	1	4.083	.825	14.314			
	2	.959	.694	6.318			
	3	1.360	.870	–4.774			
	4	– .464	.846	–4.990			
	5	–4.057	.748	–5.225			
	6	–1.971	.711	–5.642			
A		14	(32.5)				
B		7	(16.2)				
C		8	(18.6)				
D		17	(39.5)				
E		1	(2.3)				
F		0					
G		0.603					
H		0.674					

E = the number of cases for which $\hat{\lambda}$ is significantly negative (10 per cent level two-tailed test) (in parentheses are percentages)

F = the number of cases with $\lambda > 1$. (In the calculation of average $\hat{\alpha}$ and λ in the subsamples and of the correlation coefficients in rows G and H, λ was set equal to 0.95 in these cases.)

G = correlation coefficient between $\hat{\alpha}$ and π_o

H = correlation coefficient between $\hat{\alpha}$ and $\bar{\pi}$ (the average of the normalised profit rate for the entire period).

Source: Odagiri and Yamawaki (1990).

The Persistence of Profits

Table 6.5   Long-run projected profit rates relative to initial period profit rates

	Canada		FRG			France	Japan
	π_{at}	π_{bt}	π_{at}	π_{bt}	V	π_{bt}	π_{at}
Highest initial profit rates	.55	.49	.15	.19	.21	.62	.22
Lowest initial profit rates	.84	.71	.31	.32	.15	.48	.21

	Sweden	United Kingdom	United States 1950–72	United States 1964–80
	π_{bt}	π_{at}	π_{at}	π_{at}
Highest initial profit rates	.29	.21	.85	.26
Lowest initial profit rates	.35	.16	.63	.59

Notes: π_{at} Estimates based on accounting profits after taxes divided by total assets.

π_{bt} Estimates based on accounting profits before taxes divided by total assets.

V   Estimates based on the market value of the firm divided by total assets.

Source: Geroski and Mueller (1990).

Over the period 1950–72, the United States was relatively free of competition from imports. Many industries in Canada are protected by high tariffs also. The appearance of Canada and the United States in the group of countries with comparatively high permanent rents may imply that protection from international competition does facilitate the ability of firms to earn persistent rents. But Japan is arguably a rather closed economy also, and the degree of persistence measured for this country resembles that of the more open FRG, Swedish and UK economies. The estimates of permanent rents for France are also much closer to those of Canada and the United States than they are to those of its Common Market neighbour, West Germany. Thus, more than just the height of tariff and other trade barriers must be examined to explain differences in the relative levels of permanent rents across countries.

Japanese corporations have not succeeded in translating their spectacular success in capturing international markets into permanently high profit margins. The degree of permanent profits persistence in Japan is not much greater than that in the UK. It is interesting, however, that the fraction of 1948 profit differences across UK companies that are estimated to reflect differences in permanent rents is nearly the smallest of any country. The generally accepted image of UK products as being uncompetitive on world markets is confirmed by the inability of UK companies to gain persistently above normal rates of return. The performance of the UK economy, as measured by the average heights of permanent rents, comes close to that expected for an economy at a long-run competitive equilibrium. This observation further illustrates the importance of the difference between static and dynamic measures of competitive performance. It is possible for an economy to rank high in terms of modest average levels of permanent rents, and price-cost differences, and yet perform poorly in terms of generating productivity and income growth over time.

Some additional efforts to go beyond the measurement of permanent departures from average profits, and to account for their causes, were made in the other country studies. In Japan, as in the United States, firm market share (or rank in its industry) and advertising were positively related to persistent profitability. Advertising intensity was significantly related to profitability in Germany, but not in the UK. Proxies for market share in both the UK and the FRG proved to be statistically insignificant, although this may be attributable to the crudeness with which market share was estimated in these countries.

Thus, at least in Japan and the United States where the estimates of market share are most accurate, it seems that successful product differentiation, where success is measured by market share and product differentiation is measured by industry R&D or advertising, leads to persistent differences in profitability. This suggestion is reinforced by other studies which have found the combination of market share and product differentiation to be important in explaining profitability (Ravenscraft, 1983). The role played by product differentiation may also explain some of the differences in the patterns of results observed across countries. Television advertising is a major vehicle for product differentiation in the United States and Canada, but is severely constricted by the State's control of the television networks in West Germany. Brand images are thus more difficult to establish in West Germany and fewer consumer products with significant market power are found in Germany than in Canada and the US. In those industries where product differentiation is important in Germany, for example automobiles and beer, several companies with apparently permanent above normal profits do exist. But, much of German production is concentrated in capital goods industries that compete on international markets. Both Sweden and Japan are also heavily dependent on their export markets, and the UK economy has been subject to tremendous competitive pressure from imports. In internationally open markets, establishing the kind of buyer loyalty and market position which can be developed for goods facing only domestic competition is difficult, and, indeed, this difficulty may be part of the explanation for the greater degrees of persistence in Canada, France and the United States than in the FRG, Japan, Sweden, and the United Kingdom.

6.9 CONCLUSIONS

The existence of monopoly rents is a clear signal of the existence of a monopoly 'problem'. If the π_p and λ estimates in each country implied that all disequilibria quickly disappeared, no scope for public policy would be present. But some permanent rents (positive and negative) appear to exist in every country, and while the adjustment process appears to be fairly quick on average across the several countries, in some instances the λs do imply a slow adjustment to the estimated long-run equilibria. Whether the existence of these rents constitutes a sufficient condition for policy action depends on four factors: (i) the magnitude of the misallocation of resources implied by the measured rents; (ii) the costs to both the firms and the enforcement agencies of eliminating the monopoly positions that create these rents; (iii) the social waste from expenditures to protect and capture these rents; and (iv) the social benefits from new products and processes brought about through the creation of monopoly rents.

The first two factors raise no issues of controversy or novelty in antitrust enforcement. What is the cost in terms of efficiency loss from the existence of monopoly? What are the costs of eliminating it? Every country in this study, and most of those among the developed, industrialised nations, have some form of Monopoly Commission, Fair Trade Commission or similar organisation charged with curbing the social costs of monopoly, and promoting the social benefits from competition. The analysis here suggests that the first place for these organisations to look for a monopoly problem is among the firms with high π_p and λ values.

The competition or antimonopoly policies of every country are built on the presumption that the Cournot model describes the competitive process. The monopoly problem consists of too few sellers, producing too little output at too high a price. The solution to this problem is to increase the number of sellers, and/or their output, and thereby bring down industry price. In those markets where static competition with a relatively homogeneous product is a reasonable approximation, this policy remains a defensible approach to the 'monopoly' problem. But some markets are better characterised by a Schumpeterian-like model of dynamic competition. Products are heterogeneous and nonprice, investment modes of competition predominate. In these markets, more sellers may not lessen 'the monopoly problem' and might even worsen it. An appropriate policy to apply to these markets must address the third and fourth factors listed above, but, as yet, no country's antitrust authorities have given much evidence that they are even aware that other factors are involved.[11]

APPENDIX

Annual accounting data by firm are from Standard and Poor's COMPUSTAT tape and conform to its definitions. Where COMPUSTAT data were not available, data from *Moody's Industrial Manual* were substituted.

Variable Definitions

π_{it} = firm i's profit rate in year t
= (income + interest)/total assets

$$\hat{\pi}_{ip} = \frac{\hat{\alpha}_i}{1-\hat{\lambda}_i} \text{ , from } \pi_{it} = \lambda_i \pi_{it-1} + \mu_{it}$$

$$\pi_{i50} = \sum_{t=50}^{52} \pi_{it}/3$$

GAQ = growth by acquisition. Let AQ_{it} be i's assets acquired in year t, and K_{it-1} its assets at end of year $t-1$, then

$$GAQ = \sum_{t=50}^{72} AQ_{it}/K_{it-1}$$

C_4 = A projected four firm concentration ratio. Projection made by assuming concentration follows the path $C_{4t} = a + b/t$. The coefficient a is then the projected concentration at time equals infinity. Two measures of concentration were used to make the projections, the sales-weighted average C_4 for a firm in 1950 and in 1972. The 1972 figures were adjusted for imports and geographic differences in market definition as in Weiss (1981). Since the projected concentration places heavy weight on the 1972 figure, this figure was used to proxy C_4 when the 1950 figure was missing.

m = Projected market share. This projection was made in the same way C_4 was projected. To adjust for imports and geographic differences in market definition, the 1972 market share figure was multiplied by the ratio of the 1972 Weiss-adjusted C_4 to the unadjusted C_4.

ADV = Industry advertising to sales ratio. Sales-weighted average advertising-to-sales ratio based on 1963 IRS advertising and sales data. The year 1963 was chosen because it falls in the middle of the sample period.

PAT = Industry patent to sales ratio. Sales-weighted average patent-to-sales ratio from period 1966–8 as reported in NSF (1977), with 1967 Census of Manufacturing sales as deflator. Years 1966–8 were used because they are earliest reported by NSF.

Notes

* This chapter pulls together material from chapters 1, 3, 11 and 12 of my book *The Dynamics of Company Profits* (Cambridge University Press 1990). Chapter 11 was written by Hiroyuki Odagiri and Hideki Yamawaki. Chapter 12 is coauthored by Paul Geroski and myself.

1. A second important exception might appear to be the contestable market theory of Baumol, Panzar and Willig (1982). Entry and exit are the heart of Schumpeter's process of creative destruction, just as the conditions of entry and exit are central to defining the contestability of a market. But, in contrast to Schumpeter's dynamic depiction of the competitive process, the contestable market theory is entirely static. It relates *conditions* of entry to *levels* of profit in equilibrium. The dynamics of attaining equilibrium are not addressed. Testing the contestable market theory has proceeded in the tradition of other empirical work in industrial organisation by relating profit rates to market structures in cross-sectional analyses.
2. Data were taken from COMPUSTAT and *Moody's*. For definitions of variables used and list of sample firms, see Mueller (1986).
3. In Mueller (1986) firm profitability was measured as a deviation from sample mean divided by the sample mean. This definition of π_{it} gave mean λ of more than double those reported here.
4. Note that all of the λ fall between -1 and 1 implying convergence on the $\hat{\pi}_{ip}$.
5. Since π_{ip} is a ratio of two estimated parameters, its standard error must be calculated from the covariance matrix of the coefficients (Kmenta, 1971, pp. 442–8).
6. Since the dependent variable is itself a parameter, each equation is estimated using a form of GLS in which each observation is weighted by the standard error of π_p. The coefficient on the intercept is thus the coefficient on $1/\sigma_{\pi_p}$. For a discussion of this procedure, see Saxonhouse (1976).
7. This method of modelling oligopolistic interaction has been employed by Cyert and DeGroot (1973), Kuenne (1974), Shubik (1980), and Long (1982).
8. For details of the deviation, see Mueller (1986, ch. 4).
9. Estimates using a slightly different measure of $\hat{\pi}_{ip}$ are presented in Mueller (1986) ch. 4.
10. Each sub-sample in Sweden has only eleven firms in it, so that one or two firms can shift a sub-sample.
11. The cereals case, brought by the US Federal Trade Commission in the mid-1970s, indicated an appreciation of these issues and a novel attempt to attack them under existing law. It was killed by the Reagan Administration shortly after it took office.

References

Baumol, William J., John C. Panzar and Robert D. Willig, *Contestable Markets and the Theory of Industry Structure* (New York: Harcourt, Brace Jovanovich, 1982).

Clark, John M., *Competition as a Dynamic Process* (Washington, D.C.: Brookings Institution, 1961).

Cyert, Richard M. and Morris M. DeGroot, 'An Analysis of Cooperation and Learning in a Duopoly Context', *American Economic Review*, 63 (March 1973) pp. 24–37.

Gale, Bradley J. and Ben S. Branch, 'Concentration versus Market Share: Which Determines Performance and Why Does it Matter?', *Antitrust Bulletin*, 27 (Spring 1982) pp. 83–106.

Geroski, P. and R. Masson, 'Dynamic Market Models in Industrial Organization', *International Journal of Industrial Organization*, 5 (March 1987) pp. 1–14.

Geroski, Paul A. and Dennis C. Mueller, 'The Persistence of Profits in Perspective', in Dennis C. Mueller (ed.), *The Dynamics of Company Profits* (Cambridge: Cambridge University Press, 1990) ch. 12.

Gort, Michael and Steven Klepper, 'Time Paths in the Diffusion of Product Innovations', *Economic Journal*, 92 (September 1982) pp. 630–53.

Kirzner, Israel M., *Competition and Entrepreneurship* (Chicago: University of Chicago Press, 1973).

Klepper, Steven and Elizabeth Graddy, 'Industry Evolution and the Determinants of Market Structure', mimeo, Carnegie-Mellon (1984).

Kmenta, Jan, *Elements of Econometrics* (New York: Macmillan, 1971).

Kuenne, Robert E., 'Towards an Operational General Equilibrium Theory with Oligopoly: Some Experimental Results and Conjectures', *Kyklos*, 27 (1974) pp. 792–820.

Long, William F., 'Market Share, Concentration, and Profits: Intra-Industry and Inter-Industry Evidence', unpublished, Federal Trade Commission (1982).

McNulty, Paul J., 'Economic Theory and the Meaning of Competition', *Quarterly Journal of Economics*, 82 (November 1968) pp. 639–56.

Mueller, Dennis C., *Profits in the Long Run* (Cambridge: Cambridge University Press, 1986).

National Science Foundation, *Science Indicators 1976* (Washington: Government Printing Office, 1977).

Nelson, Richard R. and Sidney G. Winter, *An Evolutionary Theory of Economic Change* (Cambridge, Mass.: Harvard University Press, 1982).

Odagiri, Hiroyuki and Hideki Yamawaki, 'The Persistence of Profits: International Comparison', in Dennis C. Mueller (ed.), *The Dynamics of Company Profits* (Cambridge: Cambridge University Press, 1990) ch. 11.

Ravenscraft, David J., 'Structure–Profit Relationships at the Line of Business and Industry Level', *Review of Economics and Statistics*, 65 (February 1983) pp. 22–31.

Saxonhouse, Gary R., 'Estimated Parameters as Dependent Variables', *American Economic Review*, 66 (March 1976) pp. 178–83.

Schumpeter, Joseph A., *The Theory of Economic Development* (Cambridge, Mass.: Harvard University Press, 1934).

Schumpeter, Joseph A., *Capitalism, Socialism and Democracy*, 3rd edn (New York: Harper & Row, 1950).

Shepherd, William G., 'The Elements of Market Structure', *Review of Economics and Statistics*, 54 (February 1972) pp. 25–37.

Shepherd, William G., *The Treatment of Market Power* (New York: Columbia University Press, 1975).

Shubik, Martin, *Market Structure and Behavior* (Cambridge, Mass.: Harvard University Press, 1980).

Weiss, Leonard W., 'Corrected Concentration Ratios in Manufacturing-1972', mimeo (Washington, DC: Federal Trade Commission, 1981).

7 Profit and Wage Convergence and Capital Accumulation Among Industrialised Countries, 1963–83

Edward N. Wolff and David Dollar*

7.1 INTRODUCTION

Most economic theories, both classical and neoclassical, assume a tendency for equalisation in profit rates both among industries within a country and among countries over time.[1] Indeed, in the Heckscher-Ohlin model, the key assumption made is that factor prices, both profit rates and wage rates, will tend toward equality both among industries and among countries.[2] Moreover, most theories assume that the equilibrating mechanism is the flow of capital to the industries and countries with relatively high profit rates. Surprisingly, the evidence on both of these hypotheses is rather scant.

We use data for twelve manufacturing sectors and eight countries – Belgium, Canada, Federal Republic of Germany, Italy, Japan, the Netherlands, the United Kingdom, and the United States. Our analysis covers the period from 1963 to 1983. We investigate three questions. First, is there any evidence of convergence in profit rates either among industries or countries during the 1963–83 period? Second, is there evidence of convergence of real wages either among industries or among countries? Third, is the rate of capital accumulation higher in more profitable industries and countries or are there other factors, such as the real wage level or the rate of productivity growth, that influence capital formation?

It is, perhaps, helpful to place this study in the context of recent work of ours (Dollar and Wolff, 1988), where we investigated the labour productivity levels (an index of value added per work hour) among 28 manufacturing industries in 13 industrialised countries over the period from 1963 to 1982. We find strong evidence of convergence on the US level in virtually every industry covered by the study, though the degree of convergence varied considerably among industries. We concluded that the convergence of productivity at the industry level was the proximate cause of the convergence in aggregate labour productivity levels noted in many studies.

The empirical evidence thus strongly indicates convergence in productivity levels both on the aggregate level and the industry level among industrialised countries in the postwar period. Interestingly, there is little theoretical basis for this phenomenon, except for the Heckscher-Ohlin model. On the other hand, the theoretical basis for profit rate equalisation is quite strong, and, indeed, is a basic assumption of most models of price determination. There are, of course, many caveats. First, it is necessary to distinguish between the accounting rate of return on the one hand and the real cost of capital, the internal rate of return, and the rental rate of capital on the other. Most theories predict a tendency toward equalisation for one of the latter three measures of the rate of return; none, as far as we are aware, predicts equalisation in the accounting rate of return. Since we, as in most other studies, use the accounting rate of return, our results cannot be directly interpreted as evidence for or against such basic models of price determination.

Second, the convergence of profit rates within country is subject to many qualifications, since industry concentration and various sources of economic rent (such as proprietary technologies) will deter complete equalisation.[3] Indeed, Mueller (1986) has found persistent interindustry differences in profit rates in the US. Third, the convergence of profit rates across countries is subject to other qualifications, such as differences in the tax treatment of profits and depreciation and the degree of country risk.

With regard to wage convergence, it is first necessary to distinguish between the industry level and the country level. On the industry level, most standard models, again, assume as a basic tenet that real wages will be equalised among industries within a country. Of course, this is subject to many caveats, such as difference in the degree of concentration, unionisation, and skill levels among industries. Indeed, several recent studies of 'efficiency wage differentials' have established persistent interindustry real wage differences in the US (Krueger and Summers, 1986; or Dickens and Katz, 1986).

At the country level, there appear to be two competing hypotheses. The first derives from a standard neoclassical model, where the (real) wage is equal to the marginal product of labour. This is most easily illustrated by the case where the aggregate production function in a country is of Cobb-Douglas form:

$$Y_t = e^{gt} L_t^{\alpha} K_t^{(1-\alpha)} \tag{1}$$

Where Y_t is output at time t, L_t is labour input at time t, K_t is capital input at time t, and g is the rate of Hicks-neutral technological progress. Then, the wage w is given by:[4]

$$w = \partial Y / \partial L = \alpha e^{gt} L^{(\alpha - 1)} K^{(1 - \alpha)} = \alpha Y / L \qquad (2)$$

Insofar as the labour shares, α, tend to be relatively equal among countries, the real wage will, then, be correlated directly with the average labour productivity of the country. The second follows from the Heckscher-Ohlin model, which predicts factor price equalisation among countries. Both models may offer the same prediction for the sample of countries and period under consideration here, because of the convergence in aggregate labour productivity that has occurred.

Finally, with regard to determinants of industry capital accumulation, the main hypothesis to test is that high profits are a direct inducement to capital investment. There are, however, several other variables of interest that we shall consider. First, in previous work, a high correlation was found between the rate of productivity growth and that of the capital–labour ratio in OECD countries (Wolff, 1989). This result is consistent with the so-called 'embodiment effect', namely the embodiment of advanced technology in new capital investment. However, it is not possible to attribute causation, and the most that can be inferred from this study is that there is a strong positive relation between capital accumulation and technological change. Here, we shall consider the relation of productivity growth to the rate of capital accumulation.

Second, another finding of interest from this study is that the rate of capital accumulation was higher in the initially low productivity countries, a relation referred to as the 'accumulation effect'. In other words, a low level of productivity in a country may provide a disproportionate incentive for investment and thus be associated with a high rate of capital accumulation. It was speculated that the likely reason for this is that real wages will tend to be lower in countries with lower levels of labour productivity. Thus, from the standpoint of international trade, the low real wages of a low productivity country will be an inducement to capital investment, since the labour costs and, hence, costs of production will be lower than in high productivity economies.

A contrasting position is found in Marx (1967), who argued in Volume 1 of *Capital* that high wages induce labour-saving capital investment. In other words, high wages should create pressure for new investment. Thus, high productivity should provide a stimulus to investment and more backward countries should have lower rates of capital formation. These two opposing hypotheses can be examined with the data on hand.[5]

With the available data, we can estimate real labour compensation and relatively crude gross profit rates by sector and year among our sample of countries. The convergence in real wage rates among industrial countries has been well documented (Hooper and Larin, 1989), and we find a similar result. However, we find little convergence of wages across industries. Moreover, the results indicate considerable variation in profit rates both among countries and industries and over time. The results show some tendency toward convergence within industry and across countries but no tendency toward equalisation across industries within country. This latter finding accords with recent work by Glick and Ehrbar (1988a, 1988b, 1990), who find almost no tendency toward profit rate equalisation among manufacturing industries in the US over the postwar period and none for France, Germany, Italy, and the UK during the 1970s. We find that capital has flowed to industries with high profit rates and has been accumulated more rapidly in industries with high lagged productivity growth. Moreover, even after controlling for industry wage differences, capital investment has been higher in industries with lower productivity levels.

The remainder of the chapter is organised into four parts. The first provides a description of the data and the measurement concepts used in the chapter. The second presents the basic evidence on convergence in profit rates and real wages. In the third, results are summarised on determinants of capital accumulation both by industry and country. Concluding remarks are made in the last part.

7.2 DATA SOURCES AND CONCEPTS

Data on output and employment are from the United Nations *Yearbook of Industrial Statistics*, which are reported for 28 manufacturing industries. Our output measure is value added, which is reported in current prices, denominated in domestic currency.[6] Value added is reported net of indirect business taxes, so that it is comparable among countries. We used the GNP deflator of each country to convert output values of different years into 1983 prices, and then applied the PPP index calculated by OECD to convert all output values into 1983 US dollars.[7] Our labour input measure is employment.[8] Our capital stock data for the EEC countries come from Eurostat work sheets, for Canada from Statistics Canada (1987), for Japan from the Japan Economic Planning Agency (1988), and for the US from Musgrave (1986). Only gross capital stock data are available for the eight countries.[9]

Total employee compensation is also provided by industry for each country. This is defined as wages and salaries plus fringe benefits including contributions to social insurance (both employee and employer). The real wage series (w) was constructed by first converting employee compensation of different years into 1983 prices using the household consumption expenditure deflator and then applying the OECD PPP index to convert all values into 1983 US dollars. Real wages were then calculated by dividing total employee compensation in 1983 US dollars by industry, country, and year by the corresponding figure on total employment. No adjustment is made for differences in hours worked or the number of part-time employees.

Gross profits in current prices and domestic currency is defined as value added less employee compensation, both of which are also in current prices and domestic currency. Gross profits include retained earnings, dividends paid out, net interest paid, as well as depreciation. Gross profits are valued before corporate income taxes though net of indirect business taxes. The gross profit rate (π) is the accounting rate of return defined as the ratio of gross profits in current prices and domestic currency to gross capital stock in current prices and domestic currency. Our results on convergence in profit rates will thus be biased insofar as net profits and depreciation are subject to differences in corporate income tax treatment both across industries and across countries.

Due to data availability, the total factor productivity (TFP) index is measured as a ratio of a sector's value added (Y) to a weighted average of employment (L) and gross capital stock (K):

$$\text{TFP} = Y/[\alpha L + (1 - \alpha)K] \tag{3}$$

where α is the wage share in current prices and domestic currency. Country-specific averages of the ratio of wages to value added over the full period in each industry were used to measure the wage shares.[10] The TFP index is normalised so that the US TFP index in 1963 equals 1.0 in each industry. Two measures of total factor productivity growth are used. The first, which we call 'crude' TFP growth, is the time derivative of equation (3). The second is the Divisia measure of TFP growth, ϱ, defined as:

$$\varrho = \dot{Y}/Y - [\alpha \dot{L}/L + (1 - \alpha)\dot{K}/K] \tag{4}$$

where a superscript dot (.) indicates the time derivative. Since our data are for discrete time periods, we use the Tornqvist-Divisia index, defined using average period factor shares, for estimating TFP growth by period.

Data for computing profit rates, real wage rates, and TFP indices were available for the 1963–83 period for eight countries: Belgium, Canada, Federal Republic of Germany (Germany, for short), Italy, Japan, the Netherlands, the United Kingdom, and the United States. Due to differences in data classification schemes from the various sources, we were forced to aggregate our sectoral manufacturing data into twelve industries: ferrous and nonferrous metals (13);[11] nonmetal minerals and products (15); chemicals (17); metal products, excluding machinery and transportation (19); machinery (21 and 23); electrical goods (25); transport equipment (28); food, beverages, and tobacco (36); textiles, clothing, footwear and leather (42); paper and printing (47); rubber and plastic products (49); and other industries (48). See the Appendix for more details on data availability and sources by component.

7.3   RESULTS ON PROFIT RATE AND REAL WAGE
CONVERGENCE

Table 7.1 shows gross profit rates for the whole manufacturing sector for
selected years over the 1963–83 period. The profit rates at first glance
appear quite high, ranging for the most part between 20 and 40 per cent.
However, it should be recalled that the profits are before tax and gross of
depreciation and include all forms of property (non-wage) income. Moreover, the denominator includes only fixed capital.

Next, we look at the movement of the rate of profit over the period. In
all eight countries, with the exception of the UK, a clear downward trend is
evident for the rate of profit over the 20-year period. However, the
direction of change is not uniform over the whole period. For most
countries, the rate of profit in manufacturing rose between the early 1960s
and the early 1970s and then declined. The unweighted average (shown in
Panel A) increased from 31 per cent in 1963 to 39 per cent in 1972 and then
fell to 30 per cent in 1983. There was also a sizeable drop between 1979 and
1982, a likely consequence of the worldwide recession of 1981–2.

Four measures of inter-country dispersion are presented in Panel A. The
first, the coefficient of variation, defined as the ratio of the standard
deviation to the unweighted mean, increased from 0.28 in 1963 to 0.36 in
1970, declined to 0.21 in 1979, and then rose to 0.29 in 1983. Over the
whole period there is no discernible trend in the coefficient of variation.
The second is the ratio of the maximum rate of profit to its minimum value
in the sample. This measure of dispersion has a similar pattern, increasing
between 1963 and 1970, declining between 1970 and 1979, and then rising
in the early 1980s. If anything, there is a slight upward trend in this index of
dispersion over the full 20-year period. The third is the ratio of the
unweighted mean gross profit rate among all countries excluding the one
with the highest profit rate to that of the leader. Japan had the highest
profit rate in manufacturing in all years except 1963 and 1976–9, when the
US led. This index has a somewhat similar pattern as the other two,
declining from 1963 to 1970, rising between 1970 and 1979, and then
declining slightly between 1979 and 1983. The overall trend shows declining dispersion over the 20-year period.

Because of data availability, the sample of countries changes over the
period. We therefore show the coefficient of variation and the unweighted
mean relative to the leader for two constant sample sets of countries
(Panels B and C). The pattern is identical for the two statistics, with the
coefficient of variation increasing between 1963 and 1970, then declining
until 1979, and then rising again; and the unweighted mean relative to the
leader declining between the early 1960s and 1970, rising between 1970 and
1979, and then declining in the early 1980s.

For individual industries, the pattern is mixed, as shown in Table 7.2.

Table 7.1   Gross profit rates for the whole manufacturing sector by country for selected years, 1963–83[a]

	1963	1967	1970	1972	1979	1982	1983
Belgium	25.9%	22.3%	27.7%	NA	25.5%	16.9%	NA
Canada	23.3	22.5	20.4	21.9	24.9	NA	17.6
Germany	NA	48.3	53.0	46.2	35.8	29.1	NA
Italy	NA	NA	36.2	26.3	28.5	23.9	NA
Japan	NA	62.6	65.6	56.7	43.1	38.3	38.9
Netherlands	33.3	35.4	39.4	NA	31.8	18.3	NA
United Kingdom	25.8	NA	27.2	NA	29.7	24.7	26.7
United States	47.4	50.4	44.0	45.4	43.3	35.1	38.1

A. Summary Statistics Based on Countries with Available Data[b]

	1963	1967	1970	1972	1979	1982	1983
Unweighted mean	31.1%	40.3%	39.2%	39.3%	32.8%	26.6%	30.3%
Coeff of variation	.28	.37	.36	.33	.21	.28	.29
Maximum/ minimum	2.03	2.81	3.21	2.59	1.74	2.27	2.21
Unweighted average relative to leader	.57	.57	.54	.62	.72	.64	.71

B. Summary Statistics Based on Seven-Country Sample: Belgium, Germany, Italy, Japan, Netherlands, UK, and US

	1963	1967	1970	1974	1979	1982	1983
Coeff of variation	NA	NA	.31	.20	.19	.28	NA
Unweighted average relative to leader	NA	NA	.58	.70	.75	.64	NA

C. Summary Statistics Based on Six-Country Sample: Belgium, Canada, Germany, Japan, Netherlands, and US

	1965	1967	1970	1974	1979	1980	1983
Coeff of variation	.32	.37	.36	.22	.22	.28	NA
Unweighted average relative to leader	.67	.57	.56	.71	.74	.66	NA

Notes: [a] Results are based on the total gross profits and total capital stock for manufacturing.
[b] See Appendix for years and industries included for calculating gross profit rates in each country.

Convergence of gross profit rates among countries, as evidenced by the decline in the coefficient of variation and the increase in the unweighted average relative to the leader, occurred in chemicals (17), machinery (21/23), rubber and plastics (49), paper and printing (47), transport equipment (28), and metal products (19). There is clear evidence of divergence of gross profit rates in only the other industries category (48) and food, beverages, and tobacco (36). In the other four sectors, no clear trends are discernible or the results of the two indices are contradictory.

We have divided the industries into three groups – heavy, medium, and light – based on the unweighted average of the capital–labour ratios among the eight countries.[12] Convergence was strongest among medium industries, where the unweighted average of the coefficients of variation of industries within this group fell by almost 30 per cent over the 1963–82 period, and the (unweighted) average gross profit rate level of the other countries pulled to within three-fifths of the leader. Among light industries, the unweighted average of the coefficient of variation fell by about 20 per cent, and the average gross profit rate reached to about three-fifths of the leader. Among heavy industries, there is a very slight trend toward profit rate equalisation. Results for the unweighted average among all manufacturing industries shows that, on average, there was a moderate tendency toward profit rate equalisation among individual manufacturing industries.

The weighted averages are based on aggregate profits and capital stock for industries within each of the three large subsectors of manufacturing. The results show that gross profit rates within each of the industry groups became considerably more equal among countries over the 1963–82 period. Convergence was again strongest within medium industry, for which the coefficient of variation fell by almost two-thirds. Profit rate convergence was also strong within heavy industry and light industry. However, the gross profit rate within all manufacturing showed no tendency toward equality. The apparent contradiction is due to differences in industry mix within each country.

Table 7.3 shows another slice of the profit rate convergence issue. The data provide indices of dispersion of profit rates among individual industries within each country. In Belgium, Germany, Italy, and the United States, profit rates became more unequal among the twelve manufacturing industries over the 1963–83 period. In Japan, the Netherlands, and the UK, industry profit rates moved closer together over the 20-year period. For Canada, the two indices show contradictory trends.

In sum, there is no persuasive evidence showing a trend towards convergence in gross profit rates within total manufacturing among the eight countries in the sample over the 1963–83 period. The evidence does indicate convergence during the 1970s but a pattern of dispersion during the 1960s and early 1980s. However, there is some evidence of profit rate equalisation within individual industries. There is direct evidence for six of

Table 7.2   Indices of profit rate dispersion across countries by manufacturing industry for selected years, 1963–82[a]

	NACE	Coefficient of Variation				Unweighted average in seven countries relative to leader			
		1963	1972	1979	1982	1963	1972	1979	1982
Heavy industries									
Ferrous and nonferrous metals	13	.57	.50	.42	.61	.41	.39	.53	.43
Chemicals	17	.48	.43	.37	.33	.41	.54	.58	.59
Nonmetallic minerals	15	.46	.88	1.12	.49	.50	.26	.16	.39
Medium industries									
Machinery	21/23	.30	.33	.29	.25	.60	.52	.61	.65
Rubber and plastics	49	.86	.68	.60	.76	.29	.38	.54	.42
Paper and printing	47	.58	.62	.28	.30	.51	.34	.64	.66
Transport equipment	28	.42	.37	.30	.24	.46	.59	.71	.70
Light industries									
Metal products	19	.79	.58	.32	.27	.40	.37	.64	.67
Other industries	48	.18	.39	.23	.30	.76	.56	.67	.61
Textiles	42	.36	.41	.40	.45	.48	.55	.57	.51
Electrical goods	25	.31	.37	.27	.29	.54	.46	.61	.57
Food, beverages, tob.	36	.20	.33	.29	.42	.70	.54	.61	.60
I. Unweighted Averages[b]									
All manufacturing		.46	.49	.41	.39	.51	.46	.57	.57
Heavy industry		.50	.60	.64	.48	.44	.40	.42	.47
Medium industry		.54	.50	.37	.39	.47	.46	.63	.61
Light industry		.41	.44	.31	.33	.55	.49	.62	.59
II. Weighted Averages[c]									
All manufacturing		.28	.33	.21	.28	.57	.62	.72	.64
Heavy industry		.44	.44	.39	.29	.47	.48	.56	.65
Medium industry		.46	.36	.18	.17	.41	.63	.67	.70
Light industry		.32	.24	.24	.25	.53	.62	.68	.67

Notes:

[a] The countries included in the calculations are as follows:

continued on p. 112

Table 7.2   Notes continued

Industry 13:

1963   Belgium, Canada, UK, US.
1972, 1979 All except Netherlands.
1982   Belgium, Germany, Italy, Japan, UK, US.

Industry 17:

1963   Belgium, Canada, UK, US.
1972   All except Netherlands and UK.
1979   All except Netherlands.
1982   Belgium, Germany, Italy, Japan, UK, US.

Industry 15:

1963   Belgium, Canada, Netherlands, UK, US.
1972   All except Japan.
1979   All.
1982   All except Canada.

Industry 21, 23:

1963   Canada, UK, US.
1972, 1979 Canada, Germany, Italy, Japan, UK, US.
1982   Germany, Italy, Japan, UK, US.

Industry 49:

1963   Belgium, Canada, UK, US.
1972, 1979 Belgium, Canada, Germany, Italy, UK, US.
1982   Belgium, Germany, Italy, UK, US.

Industry 47:

1963   Belgium, Canada, Netherlands, UK, US.
1972   All except UK.
1979   All.
1982   All except Canada.

Industry 28:

1963   Canada, Netherlands, UK, US.
1972, 1979 All except Belgium.
1982   All except Canada and Belgium.

Industry 19:

1963   Canada, Netherlands, UK, US.
1972   Canada, Germany, Italy, Japan, US.
1979   All except Belgium.
1982   Germany, Italy, Japan, Netherlands, UK, US.

Industry 48:

1963   Belgium, Canada, Netherlands, UK, US.

Table 7.2   Notes continued

1972, 1979 All.
1982   All except Canada.

Industry 42

1963   Belgium, Canada, Netherlands, UK, US.
1972   All except UK.
1979   All.
1982   All except Canada.

Industry 25:

1963   Canada, Netherlands, UK, US.
1972, 1979 All except Belgium.
1982   All except Canada and Belgium.

Industry 36:
1963   Belgium, Canada, Netherlands, UK, US.
1972, 1979 All.
1982   All except Canada.

All Manufacturing:

1963   Belgium, Canada, Netherlands, UK, US.
1972   Canada, Germany, Italy, Japan, US.
1979   All.
1982   All except Canada.

Heavy Industry:

1963   Belgium, Canada, UK, US.
1972   Belgium, Canada, Germany, Italy, US.
1979   All except Netherlands.
1982   Belgium, Germany, Italy, Japan, UK, US.

Medium Industry:

1963   Canada, UK, US.
1972   Canada, Germany, Italy, US.
1979   Canada, Germany, Italy, UK, US.
1982   Germany, Italy, UK, US.

Light Industry:

1963   Canada, Netherlands, UK, US.
1972   Canada, Germany, Italy, Japan, US.
1979   All except Belgium.
1982   Germany, Italy, Japan, Netherlands, UK, US.

[b] Unweighted average of corresponding statistics in each industry group.
[c] Statistics based on aggregate gross profits and aggregate capital stock for
   industries in each industry group.

Table 7.3   Indices of dispersion of industry profit rates within country for selected years, 1963–83

	1963	1967	1970	1972	1979	1982	1983
A. Coefficient of Variation[a]							
Belgium	.74	.82	.70	.75	.86	.93	NA
Canada	.48	.53	.56	.52	.51	NA	.55
Germany	.44[c]	.46	.42	.50	.48	.47	NA
Italy	NA	.27[d]	.30	.31	.31	.37	NA
Japan	.40[c]	.38	.43	.43	.29	.34	.36
Netherlands	.60	.55	.57	.81[e]	.27[f]	.22	NA
United Kingdom	.45	.47[d]	.49	.36[e]	.38	.36	.33
United States	.33	.31	.36	.36	.28	.39	.39
B. Unweighted Average Relative to Leading Industry[b]							
Belgium	.39	.33	.36	.34	.29	.29	NA
Canada	.44	.42	.43	.37	.42	NA	.56
Germany	.60[c]	.57	.53	.45	.41	.45	NA
Italy	NA	.53[d]	.47	.55	.50	.46	NA
Japan	.36[c]	.37	.35	.36	.47	.42	.41
Netherlands	.29	.32	.18	.13[e]	.36[f]	.40	NA
United Kingdom	.46	.40[d]	.41	.45[e]	.53	.59	.61
United States	.59	.70	.51	.49	.53	.51	.51

Notes: [a] Defined as the coefficient of variation of industry profit rates for industries within each country with the requisite data. Industries for which data are not available are as follows:
Belgium: 19, 21–23, 25, and 28.
Japan: 15 and 49.
Netherlands: 13, 17, 21–23, and 49.
  [b] Defined as the ratio of the unweighted average of industry profit rates among all industries except that with the highest profit rate to the highest industry profit rate. Only industries with the requisite data are included. See note [a] for the list of industries that are excluded for each country.
  [c] 1965.
  [d] 1968.
  [e] 1973.
  [f] 1980.

the twelve industries in the sample. Moreover, within each of the three large subsectors of manufacturing, particularly medium industries, aggregate profit rates became much more equal among countries over the 1963–82 period. With regard to profit rate equalisation among different industries within the same country, the evidence is mixed. In four of the eight countries, industry profit rates became less equal over the 20-year period, and in three they became more equal.

In contrast, the evidence for convergence in real wages among countries is much more compelling. Table 7.4 shows results on mean labour compen-

Table 7.4 Mean employee compensation for the whole manufacturing sector by country for selected years, 1963–83[a]
(Index number, with US = 100)

	1963	1967	1970	1972	1979	1982	1983
Belgium	47	53	61	66	75	82	NA
Canada	84	86	96	98	102	102	103
Germany	NA	54	60	67	85	88	87
Italy	NA	NA	28	58	74	75	NA
Japan	24	33	44	49	65	71	72
Netherlands	61	69	83	85	98	99	NA
United Kingdom	54	50	63	59	67	69	70
United States	100	100	100	100	100	100	100

A. Summary Statistics Based on Countries with Available Date[b]

	1963	1967	1970	1972	1979	1982	1983
Coeff of variation	.40	.33	.35	.24	.17	.15	.16
Maximum/minimum	4.12	3.01	3.63	2.04	1.57	1.47	1.46
Unweighted average relative to US	.54	.58	.62	.69	.81	.84	.83
Unweighted average relative to leader	.54	.58	.62	.69	.79	.82	.80

B. Summary Statistics Based on Seven-Country Sample: Belgium, Canada, Germany, Japan, Netherlands, UK, and US

	1965	1967	1970	1972	1979	1982	1983
Coeff of variation	.36	.33	.27	.24	.17	.14	NA
Unweighted average relative to leader	.55	.58	.68	.71	.80	.84	NA

C. Summary Statistics Based on Six-Country Sample: Belgium, Canada, Japan, Netherlands, and US

	1963	1967	1970	1972	1979	1982	1983
Coeff of variation	.40	.35	.27	.25	.19	.16	NA
Unweighted average relative to leader	.54	.58	.69	.71	.79	.83	NA

Notes:
[a] Results are based on total employee compensation in 1983 US dollars and total employment for manufacturing.
[b] See Appendix for years and industries included for calculating mean employee compensation in each country.

sation per employee for the whole manufacturing sector. All four indices of dispersion indicate very strong equalisation in average real wages among countries.[13] The coefficient of variation dropped from 0.40 to 0.16 between 1963 and 1983, the ratio of maximum to minimum declined from 4.1 to 1.5, and the unweighted average mean employee compensation increased from 54 to 83 per cent of the US level.

Results by industry, shown in Table 7.5, are just as strong. The coefficient of variation of real wages among countries fell in every industry over the 1963–82 period, while the unweighted average real wage relative to the leader increased in each industry. However, evidence on real wage convergence among industries within country is quite mixed as seen in Table 7.6. Industry real wages moved closer together over the 1963–83 period within Italy, the Netherlands, and the UK, whereas they diverged in Canada and the US. In the other three countries, there was no clear trend. Thus, as with profit rates, barriers against real wage equalisation appear stronger between industries than among countries.

7.4 PROFITABILITY AND CAPITAL ACCUMULATION

We next investigate whether there is evidence that capital flows toward higher profit sectors or countries. We also consider several other factors that might account for patterns of capital formation both among industries and among countries. However, before doing this, it might be useful to consider what the patterns themselves look like. Table 7.7 presents basic statistics on the rate of capital accumulation by country. There is considerable dispersion among nations. Over the 1963–82 period, annual average rates of capital growth in total manufacturing ranged from a low of 2.9 per cent for the UK to 8.8 per cent for Japan. Italy's rate of capital accumulation was second lowest, at 3.2 per cent per year, while those of Belgium, Canada, Germany, the Netherlands, and the US ranged from 3.9 to 4.5 per cent. The unweighted mean among these countries was 4.5 per cent per annum.

We divided the period into two halves, 1963–72 and 1972–82. There are marked differences between them. The rate of growth of the capital stock was much stronger in the first sub-period, averaging 6.2 per cent per year, than in the second, at 3.3 per cent per year. The rate of capital accumulation fell in every country. This is consistent with the finding of Boyer and Petit (1981) of a sharp break in productivity, output, and employment growth in 1973 among EEC countries. Though Japan was still highest in the two sub-periods and the UK lowest, there were changes in rank order among the other countries. Moreover, according to the two measures of dispersion presented in the table, capital growth rates were more equal in the second half of the period than the first. The coefficient of variation fell

Table 7.5   Indices of dispersion of mean employee compensation across countries by manufacturing industry for selected years, 1963–82[a]

	NACE	Coefficient of variation				Unweighted average in seven countries relative to leader			
		1963	1972	1979	1982	1963	1972	1979	1982
Heavy industries									
Ferrous and									
nonferrous metals	13	.44	.28	.21	.19	.52	.63	.68	.73
Chemicals	17	.44	.22	.13	.14	.51	.70	.80	.79
Nonmetallic minerals	15	.49	.36	.28	.29	.48	.52	.56	.54
Medium industries									
Machinery	21/23	.44	.28	.17	.19	.53	.63	.76	.71
Rubber and plastics	49	.48	.26	.13	.13	.49	.66	.81	.77
Paper and printing	47	.40	.25	.14	.10	.62	.67	.77	.81
Transport equipment	28	.41	.28	.21	.20	.55	.62	.69	.70
Light industries									
Metal Products	19	.54	.32	.23	.20	.46	.61	.70	.76
Other Industries	48	.45	.29	.20	.16	.62	.65	.71	.80
Textiles	42	.37	.24	.22	.21	.63	.70	.65	.64
Electrical Goods	25	.43	.29	.21	.19	.53	.68	.72	.72
Food, beverages, tob.	36	.44	.28	.20	.17	.53	.70	.75	.78
I. Unweighted Averages[b]									
All manufacturing		.44	.28	.19	.18	.54	.65	.72	.73
Heavy industry		.46	.29	.21	.21	.50	.62	.68	.69
Medium industry		.43	.27	.16	.16	.55	.65	.75	.75
Light industry		.44	.28	.21	.19	.56	.67	.71	.74
II. Weighted Averages[c]									
All manufacturing		.40	.24	.17	.15	.54	.69	.79	.82
Heavy industry		.46	.28	.19	.18	.53	.64	.74	.74
Medium industry		.43	.28	.18	.17	.55	.65	.77	.77
Light industry		.41	.26	.17	.13	.56	.68	.75	.84

Notes:

[a] The countries included in the calculations are as follows:

Industry 13:

1963 Belgium, Canada, Japan, UK, US.
1972–82 All except Netherlands.

Industry 17:

1963 Belgium, Canada, Japan, UK, US.
1972–82 All except Netherlands.

Industry 15:

1963 Belgium, Canada, Japan, Netherlands, UK, US.
1972–82 All.

Table 7.5   Notes continued

Industry 21,23:

1963   Canada, Japan, UK, US.
1972–82 Canada, Germany, Italy, Japan, UK, US.

Industry 49:

1963   Belgium, Canada, Japan, UK, US.
1972–82 All except the Netherlands.

Industry 47:

1963   Belgium, Canada, Japan, Netherlands, UK, US.
1972–82 All.

Industry 28:

1963   Canada, Japan, Netherlands, UK, US.
1972–82 All except Belgium.

Industry 19:

1963   Canada, Japan, Netherlands, UK, US.
1972–82 All except Belgium.

Industry 48:

1963   Belgium, Canada, Japan, Netherlands, UK, US.
1972–82 All.

Industry 42:

1963   Belgium, Canada, Japan, Netherlands, UK, US.
1972–82 All.

Industry 25:

1963   Canada, Japan, Netherlands, UK, US.
1972–82 All except Belgium.

Industry 36:

1963   Belgium, Canada, Japan, Netherlands, UK, US.
1972–82 All.

All Manufacturing:

1963   Belgium, Canada, Japan, Netherlands, UK, US.
1972–82 All.

Heavy Industry:

1963   Belgium, Canada, Japan, Netherlands, UK, US.
1972–82 All except the Netherlands.

Medium Industry:

1963   Canada, Japan, UK, US.
1972–82 Canada, Germany, Italy, Japan, UK, US.

Table 7.5 Notes continued

Light Industry:

1963   Canada, Japan, Netherlands, UK, US.
1972–82 All except Belgium.

   [b] Unweighted average of corresponding statistics in each industry group.
   [c] Statistics based on aggregate employee compensation in 1983 US dollars and aggregate employment for industries in each industry group.

Table 7.6   Indices of dispersion of industry mean employee compensation within country for selected years, 1963–83

	1963	1967	1970	1972	1979	1982	1983
A. Coefficient of Variation[a]							
Belgium	.19	.21	.19	.20	.22	.22	NA
Canada	.17	.16	.16	.17	.16	.21	.22
Germany	.12[c]	.12	.32	.12	.13	.13	.13
Italy	NA	.17[d]	.18	.17	.12	.11	NA
Japan	.23	.20	.20	.19	.20	.21	.22
Netherlands	.26	.27	.21	.22	.20	.20	NA
United Kingdom	.23	.25	.24	.13	.13	.14	.14
United States	.17	.16	.16	.16	.20	.19	.20
B. Unweighted Average Relative to Leading Industry[b]							
Belgium	.75	.67	.72	.71	.71	.68	NA
Canada	.74	.74	.71	.71	.69	.65	.61
Germany	.80[c]	.79	.77	.81	.80	.79	.79
Italy	NA	.77[d]	.72	.74	.80	.80	NA
Japan	.67	.67	.69	.72	.72	.71	.70
Netherlands	.68	.66	.75	.76	.79	.79	NA
United Kingdom	.56	.55	.55	.83	.82	.80	.81
United States	.77	.81	.81	.78	.73	.76	.73

Notes:
   [a] Defined as the coefficient of variation of industry profit rates for industries within each country with the requisite data. Industries for which data are not available are as follows:
     Belgium: 19, 21–23, 25, and 28.
     Netherlands: 13, 17, 21–23, 25, and 29.
   [b] Defined as the ratio of the unweighted average of industry mean employee compensation among all industries except that with the highest mean employee compensation to the highest industry mean employee compensation. Only industries with the requisite data are included. See note[a] for the list of industries that are excluded for each country.
   [c] 1965.
   [d] 1968.

Table 7.7   Annual average rate of growth of the capital stock for the manufacturing sector by country for selected periods, 1963–82

A. Aggregate Capital Growth[a]

	1963–72	1972–82	1963–82
Belgium[b]	6.28%	3.14%	4.46%
Canada[c]	5.22	3.63	4.35
Germany	5.82	2.14	3.89
Italy	4.08	2.49	3.24
Japan[d]	12.93	5.82	8.75
Netherlands[e]	6.80	3.23	4.73
United Kingdom[f]	3.50	2.18	2.88
United States	4.43	3.67	4.03
Mean	6.13%	3.29%	4.54%
Coeff of variation	0.45	0.34	0.37
Unweighted average			
relative to leader	0.40	0.50	0.45

B. Unweighted Average and Coefficient of Variation among Industries within each Country[g]

	Unweighted average			Coefficient of variation		
	1963–72	1972–82	1963–82	1963–72	1972–82	1963–82
Belgium[b]	6.23%	2.79%	4.42%	.33	.49	.34
Canada[c]	5.43	3.68	4.47	.20	.41	.27
Germany	6.16	2.15	4.05	.28	.68	.37
Italy	3.88	2.44	3.12	.52	.57	.49
Japan[d]	12.98	5.52	8.59	.22	.69	.31
Netherlands[e]	5.90	3.47	4.64	.36	.57	.43
United Kingdom[f]	3.69	2.29	2.98	.30	.32	.27
United States	4.78	3.72	4.22	.31	.31	.29

Notes:

[a] Results are based on the total capital stock for manufacturing.

[b] For Belgium, 1971 is used instead of 1972.

[c] For Canada, 1983 is used instead of 1982.

[d] For Japan, 1965 is used instead of 1963.

[e] For the Netherlands, 1971 is used instead of 1972 for total manufacturing and 1973 is used instead of 1972 for industry 19.

[f] For the United Kingdom, 1973 is used instead of 1972 for industries 17, 19, 42, and 47.

[g] Results based on industries with pertinent capital stock data. See Appendix for details on data availability by industry and country.

from 0.45 to 0.34, while the unweighted average relative to the leader increased from 0.40 to 0.50

Panel B of Table 7.7 shows results on both the average and the dispersion of industry capital growth rates within country. Unweighted averages of industry capital growth rates are very similar to aggregate manufacturing growth rates, indicating very little composition effect in aggregate capital stock movements. The coefficient of variation among industries increased in every country except the US, where it remained constant. Thus, differences in rates of capital accumulation increased among industries over the 1963–82 period.

Table 7.8 shows the rate of growth of the capital stock by industry averaged across countries. As indicated above, there is considerable variation in capital growth rates among industries. For the 1963–82 period, they range from a low of 1.8 per cent per year in textiles (42) to 5.7 per cent in electrical goods (25). As for total manufacturing, the capital stock growth rate declined between the 1963–72 and the 1972–82 sub-periods in every industry, as well as for the three major subsectors of manufacturing. Whereas in the first half of the period, the rate of capital accumulation was about equal among the three subsectors, during the second half it was considerably stronger in the medium industries than in heavy or light industry. The coefficient of variation for capital growth rates is also shown by industry. Whereas the coefficient of variation fell for total manufacturing between the two sub-periods, the pattern is quite mixed by industry. For five of the 12 industries, there is a clear decline in the coefficient of variation, for five there is a substantial increase, and for the remaining two no strong trend. Moreover, the dispersion in the aggregate capital growth rate among countries increased in heavy industry and declined in light medium and industry.

In sum, the results indicate that aggregate rates of capital accumulation within total manufacturing were converging among the eight countries in our sample over the 1962–83 period. However, dispersion in capital growth rates among industries within country was increasing over the same period. Morever, for some industries, rates of capital accumulation were becoming more equal among countries, whereas for other industries they were becoming less equal.

The basic data reveal no easily discernible relation between capital accumulation by industry or country and corresponding profit rate and real wage movements. As a result, we next employ regression analysis to isolate some of the factors that influence the rate of capital accumulation. Our dependent variable is:

$CAPGRTH_{it}^{h}$, the rate of growth of the capital stock in industry i of country h in year t.

The independent variables are as follows:

$PROFRATE_{it}^{h}$, the gross profit rate in industry i of country h in year t.

$WAGERATE_{it}^{h}$, mean employee compensation in 1983 US dollars (in units of 10 000) in industry i of country h in year t.

Table 7.8   Summary statistics of the annual average rate of growth of the capital stock by industry for selected periods, 1963–83[a]

	NACE	Unweighted average among countries			Coefficient of variation among countries		
		1963–72	1972–82	1963–82	1963–72	1972–82	1963–82
Heavy industries							
Ferrous and							
nonferrous metals	13	6.18%	2.30%	4.06%	.52	.51	.47
Chemicals	17	7.03	3.84	5.31	.38	.43	.30
Nonmetallic minerals	15	5.63	2.89	4.19	.28	.33	.20
Medium industries							
Machinery	21/23	6.81	4.75	5.65	.55	.36	.43
Rubber and plastics	49	6.14	3.21	4.59	.46	.44	.42
Paper and printing	47	5.70	3.72	4.66	.39	.76	.53
Transport equipment	28	6.30	4.10	5.07	.64	.39	.51
Light industries							
Metal products	19	6.97	3.69	5.17	.73	.52	.61
Other industries	48	6.22	2.37	4.05	.55	1.07	.30
Textiles	42	3.42	0.49	1.84	.57	2.37	.71
Electrical goods	25	6.73	4.76	5.65	.33	.34	.31
Food, beverages, tob.							
	36	5.21	3.14	4.07	.56	.46	.48
Weighted averages[b]							
All manufacturing		6.13	3.29	4.54	.45	.34	.37
Heavy industry		5.37	2.75	4.00	.20	.35	.16
Medium industry		4.85	3.25	4.00	.30	.18	.23
Light industry		5.49	2.42	3.70	.57	.32	.29

Notes:

[a] All countries are included in the calculations except as follows:

Industry 13:	Netherlands.
Industry 17:	Netherlands.
Industry 21,23:	Belgium, Netherlands.
Industry 49:	Japan, Netherlands.
Industry 28:	Belgium.
Industry 19:	Belgium.
Industry 25:	Belgium.
Heavy Industry:	Japan, Netherlands.
Medium Industry:	Belgium, Japan, Netherlands.
Light Industry:	Belgium.

Periods are as indicated, except as follows:

Belgium:	1971 is used instead of 1972 for Total Manufacturing.
Canada:	1983 is used instead of 1982 for all industries.
Japan:	1965 is used instead of 1963 for all industries.
Netherlands:	1973 is used instead of 1972 for Industry 19 and Light Industry, and 1971 instead of 1972 for Total Manufacturing,

Table 7.8 Notes continued

United Kingdom: 1973 is used instead of 1972 for Industries 17, 19, 42, and 47, Total Manufacturing, Heavy Industry, Medium Industry, and Light Industry.

b Statistics based on aggregate gross profits and aggregate capital stock for industries in each industry group.

$TFPGRTH_{it}^h$,	the rate of growth of total factor productivity, based on crude TFP (equation (3)) and the Tornqvist-Divisia index (equation (4)), in industry i of country h in year t.[14]
$RELTFP_{it}^h$,	the TFP level of industry i in country h relative to that of industry i in the US at the beginning of year t.
DUM_{65-72}	dummy variable equal to 1 for the 1965–72 period and zero otherwise.

We also include lagged independent variables of the form:

$PROFRATE_{i-t-n}^h$, the gross profit rate in industry i of country h in year $t-n$, where n is one or two.

We also use dummy variables for seven of the eight countries (excluding the US) and for 11 of the 12 industries (excluding Industry 48) to capture specific country and industry effects. Because of missing data problems and substantial year-to-year fluctuations in capital growth rates and industry profit rates, we actually use two-year, three-year, and five-year averages for *CAPGRTH, PROFRATE, WAGERATE,* and *TFPGRTH.* The sample covers 8 countries and 12 industries. The two-year average variables cover 9 time periods (from 1965 to 1983), the three-year average variables cover 6 time periods (1965 to 1983), and the five-year average statistics cover 3 time periods (1965 to 1980). Lags are in terms of periods (for the two-year average variables, the lag is two years).

Results of the contemporaneous forms are shown in Table 7.9. In order to isolate the effects of certain of the variables, we present the results with variables added sequentially. The first column shows the results with capital growth as a function of the profit rate, the wage rate, and TFP growth. The profit rate is a positive and highly significant determinant of the rate of capital accumulation. This result holds true for each of the regression forms, including those in which capital growth is a function of the lagged profit rate. In this form, the coefficient of the wage rate is statistically significant and negative, indicating that capital tends to flow to low wage industries and countries. On the other hand, the contemporaneous rate of TFP growth is found to be statistically insignificant.

In the second column, the relative industry TFP level (*RELTFP*) is added to the equation. The coefficient of this variable is highly significant, and its inclusion increases the adjusted-R^2 statistic from 0.13 to 0.20. The coefficient is negative, indicating that capital tends to flow to industries in countries with relatively low productivity levels. The coefficient of this variable remains negative and significant throughout the various forms tried, with two exceptions. The results generally support the 'accumulation hypothesis', namely that capital tends to flow to technologically backward industries. However, the ostensible reason is not that real wages are lower, since this variable is already controlled. Indeed, the coefficient of *WAGE-RATE* becomes statistically insignificant when *RELTFP* is added to the equation. Another interesting result is that the coefficient of TFP growth now becomes negative and statistically significant. This result indicates that contemporaneously high rates of investment are associated with low rates of TFP growth. One possible reason is that adjustment and learning costs are associated with the new capital investment, that lowers the current rate of technological advance.

In the third column, we include the period dummy variable for the 1965–72 period. The coefficient of this variable is positive and highly significant, and the adusted-R^2 statistic jumps from 0.20 to 0.29. These results hold for each of the regression variants. They indicate that when all other effects are controlled, there still is an important period effect. Indeed, the magnitude of the coefficient indicates that, *ceteris paribus*, the rate of capital growth was 2 to 3 percentage points higher during the 1965–72 period than during the ensuing years. Another interesting finding is that the coefficient on the wage rate variable now becomes positive and statistically significant. This result lends support to Marx's argument that, *ceteris paribus*, high wages create an inducement for investment to offset the high costs of labour.

Country dummy variables are included in the next column. There is, again, a considerable increase in both the R^2 and the adjusted-R^2 statistics, as well as a corresponding reduction of the standard error of the regression. All seven of the country dummy variables have positive coefficients, indicating that each of the seven countries has a higher rate of capital growth than the US after the other factors are controlled. The estimated coefficients range from a high of 0.045 for Japan, to 0.014 for Belgium, and to less than 0.01 for all the others. However, the dummy variables for only Belgium and Japan are statistically significant.

In the next regression, shown in column 5, industry dummy variables are included but country dummy variables are not. Their inclusion also results in a sharp increase in both the R^2 and the adjusted-R^2 statistics, and a corresponding decline in the standard error of the regression. All eleven of the industry dummy coefficients, with the exception of Industry 42, are positive and statistically significant, indicating higher rates of capital

Table 7.9 Regressions of the rate of growth of the capital stock on the profit rate, the real wage rate, and TFP[a]

Independent variables	*Dependent variable: CAPGRTH$_{it}^h$*					
Constant	0.0393**	0.0354**	0.0179**	−0.0054	0.0023	0.0206*
	(7.78)	(7.25)	(3.65)	(0.61)	(0.36)	(1.96)
PROFRATE$_{it}^h$	0.0476**	0.1011**	0.0872**	0.0660**	0.1238**	0.0934**
	(8.72)	(11.4)	(10.4)	(7.97)	(11.6)	(8.58)
WAGERATE$_{it}^h$	−0.0098**	0.0027	0.0078**	0.0149**	0.0027	−0.0061
(US\$10 000)	(3.71)	(0.90)	(2.67)	(3.96)	(0.86)	(1.36)
TFPGRTH$_{it}^h$	−0.0227	−0.0457*	−0.0720**	−0.0685**	−0.0758**	−0.0691**
	(1.19)	(2.45)	(4.06)	(4.18)	(4.62)	(4.54)
RELTFP$_{it}^h$		−0.0477**	−0.0418**	−0.0307**	−0.0619**	−0.0474**
		(7.53)	(7.00)	(5.40)	(8.54)	(6.58)
DUM$_{65-72}$			0.0259**	0.0302**	0.0207**	0.0196**
			(9.75)	(11.3)	(8.24)	(7.06)
Country Dummies	excl.	excl.	excl.	incl.	excl.	incl.
Ind. Dummies	excl.	excl.	excl.	excl.	incl.	incl.
R^2	0.134	0.200	0.297	0.409	0.413	0.504
R^2	0.130	0.195	0.292	0.398	0.399	0.487
Std. Error	0.035	0.034	0.032	0.029	0.029	0.027

Notes: [a] Results are based on two-year averages for *CAPGRTH, PROFRATE, WAGERATE*, and *TFPGRTH*. The sample covers 9 time periods (from 1965 to 1982), 8 countries, and 12 industries. Excluding missing values, the sample size is 694. Estimated coefficients are shown next to the respective independent variable and the absolute value of the *t*-statistic is shown in parentheses.

** Significant at the .01 level (two-tailed test).
* Significant at the .05 level (two-tailed test).

growth than other manufacturing (Industry 48). One interesting consequence of including the industry dummy variables is that the coefficient of *WAGERATE* now becomes statistically insignificant. This is apparently due to the fact that much of the variation in wage rates is due to industry differentials, captured by the industry dummy variables. However, as noted, the inclusion of the industry dummy variables increases the adjusted-R^2 statistic substantially, indicating that there are industry specific effects above and beyond wage differentials.

In the last column, the regression results are shown when both country and industry dummy variables are included in the equation. This form gives the best fit of the six in terms of both the adjusted-R^2 statistic, at 0.49, and the standard error of the regression, at 0.027. The most interesting change is in the magnitude and even the signs of the coefficients of the country dummy variables. The dummy variable for Japan is cut in half, to

0.021, though its significance level remains unchanged, at the 1 per cent level. The coefficients of Belgium, Germany, Italy, and the UK are now all negative, and with the exception of the Belgium dummy variable, significant at the 1 per cent level. The coefficient of the Canada dummy variable remains unchanged, at 0.007, but is now significant at the 5 per cent level. However, the converse is not true. The coefficients and significance levels of the industry dummies remain virtually unchanged after the inclusion of the country dummy variables. This suggests that much of the difference in country rates of capital accumulation is due to differences in industry composition.

Table 7.10 shows the results for various lagged forms of the basic equation. The first column shows the results for the case in which the profit rate, the wage rate, and TFP growth variables are all lagged by one period (in this case, two years). There are three results of particular note. First, the goodness of fit of the model, as indicated by the adjusted-R^2 and the standard error of the regression is slightly lower than in the contemporaneous form. This suggests that capital investment responds quite quickly to current market conditions. Second, the coefficient of lagged TFP growth is now positive and highly significant. This supports the view that capital is attracted to sectors which are experiencing high rates of TFP growth. Third, the coefficient of the lagged profit rate variable is smaller in value and less significant than the contemporaneous profit rate. This result supports the view that profits are important for investment as a source of funds, since firms otherwise face financial constraints.

The second column shows the results for a two-period (4-year) lagged form. The goodness of fit for this form is decidedly poorer than either the contemporaneous form or the one-period lagged form, again implying that capital investment responds relatively quickly to market conditions.[15] Results in the next two columns are based on three-year averages for the variables. The results are very similar to the corresponding regressions with two-year average variables, except that the goodness of fit is somewhat better. The apparent reason is that three-year averages smooth the data more than two-year averages, thus reducing random noise.[16]

7.5 CONCLUSION

The evidence is not persuasive that there has been a trend towards equalisation in gross profit rates within total manufacturing among countries over the 1963–83 period. Some convergence occurred during the 1970s but a pattern of dispersion prevailed during the 1960s and early 1980s. However, there is some evidence of profit rate equalisation within individual industries. With regard to profit rate equalisation among different industries within the same country, the evidence is mixed. The results suggest that market forces for profit rate equalisation is specific to industry or to

Table 7.10 Regressions of the rate of growth of the capital stock on the lagged profit rate, the lagged real wage rate, and lagged TFP growth[a]

Dependent variable:	$CAPGRTH_{it}^h$ Two-year average values		Three-year average values	
	1-per lag ($n = 1$)	2-per lag ($n = 2$)	No lag ($n = 0$)	1-per lag ($n = 1$)
Constant	0.0198	0.0351**	0.0311**	0.0219
	(1.70)	(2.92)	(2.66)	(1.59)
$PROFRATE_{i,\,t-n}^h$	0.0733**	0.0205*	0.0687**	0.0466**
	(6.48)	(2.52)	(5.91)	(4.31)
$WAGERATE_{i,\,t-n}^h$	−0.0071	−0.0152**	−0.0083	−0.0078
(US$10 000)	(1.40)	(3.03)	(1.63)	(1.31)
$TFPGRTH_{i,\,t-n}^h$	0.1156**	0.0360	−0.1451**	0.1305**
	(6.28)	(1.57)	(6.10)	(4.46)
$RELTFP_{it}^h$	−0.0324**	0.0010	−0.0411**	−0.0176*
	(4.41)	(0.19)	(4.86)	(2.32)
DUM_{65-72}	0.0205**	0.0219**	0.0242**	0.0227**
	(6.40)	(6.33)	(8.22)	(6.72)
R^2	0.466	0.378	0.560	0.492
R^2	0.445	0.350	0.536	0.461
Std. Error	0.028	0.030	0.024	0.026
Sample Size	637	548	460	406

Notes: [a] Results are based on two-year and three-year averages for *CAPGRTH*, *PROFRATE*, *WAGERATE*, and *TFPGRTH*. The sample covers the time period from 1965 to 1982, 8 countries, and 12 industries. Lags are in terms of periods (for the two-year average variables, the lag is two years). Country and industry dummy variables are included in each country. Estimated coefficients are shown next to the respective independent variable and the absolute value of the *t*-statistic is shown in parentheses.
  ** Significant at the .01 level (two-tailed test).
  * Significant at the .05 level (two-tailed test).

groups of industry of similar capital intensity rather than to country. Intangible assets such as copyrights and specific human capital may make industries very different and act as a barrier to the equalisation of profit rates across sectors.

In contrast, the evidence for convergence in real wages among countries both within total manufacturing and by industry is much more compelling. However, evidence on real wage convergence among industries within country is quite mixed. Thus, as with profit rates, barriers against real wage equalisation appear stronger between industries than among countries.

The results also show convergence in aggregate rates of capital accumulation within total manufacturing among the eight countries over the 1962–83 period. However, dispersion in capital growth rates among industries within country was increasing over the same period.

The most important result from the regression analysis is that capital has flowed to industries with high profit rates. Moreover, the contemporaneous profit rate was statistically more important than the lagged profit rate. This result supports the view that profits are more important for investment as a source of funds rather than as a signal of future profitability. The results also generally support the 'accumulation hypothesis' proposed in Wolff (1989), namely that capital tends to flow to technologically backward industries. However, the ostensible reason is not that real wages are lower, since this variable is already controlled in the regressions. This result might be due to the lower costs of other inputs in production or to the possibility of greater potential gains in productivity in backward sectors.

Regression results for the wage rate variable are quite illuminating. Without the relative TFP level included in the regression, its coefficient is negative. However, when the relative TFP level is included, its coefficient becomes positive and significant, supporting Marx's argument that, when other factors are controlled, high wages create an inducement for investment, presumably in labour-saving technology. Furthermore, when industry dummy variables are included, the wage rate variable becomes statistically insignificant. This is apparently due to the fact that much of the variation in wage rates is due to industry differentials, captured by the industry dummy variables. This is consistent with our finding that variation of mean employee compensation across industries has shown little sign of convergence over the 1962–83 period, while wage rates have converged strongly among countries.

The regression results for TFP growth are also quite interesting. In the contemporaneous regressions, high rates of investment are associated with low rates of TFP growth. The likely reason is that adjustment and learning costs are associated with the new capital investment, thus lowering the current rate of technological advance. On the other hand, lagged TFP growth is a significant and positive determinant of capital investment. This result lends support to the argument proposed in Wolff (1989) that high rates of technical advance might themselves act as a stimulus to capital accumulation.

The results also indicate that once other effects are controlled, the rate of capital growth was 2 to 3 percentage points higher during the 1965–72 period than during the 1972–82 years. This is consistent with the basic data which show a pronounced slowdown in capital accumulation during the second sub-period. They also point to industry-specific effects on capital accumulation above and beyond wage differentials. Moreover, without industry effects, the US had the lowest rate of capital accumulation of the eight countries, after adjustment for other factors. However, once industry-specific effects are included, US investment performance appears much stronger. Indeed, now only Japan and Canada have statistically significant higher rates of capital formation, while Germany, Italy, and the UK have statistically significant lower rates. This implies that part of the lower overall capital performance of the US in manufacturing was due to industrial composition. Finally, the regression results also support the view that capital investment responds rather quickly (with at most a two- to three-year lag) to market conditions, as indicated by the rate of profit, the real wage rate, and the rate of productivity growth.

APPENDIX: DATA SOURCES AND AVAILABILITY

Table 7.A1 Manufacturing industry NACE codes

13	Ferrous and nonferrous metals.
15	Nonmetal minerals and products.
17	Chemicals.
19	Metal products, except machinery and transportation equipment.
21/23	Machinery.
25	Electrical goods.
28	Transport equipment.
36	Food, beverages, and tobacco products.
42	Textiles, clothing, footwear, and leather goods.
47	Paper and printing.
49	Rubber and plastics.
48	Other manufacturing.

Table 7.A2 Capital stock data availability by country and industry

	Belgium	*Canada*	*Germany*	*Italy*
Industry				
13	1963–83	1963–81, 83	1963–83	1963–83
15	1963–83	1963–81, 83	1963–83	1963–83
17	1963–83	1963–81, 83	1963–83	1963–83
19	NA	1963–81, 83	1963–83	1963–83
21, 23	NA	1963–81, 83	1963–83	1963–83
25	NA	1963–81, 83	1963–83	1963–83
28	NA	1963–81, 83	1963–83	1963–83
36	1963–83	1963–81, 83	1963–83	1963–83
42	1963–71, 73–83	1963–81, 83	1963–83	1963–83
47	1963–83	1963–81, 83	1963–83	1963–83
49	1963–83	1963–81, 83	1963–83	1963–83
48	1963–83	1963–81, 83	1963–83	1963–83
All manuf.	1963–71, 74–83	1963–81, 83	1963–83	1963–83
Heavy ind.	1963–83	1963–81, 83	1963–83	1963–83
Medium ind.	NA	1963–81, 83	1963–83	1963–83
Light ind.	NA	1963–81, 83	1963–83	1963–83

continued on page 130

Table 7.A2   continued

	Japan	*Netherlands*	*UK*	*US*
Industry				
13	1965–83	NA	1963–83	1963–83
15	1975–83	1963–83	1963–83	1963–83
17	1965–83	NA	1963–71, 73–83	1963–83
19	1965–83	1963–71, 73–83	1963–71, 73–83	1963–83
21, 23	1965–83	NA	1963–83	1963–83
25	1965–83	1963–83	1963–83	1963–83
28	1965–83	1963–83	1963–83	1963–83
36	1965–83	1963–83	1963–83	1963–83
42	1965–83	1963–83	1963–71, 73–83	1963–83
47	1965–83	1963–77, 79–83	1963–71, 73–83	1963–83
49	NA	NA	1963–83	1963–83
48	1965–83	1963–83	1963–83	1963–83
All manuf.	1965–83	1963–71, 74–77, 79–83	1963–71, 73–83	1963–83
Heavy ind.	1975–83	NA	1963–71, 73–83	1963–83
Medium ind.	NA	NA	1963–71, 73–83	1963–83
Light ind.	1965–83	1963–71, 73–83	1963–71, 73–83	1963–83

Sources:
Belgium: Eurostat worksheets.
Canada: For 1983, Statistics Canada, Science, Technology and Capital Stock Division, *Fixed Capital Flows and Stocks* (September 1987); other years are from Statistics Canada worksheets.
France: Eurostat worksheets.
Germany: Eurostat worksheets.
Italy: Eurostat worksheets.
Japan: Economic Planning Agency, Department of National Accounts, Economic Research Institute, *Gross Capital Stock of Private Enterprises, 1965–86* (February 1988).
Netherlands: Eurostat worksheets.
UK: Eurostat worksheets.
US: John C. Musgrave, 'Fixed Reproducible Tangible Wealth in the United States: Revised Estimates', *Survey of Current Business*, vol. 66, no. 1 (January 1986) pp. 51–75

Table 7.A3   Employment data availability by country and industry

	Belgium	*Canada*	*Germany*	*Italy*
Industry				
13	1963, 65–83	1963, 65–83	1965–83	1967–82
15	1963, 65–83	1963, 65–83	1965–83	1967–82
17	1963, 65–83	1963, 65–83	1965–83	1967–82
19	NA	1963, 65–83	1965–83	1967–82
21, 23	NA	1963, 65–83	1965–83	1967–82
25	NA	1963, 65–83	1965–83	1967–82

Table 7.A3   continued

	Belgium	Canada	Germany	Italy
28	NA	1963, 65–83	1965–83	1967–82
36	1963, 65–83	1963, 65–83	1965–83	1967–82
42	1963, 65–83	1963, 65–83	1965–83	1967–82
47	1963, 65–83	1963, 65–83	1965–83	1967–82
49	1963, 65–83	1963, 65–83	1965–83	1967–82
48	1963, 65–83	1963, 65–83	1965–83	1967–82
All manuf.	1963, 65–83	1963, 65–83	1965–83	1967–82
Heavy ind.	1963, 65–83	1963, 65–83	1965–83	1967–82
Medium ind.	NA	1963, 65–83	1965–83	1967–82
Light ind.	NA	1963, 65–83	1965–83	1967–82

	Japan	Netherlands	UK	US
Industry				
13	1963, 65–83	NA	1963, 65–83	1963, 65–83
15	1963, 65–83	1963, 65–83	1963, 65–83	1963, 65–83
17	1963, 65–83	NA	1963, 65–83	1963, 65–83
19	1963, 65–83	1963, 65–83	1963, 65–83	1963, 65–83
21, 23	1963, 65–83	NA	1963, 65–83	1963, 65–83
25	1963, 65–83	1963, 65–83	1963, 65–83	1963, 65–83
28	1963, 65–83	1963, 65–83	1963, 65–83	1963, 65–83
36	1963, 65–83	1963, 65–83	1963, 65–79, 81	1963, 65–83
42	1963, 65–83	1963, 65–83	1963, 65–83	1963, 65–83
47	1963, 65–83	1963, 65–83	1963, 65–83	1963, 65–83
49	1963, 65–83	NA	1963, 65–83	1963, 65–83
48	1963, 65–83	1963, 65–83	1963, 65–83	1963, 65–83
All manuf.	1963, 65–83	1963, 65–83	1963, 65–83	1963, 65–83
Heavy ind.	1963, 65–83	NA	1963, 65–83	1963, 65–83
Medium ind.	1963, 65–83	NA	1963, 65–83	1963, 65–83
Light ind.	1963, 65–83	1963, 65–83	1963, 65–83	1963, 65–83

Source: United Nations, *Yearbook of Industrial Statistics*.

Table 7.A4   Value added data availability by country and industry

	Belgium	Canada	Germany	Italy
Industry				
13	1963, 65–83	1963, 65–83	1965–82	1963, 65–82
15	1963, 65–83	1963, 65–83	1965–82	1963, 65–82
17	1963, 65–83	1963, 65–83	1965–82	1963, 65–82
19	NA	1963, 65–83	1965–82	1963, 65–82
21, 23	NA	1963, 65–83	1965–82	1963, 65–82
25	NA	1963, 65–83	1965–82	1963, 65–82
28	NA	1963, 65–83	1965–82	1963, 65–82
36	1963, 65–83	1963, 65–83	1965–82	1963, 65–82

continued on page 132

Table 7.A4   continued

	Belgium	Canada	Germany	Italy
42	1963, 65–83	1963, 65–83	1965–82	1963, 65–82
47	1963, 65–83	1963, 65–83	1965–82	1963, 65–82
49	1963, 65–83	1963, 65–83	1965–82	1963, 65–82
48	1963, .65–83	1963, 65–83	1965–82	1963, 65–82
All manuf.	1963, 65–83	1963, 65–83	1965–82	1963, 65–82
Heavy ind.	1963, 65–83	1963, 65–83	1965–82	1963, 65–82
Medium ind.	NA	1963, 65–83	1965–82	1963, 65–82
Light ind.	NA	1963, 65–83	1965–82	1963, 65–82

	Japan	Netherlands	UK	US
Industry				
13	1963, 65–83	NA	1963, 68, 70–83	1963, 65–83
15	1963, 65–83	1963, 65–82	1963, 68, 70–83	1963, 65–83
17	1963, 65–83	NA	1963, 68, 70–83	1963, 65–83
19	1963, 65–83	1963, 65–82	1963, 68, 70–83	1963, 65–83
21, 23	1963, 65–83	NA	1963, 68, 70–83	1963, 65–83
25	1963, 65–83	1963, 65–82	1963, 68, 70–83	1963, 65–83
28	1963, 65–83	1963, 65–82	1963, 68, 70–83	1963, 65–83
36	1963, 65–83	1963, 65–82	1963, 68, 70–83	1963, 65–83
42	1963, 65–83	1963, 65–82	1963, 68, 70–83	1963, 65–83
47	1963, 65–83	1963, 65–82	1963, 68, 70–83	1963, 65–83
49	1963, 65–83	NA	1963, 68, 70–83	1963, 65–83
48	1963, 65–83	1963, 65–82	1963, 68, 70–83	1963, 65–83
All manuf.	1963, 65–83	1963, 65–82	1963, 68, 70–83	1963, 65–83
Heavy ind.	1963, 65–83	NA	1963, 68, 70–83	1963, 65–83
Medium ind.	1963, 65–83	NA	1963, 68, 70–83	1963, 65–83
Light ind.	1963, 65–83	1963, 65–82	1963, 68, 70–83	1963, 65–83

Source: United Nations, *Yearbook of Industrial Statistics*.

Table 7.A5   Employee compensation data availability by country and industry

	Belgium	Canada	Germany	Italy
Industry				
13	1963, 65–82	1963, 65–83	1965–83	1968–82
15	1963, 65–82	1963, 65–83	1965–83	1968–82
17	1963, 65–82	1963, 65–83	1965–83	1968–82
19	NA	1963, 65–83	1965–83	1968–82
21, 23	NA	1963, 65–83	1965–83	1968–82
25	NA	1963, 65–83	1965–83	1968–82
28	NA	1963, 65–83	1965–83	1968–82
36	1963, 65–82	1963, 65–83	1965–83	1968–82
42	1963, 65–82	1963, 65–83	1965–83	1968–82
47	1963, 65–82	1963, 65–83	1965–83	1968–82

Table 7.A5   continued

	Belgium	Canada	Germany	Italy
49	1963, 65–82	1963, 65–83	1965–83	1968–82
48	1963, 65–82	1963, 65–83	1965–83	1968–82
All manuf.	1963, 65–82	1963, 65–83	1965–83	1968–82
Heavy ind.	1963, 65–82	1963, 65–83	1965–83	1968–82
Medium ind.	NA	1963, 65–83	1965–83	1968–82
Light ind.	NA	1963, 65–83	1965–83	1968–82

	Japan	Netherlands	UK	US
Industry				
13	1963, 65–83	NA	1963, 65–83	1963, 65–83
15	1963, 65–83	1963, 65–82	1963, 65–83	1963, 65–83
17	1963, 65–83	NA	1963, 65–83	1963, 65–83
19	1963, 65–83	1963, 65–82	1963, 65–83	1963, 65–83
21, 23	1963, 65–83	NA	1963, 65–83	1963, 65–83
25	1963, 65–83	1963, 65–82	1963, 65–83	1963, 65–83
28	1963, 65–83	1963, 65–82	1963, 65–83	1963, 65–83
36	1963, 65–83	1963, 65–82	1963, 65–83	1963, 65–83
42	1963, 65–83	1963, 65–82	1963, 65–83	1963, 65–83
47	1963, 65–83	1963, 65–82	1963, 65–83	1963, 65–83
49	1963, 65–83	NA	1963, 65–83	1963, 65–83
48	1963, 65–83	1963, 65–82	1963, 65–83	1963, 65–83
All manuf.	1963, 65–83	1963, 65–82	1963, 65–83	1963, 65–83
Heavy ind.	1963, 65–83	NA	1963, 65–83	1963, 65–83
Medium ind.	1963, 65–83	NA	1963, 65–83	1963, 65–83
Light ind.	1963, 65–83	1963, 65–82	1963, 65–83	1963, 65–83

Source: United Nations, *Yearbook of Industrial Statistics*.

Notes

* It should be noted that the views expressed in this chapter are those of the authors and do not necessarily reflect the views of the World Bank. We would like to acknowledge the excellent research assistance of Maury Gittleman and the helpful comments of Tom Michl and Willi Semmler.
1. See, for example, Smith (1965), Ricardo (1981), Marx, volume 3 (1967), Bain (1951), Stigler (1963), and Hirshleifer (1976).
2. See Dollar, Wolff and Baumol (1987) and Dollar and Wolff (1988) for a discussion of the factor-price equalisation theorem.
3. See, for example, Glick and Ehrbar (1990) for a discussion of several of these issues.
4. In such a one-commodity model, the real wage and money wage are identical.
5. There are, of course, many other factors which influence the domestic investment rate, which fall beyond the scope of the present paper. See Baumol, Blackman and Wolff (1989) for a more extended discussion.

6. It would be preferable to use gross output, together with a third input, material, in the TFP measure. However, neither a gross output series nor material input series is available for the requisite period, set of industries, and set of countries. The use of value added and the exclusion of material inputs may bias the TFP indices if materials prices change significantly and countries differ in their dependence on materials. However, experiments with US input–output data indicate that our two-factor TFP index, with value added as the output measure, shows very similar trends for manufacturing industries as a three-factor index, with gross output as the numerator.

7. The PPP indices were obtained from Ward (1985). It would be preferable to deflate the output measures with industry-specific price deflators and then to convert to a common currency with PPP exchange rates for tradable goods. However, the pertinent data are not available.

8. The ideal labour input measure would be hours worked. Unfortunately, such data are not available on the industry level. However, data on average hours worked per year are available by country from Maddison (1982). Adjustment by these data did not significantly alter our results.

9. See the Appendix for details. It should be noted that the use of different life times and scrapping assumptions between the different sources may distort some of the international comparisons, though, since we use gross capital stock in the analysis, differences in depreciation schedules between countries do not affect the results. Difficulties in concordance between the industry classification schemes of the output data and the capital stock data may also distort some of the results. We explored the use of a fully concorded set of data from OECD, but these series begin only in 1970.

10. See the Appendix for details on data availability for the wage share calculation by industry and country.

11. NACE numbers are shown in parentheses.

12. The food, beverages, and tobacco industry does not fit easily into this three-way division because of several anomalies and, as a result, is tabulated separately.

13. We shall use the terms 'real wages' interchangeably with real employee compensation for heuristic convenience.

14. Because the results for crude and Divisia-Tornqvist TFP growth are so similar, results are shown below only for the latter.

15. We included one additional variable, suggested by Willi Semmler, the lagged rate of change in the profit rate. The argument is that increasing rates of profit, rather than the actual level of the profit rate, may serve as an inducement to invest in a particular firm or industry. However, the variable was generally statistically insignificant.

16. The same set of regressions were also run with five-year averages. The signs and significance levels of the coefficients for the contemporaneous forms were, with one or two exceptions, identical to the corresponding regressions with three-year averages. However, the R^2 and adjusted-R^2 statistics were substantially higher, and the standard error of the regression lower. This indicates that smoothing the data through averaging improves the goodness of fit of the model. On the other hand, the goodness of fit for the lagged forms was decidedly lower, implying that capital investment responds in a shorter period of time to the profit rate, the wage rate, and TFP growth than five years.

References

Bain, Joseph S., 'Relation of Profit Rate to Industry Concentration: American Manufacturing, 1936–1940', *Quarterly Journal of Economics*, vol. 65 (1951) pp. 293–324.

Baumol, William J., Sue Anne Blackman and Edward N. Wolff, *Productivity and US Leadership: The Long View* (Cambridge, Mass.: MIT Press, 1989).

Boyer, Robert and Pascal Petit, 'Employment and Productivity in the EEC', *Cambridge Journal of Economics*, vol. 5 (1981) pp. 47–58.

Dickens, William T. and Lawrence Katz, 'Industry Characteristics and Interindustry Wage Differentials', in Kevin Lang and Jonathan S. Leonard (eds), *Unemployment and the Structure of Labour Markets* (New York: Basil Blackwell, 1986).

Dollar, David and Edward N. Wolff, *Review of Economics and Statistics*, vol. 70, no. 4 (November 1988) pp. 549–58.

Dollar, David, Edward N. Wolff and William J. Baumol, 'Factor Price Equalization Model and Industry Labour Productivity: An Empirical Test Across Countries', in R. Feenstra (ed.), *Empirical Methods for International Trade* (Cambridge, Mass.: MIT Press, 1987).

Glick, Mark and Hans Ehrbar, 'Profit Rate Equalization in the US and Europe: An Econometric Investigation', *European Journal of Political Economy*, special issue, vol. 4 (1988a) pp. 179–201.

Glick, Mark and Hans Ehrbar, 'Structural Change in Profit Rate Differentials: The Post War II US Economy', *British Review of Economic Issues*, vol. 10 (Spring 1988b) pp. 81–102.

Glick, Mark and Hans Ehrbar, 'Long-Run Equilibrium in the Empirical Study of Monopoly and Competition', *Economic Inquiry*, vol. 28 (January 1990) pp. 151–162.

Hirshleifer, J., *Price Theory and Applications* (Englewood Cliffs, N.J.: Prentice Hall, 1976).

Hooper, Peter and Kathryn A. Larin, 'International Comparisons of Labour Costs in Manufacturing', *Review of Income and Wealth*, series 35 (December 1989).

Japan Economic Planning Agency, Department of National Accounts, Economic Research Institute, *Gross Capital Stock of Private Enterprises, 1965–1986* (February 1988).

Katz, Lawrence F., 'Efficiency Wage Theories: A Partial Evaluation', in S. Fischer (ed.), *NBER Macroeconomics Annual 1986* (Cambridge, Mass.: MIT Press, 1986).

Krueger, Alan B. and Lawrence H. Summers, 'Reflections on the Inter-industry Wage Structure', in Kevin Lang and Jonathan S. Leonard (eds), *Unemployment and the Structure of Labour Markets* (New York: Basil Blackwell, 1986).

Maddison, Angus, *Phases of Capitalist Development* (Oxford: Oxford University Press, 1982).

Marx, Karl, *Capital*, vols. 1 and 3 (New York: International Publishers, 1967).

Mueller, Dennis C., *Profits in the Long Run* (Cambridge: Cambridge University Press, 1986).

Musgrave, John C., 'Fixed Reproducible Tangible Wealth in the United States: Revised Estimates', *Survey of Current Business*, vol. 66, no. 1 (January 1986) pp. 51–75.

Ricardo, David, *On the Principles of Political Economy and Taxation* (Cambridge: Cambridge University Press, 1981).

Smith, Adam, *The Wealth of Nations* (New York: Random House, 1965).

Stigler, George, *Capital and Rates of Return in Manufacturing Industries* (Princeton: Princeton University Press, 1963).

Summers, Robert and Allan Heston, 'A New Set of International Comparisons of Real Product and Prices: Estimates for 130 Countries, 1950–1985', *Review of Income and Wealth*, series 34 (March 1988) pp. 1–26.

Statistics Canada, Science, Technology and Capital Stock Division, *Fixed Capital Flows and Stocks* (September 1987).

Ward, Michael, *Purchasing Power Parities and Real Expenditures in the OECD* (Paris: Organization for Economic Cooperation and Development, 1985).

Wolff, Edward N., 'Capital Formation and Productivity Convergence', mimeo (1989).

COMMENT

Thomas R. Michl

This is a rich chapter in which Edward Wolff and David Dollar cover a wide range of hypotheses and evidence, and uncover an interesting set of patterns in the data. The evidence that profit rate convergence occurs within industries across countries but not within countries is perhaps the most interesting and most problematic finding, and I begin with it.

There are two potentially distinct mechanisms for profit rate convergence considered: capital flows and 'catching up'. In classical price theory (meaning the tradition of Smith, Ricardo, Marx and Sraffa), profit rate equalisation operates tendentiously through capital flows, and prices of production (the uniform profit rate price vector) are sometimes said to constitute the centres of gravity around which actual prices fluctuate. From this theory it does not follow, it would seem, that the dispersion of profit rates should necessarily have any long-run tendency, unless imperfections, such as barriers to entry, were vanishing over time. Thus, I question the implication of the chapter that the presence or absence of profit rate convergence within countries tests the predictions of this price theory.

The second mechanism is that technology transfer drives a convergence in productivity levels, or 'catching up'. The evidence presented here shows that this process (which is well-established for industrialised countries) is mirrored in real wage levels, so one might expect to see converging wage shares as well. If capital–output ratios do not diverge, catching up will compress the world structure of profit rates, independently of capital flows. (Capital flows could speed things up, but they are not a necessary condition. The chapter does present a mechanism for catching up that involves capital accumulation, which is shown to occur faster in industries with low efficiency relative to best practice.) Since catching up has been shown by the authors in other work to occur at the industry level, it could explain why profit rates are converging across industries at the world level.

The chapter whet my appetite for a more detailed picture of the relative importance of labour productivity, capital productivity (output–capital ratio) and wages in the profitability convergence process. A general question I would raise in this connection is what role endogenous technical progress, along Kaldorian lines, might play. The catching up thesis treats tehnical change as autonomous to an individual country, and one wonders if there are not significant amounts of endogenous technical progress that arise from growth of production.

How compelling is the evidence for profit rate convergence? Comparisons of gross average accounting rates of return (GAARR), which the chapter uses, are hazardous for two reasons. First, there may be incomparabilities in methods used in different countries. Second, accounting rates of return are known to be imperfect measures of the ideal measure, the internal rate of return. Comparisons across industries and countries amplify the imperfections. For example, if returns on capital projects are higher in the early years of service life, and then decline, the GAARR will under some conditions be an increasing function of the rate of capital accumulation. Faster accumulation increases the weight of younger projects. If capital growth rates converge, so too will GAARRs. As the chapter shows, rates of accumulation do converge across countries, but not within countries across industries. Overall manufacturing GAARRs converge across countries during the 1970s, but diverge in the 1960s and 1980s; within countries, GAARRs do not converge very much across industries. Because Tables 7.1 and 7.2 (profit rates) and Tables 7.7 and 7.8 (accumulation) present data by years and intervals, respectively, it is not possible to say whether the patterns of accumulation and profitability correspond, but it is possible that some of the convergence in the latter is a statistical artifact of AARRs. Unfortunately, the relation between accounting and internal rates of return is enormously complicated, and this is the kind of problem that can be pointed out more easily than it can be resolved.

Another obstacle to interpreting the results on profit rate convergence is the absence of cyclical adjustment. If all the countries experienced the same demand-shock in the 1970s, for example, one might expect profit rate convergence simply because the business cycles were synchronised. The drop in across-country variation in the 1970s may reflect this kind of effect, although the years shown, 1972 and 1979, were not slump years. The fact that convergence is stronger in light and medium industry, compared to heavy industry, also suggests that the lack of utilisation adjustments is not a serious problem.

The rigidity of the industry wage structure within a country found here reproduces a finding originally due to 1950s Institutionalists that has been lately rediscovered by labour economists. Two explanations for wage differentials that defy conventional human capital models are that employment rents are high where supervision is costly, and that high wages partly reflect a form of monopoly rent. The first suggests that the wage structure and profit structure across industries will be independent, while the latter suggests a positive correlation insofar as labour and capital share monopoly rents. It would be interesting to explore rank correlations between the industry wage and profit rate structure with this in mind. It would also be of interest to know if the industry profit rate structure in a country remains very stable over time, for example, by rank correlations over time. If there is a persistent hierarchy of profit rates, this would call into question the notion that prices of production are centres of gravity.

Finally, I conclude with some random comments on the regression results, which present evidence for a kind of profitability-cum-accelerator investment model. The most interesting finding here is that accumulation is faster in industries with low levels of relative total factor productivity, which suggests that much catching up occurs via embodied technical change. Again, my curiosity about the effects of accumulation on capital–output ratios was aroused, and it would be of some interest to relate the model to this question. Second, adding growth of output to the lagged-form equations caused the coefficient on the growth of total factor productivity to change signs, suggesting substantial collinearity between these variables. Could this be a signal that productivity growth is partly determined by output growth, as Kaldor might say? Third, the significance of period dummies for 1965–72 suggests that investment has a sizeable exogenous component, along Keynesian 'animal spirits' lines. Fourth, the fit or profitability is stronger for contemporary as opposed to lagged profitability, suggesting that financial constraints explain, to some degree, why profitability matters in an investment equation.

8 The Flow of Profits: Insights from the *Ex Ante* Approach

Albert Gailord Hart

8.1 THE EXPECTATIONAL APPROACH TO ECONOMICS

At the 1988 meeting of the American Economic Association, Robert Eisner used the first few minutes of his presidential address to urge economists to make expectational dynamics a major focus of attention. In particular, he reminded us that when we

> introduce as arguments in an investment function such variables as current and past output, sales, or utilisation of capacity, current or past profits, cash flow or measures of liquidity, and current or past interest rates, depreciation rates, and relative rental price or user costs of capital, . . . our theory tells us that the arguments we generally need are . . . the expected future values of those variables. Firms should invest if they expect the future demand for output to be high, if they expect the cost of capital to be higher in the future than now, and if they look to higher future profits as a consequence of current investment, but little if at all in response to current or past values of these variables. (Eisner, 1989, pp. 1–2)

The present chapter is a progress report on research of just this character, using actual *ex ante* data from surveys along with well-known *ex post* series. The *ex ante* data come chiefly from a survey which Eisner himself has used to good effect in one of his most important works (1978).

Too little appreciated by economists is the growing archive of survey data on investment plans and on expectations about related variables. Of pivotal importance are the data (from 1954 to date) in reports of the McGraw-Hill survey of plans for plant and equipment expenditure. I myself have been engaged since the 1960s on a long-term project which I call 'CID' (Crystallisation of the Investment Decision), and am now pulling together a comprehensive report.

8.1.1 'Rational Expectations' as Substitute for Ex Ante Data

A wave of fashion in economic research, which now seems to be ebbing, has been the use of so-called 'rational expectations'. These were constructs out of *ex post* data, rather than statements from decision-makers themselves about their intentions and forecasts.

In principle, the rational-expectations approach was holistic – assuming that decision-makers when looking at the future take into account all the past experience which economists might deem relevant to forecasting. In practice it tended to be simplistic – assuming that decision-makers infer the future of Variable X from the history of Variable X.

While this approach gave *pro forma* recognition to the importance of expectations, it actually was an evasion of the need to find out what decision-makers expect. It did not pay any attention to the voluminous evidence (obtainable for instance in the curriculum materials of business schools which train forecasters) as to how future prospects are analysed by the young people whom decision-makers hire to collate the available evidence.[1]

8.1.2 Advantages of Ex Ante Data

As explanatory variables, *ex ante* series have several advantages for studies of fixed investment and the like, as compared with 'rational expectations' or with other formulations which use only *ex post* evidence. Notably:

(a) Plans and forecasts incorporate the effect (as perceived by decision-makers) of variables which operate discontinuously or even only on one occasion, like the oil shock of 1973. In *ex post* time-series analysis, such variables can be dealt with only by the clumsy device of dummy variables.

(b) In studies for which few observations are available, plans and forecasts offer 'portmanteau variables' – using up only one degree of freedom while embodying information from a number of indicators which decision-makers take into account. In *ex post* analysis, each such indicator has to be treated as a distinct variable.

(c) Survey-reported plans and forecasts have a certain temporal crispness: they represent the situation as viewed by respondents at the survey date. In the case of the McGraw-Hill 'spring surveys' of investment plans, taken in the early weeks of each calendar year, they presumably reflect capital-budget evaluations. As 'portmanteaus', they reflect experience with a variety of indicators down to the beginning of the survey year, excluding all evidence of later date. Thus, they permit gauging the effects on the year's investment of sales, interest rates and so on during the year, brought in separately as *surprise variables*.

(d) *Ex ante* data lend themselves to the sorting out of 'stages' in the process of investment decision. The Modigliani recursive schema of 'forecast function, planning function and realisation function' – widely praised, but insufficiently applied – was designed with an eye to this characteristic of investment-plan surveys. (Modigliani, 1960, pp. 4–7)

8.1.3 Eisner's Results for 1955–68

A handsome example of analysis along these lines is provided by Robert Eisner – using unpublished micro-data from the McGraw-Hill survey data, in combination with company-report data – for the fourteen years 1955–68. Eisner fitted a realisation function in which expenditures of each are explained by investment plans as reported at the start of that year, actual investment during the previous year, profits during the survey year, and the sales-change to the survey year from the previous year.

Pooling 'industry time series' across eleven industries, Eisner found that the *ex post* sales-change and profit variables both had positive and significant regression coefficients – 2.0 and 4.2 times standard error, respectively. The previous year's expenditure had a partial regression coefficient of *minus* 0.086 (2.3 times its standard error). But though significant, the contributions of these variables to the explanation of realised investment are dwarfed by the contribution of the start-of-year investment plan. In the presence of sales-change and profits, and of the previous year's actual expenditure, the partial regression coefficient of the start-of-year plan is 1.022 (astoundingly close to the ideal value of unity, and 25.5 times its standard error). The equation as a whole yields an adjusted multiple R-squared of 0.926, and the adjusted partial R-squared for the start-of-year plan is 0.903.[2]

8.1.4 Profits in Relation to Investment

The present chapter deals chiefly with the *ex ante* view of profits, in the context of decisions about investment expenditures for plant and equipment. As Eisner indicates, it is expectations about *future* profit flows which motivate investment. More strictly, a decision about investment, to be rational, must rest upon *comparisons* between the future profit flows to be expected under each of a set of alternative lines of investment.

Investment decision may be seen as having two aspects:

(a) *Commitment* for specific installations, ordinarily covered by a contract with a supplier.
(b) *Provisional planning* for installations on which it is not yet time to make commitments.

To get things actually done, commitments have to be made. But because of uncertainty, *premature* commitment has to be avoided, and options held open. Plans for items beyond the very near future are inherently contingent. Which path should be taken after the next step will depend on the development of new products and processes, the development of markets for outputs and inputs, and the development of sources of financing.

The two aspects of decision intersect:

(a) Unless appropriate commitments are made now, the door will not be open for many of the later moves a company has under consideration. And

(b) Unless it prepares the way for some specifiable range of future moves for the company, a commitment now makes no sense.

If a new process is about to be unveiled, it is wasteful to make a commitment now for new machinery: what is now available will soon become obsolete. But if new-model equipment is to be installed when it becomes available (perhaps next year) new structures ('plant') may be needed before the installation. To decide when and where to commit itself to new plant, management must ask how far suitable space is available in existing plant, whether the new location is appropriate for the geographical structure of markets for materials and products, and so forth.

The upshot of this reasoning is that rational decision calls for estimates of future profit flows along several different tracks. Different scenarios must be examined for alternative ways in which the commitment now up for decision can be handled – including variations of scale and form, timetable, and possible postponement of the decision. These scenarios will have branches for different ways in which the installation under the present commitment may be followed up. Further branching is called for to allow for different possibilities as to sales volume of various products, financing, availability of inputs and so on.

At this point a paradox emerges: it is irrational to be too perfectionist about 'rational' working-out of details in the image of the future. Uncertainties abound, and there is no way to be sure the right probabilities are assigned to different branches of the various scenarios. Excessive detail will mean ponderous organisation and heavy costs – plus a risk that decision may be so slow that the company will miss the boat.

Indications as to the way thinking about the future is reflected in survey results will be examined in the next section of the chapter. It seems that drastic simplification of the image of the future is typical.

8.2 INVESTMENT AND PROFIT IN THE EX ANTE DATA ARCHIVE

A large body of useful survey material on investment plans (particularly for US manufacturing, disaggregated to 2-digit industries) is available for analysis. On the side of profit expectations, however, the only survey data of which I am aware come from a special McGraw-Hill survey which ran from 1966 through 1980, and which will be examined in the fourth section of this chapter.[3]

8.2.1 Single-Valued Versus Contingent Images of the Future

The material collected by expectational surveys consists almost entirely of single-valued statements about future levels or percent changes, for variables like plant and equipment expenditure, capacity and sales. Only rarely do we find statements about the way actions or prospects would be affected by such factors as pending tax changes.

It would be very illuminating if we could know in relation to the investment plans of (say) each year from 1955 through 1985 – or even for a few of those years –

- how wide was the range respondents perceived as 'likely' for deviations of the oncoming year's sales from the forecast level;
- how wide a range of variation they perceived as 'likely' for variables on which respondents were not asked to report their forecasts – such as interest rates or prices of inputs;
- how much scope respondents felt they had to scale investment up or down on short notice in response to surprises about the above variables.[4]

8.2.2 Inferences from Plan Revision on Contingent Planning

The dearth of multi-valued estimates in survey reports probably arises from a focusing of managerial attention on the planned line of action 'adopted' by top management of the reporting companies. In the capital-budget materials on which respondents presumably draw, a good deal of documentation on alternatives to the plan finally adopted clearly must exist in company archives. The individuals assigned to fill out survey questionnaires must in many cases be well informed about such alternatives. But this information is probably too variable as between companies and as between different states of the economy to support any standard pattern of questions and tabulations.

Despite the lack of explicit *ex ante* data on contingencies, much can be learned about the way uncertainty is dealt with by decision-makers. Important clues exist in the data which show *revisions* in sales forecasts, capacity targets, and capital-expenditure plans. In the survey of McGraw-Hill, the horizon of expectations and plans for these variables runs four years ahead from the date of the survey. Hence we can compare the plans reported (for instance) at the opening of 1980 with the 'provisional plans' for 1980 that had been reported at the opening of 1979. Regressing the revision of investment plans between successive viewpoints upon sales-surprises between the two viewpoints (and other surprise-variables), we can figure out the degree to which plans were *contingent* on the course of explanatory variables.

For the available profit-forecast data, unfortunately, such contingency-analysis is not feasible because profit forecasts of horizons beyond one year were not collected. Profit is one of the weak areas of the survey material, and the value of *ex ante* studies should not be judged by the materials reported in the fourth section of this chapter. Nevertheless, the profit forecasts of this McGraw-Hill survey turn out to have considerable interest. As will be argued in the final section, it is feasible and well worthwhile to start in the near future more effective studies of profit forecasts.

8.3 PROFITS AND CASH FLOW EX POST

Before going into the *ex ante* data on 'profits', it will be illuminating to examine the *ex post* data. In the context of the essays included in this volume, this examination may be taken as cautionary.

There seems to be a rather casual consensus that whatever reinforces profit will quasi-automatically generate fixed investment and thus enhance the productivity of the economy. The standard view among experts on investment decision, of course, is that investment is best explained by a considerably more complex 'accelerator/finance' model, of the sort indicated by Eisner's remarks quoted above. Yet profits are very responsive to the demand for products, and strong profits not only constitute a source of capital, but also enhance the borrowing power of producing enterprises. Hence realised profits could be a rather strong portmanteau variable, representing several of the other variables in the accelerator/finance model.

Thus, a simplistic hypothesis that fixed investment is determined solely by realised profit might in principle be a workable simplification of the accelerator/finance hypothesis – enormously useful if strongly supported by the facts. For convenience, this hypothesis will be called 'Hypothesis S'.

8.3.1 Fixed Investment and Net Cash Flow in Manufacturing (Graphical Overview)

An overview of the relation between 'cash flow' and plant and equipment expenditure is offered by a set of time-series graphs. All the cash flow data in these graphs are 'realised' (*ex post*) figures in 1972 dollars. The expenditure data, however, include planned (*ex ante*) figures. For manufacturing, the graphs are backed up by regression analysis.

All variables on the figures are graphed on a semi-logarithmic scale, so that gradients along each curve reflect year-to-year percentage changes and vertical distances reflect ratios of the magnitudes involved. Because of lags

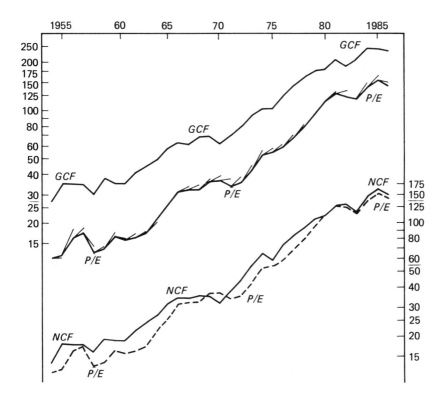

Figure 8.1   All US manufacturing. Gross cash flow, actual and planned plant
and equipment expenditure, and net cash flow, 1954–86
(Billions of dollars at current prices)

in reporting of data for some variables, the series studied terminate at
dates ranging from 1985 to 1988.

By way of preliminary, Figure 8.1 shows flows stated in current dollars
for fixed investment and cash flow in the industry group 'manufacturing'.[5]
At the bottom of the figure are two intertwining curves, for plant and
equipment expenditure (*P/E*) and for net cash flow (*NCF*). At the top is a
curve for an aggregate called 'gross cash flow' (*GCF*). *P/E* expenditures are
graphed in the middle of the figure, on the same dollar scale as *GCF*.[6]

A certain rough parallelism appears between *P/E* and *NCF* – and also
between *P/E* and *GCF*, though *GCF* has been much larger than *P/E*
throughout. *P/E* has outgrown *GCF* – presumably because of increased
reliance on debt financing. This change in financing has been dramatised in
recent years by the clamour about corporate 'leverage', but actually has
been taking place continuously over several decades.[7]

Closer inspection of the curves shows, however, that the 'rough parallelism' is not strong enough to validate Hypothesis *S*. At a number of points,

cash flow was falling while *P/E* was rising. This countermovement appears from 1955 to 1957, and from 1968 to 1970 for both *GCF* and *NCF* – and from 1974 to 1975 for *NCF*. Peaks and troughs visible both in cash flow and in *P/E* sometimes came in the same year, sometimes a year apart.

A further indication that Hypothesis *S* is not a serviceable 'explanation' of fixed investment may be seen by close examination of the *P/E* curve presented along with the *GCF* curve. Here a series of stub lines (attached at the left to the *P/E* curve, but free-floating above or below that curve at the right) shows the prediction of *P/E* offered by the investment plans reported in the McGraw-Hill investment survey.[8]

8.3.2 Regression Analysis of *P/E* and Cash Flow for Manufacturing

The results of a regression analysis to 'explain' plant and equipment expenditures appear in Table 8.1. Here '*NCF*' is taken as the measure of cash flow. Additional sets of regressions, with cash flow measured by '*GCF*' and by two intermediate indices with first (taxes) and then (taxes plus interest) excluded, are so closely parallel that it is needless to present them here.

The first group of equations presented (numbered 1 to 5) are simple correlations. A mere linear trend (equation 1) purports to explain 96.362 per cent of the variance in expenditures. The lagged dependent variable (base-year capital expenditure) purports to explain 97.834 per cent; viewpoint-year cash flow, 97.881 per cent; base-year cash flow 98.899 per cent; the reported expenditure plan for the viewpoint year, 99.776 per cent.

For all the variables except trend, the partial regression coefficients (being logarithmic) have the dimension of elasticities. All these coefficients in the first group of equations give elasticities close to unity. Closest is the elasticity for the investment plan, which comes out at 1.0011, with a standard error of 0.0084.

The second group of equations (numbered 6 to 9) offer explanations which use two or three of the listed variables, but leave out the expenditure plan. The base-year cash flow and expenditure levels (equation 6) purport to explain 99.004 per cent of the variance. The combination of base-year and viewpoint-year cash flow (equation 7) purports to explain 99.022 per cent; the combination of base-year cash flow and base-year expenditure (equation 8), 99.023 per cent; the combination of base-year cash flow and expenditure plus viewpoint-year cash flow (equation 9), 99.173 per cent. Equations using trend along with these combinations of variables uniformly fail to show any significant contribution from the trend.

The elasticities of expenditures on the base-year cash flow in this group of equations are considerably below unity. On the other variables, elasticities are much lower – ranging downward from the level of 0.319.

Table 8.1 'Explanation' of plant and equipment expenditures in US manufacturing from cash flow and investment plans, 1955–86

(Logarithms of current dollar flows in billions; Cash flow represented by NCF)

Equation	Adjusted	Intercept	Regression coefficients (T-value)				
			B-year cash flow	V-year cash flow	Trend	B-year P/E	Planned V-year P/E
		Single explanatory variable					
1	0.96362	+3.701 (136.1)	-----	-----	0.086 (29.1)	-----	-----
2	.97834	+0.088 (+0.9)				0.997 (38.1)	
3	.97881	−0.369 (−3.4)		1.062 (38.5)			
4	.98899	−0.314 (−4.1)	1.068 (53.6)				
5	.99776	−0.047 (−1.1)				1.001 (119.4)	
		Two or three explanatory variables, without expenditure plan					
6	.99004	−0.227 (−4.7)	0.800 (6.0)			0.254 (2.2)	
7	.99022	−0.345 (−4.7)	0.785 (6.0)	0.286 (2.2)			
8	.99023	−0.187 (−2.4)	0.542 (6.1)			0.023 (1.9)	
9	.99173	−0.251 (−3.2)	0.450 (5.0)	0.319 (1.8)		0.287 (2.5)	
		Two or three explanatory variables, including expenditure plan					
10	.99791	−0.089 (−2.3)	0.146 (1.8)				0.865 (11.4)
11	.99817	−0.047 (−2.9)		0.145 (2.8)			0.867 (17.9)

In equations which use the planned expenditure level as an explanatory variable, not only the trend but also the base-year expenditure uniformly fail to show any significant contribution. In the two equations which are included in the table because all variables are significant, base-year cash flow (in equation 10) is marginally significant with a *T*-value of 1.80, while viewpoint-year cash flow (in equation 11) is moderately significant, with a *T*-value of 2.79. This outcome is logical since base-year cash flow was known to respondents at the time when the investment plan was formulated, while viewpoint-year cash flow was not then known and has the status of a surprise variable.[9]

These equation-fittings for the period 1955–86 agree with Robert Eisner's results for 1955–68 (cited above). When the investment plan for the viewpoint-year is taken into account, the apparent power of profit variable to predict investment evaporates almost completely.

8.3.3   Cash Flow and *P/E* Outside Manufacturing (Graphical Overview)

Important as is investment by manufacturing companies, a larger flow of investment in the United States takes place in other industries. According to statistics from the Bureau of Economic Analysis, 'total non-farm business' invested \$437 billion in plant and equipment in 1987, of which manufacturing accounted for only \$146 billion and non-manufacturing industries for \$291 billion (*Survey of Current Business*, Sept 1988, p. 19).

Eliminating the 'finance and insurance' sector because its cash flow data are very hard to interpret, we still have \$235 billion in the industry group called in this chapter 'NFFM' (non-farm, non-financial, non-manufacturing). A graphical overview for this group is provided in a series of figures.

In Figure 8.2, we have a counterpart for 'NFFM' of Figure 8.1 presented for manufacturing. As before, gross cash flow is graphed at the top of the figure and net cash flow at the bottom. As before, the centre of the figure is occupied by a curve which traces plant and equipment expenditures, with stub lines to show how each year's *P/E* would have moved if the plan reported by the McGraw-Hill survey from the start of the year had been correct.

One surprising difference exists between Figure 8.1 and 8.2, however. In both figures, the curve for *P/E* is intertwined with a cash flow curve. But while *P/E* for manufacturing was sometimes above and sometimes below *net* cash flow, *P/E* for 'NFFM' was sometimes above and sometimes below *gross* cash flow and always far above net cash flow. At this point, the simplistic Hypothesis *S* breaks down badly. When we allow for the fact that an appreciable part of *GCF* was committed to payment of taxes and a substantial and growing part to payment of interest, it is evident that *P/E* expenditures in group 'NFFM' were financed primarily from external borrowing rather than from internal funds.

In Figure 8.3, cash flow and *P/E* expenditures in group 'NFFM' are measured in 'real' units – plant and equipment dollars of 1972. This basis gives a view of the behaviour of the variables across 'growth cycles'.[10]

Growth-cycle analysis starts with the location of 'unsubmerged peaks', – using a procedure which parallels the 'Wharton method' of determining growth in capacity. The points flagged by letters *A*, *C*, *E*, *G*, and *I* determine an envelope curve which may be regarded as representing 'full-activity' levels of the variables, while the peaks between *A* and *C* and between *C* and *E* are regarded as 'submerged'. To guide the eye, parallel lines located 10 per cent and 20 per cent below 'full' are drawn between the curves and the 'full' levels.

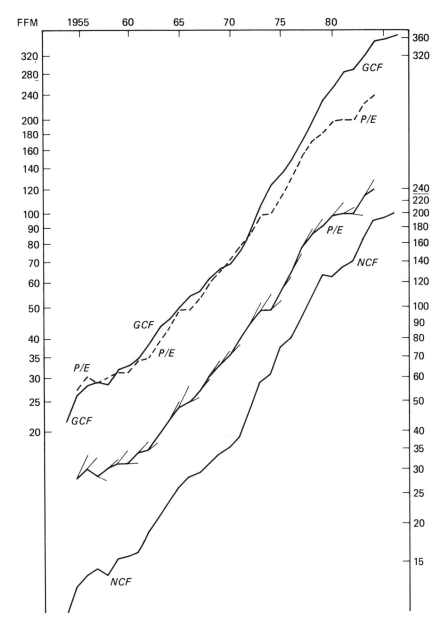

Figure 8.2   US business excluding farming, finance, and manufacturing
('industry group NFFM'). Gross cash flow, actual and planned plant and
equipment expenditure, and net cash flow, 1954–86
(Billions of dollars at current prices)

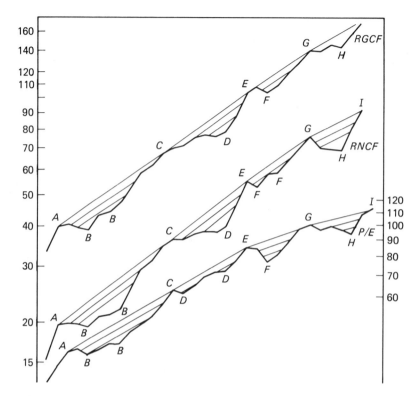

Figure 8.3   US business excluding farming, finance, and manufacturing
('industry group NFFM'). Real gross cash flow, real net cash flow and real plant
and equipment expenditure, 1954–86
(Billions of 'plant-and-equipment dollars of 1972')

The *RP/E* curve shows marked retardation in the growth of real investment after point *E* (1973) and again after point *G* (1979). Both *RGCF* and
RNCF show substantially linear peak-to-peak growth down to 1979. After
1979 we see a slight retardation in *RGCF* and a marked retardation in
RNCF. The difference between these curves is traceable to the increased
commitment of *RGCF* to the payment of interest.

Comparing the growth-cycle movements of the two cash flow curves, we
find that they agree as to the dating of the unsubmerged peaks, with one
exception: on the *RGCF* curve it is a close decision whether to flag 1973 or
1974 as the full-peak year, whereas on the *RNCF* curve 1974 appears as a
trough. With the same exception for year 1974, the *RGCF* and *RNCF*
curves agree also as to the dating of troughs. The shortfall from the 'full'
level at troughs is appreciably greater for *RNCF* than for *RGCF*.

When we compare the curve for expenditures (*RP/E*) with the curves for
cash flow, interesting differences in timing meet the eye. Peak *A*, the

second part of the double trough B, trough F, trough H and peak I all come one year later on the RP/E curve than on $RNCF$. At F and I, however, the timing of RP/E matches better with $RGCF$ than with $RNCF$.

8.3.4 Tentative Findings on Linkage of Investment and Cash Flow

The evidence examined in this section of the chapter indicates that Hypothesis S is seriously misleading. If it were true that cash flow 'semiautomatically' generates investment in plant and equipment, the cash flow variables should yield predictions of P/E expenditure that would be serious competitors with the prediction offered by investment plans. Furthermore, it should be NCF rather than GCF that would intertwine with the P/E curve on Figure 8.2.

The regression analysis for manufacturing indicates that in the realisation of investment plans the course of cash flow during the year AI (may) be useful as an explanation of deviations from plan. But it must be emphasised that cash flow is only one of several surprise variables which can influence deviations, and must be evaluated in models which incorporate (notably) interest rates and deviations of sales from forecasts. Whether cash flow will show a significant partial correlation of T-value in the presence of these variables must be regarded as doubtful, through Eisner's results for 1955–68 give some encouragement.

8.4 THE McGRAW-HILL SURVEY OF PROFIT FORECASTS, 1966–80

The McGraw-Hill collection of *ex ante* data, as was mentioned, includes a *Survey of Corporate Profit Trends*, which ran from 1966 through 1980. The tables released by McGraw-Hill include:

CORPORATE PROFITS BEFORE TAXES (*not* including agriculture. forestry, fisheries or profits earned overseas);
HOW MUCH CORPORATIONS EXPECT THEIR PROFITS WILL RISE (percentages of number of reporting companies estimating 'higher, lower or same');
HOW CORPORATIONS EXPECT (the survey year's) PROFIT MARGINS WILL COMPARE WITH (previous year's);
DEPRECIATION ALLOWANCES
CASH FLOW (Expected percent change).

This survey constitutes one of the weakest elements in the McGraw-Hill collection of *ex ante* estimates. But examination, industry by industry, of the data on profits before tax offers some very interesting clues to the decision-maker's view of the future.[11]

8.4.1 Predictive Power of Forecasts of Profit Before Tax

Examination of the regression results for the McGraw-Hill survey forecasts of profit before tax shows that in a number of industries the forecasts show a high correlation with profit realisations. But when we compare the *ex ante* levels of profit with estimates from trend and base-year profit, few industries show an appreciable *net* contribution of the forecasts to the explanation of realised profit. The evidence for these statements is presented in Table 8.2.[12]

If we look only at the ARSQs for equations using *ex ante* data, the correlations of realised with forecast profit before tax are not unimpressive. The *R*-squared adjusted for degrees of freedom exceeds 0.75 for industries 20, 26, '3438', 35, 29 and 'NEC'. Entries of 0.70472 and 0.62536 appear for industries 32 and 36. Three industries (22, 30 and 33) show entries in a range between 0.46 and 0.29. Industry 37B alone shows a derisory ARSQ (0.07843).[13]

8.4.2 Low Partial Contribution of PBT Forecasts

A second look at Table 8.2 shows that industry by industry the 'best' equation making no use of the *ex ante* variable yields an ARSQ rather close to that of the 'best' equation which *does* use the *ex ante* data. In fact for several industries the allowance for the difference in the number of degrees of freedom causes the ARSQ for the *ex post* equations to exceed by a narrow margin the *ex ante* data.

In the right-hand column of the table, we find that the largest partial contribution of the *ex ante* data is 0.1624, for industry 32 (stone, clay and glass). For industries 28, 30, '3438', 35 and 37B, the ARSQ of the best equation without *ex ante* evidence exceeds that with *ex ante* evidence, so that the net contribution is nil.

8.4.3 Surmises on the Failure of Forecasts of PBT

It would be hard to imagine a more abject failure of *ex ante* data to predict than the one just examined. This failure is surprising in view of the power of the *ex ante* data for plant and equipment expenditure which was demonstrated earlier in this chapter.

In a sense the failure may reflect the fact that it is easy to make 'in-the-ballpark' forecasts of profit before tax. In the left-hand part of Table 8.2, we find ARSQ above 0.80 in industries 20, '3438', 35, 29 and NEC – and also above 0.75 in industries 26 and 28. If it had seemed important to decision-makers to estimate year-to-year changes in profit, they surely would have introduced better estimation procedures and sharpened up their forecasts. But so long as they were not grossly in error as to

Table 8.2 'Explanation' of realised profit before tax in US manufacturing industries: correlations in specific industries for 'best' equations which do or do not include *ex ante* evidence, 1966–80*

(All profit measurements in logarithms of current dollars)

SIC	Adjusted R-squared for equations not using Ex ante variable		Adjusted R-squared for equations using Ex ante variable		Partial contribution of Ex ante
	Equation	*ARSQ*	*Equation*	*ARSQ*	
All manufacturing					
Sum	4	0.87206	6	0.873297	0.0072
Non-durable goods industries, excluding petroleum					
20	4	.90875	6	.91401	.0577
22	4	.43234	6	.46232	.1434
26	4	.76796	6	.75492	.0053
28	4	.78036	7	.76686	nil
30	1	.38471	6	.37187	nil
Durable goods industries					
32	1	.64730	7	.70474	.1624
33	4	.28734	6	.29136	.0017
3438	4	.80876	6	.79369	nil
35	4	.88045	6	.87981	nil
36	4	.59292	7	.62536	.0797
37A No results because of negative profit before tax in 1980					
37B	4	.09875	6	.07843	nil
Other manufacturing					
29	4	.89907	7	.91167	.1249
NEC	6	.86484	6	.87041	.0150

Note: * The SIC and equation numbers refer to the fitted equations whose parameters are reported in Table 8.A1 in the appendix. The original fittings ran a set of 10 equations for each industry.

the level of profits, financing on the market for corporate debt could always be used to cover investment needs.

8.4.4 Use of Broad As Against Specific Indicators in Profit Estimates

Important clues to the nature of information used by decision-makers to form their estimates of future profits are offered by another set of regression fittings which take the forecasts as objects of explanation. The results are presented in Table 8.3.

To analyse these results, we may start with the left-hand half of the

Table 8.3 'Explanation' of forecasts for profit before tax in specific manufacturing industries from trend and forecast averaged over total manufacturing, 1966–80*

(Data stated in logs of current-dollar PBT)

SIC	Equations using no trend			Equations using trend		
	Equation	ARSQ	Elasticity	Equation	ARSQ	Elasticity
Non-durable goods industries, excluding petroleum						
20	9	0.8054	0.881	10	0.9126	0.335
22	9	.5181	0.675	10	.5285	0.995
26	9	.8989	1.044	10	.9128	0.782
28	9	.9202	0.712	10	.9349	0.539
30	9	.8245	0.915	10	.8117	0.855
Durable good industries						
32	9	.8497	1.011	10	.8372	1.004
33	9	.2672	0.792	10	.4287	1.787
3438	9	.9603	0.983	10	.9625	1.102
35	9	.9847	1.066	10	.9834	1.070
36	9	.7089	1.049	10	.8006	1.714
37A No results because negative PBT in 1980 aborted programme						
37B	9	nil	————	10	.4588	1.612
Other manufacturing						
29	9	.8586	1.726	10	.8939	1.083
NEC	9	.9099	1.066	10	.9405	0.708

Note: * For the full set of parameters, see table 8.A2 in the appendix.

table, which presents simple OLS regressions between industry forecasts and the all-manufacturing forecast. Of all the industries tabulated, only two show low adjusted R-squared. These two are SIC 33 (primary metals, with ARSQ of 0.2672) and SIC 22 (textiles, with ARSQ of 0.5181). ARSQ ranges for the other industries from 0.7089 to 0.9603, with half lying in a central range from 0.8245 up to 0.9099.

In these equations using no trend, the elasticity of the industry forecast on the all-manufacturing forecast ranges from 0.675 for SIC 22 up to 1.066 for SIC 35 and NEC – with an outlier for SIC 29 (petroleum refining) of 1.726. Half of the thirteen elasticity coefficients lie in a central range from 0.915 to 1.049.[14]

The ARSQ may be interpreted as showing the proportion of the information content of the industry forecast which is shared with the all-manufacturing average. Then (1-ARSQ) measured the proportion of information content which is specific to the industry of the respondent – or to his company. On this reading, over 80 per cent of the information content of industry forecasts during 1966–80 was common to the industry forecast and the all-manufacturing forecast in nine out of the twelve industries covered.

Since it is certainly possible that the relative weight of broad indicators may vary through time, the inclusion of a trend term may be appropriate. Equations with 'trend' and the all-manufacturing average as explanatory variables are reported in the right-hand half of the table. They do show higher ARSQ for most industries, and raise the ARSQ for the bottom outlier SIC 33 from 0.2672 to 0.4287. But they yield elasticity estimates far above unity for three of the six durable goods industries. The left-hand half of the table thus seems the appropriate basis for interpretation.

8.5 EXPECTATIONAL RESEARCH PROBLEMATICS

To arrive at a satisfactory understanding of the role of profits in the US economy, a number of questions about profit expectations need study. Some topics in this area which deserve serious research may be listed as follows:

1. *Further examination of McGraw-Hill survey data.* The sort of analysis applied in section 8.4 of this chapter to the MGH series of profit before tax forecasts should be extended to the MGH survey reports on forecasts of cash flow. In particular, it is worth testing on this second set of forecasts the indication that decision-makers base their forecasts on general economic indicators rather than on industry-specific or company-specific information.[15]
2. *Systematic use of new inquiries on companies' profit forecasts.* Since financial markets are so much concerned with the profit prospects of individual companies, access to the view of the future held by top managements has been a great advantage for favoured speculators; and skill in translating the cryptic statements offered at meetings of financial analysts with management representatives has been highly valued.

   One of the paradoxes of the recent period of financial deregulations has been the active pursuit by the SEC and by federal and state prosecutors of misuses of 'inside information'. The evolving standard of equal access to information has led the SEC in recent years to require reports of company profit forecasts (or of substantial revisions of such forecasts).

   With so much information from these reports widely available through electronic data services, a good deal of individual company analysis of profit forecasts has plainly been carried on in financial circles. It would not be unduly difficult to programme, for purposes of econometric analysis, compilations of profit forecasts and related variables over stratified samples of companies, broken down into sub-samples by industry.

It is not unlikely that such sampling studies have been in progress but have escaped my attention. But it is very unlikely that such studies will have exhausted this vein of ore. With an orientation toward understanding fixed investment, a research project in this area would have very bright prospects of usefulness.

3. *Cash flow and investment as elements in a joint decision*. The apparent rather close relationship of net cash flow and fixed investment could well arise in good part from decisions to alter net cash flow. Managements have more scope than is generally recognised by economists for adaptation of cash flow to needs for internal financing of investment.

It may prove feasible by such methods as canonic correlation to deal jointly with fixed investment and some suitably defined cash-flow measure (I would suggest cash flow ex taxes and interest), at the 2-digit-industry level of aggregation. It is likely that the hypothesis of joint determination will work well for some industries and badly for others. Hypotheses as to the industries where joint determination is an important characteristic should presumably be specified before working out the numbers.

4. *Company reports as evidence on profit expectations*. Over many decades, publicly owned companies have been distributing annual and quarterly reports to all stockholders. These reports naturally are rich in comments on profit prospects. They deal with the company as a whole and also with its major activities. Investment plans are sketched, and the prospects of new products and processes are indicated. Thus the amount of *ex ante* material in these reports is enormous. If these materials can be systematised and transformed for econometric analysis into orderly sets of numbers for well-defined industry samples, our understanding of profits and of investment can be greatly deepened.

5. *Budgets, plans, appropriations*. In the economics of investment decisions, a number of forward-looking concepts are treated as separate domains. An integrated view of capital budgeting, investment planning, capacity targets, appropriations, contracts and orders for plant and equipment, etc. is urgently needed.[16]

APPENDIX

Table 8.A1 'Explanation' of realised profit before tax in specific manufacturing industries from trend, base-year profit and expected viewpoint-year profit, 1966–80

(Logarithms of current-dollar estimates)

SIC	Eq. no.	ARSQ	Intercept	Partial regression coefficients (T-Values)		
			Profit	Trend profit	Base-year	Expected
			Manufacturing			
A11	3	0.8497	0.046 (0.1)	-----	-----	0.986 (9.3)
	4	.8721	1.486 (1.9)	0.033 (2.0)	0.641 (3.3)	-----
	6	.8729	1.348 (1.7)	0.032 (1.8)	-----	0.665 (3.3)
			Non-durable goods			
20	3	0.9106	0.025 (0.2)	-----	-----	0.0984 (12.4)
	4	.9087	0.704 (2.0)	0.034 (1.8)	0.586 (2.6)	-----
22	3	.3813	0.056 (0.7)	-----	-----	0.655 (3.5)
	4	.3723	0.146 (1.8)	0.033 (1.8)	0.335 (1.3)	-----
	7	.5586	0.084 (1.2)	0.038 (2.4)	–1.416 (–1.9)	1.671 (2.5)
26	1	.7342	0.755 (12.7)	0.091 (6.6)	-----	-----
	3	.7429	0.025 (0.2)	-----	-----	0.967 (6.7)
	4	.7549	0.492 (2.6)	0.056 (2.1)	0.382 (1.4)	-----
	6	.7680	0.354 (1.5)	0.046 (1.5)	-----	0.531 (1.7)
28	3	.7318	0.174 (0.7)	-----	-----	0.883 (6.6)
	4	.8243	0.027 (1.50)	-----	0.501 (1.8)	-----
	7	.7669	1.061 (1.9)	0.030 (1.6)	0.924 (1.1)	–0.477 (–0.5)

The Flow of Profits

Table 8.A1   continued

SIC	Eq. no.	ARSQ	Intercept Profit	Trend profit	Base-year	Expected
			Non-durable goods			
30	1	.3847	−0.033	0.054	-----	-----
			(−0.5)	(3.4)		
	3	.3505	−.065	-----	-----	0.614
			(−0.9)			(3.2)
	4	.3435	−0.024	0.044	0.145	-----
			(−0.3)	(1.6)	(0.4)	
	6	.3719	−0.048	0.034	-----	0.285
			(−0.7)	(1.2)		(0.9)
			Durable goods industries			
32	1	.6473	0.339	0.079	-----	-----
			(5.4)	(5.4)		
	6	.6675	0.209	0.053	-----	0.351
			(1.8)	(2.1)		(1.3)
	7	.7047	0.143	0.060	−1.551	1.838
			(1.2)	(2.5)	(−1.6)	(1.9)
33	3	.2847	0.258	-----	-----	0.692
			(0.9)			(2.8)
	4	.2873	0.460	0.034	0.527	-----
			(1.8)	(1.2)	(2.3)	
	6	.2994	0.352	0.033	-----	0.599
			(1.2)	(1.1)		(2.3)
3438	3	.7688	0.174	0.875	-----	-----
			(0.9)	(7.2)		
	4	.8088	0.563	0.025	0.675	-----
			(1.7)	(1.4)	(3.2)	
	6	.7937	0.615	0.028	-----	0.605
			(1.8)	(1.6)		(3.0)
35	3	.8739	0.021	-----	-----	0.974
			(0.1)			(10.3)
	4	.8805	0.522	0.027	0.734	-----
			(1.7)	(1.6)	(4.2)	
	6	.8798	0.393	0.022	-----	0.769
			(1.2)	(1.3)		(4.1)
36	3	.5772	0.200	-----	-----	0.822
			(0.9)			(4.7)
	4	.5929	0.514	0.036	0.604	-----
			(1.9)	(1.6)	(2.7)	
	6	.6285	0.451	0.035	-----	0.618

Table 8.A1 continued

SIC	Eq. no.	ARSQ	Intercept	Partial regression coefficients (T-Values)		
			Profit	Trend profit	Base-year	Expected
			Durable goods industries			
			(1.7)	(1.6)		(3.0)
	7	.6254	0.423	0.039	−1.502	2.051
			(1.6)	(1.8)	(−1.0)	(1.4)

37A Presence of a negative entry for realised PBT in 1980 prevents use of umbrella function because log of a negative number does not exist.

SIC	Eq. no.	ARSQ	Profit	Trend profit	Base-year	Expected
37B	2	.0880	−0.135	0.636	-----	-----
			(−1.0)	(1.9)		
	3	.0503	−0.175	0.559	-----	-----
			(−1.3)	(1.7)		
	4	.0987	−0.136	-----	0.607	-----
			(−1.1)		(1.8)	
	6	.0784	−0.175	−0.035	-----	0.553
			(−1.4)	(−1.1)		(1.7)
			Other manufacturing industries			
29	1	.8379	.1983	0.168	-----	-----
			(24.3)	(8.9)		
	2	.8780	0.058	1.057	-----	-----
			(0.2)	(10.5)		
	3	.8912	−0.062	-----	1.086	-----
			(−0.3)		(11.2)	
	4	.8991	0.773	0.070	0.665	-----
			(1.9)	(1.9)	(3.0)	
	5	.8938	−0.277	−2.161	-----	3.290
			(−1.0)	(−1.1)		(1.7)
	6	.9076	0.624	0.063	-----	0.722
			(1.5)	(1.8)		(3.3)
	7	.9117	0.409	0.063	−2.128	2.903
			(0.9)	(1.9)	(−1.2)	(1.6)
			NEC: Manufacturing not elsewhere classified:			
	1	.8541	2.110	0.088	-----	-----
			(52.8)	(9.5)		
	3	.8255	0.208	-----	-----	0.902
			(0.9)			(8.5)
	4	.8684	1.270	0.051	0.412	-----
			(2.3)	(2.1)	(1.6)	
	6	.8704	1.296	0.053	-----	0.386
			(2.6)	(2.3)		(1.6)

Table 8.A2   'Explanaton' *ex ante* levels of profit before tax in specific manufacturing industries from *ex ante* levels for manufacturing, 1966–80

(Logarithms of current-dollar estimates)

SIC	Eq.	ARSQ	Regression parameters (T-values)		
			Intercept	Trend	Estimated level for all manufacturing
All mfg	8	0.7274	4.05 (80.6)	0.075 (6.5)	-----
Non-durable goods industries					
20	9	.8054	−1.96 (−4.4)	-----	0.881 (8.0)
	10	.9126	0.25 (0.4)	0.053 (4.1)	0.335 (2.2)
22	9	.5181	−2.50 (−3.9)	-----	0.675 (4.3)
	10	.5285	−3.79 (−2.9)	−0.032 (−1.1)	0.995 (3.1)
26	9	.8989	−3.47 (−9.4)	-----	1.044 (11.6)
	10	.9128	−2.41 (−3.5)	0.027 (1.7)	0.782 (4.6)
28	9	.9202	−1.01 (−4.6)	-----	0.712 (13.2)
	10	.9349	−0.31 (−0.8)	0.017 (2.0)	0.539 (5.4)
30	9	.8245	−3.65 (−8.4)	-----	0.915 (8.5)
Durable goods industries					
32	9	.8497	−3.72 (−8.4)	-----	1.011 (9.3)
33	10	.4287	−6.21 (−2.9)	−0.10 (−2.1)	1.787 (3.4)
3438	9	.9602	−2.34 (−11.2)	-----	0.983 (19.1)
	10	.9624	−2.83 (−6.8)	−0.011 (−1.3)	1.103 (10.7)
35	10	.9847	−2.50 (−17.9)	-----	1.066 (31.1)

Table 8.A2   continued

SIC	Eq.	ARSQ	Regression parameters (T-values)		
			Intercept	Trend	Estimated level for all manufacturing
36	9	.7089	−3.01 (−4.4)	-----	1.049 (6.2)
	10	.8006	−5.71 (−4.9)	−0.066 (−2.6)	1.713 (6.0)
37A	*Negative VPB for 1980 block use of umbrella programme*				
37B	10	.4588	−6.53 (−3.9)	−0.123 (−3.5)	1.621 (4.0)
	Other manufacturing industries				
29	10	.8939	−2.50 (−1.9)	0.063 (2.3)	1.083 (3.4)
NEC	10	.9405	−0.80 (−1.4)	0.034 (2.8)	0.718 (5.0)

Notes

1. Another place to look for evidence might be the formulas built into certain now-fashionable pieces of computer software, which are advertised as enabling any user of a personal computer or work station to forecast almost any economic variable.
2. See Eisner (1978) pp. 142–3. Using the same variable on an alternative footing which he calls 'aggregate time series', Eisner found a partial regression coefficient for the start-of-year plan of 0.978 (11.1 times its standard error) and an adjusted partial R-squared for the plan of 0.943. Positive partial coefficients for sales-change and profit were 2.0 and 2.3 times their standard errors, while the partial regression of the previous year's investment was essentially zero – 0.03 per cent of its standard error.
3. Laurie Rutherford, an economist at Data Resources, has unearthed in the DRI files of McGraw-Hill surveys, a paper on this profits survey by its founder (Douglas Greenwald) with Margaret K. Matulis, whom Eisner describes as the person who 'for many years conducted the [investment-plan] surveys'. See Eisner (1978, p. xxii). The Greenwald and Matulis paper, presumably framed for presentation at the Federal Statistical Users Conference, is devoted largely to explaining away the very weak predictive value of the first two profit surveys by a careful analysis of the factors that make profit hard to forecast and of the surprises experienced by manufacturers during 1966 and 1967. Greenwald and Matulis stress, as Eisner puts it, a difficulty 'inherent in the survey itself' – that 'there is no way of telling what assumptions the respondent has made about the economic outlook which in turn is the framework upon which his profits

expectations sit'. This flaw could easily have been remedied by asking respondents' permission for simultaneous use of their answers to both the profit survey and the survey of plans for plant and equipment expenditures – taken by MGH almost simultaneously. This device would have enabled MGH to link sales forecasts and expenditure plans to profit forecasts, with no increased burden upon respondents.

4. Some years ago, at an NBER conference on forecasting, I expressed surprise at the fact that participants focused upon knowing as soon as possible *whether* a downturn was imminent or had just occurred – but showed little concern for gauging *how intense* the ensuing downswing was likely to be. 'Why,' said one business economist, 'that's simple. If there is to be a downswing – even a mild one – we can't go wrong in cancelling or postponing all the projects where we have any choice.'

5. Because of peculiarities in the companies constituting manufacturing industry 29 (petroleum refining), it might be preferable to work data for 'industry group MXP', excluding petroleum. But data deficiencies block the measurement of 'gross cash flow' for component industries in manufacturing.

6. Net cash flow (*NCF*) is the sum of undistributed profits plus capital consumption allowances. Gross cash flow (*GCF*) corresponds roughly to what is called 'gross operating income' in the *Quarterly Financial Report* published by FTC/SEC, plus income from overseas subsidiaries and the like. The difference between gross and net cash flow has three components: corporate profit taxes, federal, state and local, net interest paid and dividends paid. The sum of net interest and dividends, which may be called 'payouts', appears in another chart.

7. In 1938, when I prepared the report *Debts and Recovery* for the Twentieth Century Fund, I as well as the Committee on Debt Adjustment was much concerned over the danger that the interest loophole in the corporate income tax (then at a 16 per cent rate!) would induce a shift toward risky debt financing. The tax rate of almost 50 per cent which has applied ever since the end of the Korean War has offered a much more intense incentive for a shift toward debt. This incentive was of course quite apparent to corporate managers. Hence we should not be surprised that the ratio of taxes to *GCF* has dropped fairly rapidly ever since 1955, even though the ratio of taxes to 'corporate income before tax' has been rather steady at a level somewhat above 40 per cent.

8. Each of these stub lines shows how *P/E* would have moved during the year had the plans reported at the start of each year been exactly fulfilled. With a few exceptions (notably at 1971 and 1982), these plans offered close predictions of changes in realised *P/E*. As will appear in the regression analysis, these predictions completely dominate those which could be made from cash flow, with or without supplementary *ex post* evidence from the history of realised *P/E*.

9. In an equation where both cash flow terms enter along with the investment plan, the *T*-values are 0.73 for base-year cash flow and 2.14 for viewpoint-year cash flow. This outcome is compatible with the view that surprises as to cash flow are a significant factor in investment. But the elasticity of expenditure on viewpoint-year cash flow, according to this equation, is only 0.126.

For a real test of the role of cash flow in the viewpoint-year as a surprise variable, it would be essential to bring in several other surprise variables. This would carry us far beyond the limits appropriate for this chapter.

10. The corresponding chart for manufacturing is omitted to save space. It differs

from that for group 'NFFM' in that RP/E expenditure shows acceleration rather than retardation after 1973, while $RNCF$ shows acceleration after 1979.

11. I examined the *ex ante* on sales – hoping that they could be used as a proxy for profit prospects. This enterprise was not very rewarding – particularly since published data on realised sales are for industries conceived as sets of establishments, while the *ex ante* sales data are for industries conceived as sets of companies. My use of a provisional COMSET production index as proxy for sales had several drawbacks – not least, the difficulty of dealing with the price of goods sold.
12. The parameters of the underlying equations are stated in Table 8.A1, appended to this chapter.
13. No entry appears for industry 37A (motor vehicles) because the presence of a negative realised profit figure in 1980 blocks use of the logarithmic umbrella function that drives the regressions.
14. The 'elasticity' mentioned here is taken to be identical with the regression coefficient of the industry forecast on the all-manufacturing forecast. This identification is appropriate because both variables are measured in logarithms.
15. The forecasts of depreciation also deserve scrutiny. This is an area where it should be easy to forecast rather precisely. Whether or not these forecasts are close to the mark can tell us whether or not the respondents were trying to produce valid *ex ante* figures.
16. The nearest thing to an integrated treatment that I have found is Eliasson (1967). But even Gunnar Eliasson has paid little attention to realisations as against *ex ante* formulations, and (within the *ex ante* field) to appropriations and commitments as against budgets and plans.

References

Eisner, Robert, *Factors in Business Investment* (Cambridge, Mass.: Ballinger Publishing Company for the National Bureau of Economic Research, 1978).

Eisner, Robert, 'Divergences of Measurement and Theory and Some Implications for Economic Policy', *American Economic Review*, vol. 79 (March 1989) pp. 1–13.

Eliasson, Gunnar, *Business Economic Planning* (New York: John Wiley & Sons, 1976).

Hart, Albert G., *Debts and Recovery, 1929/1937* (New York: Twentieth Century Fund, 1938).

Modigliani, Franco, 'Introduction to Albert Gailord Hart', in Franco Modigliani and Guy C. Orcutt (eds), *Quality and Economic Significance of Anticipations Data* (Princeton: Princeton University Press, 1960).

9 The Impact of Changing Profitability on the Supply Side of the Economy

John Hudson

In this chapter we shall be looking at work which has been done on corporate births and deaths. We shall also be presenting new work which looks at the determinants of the average liabilities with which firms fail. We hope to show that profits perform a crucial role in the Schumpeterian cycle, encouraging the establishment of new firms, as well as ensuring that the inefficient firm or the firm in a declining industry does not utilise scarce resources which could be better employed elsewhere. However, we will also be arguing that this role is not performed as efficiently as it might be and that government restrictions on the invisible hand can actually improve the efficiency of the supply side of the economy. In particular we will argue that bankruptcies impose costs upon an economy, costs which the American bankruptcy system does more to minimise than European systems.

The data on company births are shown in Figure 9.1. This represents the total number of stock corporations which issued charters under the general business laws of the various states. These include completely new businesses which are incorporated, existing businesses which are changed from the non-corporate form to the corporate form of organisation, and existing corporations that have been given certificates of authority to operate in another state. Thus it can be seen that the massive number of 683 686 corporations in 1987 would not all be totally new enterprises. Similarly, there will be many businesses which start in non-corporate form which are not captured by this data. Nonetheless, this is still a valuable indicator of new corporate development and the rapid rise in this series since 1970 is impressive. The figure shows births expressed as a proportion of total firms on the Dun & Bradstreet register.

Figure 9.1 also shows the failure rate of US firms per 10 000 listed industrial and commercial enterprises. A failure is defined as a concern that is involved in a court proceeding or a voluntary action that is likely to end in loss to creditors. All industrial and commercial enterprises that are petitioned into the Federal Bankruptcy Courts are included in the failure records, as well as certain other closures, e.g. voluntary discontinuances with known loss to creditors. The series follows a somewhat unusual pattern. It rises almost continuously until 1961, following which there is an

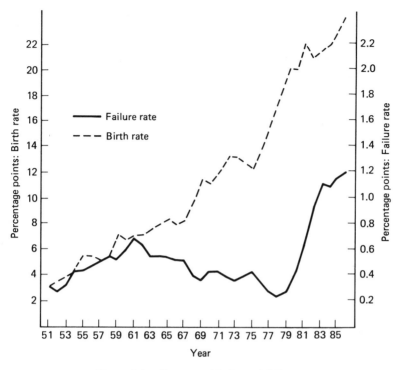

Figure 9.1   Company births and failures

equally marked downward trend until 1978–9, when there is a dramatic increase. It is interesting to note that this most recent upturn coincides with the introduction of the new Bankruptcy Code, and it may be that the new Code has in some way tended to increase the number of bankruptcies.

9.1   PREVIOUS WORK ON COMPANY BIRTHS AND DEATHS

In this section we will summarise the results of previous work (Hudson, 1988 and forthcoming). It was argued that the number of corporate births will be positively correlated with profits. No great leap of the imagination is required to see why this should be so. Individuals will start a business if the expected rewards exceed those from staying in paid employment after having adjusted for differing degrees of risk. These rewards are directly related to profitability, whilst the rewards from paid employment may be expected to be inversely related to profitability. Hence we would expect that as profits increase the number of new corporate businesses also increases. It was also argued that the unemployed are more likely to set up new firms than the employed. For an unemployed person current income will equal any benefits received whilst unemployed. Future income will depend upon how soon he can expect to get a job and at what wage. Standard search theory would suggest that both of these will depend upon the number of relevant vacancies and the number of job searchers competing with him for those vacancies. If we ignore on the job search, the latter can be proxied by the number of unemployed. The more vacancies and the fewer unemployed, the quicker he can expect to find a job and the higher also will be the expected wage at which it will be offered. Thus, both because of the greater uncertainty, the lower expected income stream and the fact that the bulk of this income stream is in the future we would expect the probability of an individual setting up in business to increase if he becomes unemployed, and the more slack in the labour market the greater will be this increase.

In many cases, whether the individual sets up in business or not may depend upon whether he can get the appropriate credit from the bank or some other agency. Some, of course, will not need such facilities: either the company does not need substantial sums of money to establish, or alternatively the individual has the necessary finance himself. But many businesses will need such facilities and the banks are unlikely to give money to all who ask. The decision is likely to depend upon the rate of interest. A rise in the general level of interest rates will reduce the net present value of the new firm's potential profits and make it less likely that new entrepreneurs will be able to get a loan from the bank.

Therefore, the probability that an individual will start a firm will be determined by the ratio of expected profits to current income, labour market conditions and the rate of interest. The profits expected from setting up a new firm may be linked to the average profitability of existing firms together with some variable, or variables, proxying the number of potential opportunities for new businesses. In the empirical work which follows, real consumers' expenditure will be used for this. In addition, it is possible that the death of one firm may provide an opening for other firms to fill, thus we shall also include the total liabilities in real terms of bankrupt companies lagged one period (RTL_{t-1}) as an independent variable. Data on vacancies is not available for much of the sample period, hence labour market conditions will be proxied by unemployment alone. Finally a lagged dependent variable will be included, allowing for a partial adjustment mechanism. In addition, with nearly all these variables we shall be looking at the possible significance of lagged values to allow for possible lags in behaviour.

Hence the equation we shall be estimating is

$$BIRN_t = \beta_0 + \beta_1 U_t + \beta_2 \pi_t + \beta_3 C_t + \beta_4 r_t + \beta_5 RTL_{t-1}$$
$$+ \beta_6 BIRN_{t-1} \tag{1}$$

where $BIRN_t$ is the number of births in period t, U_t the level of unemployment, π_t a measure of profits, and C_t consumers expenditure. r_t represents a vector of interest rate variables intended to capture the risk adjusted rates at which banks lend to new firms. In addition to the real rate based on Moody's Aaa corporate bonds, referred to in the regression results as r_t, we will also include two interest rate spread variables, $RANR$ and $RANRC$, both of which are defined in an appendix.

Turning now to company deaths we argued that a situation of immediate financial crisis is likely to be preceded by negative trading profits. Faced with this situation the firm is likely to try and secure further credit from its bank. The bank may give this because the firm can issue a debenture which gives the bank security in the form of a charge on its assets. This will ensure that in any liquidation the bank is ahead of other, unsecured creditors in the distribution of assets. This was the position until 1978. However, the introduction of the new Bankruptcy Code will have affected this. For there is now the risk that a firm may go into a 'Chapter 11' bankruptcy, thus preventing the bank from realising its assets. This will probably result in an increase in the risk adjusted rate of interest the bank uses to evaluate the firm's position. It should also cause the banks to consider in more detail the long-term viability of the firm. Thus the net effect of the introduction of the new Bankruptcy Code will be to both shift upwards the band of interest rates at which banks lend to troubled firms and to make it less likely that they will do so. An increase in the average interest rate will also increase risk adjusted interest rates and this can be regarded as either increasing the payments due to the bank in future periods or further reducing the present value of any future profits. In any case it too will reduce the likelihood that the bank will give credit to the firm.

Thus, given the institutional framework within which the firm operates, the probability of it going into bankruptcy is determined primarily by past and current profits, together with the rate of interest. I shall assume that the former will be a function of aggregate profitability, the firm's age and a vector of firm specific factors such as innate entrepreneurial skill and location. Age is likely to be important as a new firm is unlikely to reach an equilibrium level of profits immediately. The owners will be on a learning curve, where they find not only potential customers, but gain the knowledge necessary to run the business. Secondly, the fact that a company has been in existence a number of years is an indication that the owners are capable entrepreneurs and the industry is a viable one. Thus, age also acts as a proxy for other firm specific factors. However, it takes time for a firm to build up debts, for creditors to perceive that the company cannot pay and for bankruptcy proceedings to begin. We might therefore also expect to see an initial 'honeymoon period' between a company being established and it getting into difficulties. Support for both of these hypotheses can be found in Altman (1983). In a study using quarterly data on American business failures he found evidence for both a 'honeymoon period' and a subsequent period of high risk.

In analysing company births it was argued that an unemployed worker will be more likely to start a new firm than an employed worker. Many of these firms will be more marginal in two senses. Firstly, their prospects for success may be less than for other firms. They may be setting up in industries or areas which will make it difficult for the firm to grow and survive. In many cases the expected profits will be such that had the owner been in employment he would not have considered setting the firm up. Secondly, such people may be less well suited to the role of entrepreneur than those who give up paid employment to start a new firm. They may also have had less relevant experience. For all these reasons we might expect a particularly high failure rate amongst such firms. To allow for this we shall be including the average of unemployment (AU_t) in years $t-1$ to $t-2$ when analysing company failures in period t. This is, in effect, acting as a proxy for entrepreneurial skill. We will also be including a variable to take account of any supply side multiplier. This will occur if one bankruptcy has knock-on effects on other firms. As in the births' equation this variable will be the real total liabilities of bankrupt firms lagged one period. Finally, we will be including the percentage change in GDP in those years when it was negative (FY), i.e. when GDP fell, in other years it being zero. The argument for this is a Schumpeterian one, that during such periods of severe recession, large, established firms in declining industries are most at risk. The expectation is that this will not have a very large effect on the number of bankruptcies, as there are not many such firms, but the average liabilities of bankrupt firms will be increased at such times. Hence the equation we shall be estimating is:

$$FAIL_t = \varepsilon_0 + \varepsilon_1 AU_t + \varepsilon_2 \pi_t + \varepsilon_3 r_t + \varepsilon_4 LAWD + \varepsilon_5(L)BIR_t$$
$$+ \varepsilon_6 RTL_{t-1} + \varepsilon_7 FY_t \qquad (2)$$

where $\varepsilon_5(L)$ denotes the lagged operator and $LAWD$ is a dummy variable proxying the introduction of the new Bankruptcy Code. Unlike the births' equation this contains no lagged dependent variable. A more rapid adjustment to changes in the state of the world is to be expected in the case of failures where businessmen are forced by losses into bankruptcy. There are no such pressures forcing them to set up firms. Also unlike births the dependent variable is expressed as a proportion of existing firms, because this is the population from which those deaths must be drawn.

9.2 THE EMPIRICAL WORK ON BIRTHS AND DEATHS

The variables used in the empirical work are summarised in an appendix. The regression results relating to company births are shown in equation (3). These were estimated jointly with a failure rate equation using Zellner's (1962) seemingly unrelated regression technique. This was done as it is possible that the error terms between the two equations are co-temporaneously correlated through time. A shock which increases bankruptcies might also be expected to reduce the number of new firms being registered. With the exception of the interest rate variables, all coefficients are correctly significant at the 5 per cent level. The interest rate itself is correctly signed and significant at the 10 per cent level of significance, although neither of the two interest rate spread variables are significant at the 10 per cent level. We have used interest rates lagged one year in all the equations. Unemployment has also been lagged one period, which suggests that those unemployed who do set up firms do not do so immediately upon becoming unemployed. Lagged real total liabilities of bankrupt firms was not significant, even though we experimented with a lag structure of up to three years, and has been omitted from the results. This suggests that if failures do leave a void which new firms fill the process takes several years. Alternatively, it is possible that such a process takes place indirectly, with the void in supply side capacity first increasing profits, which then increase births. The explanatory power of the equation is very high, but with a lagged dependent variable included in the regression this is only to be expected.

$$BIR_t = -146990 + 4981U_{t-1} + 6754\pi_t + 205.6C_t - 2646r_{t-1}$$
$$\qquad\quad (3.29) \qquad (2.38) \qquad (2.17) \qquad (3.76) \qquad (1.79)$$

$$+ 7200RANR_t - 5974RANRC_t + 0.782BIR_{t-1} \qquad\qquad (3)$$
$$\quad (1.39) \qquad\qquad (0.50) \qquad\qquad (8.11)$$

$R^2 = 0.99$, Durbin's h statistic $= 0.887$, $Q(15) = 22.32$, $X^2(3)$ $= 3.99$, estimation period 1952–83.

The $X^2(3)$ figure relates to a test for one step ahead forecasting accuracy (see Davidson *et al.*, 1978). It is based on forecasts for the years 1984–6, distributed as chi-square and is insignificant at the 5 per cent level, providing confirmation of the equation's continuing validity outside its estimation period. Durbin's h statistic suggests that there is no serial correlation at the 5 per cent level of significance. The Ljung-Box Q-statistic is a more general test for serial correlation, it is distributed as chi square, and it too suggests no serial correlation at the 5 per cent level of significance. The correlation between the error terms from this equation and the corresponding one for failures, in equation (4), is −0.018. This is very small, nonetheless the efficiency gain from using the seemingly unrelated regressions method of estimation, in terms of reduced standard errors, was noticeable. These results closely match those of a similar equation estimated for the UK (Hudson, 1988). In particular the profits variable is correctly signed and significant, as is the unemployment variable. However, the significance, albeit the weak significance, of the rate of interest contrasts to the UK study where it was not significant.

The results relating to failures are shown in equation (4). All the summary statistics are satisfactory and all the variables are correctly signed and significant at the 1 per cent level, except the two interest rate spread variables and the asymmetric decline in GDP variable (*FY*). The significance of the unemployment variable is again supportive of the hypothesis that the unemployed are more likely to set up in business than the employed. But, this time there is the added implication that such firms are subsequently more likely to fail. The significance of the positive coefficient on *LAWD* suggests that the recent changes in the bankruptcy legislation have increased the number of firms becoming bankrupt. Although the variable does not become operative until 1980 which suggests that the impact of the new Code was not

$$FAIL_t = 113.50 + 4.298AU_t - 6.020\pi_t + 2.306r_{t-1} - 0.333RANR_t$$

$$(5.63) \quad (3.09) \quad\quad (3.64) \quad\quad (3.24) \quad\quad (0.13)$$

$$- 4.161RANRC_t + 45.00LAWD - 1.541BIRL14$$

$$(0.66) \quad\quad\quad (6.73) \quad\quad\quad (7.92) \quad\quad\quad\quad\quad (4)$$

$$+ 0.00000868RTL_{t-1} + 3.235FY_t$$

$$(4.88) \quad\quad\quad\quad (1.00)$$

$R^2 = 0.87$, Durbin Watson statistic = 2.04, $Q(15) = 19.12$, $X^2(3)$ = 0.35, estimation period 1952–83.

immediate. Evaluating the numerical effect of this is slightly difficult as Dun & Bradstreet increased the sample size of firms used to calculate the failure rate in 1984. However, taking the 1980 figure, the size of the coefficient on *LAWD* in equation (4) indicates that the annual increase in the number of companies going into bankruptcy as a result of the introduction of the new code was about 11 626. As Table 9.1 shows, this figure is not inconsistent with the hypothesis that the increase is primarily due to more firms going into re-organisation.

Table 9.1   Number of firms going into reorganisation

Year	1974	1975	1976	1977	1978	1979	1980	1981	1982	1983	1984
	2171	3506	3235	3046	3266	3042	5302	7828	14059	21207	19913

Source: Administrative Office of the US Courts, Annual Report of the Director.

The hypothesis of a honeymoon period in the life cycle of a company receives some support from the negative coefficient on *BIRL*14, the sum of births lagged one to four years as a proportion of the current number of companies. However, this suggests a much longer lag than that indicated by Dun & Bradstreet data and also by the previous study Hudson (1988). Whereas no evidence at all was found for a subsequent period of high risk. This must be regarded as unsatisfactory.

9.3   THE AVERAGE LIABILITY OF BANKRUPT FIRMS

We now turn to examine the average liability of bankrupt firms. This is an important area, for the impact of bankruptcies on both the economy and individuals will depend not just on the number of bankruptcies, but also upon the losses each of these incur. If this average loss increases then the economic costs of bankruptcies will also increase even if the number of bankruptcies stays the same. These costs arise in several ways. Firstly, there are the direct losses borne by individual creditors, which will result in a reduction in their wealth which will then have multiplier effects throughout the rest of the economy. Individuals will cut back on spending, which in a standard Keynesian analysis will reduce aggregate expenditure and output and lead to unemployment. In addition to the demand side effects there will also be supply side ones, which are not so specific to Keynesian analysis. If the firm not only goes bankrupt, but in the process closes down as a producing unit, jobs will be lost. The effect of this on the level of output and employment will depend upon the speed with which new and existing firms can utilise the resources thus released. On the capital side such resources may never be utilised. In many cases the buildings the firm utilised will be demolished and new structures may appear on the site, whilst much of the plant and equipment may be scrapped. The labour force may be more easily transferred to new productive processes, but even here retraining may be necessary, and middle-aged workers may be deemed too old to be retrained. In addition to the traditional demand side multiplier there will also be a supply side multiplier if some of the firm's creditors are themselves firms who are also forced to close, possibly in a bankrupt state, because of the losses they have suffered. These further closures will then also have additional demand and supply side effects.

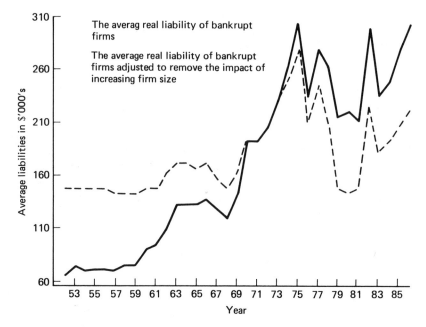

Figure 9.2   The average real liabilities of bankrupt firms in 1972 prices

The data on the average real liability of bankrupt firms are shown in Figure 9.2 and a full definition is given in an appendix. They do not take into account offsetting assets. Thus these do not correspond to actual losses incurred by creditors, which will be less than this. Nonetheless the two series are likely to be directly related. In order to obtain a real measure of average liabilities over time, the data have been deflated by the GNP price deflator whose 1972 value is a 100. To obtain an average, total liabilities are divided by the number of failures. It can be seen that in general the data follows a cyclical pattern around a steady upward trend. It should be emphasised that this implies that the average liability of a bankrupt firm in real terms has increased substantially over time. Until 1968 this upward trend was a relatively modest one. However the period 1969–75, in particular, saw a rapid increase in average liabilities. These fluctuations have continued since then, although with the 1975 figure forming an effective ceiling. It is interesting to note the apparent correlation with profits and this too is something we shall be exploring in subsequent sections. We shall also be interested in any possible impact of the introduction of the new Bankruptcy Code.

In order to simplify the analysis we shall assume that there are just two sizes of firm which go into liquidation, which may be thought of as being small and large. AL_s and AL_l denote the average size of liabilities of these two classes of firms. The average liability (AL) of these firms can then be expressed as

$$AL = \frac{N_s\,AL_s + N_l\,AL_l}{N_s + N_l} \tag{5}$$

$$= P_sL_s + (1 - P_s)L_l \tag{6}$$

where N_s denotes the number of small firms going into liquidation, N_l the number of large firms and P_s the proportion of small firms amongst the total number of bankrupt firms.

Let us look first at the liabilities faced by a bankrupt small firm. We will assume firstly that there is a fixed and unchanging time period (G) between a firm first getting into difficulties, in the sense of being unable to meet payments at a due date, and the firm being placed into bankruptcy. We will also assume that during this time period new liabilities will be built up in direct proportion to the firm's losses over this trading period. That is, if the firm is only making minor losses it will be able to carry on trading without adding excessively to its liabilities. If on the other hand it is making large losses then it will be expected to add considerably to its liabilities. Mathematically we may express this assumption as

$$L_{st} = \int_0^G \pi(t)\,dt + L_{s0} \tag{7}$$

where π represents profits, which if the firm is making losses will be negative, L_{s0} liabilities at the beginning of the period, L_{st} liabilities at the end of the period. We shall further assume that for a small firm these negative profits will be linked to profitability in general, as Figure 9.3 shows. This shows the assumed distribution of profits across all small firms. It is approximately normal, but due to the fact that there are a finite number of firms, with given and known losses the two tails of the distribution touch the horizontal axis at some point. The proportion of firms making losses is shown by the shaded region of the diagram, i.e. it covers all firms with profits less than zero. Provided the variance of the distribution is constant, a shift in the mean towards the left, that is, a reduction in average profitability, will both increase the number of firms making losses, *and* increase the average loss. Moreover, it will increase the latter in a nonlinear manner. In the normal case when the majority of firms are making positive profits the relationship will be such that average losses will increase at an increasing rate as the mean level of profits declines.

A further factor which will determine the profitability of a typical small firm will be the quality of its entrepreneur. As before we shall proxy this at

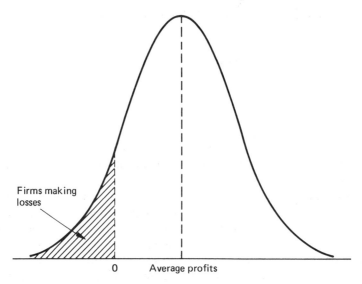

Figure 9.3   The distribution of profits

the aggregate level by lagged functions of unemployment and company births. A failing firm will, as we have seen, attempt to obtain credit from the bank. If it is successful in this, it will, in effect, increase G, the period between a firm getting into trouble and it going into bankruptcy. Thus a reduction in interest rates in the past, which led to more bankrupt firms being kept alive, only to go bankrupt in the current period, will increase the average liability of a bankrupt firm. However, the new bankruptcy legislation in making it less likely that the bank will keep open failed firms, may well have reduced the average liability of bankrupt firms.

Thus we may write the average liability of small bankrupt firms (AL_s) as a nonlinear function of aggregate profitability, lagged levels of unemployment, the rate of interest, lagged births as a proportion of the current firm population (Bir), and a zero-one dummy variable ($LAWD1$) relating to the introduction of the new Bankruptcy Code in 1978. Because there may have been a lag before the banks realised the full implications of the new code and changed their decision-making process, we will try different lags on this variable, which need not be the same as in the failures' equation. Lagged real total liabilities for all firms will again be included to proxy the possible knock-on effects of previous liquidations. If there have been large losses in the previous period this may mean that some firms this period will experience exceptionally large losses due to bad debts. This, in essence, is the supply side multiplier, similar to the Keynesian multiplier on the demand side, which we discussed earlier. Hence the equation we shall be estimating will be

$$AL_s = \delta_0 + \delta_1\pi_t + \delta_2\pi_t^2 + \delta_3(L)U_t + \delta_4 r_t + \delta_5(L)Bir_t$$
$$+ \delta_6 LAWD1 + \delta_7 RTL_{t-1} \tag{8}$$

Turning now to large firms, we will now assume that the liabilities with which they fail are determined by similar factors to those for a small firm. However, there will be differences. We have no measure of large firm entrepreneurial ability; certainly these firms will not have been recently started and therefore the recent levels of unemployment and corporate births are irrelevant for this part of the analysis. However, the assumption of a fixed time period between a firm getting into difficulties and the decision being taken to go into bankruptcy will still be made. This need not be the same amount of time as applies to a small firm; we need merely assume it is constant across all large firms. It is during this period that firms will add to their liabilities in a manner similar to that indicated by equation (7). The Schumpeterian process of decline will hit large established firms in decaying industries particularly hard regardless of the state of profitability in the economy as a whole. This decay part of the Schumpeterian cycle is likely to be correlated with a strong recession. Thus, in the empirical work which follows we will again proxy this longer term cycle by *FY*. Thus we may write the average liability of large firms (AL_l) as a similar function as that for small firms in (8), but with the lagged functions on unemployment and births omitted and *FY* added.

$$AL_1 = \alpha_0 + \alpha_1\pi_t + \alpha_2\pi_t^2 + \alpha_3 FY_t + \alpha_4 r_t + \alpha_5 LAWD1$$
$$+ \alpha_6 RTL_{t-1} \tag{9}$$

Equation (6) also implies that bankrupt firms' average liability will depend upon the proportion of small firms going bankrupt *vis-à-vis* large firms. It has already been shown that new firms and particularly new firms started by the unemployed are more susceptible to bankruptcy than established firms. Thus, assuming that most new firms are small, it follows that a recent increase in the number of corporate births will, other things being equal, see an increase in the proportion of bankrupt firms which are small, as indeed will an increase in the number of firms started by the unemployed. We will again proxy the latter by an average of past unemployment.

We will assume, as with average liabilities for large firms, that there are two cyclical effects which affect the bankruptcy rate amongst firms. These are the business cycle and something akin to the Schumpeterian cycle. The business cycle will be characterised by fluctuations in output around an upward trend, but not sharp falls in the level of output, and profits. The evidence provided by Dun & Bradstreet is that many small firms which go bankrupt do so through management faults of inexperience or incompetence. Such firms are likely to go bankrupt regardless of whether the economy is in a boom or a recession. Thus the number of such firms will be relatively insensitive to changing profit levels. On the other hand the number of firms who go bankrupt for reasons other than incompetence or inexperience will prove more sensitive to changing profitability and the Schumpeterian cycle. Thus we would expect the proportion of large bankrupt firms to rise both as profits decline and with the onset of a recession as measured by *FY*. We shall also be including interest rates and the Bankruptcy Code dummy variable to allow for differences in the impact of bank lending and variations in bank lending between small and large firms. Hence the proportion of small firms in the total of all bankrupt firms will be given by the following function

$$P_{st} = \theta_0 + \theta_1 \pi_t + \theta_2 \pi_t^2 + \theta_3(L)U_t + \theta_4 FY_t + \theta_5 TREND_t$$
$$+ \theta_6 r_t + \theta_7(L)Bir_t + \theta_8 LAWD1 \tag{10}$$

The trend variable represents a possible secular shift in the size structure of corporate business over the sample period. It is important to be clear about what these assumptions about the two cycles imply. We are not assuming that the number of small firms going bankrupt does not increase as profits decline, merely that larger firms are proportionately harder hit and that the proportion of small firms in the bankrupt population declines. Similarly, we are not assuming that small firms do not go bankrupt in larger numbers in severe recessions, merely that larger firms are relatively more severely hit.

We could substitute (8), (9) and (10) into (6) to get a general function linking average liabilities to all the dependent variables. But this would obscure one of the central points of our argument, that average liabilities are dependent both upon the relative proportion of small to large firms in the population of bankrupt firms as well as the average liabilities of small and large firms respectively. Thus, the average liability can change either as a result of a change in the average liability of either small or large firms, or the relative proportion of small to large firms in the bankrupt population. In order to test this hypothesis we shall include the proportion of large firms in the bankrupt population as a separate explanatory variable explaining the average liability of all firms.

$$AL_t = \mu_0 + \mu_1 \pi_t + \mu_2 \pi_t^2 + \mu_3(L)U_t + \mu_4 FY_t + \mu_5 r_t + \mu_6(L)Bir_t$$
$$+ \mu_7 LAWD1 + \mu_8 RTL_{t-1} + \mu_9 P_{lt} \tag{11}$$

9.4 THE EMPIRICAL ANALYSIS

The theoretical work distinguished between small and large firms. In reality the analysis is not so simple as there will be more or less a continual spectrum of bankrupt firms defined by size. Thus any dividing line between 'small' and 'large' is bound to be arbitrary. For our purposes, however, we have defined small firms as ones with liabilities of less than one hundred thousand dollars. There are obvious disadvantages with basing our definition of size on liabilities. For example, an increase in the average liability of small firms will push some of them into the large firm category. Whereas theoretically a 'small firm' is a small firm and this should not happen. Partly because of this we would expect the error terms in the two equations (10) and (11) to be correlated, which is something we shall take account of when estimating the equations.

The first task was to estimate an equation by ordinary least squares with the proportion of large firms in the bankrupt population as the dependent variable. This is necessary in order to be able to derive an estimate of the proportion of large firms which is independent of the price level. Being as the proportion of large firms amongst the bankrupt population is simply equal to one minus the proportion of small firms the dependent variables explaining the former will be the same as in equation (10), although the signs of the coefficients will of course be reversed. This proportion is shown in Figure 9.4, and as can be seen has been steadily increasing over time. This is not surprising as in real terms a hundred thousand dollars represented a larger amount in 1952 than in 1983. Hence in addition to the other variables specified in equation (10) we have included the price level, and we expect this to have a positive coefficient. Not surprisingly this is in fact the case as can be seen from equation (12), with it being significant

$$LP_{lt} = 5.086 + 0.695 \text{Log}(P_t) - 0.198\pi_t + 0.0107\pi_t^2 - 0.0118AU_t$$
$$\quad (3.82) \quad (2.13) \quad\quad (1.37) \quad\quad (1.38) \quad\quad (0.61)$$

$$\quad + 0.0645FY_t + 0.0701TREND - 0.0184r_{t-1} + 0.0265RANR_t$$
$$\quad\quad (1.29) \quad\quad (5.33) \quad\quad\quad (1.76) \quad\quad (0.69)$$

$$\quad - 0.111RANRC_t - 0.269LAWD1 \quad\quad\quad\quad\quad\quad (12)$$
$$\quad\quad (1.28) \quad\quad\quad (1.78)$$

$R^2 = 0.99$, $DW = 1.68$, $Q(15) = 13.88$, estimation period 1952–83.

at the 5 per cent level. The dependent variable in this equation is not the proportion of large firms, as this lies within a bounded interval between 0 and 1, rather it is the logit transform of this proportion. We shall delay interpretation of this equation until later. For now we shall concentrate upon calculating a figure for the proportion of large firms in the bankrupt population which is adjusted to take account of movements in the price level, that is an estimate of the proportion of large firms which we would get if the price level was fixed at its 1972 level throughout the period. This is calculated in two stages. Firstly the value of the dependent variable in equation (12) is calculated with prices fixed at their 1972 level.

$$LP_{lt}^* = LP_{lt} - 0.695(\text{Log}(P_{1972}) - \text{Log}(P_t)) \tag{13}$$

However, the dependent variable in (12) is only the logit transform of the proportion of large firms, thus we need to invert the logit transform to get:

$$P_{lt}^* = 100(\exp(LP_{lt}^*)/(1 + \exp(LP_{lt}^*)) \tag{14}$$

This variable can then be included in equation (11) which is estimated jointly with equation (10) in a two equation system. There is no simultaneity in the system, but, as we have already seen, the error terms are likely to be correlated and again Zellner's (1962) seemingly unrelated regression approach (*SUR*) should yield more efficient results than estimating the equations separately with *OLS*. The results are shown below. Equation (15) relates to the proportion of small firms in the bankrupt population, the dependent variable again being the logit transform of this proportion. To a large extent this equation is a mirror image of equation (12) which was estimated by *OLS*, and the improvement in the *t* statistics is a measure of the improvement in efficiency gained by using *SUR* instead of *OLS*.

$$LP_{st} = 5.089 - 0.696\text{Log}(P_t) + 0.198\pi_t - 0.0107\pi_t^2 + 0.0118AU_t$$
$$\quad\quad (4.72) \quad (2.64) \quad\quad\quad (1.70) \quad\quad (1.71) \quad\quad\quad (0.75)$$

$$\quad - 0.0657FY_t - 0.0701TREND + 0.0184r_{t-1} - 0.0264RANR_t$$
$$\quad\quad (1.60) \quad\quad\quad (6.57) \quad\quad\quad\quad (2.17) \quad\quad\quad (0.84)$$

$$\quad + 0.111RANRC_t + 0.269LAWD1 \tag{15}$$
$$\quad\quad (1.59) \quad\quad\quad\quad (2.19)$$

$R^2 = 0.99$, $DW = 1.68$, $Q(15) = 13.86$, $X^2(3) = 113.5$, estimation period 1952–83.

In terms of significant variables this is the weakest of the regressions, although the overall explanatory power of the equation is high. Lagged births were omitted from the equation because they were not significant.

Neither of the two profits variables are significant at the 10 per cent level, although they are both very close to being so. Of the interest rate variables only the real interest rate itself was significant at the 5 per cent level. The significance of this variable suggests that a rise in interest rates, which leads banks to view credit requests from troubled firms more critically, tends to hit the smallest firms hardest. This is reinforced by the significance of the dummy variable proxying the introduction of the new Bankruptcy Code. This takes a value of one from 1982 onwards, this date providing the most satisfactory results, which suggests that there was a lag between its introduction and it having an impact upon banks' behaviour. The coefficient is again positive and suggests that during this period the proportion of small firms out of the bankrupt population has increased. However, neither of these results necessarily implies that small firms suffer most from the banks. An alternative possibility is that firms will build up extra liabilities if allowed to continue trading by the bank granting them credit. Those firms with liabilities close to the border we have defined between large and small may well then be pushed over that border and be classified as large; whilst if the bank does not grant them credit they will have to close immediately and be classified as small. Thus, e.g. the significance and sign of the Bankruptcy Code dummy may simply denote the banks now giving less credit to all firms including those which in terms of size are marginal. Finally, the coefficient on the time trend is also negatively signed and significant at the 1 per cent level and suggests that there has been a steady decline in the proportion of small firms amongst those going bankrupt over time. As outlined in the theory this is probably linked with an increase in the number of large firms in the economy.

The summary statistics are all satisfactory with the exception of the X^2 test for forecasting performance which is significant at the 1 per cent level. If we look at Figure 9.4 we can see the very large jump in 1984 in the proportion of small firms and thus this appears to be a case of the changes Dun & Bradstreet have made in the manner they collect their data having made the variable incomparable with the data prior to 1984. Figure 9.4 also shows the proportion of small firms in the sample having corrected for the downward drift in the proportion because of rising prices. This then is an estimate of the proportion of firms with liabilities less than one hundred thousand dollars in 1972 prices. There are two things to note. Firstly there has still been a substantial downward shift in this measure of the number of small firms. Secondly, we do get an increase in the proportion around 1982–3 which probably reflects the banks' behaviour in giving less credit to troubled firms forcing them to close earlier with less debts. This adjusted measure of the proportion of small firms in the bankrupt population is based on the predicted values derived from the right hand side of equation (15), and it is therefore unaffected by Dun & Bradstreet's changes in data collection from 1984 onwards.

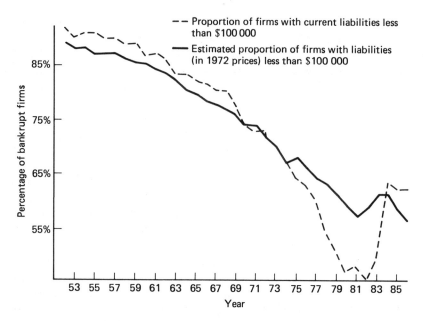

Figure 9.4   The proportion of small firms in the bankrupt population

Turning now to equation (16), which relates to average liabilities and is in a sense the most important of the equations, we see that all the variables are significant at the 1 per cent level with the exception of interest rates and *RANRC*, one of the interest rate spread variables, with interest rates being significant at the 5 per cent level. The profit variables are both significant at the 1 per cent level and with the expected signs which suggest that liabilities increase at an increasing rate as aggregate profits decline. The *FY* variable is also positively signed and strongly significant. The strong significance of this in this equation and nowhere else supports the hypothesis that large firms, of which there are not many, in old declining industries tend to be most at risk in major recessions, rather than during the normal business cycle. A reduction in interest rates results in an increase in average liabilities because banks become less willing to lend to bankrupt firms, allowing them to continue trading thereby increasing their liabilities. However, the significance of *LAWD*1 suggests that they have been less willing to do this following the introduction of the new Bankruptcy Code. It is interesting to note that this variable becomes operative in 1982, some two years after the related dummy variable in the failures' equation. This suggests that banks reacted to an increasing number of firms going into Chapter 11, rather than anticipating the effect following the introduction of the new Code in 1978. In this equation *RANR*, the difference between the banks' prime rate of interest on short-term loans and that on three-month Treasury bills is significant at the 1 per cent level. This was included as an indication of risk premiums and the negative coefficient suggests that as this difference increases average liabilities decline. The unemployment variable is also positive and significant at the 1 per cent level, thus supporting the theoretical arguments that firms started by the unemployed are not only more likely to go bankrupt but to do so with larger liabilities than other small firms. Finally, the significance of lagged real total liabilities provides further confirmation for the existence of a supply side multiplier by which bankruptcies have knock-on effects leading to further bankruptcies. The Durbin–Watson statistic and the Ljung-Box Q-statistic suggest no serial correlation at the 5 per cent level of significance. The $X^2(3)$ figure also suggests that the changes in the way the dependent variable has been measured have not significantly altered its value, that is it also still appears to be comparable with the variable as measured before 1984. This may seem incompatible with the previous finding that there has been a significant change in the proportion of firms with liabilities less than $100 000. However, close inspection of the Dun & Bradstreet data reveal that in addition to these changes having increased the proportion of small firms it has also increased the proportion of very large firms, i.e. those with liabilities in excess of one million dollars. These two conflicting influences appear to have cancelled each other out in determining average liabilities. Whether they will continue to do so is another question.

$$AL_t = 673.43 - 135.50\pi_t + 6.444\pi_t^2 + 17.677AU_t + 79.808FY_t$$
$$\quad\ (5.57)\quad\ (5.34)\quad\ \ (4.85)\quad\ \ (5.37)\quad\quad\ (8.69)$$

$$\quad - 3.559r_t \quad - 37.556RANR_t \quad - 5.450RANRC_t$$
$$\quad\ \ (2.23)\quad\quad\ (7.55)\quad\quad\quad\ (0.39)$$

$$\quad - 245.28LAWD1 + 5.018P_{it}^* + 0.0000194RTL_{t-1} \quad\quad (16)$$
$$\quad\quad\ (7.70)\quad\quad\quad\quad\ (8.77)\quad\quad\ (3.93)$$

$R^2 = 0.97$, DW Statistic $= 1.98$, $Q(15) = 10.36$, $X^2(3) = 4.09$, estimation period 1952–83.

Using this equation we can derive a measure of average liabilities based on a constant proportion of small firms. This is shown in Figure 9.2, with 1972 again being the reference year. We can see that average liabilities amended in this way have been remarkably stable. There is perhaps some indication of a small upward drift over time. More noticeable, however, is the sharp upward shift in the early 1970s together with a smaller peak in the early

1980s. But on the basis of this evidence we can tentatively suggest that much of the increase in the real average liabilities of bankrupt firms is caused by a steady shift from small to large firms in the bankrupt population.

9.5 CONCLUSIONS

The chapter has shown that profits both influence the number of corporate births and deaths. They also determine the liabilities with which bankrupt firms fail. By itself this does not give us a theory of stability on the supply side of the economy. But it would not be hard to construct such a theory. We simply need profits to move in a manner in inverse proportion to supply side capacity. That is, suppose profits decline for some reason. Our results show that the supply side of the economy will shrink. There will be an increase in the number of firms which go bankrupt and an increase in their liabilities. There will also be knock-on effects as both supply and demand side multipliers expand the initial impact of the decline in profits. This concept of a supply side multiplier is new to the literature. It arises because when a firm fails with bad debts some of its creditors are likely to be other firms who may then also fail. It is also a multiplier which operates in one direction only, that is bankruptcies lead to further bankruptcies, but corporate births do not spawn other births. Now if profits begin to increase because of shortages in supply this will encourage the growth of new firms and also reduce the number of failures. Thus the supply side of the economy can be seen to be restoring itself back towards an equilibrium level following some initial adverse shock. The driving mechanism behind this recovery is profits. Profits affect both births and deaths – although they are aided in this by possible favourable movements in interest rates and also by the behaviour of the unemployed who seek to find work for themselves. (It is also worth emphasising that such a theory to be complete would need to take account of the growth of firms and also plant closures.)

However, it is a long way from the conclusion that profits are the means which secure supply side equilibrium to the conclusion that the process by which this is achieved is efficient and cannot be improved upon. Indeed, we have seen that it appears to be far from efficient: the reason being that no effective filter is applied to entrepreneurial talent. Anybody who wants to set up in business can. Almost uniquely for any form of employment, entrepreneurs need no training, no skills and need possess no special expertise. Needless to say many of them do not survive. They fail with costs not just to themselves but also to the economy as well. *Thus one step which could be taken to ensure that fewer new firms fail would be to require of all new entrepreneurs attendance at some government acredited course aimed at teaching them the basics of starting in business.* Similarly firms can go bankrupt not because their long-term prospects are not good, but because of some temporary shock or possibly managerial misjudgement. If capital markets worked perfectly it is probable that such firms would be saved from closing down. But the evidence, certainly in Europe, is that such firms do close down with a permanent loss of resources to the economy. In the US this happens much less due to Chapter 11 of the Bankruptcy Code which can force reorganisation of the firm against creditors who might otherwise wish to see it closed and its assets liquidated. Thus the US system seems much more geared to retaining supply side capacity in a recession than does Europe.

Of course this is a delicate line to walk. Supply side capacity should not be protected in industries which are in serious decline. But with the onset of a recession and declining profitability many more firms than just those in declining industries are at risk. In Europe such firms close down, their capital stock frequently being scrapped. Thus when the recession recedes and profits and demand increase, supply side capacity is not available to meet it. This may well be one of the reasons why unemployment stayed at such high levels in Europe throughout the 1980s. In other words it is not a lack of effective demand which is prolonging European unemployment, although it may have been the initial cause, it is the lack of supply side capacity sufficient to employ all the labour force. Viewed in this light the Chapter 11 legislation may also be one of the reasons unemployment was able to fall so rapidly in the US in the 1980s. Finally it should be emphasised that this is rather a different way of looking at the macro-economy than is usual. Those who have looked at unemployment from an interventionist perspective have frequently seen it as being caused by demand deficiency. We see it as being caused potentially by both demand and supply side deficiencies, which interact and reinforce one another, whereas those who have looked at the supply side have tended to concentrate on the long-run growth or welfare implications of an economy in equilibrium. These arguments are expanded further elsewhere (Hudson, 1988).

APPENDIX: DATA SOURCES AND DEFINITIONS

AL   The average real liability of bankrupt firms. They represent current liabilities, i.e. all accounts and notes payable and all obligations, whether in secured form or not, known to be held by banks, officers, affiliated companies, supplying companies, or the Government. They do not include long-term publicly held obligations. Nor do they take into account offsetting assets.

BIRL14   The average of new business incorporations in periods t-1, t-2, t-3 and t-4 as a proportion of the number of industrial and commercial enterprises listed in the Dun and Bradstreet Reference Book in period t.

BIRN   Figures for new business incorporations represent the total number of stock corporations issued charters under the general business corporation laws of the United States and the District of Columbia.

FAIL   An index of business failures relating the number of failures to the number of industrial and commercial enterprises listed in the Dun & Bradstreet Reference Book. The index is expressed as the annual number of failures per 10 000 listed industrial and commercial enterprises. A failure is defined as 'a concern that is involved in a court proceeding or a voluntary action that is likely to end in loss to creditors'.

P_s The proportion of small firms in the economy, defined as those with liabilities less than $100 000.

P_l The proportion of large firms in the economy, defined as those with liabilities more than $100 000.

π (Net Profit/Net GDP)*100   Net profit is domestic profits adjusted for industry valuation plus capital consumption adjustment. Net GDP is similarly adjusted.

r   The real rate of interest equals the nominal rate on Moody's Aaa corporate bonds less the rate of inflation in the previous period, which proxies the expected rate of inflation.

RANR   The difference between the rate of interest on the banks' prime rate on short-term loans and that on 3-month US Treasury bills.

RANRC   The difference between the rate of interest on Moody's Aaa and Baa corporate bonds.

C   Personal consumption expenditures in billions of 1972 dollars.

AU   The average of unemployment, in the civilian labour force as a percentage of the civilian labour force, in the previous two years.

LAWD   A dummy variable proxying the impact of the Bankruptcy Code introduced in 1978. It was operative from 1980 onwards.

LAWD1   A dummy variable proxying the reaction of the banks to the introduction of the Bankruptcy Code. It was operative from 1982 onwards.

FY   A dummy variable taking the absolute value of the percentage change in real GDP when GNP is falling and zero otherwise.

Sources: *Business Statistics*, 1986 and various issues of the *Survey of Current Business*. The original source for the company failure and births data was Dun & Bradstreet Inc. Dun & Bradstreet's *Business Failure Record* was also the source for the data on liabilities and the relative proportions of small and large firms amongst the bankrupt population.

References

Altman, E. I., *Corporate Financial Distress* (New York: John Wiley, 1983).
Davidson, J. H., D. F. Hendry, F. Sbra and S. Yeo, 'Econometric Modelling of the Aggregate Time-Series Relationship Between Consumer's Expenditure and

Income in the United Kingdom', *Economic Journal*, 88 (Dec. 1978) pp. 661–92.

Hudson, J., 'An Analysis of Company Liquidations', *Applied Economics*, 18 (Feb. 1986) pp. 219–35.

Hudson, J., *Unemployment After Keynes: Towards a New General Theory* (New York: St. Martin's Press, 1988).

Hudson, J., 'The Birth and Death of Firms', *The Quarterly Review of Economics and Business*, (forthcoming).

Zellner, A., 'An Efficient Method of Estimating Seemingly Unrelated Regressions and Tests for Aggregation Bias', *Journal of the American Statistical Association*, 57 (June 1962) pp. 348–68.

Part II
Deficits

10 The Quality of Debt

Charles P. Kindleberger

Much of macroeconomic analysis, outside of fiscal policy, runs in terms of the quantity of money. Velocity is assumed to be constant, or to vary only within narrow limits. Control the money supply, the monetarists claim, and you control national income, more or less, but at any rate within a comfortable range.

There are several problems with the monetarist position. First is the question of defining money: does one take currency plus demand deposits, M_1, or add in savings deposits, making the total M_2? There are many more definitions, in some accounts reaching up to M_7. Second, if the market gets the bit in its teeth and 'money', properly defined for the recent past is held constant, the market will devise a new medium of exchange, bank notes when money was coin, bank deposits when money consisted of coin and banknotes, and so on. Third, even if one had the right definition of money, the idea that the quantity of money determines national income is highly dubious in the short run, and raises a serious identification problem in the long run. Which is the dependent and which the independent variable? Does a rise in income produce more money, or more money produce the rise in income, with the converse holding for declines in the money supply and in income? There abides the perennial problem of cause and effect, the chicken and the egg.

Some economic analysts seek escape from these dilemmas in calculating the quantity of credit or debt. Henry Kaufman (1986), the Wall Street economist, says 'Money matters, but credit counts.' Benjamin Friedman (1983), not to be confused with the monetarist, Milton Friedman, the former from Harvard University, the latter emeritus from the University of Chicago, wants to measure the ratio of debt to income, to obtain an analogue to monetary velocity. There are many forms of debt. Money in most of its forms – all except coin – is debt. There are others, of households, non-financial firms, financial firms, of governments. If debt is expanding rapidly, spending and national income are likely to rise; if contracting, to fall. But debt is an *ex post* concept. I once heard Arthur Laffer say in conversation that what we should measure is the unused credit of spending bodies, to get a sense, *ex ante*, of how much debt could expand. John Stuart Mill said something of the same sort for individuals, some years ago:

> The purchasing power of an individual at any moment is not measured by the money actually in his pocket, whether we mean by money the

metals or include bank notes. It consists, first, of the money in his possession; secondly, of the money at this banker's, and all other money due him and payable on demand; thirdly, of whatever credit he happens to possess. (*Westminster Review*, 1844, quoted in Jacob Viner, *Studies in the Theory of International Trade*, 1937, p. 246.)

Mill's focus on the individual underlines that there is an aggregation problem, sometimes referred to as an illustration of the fallacy of composition. The debt or credit of each individual can be measured primarily on the assumption that everything else is unchanged. If the debts of other firms rise, the capacity of a firm to borrow may decline *ex ante*. And the mention of 'at any moment' implies that the credit possessed by an individual is conditioned by a host of other factors: the economic outlook, the state of animal spirits (to use a phrase of Keynes) of bankers and other lenders, the fears and hopes of the monetary authorities, including bank regulators, the rate of interest, or perhaps more accurately, the term structure of interest rates.

In addition, the quantity of credit or debt is subject to some of the same definitional difficulties that render the quantity of money problematic. Definitions will vary. Some analysts are interested only in the credit of non-financial institutions, and omit interbank loans and deposits, plus what Kaufman (1986) calls 'hidden debt, swaps, futures, repos, futures, and a host of other off-balance sheet items'. One suggestion of Ian Giddy (1985) is that, for measuring the ratio of capital to debt of a bank, the off-balance sheet items be valued as if they were options, the value of which have been reduced by the financial pundits to a formula. This ingenious suggestion is perhaps too sophisticated to gain widespread acceptance. Should one count domestic debt and foreign debt the same? add household, small firm and large firm debt to one another, dollar for dollar? government debt and private debt?

Like money, debt expands rapidly and elastically with economic euphoria. Adam Smith has a famous passage discussing what is called in the index, but not in the text, the 'pernicious practice' of drawing and redrawing bills of exchange. He apologises for describing it in detail on the ground that it is well known to all men of business. A in Edinburgh draws on B in London, a bill payable two months after date. B in London accepts the bill on the understanding that he can pay it off by drawing a bill on A with a similar maturity. The two are careful to use different banks, and sometimes to bring others into the process, in chains. The Dutch had the same practice with the unpronounceable name of *Wisselruitij*. By such devices credit can be expanded many times on the basis of a small capital base. Sir Francis Baring knew of clerks (about 1808) who were not worth £100 but who were allowed discount of £5000 to £10 000. In 1857 a London accountant claimed to know of firms with capital of less than £10 000 and obligations of £900 000 and held that this was not untypical. Using very different techniques of pyramiding credit on the basis of real estate, one banker, whose suicide was reported in the *New York Times* last summer, owed $475 million but had been jailed because he was unable to raise bail – whether cash or a bond was not stated – of $750 000. As debt rises and falls, its quality varies inversely. Henry Kaufman worries that the volume of debt in the United States approached $8 trillion in 1985; a letter-writer to the *New York Times* on 12 August 1988 that it was getting close to $10 trillion. The quantity of debt is a subject of interest in its own right and as a proxy for the quality of debt. It may be useful, however, to approach the quality of debt directly.

By way of a diversionary excursus, I am also interested in the quality of money because of Gresham's law. Innovations producing new kinds of money do not inevitably match old monies in quality, and if bad money drives good money into hoarding or export, the quantity of money can become unstable. This was a crucial issue for the Currency School in Britain in the first half of the nineteenth century that insisted that Bank of England notes be backed, pound for pound above a small fiduciary issue, in gold and silver. It surfaced again in the United States in the twentieth century in the advocacy of 100 per cent reserves against bank deposits. I shall come back to these questions later. At the moment, however, I want to mention as part of this parenthesis that the Austrian school of free banking, including a great many non-Austrians, wants to rid banks of all regulation, relying on the opposite of Gresham's law – that is, good money will drive out bad. I am prepared to concede that this is a theoretical possibility, and may even have occurred on one or two occasions. In a seller's market, with goods short, the seller can demand the money of his choice, and will rationally insist on good money. But in buyers' markets, which seem to have prevailed over the last millenium, the buyer chooses the money he spends, and understandably holds back the good.

The quality of money and the quality of debt were considered by economists long before the collection of statistics on financial quantities including national income. Along with the Currency School, the French wanted money as good as gold, and clung to that position down through to the Fifth Republic, as set forth by Jacques Rueff and President Charles deGaulle. The rival to the Currency School, the Banking School, led by the Bank of England and Thomas Tooke, was interested in the quality of debt, wanting bank credit extended only on 'real bills', that is, bills of exchange drawn by a seller of merchandise on a buyer, with the goods already moving in transport, and title to the goods represented by a bill of lading often attached to the bill of exchange. The Bank of England in principle discounted only bills of exchange with two good London names, generally those of the seller's bank and the buyer's. The Bank of France wanted three names, and in the crisis of 1848 created Comptoirs d'Escompte (discount offices) to add the third name. (As an aside it may be mentioned that a distinguished international banker, Louis Raphael Bischoffsheim in 1867, told a Commission in Paris investigating monetary practices that he favoured one good name over twenty mediocre ones, foreshadowing the famous remark of J. P. Morgan that he loaned not on balance sheets or collateral, but on character. As a still wider diversion, it may be observed that Thomas Ashton has written that Lancashire in the early nineteenth century disliked banknotes as money because of some unhappy experience with failed banks, and used bills of exchange instead, each recipient adding his name, the notes often for odd amounts and bearing ten to twenty names, some of them of bankrupts.) The real-bills doctrine was upheld in the United States by J. Laurence Laughlin of the University of Chicago to 1916 and by my own banking professor at Columbia University, H. Parker Willis, in the 1920s and 1930s.

The Banking School and its real-bills followers had an interest in the quality of credit which was laudable, but disregarded its quantity. They failed to appreciate that as more and more real bills operated as money, they raised prices and made possible the issuance of bills of higher monetary amounts. The process could readily become self-perpetuating, or a positive feedback one, leading to inflation, and in the famous debates in Britain during the Napoleonic War, to depreciation of the exchange rate. They were, moreover, as Hawtrey has indicated, a little severe on some loans not based on bills of exchange: loans to finance inventory, for example, and the process by which bills of exchange became separated from underlying trade shipments was an entirely natural one. As described by the Swedish economic historian, Kurt Samuelsson (1955), the firm of Carlos and Claes Grill in Stockholm would continuously ship goods to their London correspondent and continuously draw bills on him. After a time, particular bills became disassociated from particular shipments, and the Grills drew on London when they needed the money. Real-bills enthusiasts regarded drafts not associated with trade as 'finance bills', or even more pejoratively as 'accommodation paper', drafts designed to accommodate a borrower in general rather than to promote a given sale. Sometimes finance bills were written for odd amounts to disguise their character. A banking manual of the mid nineteenth century records a conversation among bank directors in which one director speaks against a loan to a rich client to finance a new house and furnishings, saying that it is not a *bona fide* commercial note that will be paid when due, but accommodation paper! The exclamation point indicating how outrageous it was thought to be.

The contemporary macroeconomist who is concerned with debt structures and the quality of debt is Hyman P. Minsky of the Jerome Levy Economics Institute, New York, whose taxonomy, however, has evoked strong controversy. Minsky divides debt into three categories: hedge finance, speculative finance and Ponzi finance, the last characterisation giving rise to criticism because Charles Ponzi was a swindler. Hedge finance consists in borrowing under conditions where the cash flow in from operations exceeds the payment commitments of the future, including debt repayment. Speculative finance involves payment commitments in excess of cash inflow from operations. These may be banks which expect to continue to receive deposits or non-financial firms that roll over their debt or paper. The word 'speculative' in the characterisation involves specula-tion primarily on the rate of interest. If a firm needs to roll over debt and interest rates rise, its initial calculations may prove to have been optimistic. Speculative finance as a term, however, seems to imply something more in the way of risk. Ponzi finance, according to Minsky, is a special kind of speculative finance in which cash outflow exceeds cash inflow for an extended period at the end of which, presumably, a surge in cash inflow, such as from the sale of a capital asset under construction, will enable payment commitments to be made good. There are, of course, many normal financial operations of this sort, such as construction loans, and it is misleading to attach the name of a swindler to them. Ponzi paid off initial investors in a fictitious foreign-exchange operation, on which he promised a 45 per cent return, with the monies received from new investors – a swindle. I would prefer to call Minsky's categories by less value-loaded names. In any event, the categories chosen are too limited to do justice to the wealth of gradations in the quality of debt.

The quality of debt must be judged by many more variables than the three which go to make up the Minsky scheme, focused on the purpose of the borrowing. Some relate to the terms of the loan, and whether the interest return compensates properly for the risk, the maturity of the debt, the presence or absence of amortisation, any claim on assets, or collateral, in the case of liquidation, and sometimes from the point of view of the lender, whether or not it is callable. The size of the debt in relation to the net worth of the borrower is an important consideration, and the size of debt service relative to gross earnings – interest and dividends – of the borrowing corporation. Other considerations are whether or not a debt is guaranteed by a third party, the currency it is denominated in if borrower and lender are in different countries. In the case of financial corporations, an informed depositor should be interested in the capital/deposit ratio, the reserve to deposit ratio, the concentration or diversification of loans and investments, and the nature of the relationships between bank officers and its borrowers – whether, for example, there are loans to directors, officers or their families in excess of proper business dealings.

These facets of debt evaluation are so numerous and varied that it is impossible in my view to compress them into a single schema. One can perhaps throw light on one and another aspect, however.

Take, for example, so-called 'junk bonds', bonds sold to the public at high rates of interest that are well short of investment grade, bonds rated AA or better by Moodys or Standard & Poors investment advisory services because debt service is covered by gross profits of interest and dividends less than several times. These have become popular in the purchase of the equity of corporations being taken over in leveraged buy-outs, generally in combination with bank debt raised for the purpose. They bear high rates of interest to compensate for their greater risk, along the lines of the risk return tradeoff of the Tobin-Markowitz model for which Tobin received the Nobel Prize. Junk bonds can be diversified through mutual funds which hold various of them and count on the default of a few among them. In one of the first such default, that of the REVCO D.S. Inc. drugstore chain in August 1988, which proved unable to meet interest payments of $46 million on $703.5 million of junk bonds, the judge under Chapter 11 bankruptcy proceedings put trade creditors and bank creditors ahead of all other parties, including unsecured creditors, bondholders and shareholders should the company ultimately be liquidated.

The *Boston Globe* made the point that Kohlberg, Kravis and Roberts who undertook a leveraged buy out of RJR-Nabisco because of difficulty in selling their low grade bonds have had to resort to sweeteners of various sorts – what the history of finance calls in French '*douceurs*' – to get them placed. To the extent that the discharge of the debt requires selling off assets we get close to Minsky's definition of Ponzi finance. A further point should be noted that the announcement of the KKR bond issues drove down the prices of $5 billion of outstanding RJR-Nabisco bonds to such an extent that two insurance companies, Metropolitan and Equitable, sued unsuccessfully to halt the process. The episode makes clear that the quality of debt is not a simple function of the quantity.

Another aspect of the rate of return is whether it is fixed or adjustable, and if adjustable, under what conditions. In a straight fixed rate loan, there are two risks: a default risk that the debtor will be unable to meet his obligation, and an interest rate risk – that is, the risk of a rise in interest rates which will depress the market value of the loan. The longer the loan to maturity, the greater the interest rate risk for a fixed rate mortgage. It is this effect which has been hard on banks and savings banks in the southwest of the United States in recent years, starting with the sharp rise in interest rates at the beginning of the 1980s. This rise not only knocked down the value of fixed rate mortgages, but lost deposits subject by regulation to a ceiling rate of return as depositors withdrew from banks and thrifts to put their money into unregulated money funds. A shift to adjustable rate mortgages helped at the margin, but did not eliminate the interest rate risk so much as to transfer it from the bank to the borrower, thereby increasing the default risk. Interest rates declined through most of the 1980s down to 1988 when they started up again. What effect adjustable rate mortgages and the recent popularity of home equity loans which ate up part of the accumulated amortisation of many mortgages will have on household capacity to service home debt poses a riveting and important question.

Government deregulation of savings and loan associations in 1986, allowing them to pay higher interest than 5½ per cent to hold their deposits, encouraged some, first to offer high rates to attract funds, and then to take on risky loans to earn the requisite returns. Many of the problems of thrift institutions today stem from the one–two punch of first disintermediation and then deregulation. The fact that deposits were insured below $100 000 also proved dysfunctional: a group of deposit brokers came into being, taking sums such as $5 million and spreading it around among risky, high interest paying banks in $95 000 bundles to get both the high returns and FDIC insurance.

The complex nature of the quality of debt can be illustrated with the numerous variables affecting an automobile loan. Among the variables are the amount of the down payment, the length of the loan, the net worth of the borrower, his or her employment and its stability, the quality of the automobile, and the extent to which its price holds up in the second-hand market. When the market for automobile loans indulges in overtrading, down payments fall, terms become stretched to four years from the standard two or three. If a bank 'securitises' its automobile loans, aggregating a large number so as to diversify risk, and selling off shares in the pool, this improves the quality of the automobile paper, especially if the bank furnishes an implicit or explicit guarantee against possible individual defaults where the repossessed car has fallen in value below the amount remaining of the loan.

It is of interest in this connection that banks charging high rates on auto loans in recent years have had little trouble, while the automobile companies themselves – pushing sales by 4.9 per cent and similar financing over 60 months – have found themselves having to repossess some vehicles from which buyers have walked away with the value of the car depreciated below the remaining loan. In the cases of two companies – Ford and General Motors – write-offs on losses from these bad debts amounted in 1988 to more than $100 million each.

In the home mortgage field, practice in the 1920s was to lend on fixed amount mortgages for terms such as three years. At the end of the period, it was not expected that the loan would be paid off, as in the case of an automobile loan, but that it would be rolled over for an equal period. In some circumstances, if the condition of credit markets had changed substantially, there might be negotiation for a change in terms, largely the new interest rate, but on some occasions the amount of the loan. If markets were tighter, the lender might raise the rate and possibly ask for some reduction of principal. Or with easier money, the debtor might ask for and get a lower interest rate. Like many contracts with fixed periods to run, like those between trade unions and employers, or tenant and landlord, renewal was the rule. In the depression of the 1930s, however, default was so widespread that financial institutions moved to amortise mortgages, with much longer periods, twenty or thirty years. Interest and amortisation were paid together at a flat rate, with interest starting high and declining as the debt shrank in size, and amortisation picking up gradually. After a stretch of years of accumulated amortisation, the owner's equity had built up and the debt fallen, to raise the equity/debt ratio and improve the quality of the obligation. But the attraction of this sort of finance, and its superiority over old flat rate short-term mortgages have lately been called into question by offers by banks of what are called 'home equity loans', loans against the owner's rising equity. These are the equivalent of what used to be known as second mortgages. They clearly reduce the quality of the mortgage, less, to be sure, if the new monies are used for improvements to the property than if they are spent otherwise.

Consumer debt quality is judged by rating bureaus after the fact, on the basis of whether a given household is punctilious in paying off debts or slow pay. There are those who advocate that a young person start out in life by borrowing a substantial sum, put it into a savings account, and pay it back on maturity, regarding the spread between the interest paid and the interest received as a payment for a good credit standing. In many instances, a consumer has to fill out applications for charge account, credit cards and the like, detailing assets, debt, income, employment and so on. Old-fashioned bankers have difficulty in understanding the thinking of banks that mail out credit cards to lists of people without checking their credit standing. Widespread use of credit cards in the United States is partly responsible for the decline in personal savings, as credit extended to consumers representing dissavings, rises net after pay-downs, each month, some months more, some less. Franco Modigliani won the Nobel Prize for his life-cycle consumption function, in which people save when young, dissave when older. That may have been true once in this country, and may be true today in some countries like Switzerland. For the most part, young people run up substantial debts, for education, house buying and furnishing, and pay them off as they get older and their preoccupation with possessions wanes. Older people do spend, to be sure, on travel and medical outlays, but few of them eat up their savings completely in wasting annuities.

There is also the question of the nature of debt as affected by exchange rates. Under a fixed-rate system, of course, the choice of currency in which the debt is fixed is reduced in importance, although some particularly attractive investments in the 1920s and early 1930s were payable in the creditors' choice among two or three currencies. Debts fixed in gold proved unable to withstand the depreciation of the dollar in 1933. Where debt is denominated in a foreign currency, there may be something akin to the

Miller-Modigliani theorem that risks are shifted rather than reduced. In 1932, Colombia had maintained debt service on its dollar bonds until it depreciated the peso. This made the domestic budgetary problem so acute that the government defaulted. In the United States most foreign borrowing has been in dollars, apart from Roosa bonds with an explicit, and swaps with an implicit, exchange guarantee. But if the United States budget and trade deficits keep up much longer, I anticipate that Japanese insurance companies, for one, will become restless in buying US treasury obligations denominated in dollars, and will insist on some sort of exchange guarantee. It is true that the spread between US and Japanese interest rates provides some protection against exchange loss. I should think not enough, however.

Fraud and swindles are a prime source of bad debt. I have written a chapter on the subject in *Manias, Panics and Crashes* (1978), and believe that my judgement then that swindles grow with the boom phase of a cycle of overtrading followed by crash, and peak after the crash, has been borne out by the decade or more of experience since the writing of the first edition. On the upswing, swindles are demand led. Many people get upset seeing others make money, and blindly rush into dishonest schemes that appear to pay large returns. After the crash, it is a different group that does the swindling, financial people in trouble that try to cheat their way out of it. This follows a supply led model. Most of these are Ponzi schemes, promising high returns and paying off the early comers with the subscriptions of the late. Collapse seems almost inevitable.

Before turning to what, if anything, to do about quality of debt, I should like to make a point about the predilection for risky investments of latecomers in an industry, thrusting upstarts from the point of view of the Establishment, who try to elbow their way to wealth when most of the good risks have settled into continuing relationships with established banks or investment houses. Examples of such latecomers can be multiplied by the dozen: Jay Cooke who moved into railroad finance in the 1870s after the profitable roads had been sewed up by other bankers, and was left with the Northern Pacific; Caldwell & Company in municipal finance in Tennessee, Kentucky, Arkansas; the Bank of the United States in third grade mortgages in New York; the Franklin National Bank in New York in foreign exchange, the Butcher banks in Tennessee, Penn Square in oil exploration . . . one could go on.

Somewhat tangentially related to the newcomer, late-start thruster is a class noted by Francois Crouzet (1988) in a paper on the Codman Brothers of Boston and Lincoln, Massachusetts, the younger brother of a successful businessman or banker, who brings a firm to the brink of disaster by indiscretions both of high living and poor investments. Crouzet observes that the account of the Codmans may strike some as anecdotal, but he believes that time and again firms have been jeopardised or ruined by lax junior partners. Two prominent historical examples that spring to mind are Jay Cooke's younger brother, Henry, in charge of the Washington office of the firm, and D. W. Chapman of Overend, Gurney & Co., after it had gone public and the Gurneys had retired. Crouzet observes that family relationships have served positive roles in business – nepotism is often a sound practice in a world where a principal cannot trust an agent – but that misplaced confidence or a reluctance to distrust a close relative can end in disaster.

I forbear from trying to outline a comprehensive scheme of the quality of debt, given the number and disparity of the variables involved, but conclude by discussing what, if anything, should be done about it. There are those who say nothing, believers in the efficacy of the market as an evolutionary device to promote the fittest. There are those who advocate free banking, let both the borrower and the lender beware, do nothing beyond the enforcement of contracts and the policing of fraud. Perhaps leave it to the private agencies, the credit bureaus, rating services, print media, to produce the necessary disclosure. Or leave it to the accounting profession to establish standards.

At the other end of the spectrum are the regulators who would enforce a variety of rules to which banks and other financial institutions would have to conform: full disclosure in bond prospectuses, predetermined ratios of reserves of different sorts to deposits of different sorts, set capital ratios, separation of commercial banking and security underwriting, prohibitions against lending more than a certain percentage to any one borrower, limits on loans, to officers and directors. A requirement that banks, for example, 'mark to market', write-off their loans and investments down from cost to their market valuation, is more often honoured in the breach than in the observance; in many cases, say for loans, there is no market, or, as in the case of Third World syndicated bank debt, the market is thin and riddled with airpockets. Mark to market should have been observed more widely in say southwestern United States mortgage lending by thrift institutions, but as a universal rule it is a counsel of perfection. Regulation of all kinds is aimed at promoting customers' confidence and convenience in financial firms' products by certifying the integrity and competence of individual institutions, reducing transactions costs of both financial firms and their clients.

One extreme schema for regulating the quality of debt is that proposed in the 1930s by Henry Simons, (1948) the Chicago monetarist. He wanted 100 per cent reserves against bank deposits, which he combined with a vigorous attempt to stamp out elasticity of credit throughout the financial system, and not only in banks. This meant restriction of open book credit of non-financial firms and of instalment loans, limiting government debt to non-interest bearing forms (money) at one end of the spectrum and very long-term debt at the other – ideally perpetual debt or consols. He advocated that all other financial wealth be held in equity form, and would explicitly ban fixed monetary contracts so that no institution that was not a bank could create effective money substitutes. This, he claimed, would especially limit the short-term, non-bank borrowing and lending that made society vulnerable to quixotic changes in business confidence. Movements such as the use of large-scale bank borrowing and the issuance of junk bonds to finance mergers and acquisitions that have added to debt in the United States and shrank the volume of equity held by the market would have been especially anathema.

These views are more royalist than the king, more Chicagoan than the regular Chicago school which has sought 100 per cent reserve banking from time to time, but has wanted at the same time to preserve the greatest possible freedom for persons and firms to advance their own interests within a system of what Adam Smith called 'magistracy'. This then means regulation.

It is not my task to propose an ideal system of regulation to ensure the quality of debt. If I were able to, as I am not, it would be subject to entropy, the propensity of all systems of organisation, especially taxation, to lose efficiency over time as loopholes and end runs develop. Institutional organisation is a labour of Sisyphus, *perpetuum mobile*. Edward Kane (1988) of Ohio State University has developed a model of financial regulation that resembles a market, with demands for and supplies of regulation, a number of regulators competing with one another, and something of a cobweb in which the regulators lag behind the regulatees. Competition among regulators is justified by the fear of over-regulation that he sees likely as a result of a single regulator or a regulatory cartel. It is not clear to me that such a result inevitably follows: there might well develop symbiosis between regulators and regulatees, such as characterised the Interstate Commerce Commission and the railroads, the Federal Communications Commission and the radio and television industry, the Maritime Commission and shipping interests, and perhaps some public utilities commissions and the utilities. A third possibility is that the lag in regulation behind financial innovation lengthens through the inattention of regulators, like the sleep that seems to have prevailed in the control rooms of nuclear power plants. When problems are few, there would likely be a drift of top flight personnel into more challenging fields out of the regulatory agencies, leaving them handicapped when a boom supervenes with its push to reduce lending and investing standards.

It would be convenient if one could devise a numerical measure of debt quality overall, like air or water quality. There are those who say that if you cannot measure something, it doesn't exist. The Harry Trumans of the world don't want a discussion of a problem, with 'on the one hand' and 'on the other': they want a number.

A valiant attempt at producing a number is Raymond Goldsmith's

(1969) Financial Interrelation Ratio (FIR), representing the volume of all financial assets, including those of financial institutions, household and government bodies, compared with gross national product. Goldsmith's interest was in development, and he determined that this ratio started at about 0.20 in underdeveloped economies and rose with development to about 1.5 when it levelled off. This was an empirical finding published in 1969, when Goldsmith wrote of a 'full complement of financial institutions' before the flowering of the Euro-currency market, credit cards, money market funds, repurchase agreements ('repos'), negotiable orders of withdrawal ('NOW' accounts), certificates of deposit (CDs), options, futures, Third World syndicated bank loans and the like. Debt in the United States grew rapidly from the 1970s, and now runs about three times gross national product. This takes us back to the quantity of debt, as discussed by Benjamin Friedman and Henry Kaufman, an advance over the concentration on the quantity of money, but still short of adequate attention to quality. Rapid increases in quantity are doubtless associated with declines in quality. Kaufman is properly concerned about the substitution of debt for equity – leading away from the stern line of Henry Simons. But Minsky's (1982) concern with debt structures, flawed though his taxonomy may be, calls attention to a critical dimension of an economy's stability or fragility.

Is it proper to call attention to a problem if one lacks all solution except for continuous surveillance and action to contain financial quality when it threatens to get out of hand? I think so. I hope so.

References

Crouzet, F., 'Opportunity and Risk in Atlantic Trade during the French Revolution', a paper presented to the International Symposium in honour of Professor Wolfram Fischer, Berlin (6–7 May 1988).
Friedman, B. J., 'The Roles of Money and Credit in Economic Analysis', in James Tobin (ed.), *Macroeconomics, Prices and Quantities: Essays in Memory of Arthur M. Okun* (Washington, D.C.: Brookings, 1983).
Friedman, Milton, *The Optimum Quantity of Money and Other Essays* (Chicago: Aldine, 1963).
Giddy, Ian, 'Regulation of Off-Balance Sheet Banking', in Federal Reserve Bank of San Francisco, *The Search for Financial Stability: The Last Fifty Years* (San Francisco, 1985).
Goldsmith, R., *Financial Structure and Development* (New Haven: Yale University Press, 1969).
Hawtry, R. G., *Currency and Credit* (London: Longmans, Green, 1919).
Kane, E., 'How Market Forces Influence the Structure of Financial Regulation', paper for the American Enterprise Institute's Financial Market Project (February 1988).

Kaufman, H., *Interest Rates, the Markets, and the New Financial World* (New York: Times Brooks, 1986).

Kindleberger, Charles P., *Manias, Panics and Crashes: A History of Financial Crises* (New York: Basic Books, 1978).

Minsky, H. P., 'The Financial-Instability Hypothesis: Capitalist Processes and the Behavior of the Economy', in C. P. Kindleberger and J. P. Laffargue (eds), *Financial Crises: Theory, History and Policy* (Cambridge: Cambridge University Press, 1982).

Samuelsson, Kurt, 'International Payments and Credit Movements by Swedish Merchant-Houses, 1730–1815'. *Scandinavian Economic History Review*, vol. 3 (1955).

Simons, H., *Economic Policy for a Free Society* (Chicago: University of Chicago Press, 1948).

11 Rising Debt in the Private Sector: A Cause for Concern?

John Caskey and Steven Fazzari*

11.1 INTRODUCTION

One of the most striking developments in the US economy over the past decade has been the growth of private sector debt. Highly publicised leveraged buy-outs and financial restructurings have saddled the corporate sector with levels of debt that are unprecedented in the post-war period. High consumer spending has fuelled the long expansion of the mid-1980s, but it has been financed with credit, putting the household sector deeply in debt.

This chapter tries to make sense of widely voiced concerns about the macroeconomic significance of the rising indebtedness. This issue is prominently discussed in the press, and it often appears in statements of economic policy-makers. Most modern theoretical and empirical research in macroeconomics, however, has little if anything to say about the implications of high and growing debt levels for the performance of the economy.

We begin with a brief summary of evidence that shows a recent sharp increase in private sector indebtedness and we note some of the concerns about this development voiced by market analysts and policy-makers. Subsequently, we argue that, in spite of the relative neglect of debt in mainstream theory, there are good theoretical grounds for believing that high private sector debt levels can magnify the severity of economic downturns and weaken, even overcome, the stabilising economic forces assumed to operate in conventional macroeconomic theory. In the third section, we present some preliminary empirical research supporting the claim that current US private sector debt may indeed adversely affect future macroeconomic performance. In the final section, we discuss some public policy implications of our conclusion that high private sector indebtedness poses significant macroeconomic risks.

11.2 CONCERN OVER GROWING PRIVATE DEBT

Since the mid-1980s, a number of economists on Wall Street, in government, and in academia have expressed concern over growing private sector

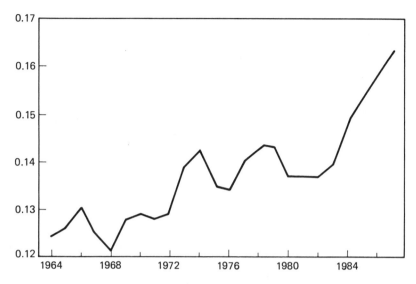

Figure 11.1 Household debt/asset ratio

debt. This increase in indebtedness is evident in a variety of measures. As shown in Figure 11.1, the household debt-to-asset ratio has trended upward over the last two decades, and its growth has accelerated sharply since 1982.[1] This observation is generally consistent with past experience in expansions (note the fast growth in the household debt-to-asset ratio in 1972–4 and 1976–8). But the recent increase in this measure of household indebtedness seems especially large. The debt-to-asset ratio for nonfinancial corporate business (Figure 11.2) fell throughout the 1970s. But again, the growth in this measure has been dramatic since 1982.

Some economists who have examined these data have seen no cause for alarm. For example, they point out that the Federal Reserve's balance sheet data values firms' tangible assets at replacement cost, not market value. Using market values would undoubtedly reduce the post-1982 debt-to-asset ratios for firms. Moreover, businesses (by either valuation method) and household are far from insolvent.

Concern about rising private sector debt, however, is not just based on debt-to-asset ratios, but also on debt-to-income and debt service-to-income ratios. Debt-to-asset ratios determine the solvency of economic agents at a point in time. If many firms and households needed to sell assets simultaneously to service debt in a crisis, asset prices could tumble and solvent units might quickly become insolvent.[2] Therefore, the risk of a systematic crisis may be better measured by the ratio of debt or debt service to income flows that reflect the ability of agents to make ongoing payments on their obligations.[3] This emphasis is particularly appropriate in a paper for the Levy Institute; Jerome Levy's economic research focused on the crucial

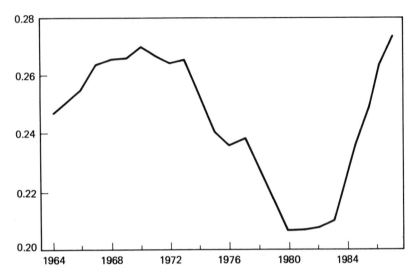

Figure 11.2   Nonfinancial corporate debt/asset ratio

role of profit *flows* as the basis for economic analysis.[4]

As shown in Figures 11.3 through 11.7, debt-to-income and debt service-to-income ratios are at very high levels relative to post-war experience. The private sector debt to GNP ratio, shown in Figure 11.3, stabilised at a level a little above 1.1 during the 1970s. Between 1981 and 1987, however, it shot up above 1.4. Figures 11.4 and 11.5 show similar patterns for household and business debt-to-income ratios. The ratio of interest payments to income, a flow measure of solvency, has practically doubled for households since the mid-1970s and the ratio of interest expense to profits plus interest (a cash flow proxy) has tripled for businesses, as shown in Figures 11.6 and 11.7.

These trends have led some business economists to express public concern about potentially serious economic risks created by rising debt-to-income ratios. Henry Kaufman (1986, p. 22) has warned that 'huge debt will add a very troubling dimension to the next business recession'. More explicitly, Mickey D. Levy, chief economist of First Fidelity Bancorp in Philadelphia warned that, '[o]nce the economy begins to weaken, as it sooner or later will, the high levels of corporate debt will exacerbate the downturn. A company in trouble can simply cut or suspend dividend payments on stock, but it will go bankrupt if it can't service its debt.'[5]

Policy-makers are typically more circumspect in expressing their views about danger signs in the economy. Nevertheless, shortly before his departure from the Federal Reserve Board of Governors, Paul Volcker added his voice to those concerned about declining financial margins of safety: 'the overall data do strongly suggest greater "leveraging" among

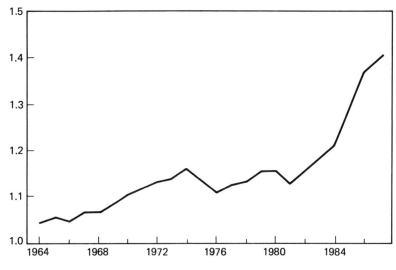

Figure 11.3 Private sector debt/GNP ratio

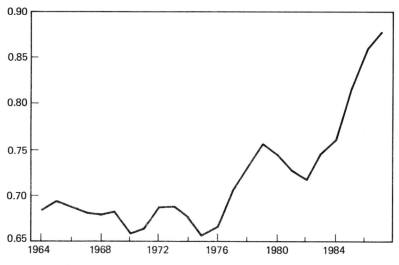

Figure 11.4 Household debt/disposable income ratio

borrowers; that is, a larger burden of principal and interest payments relative to net worth and income streams. . . . Increased leveraging implies smaller safety margins to deal with economic adversity. . . . The vulnerability of the economy to unanticipated increases in interest rates or a shortfall in income appears to be increasing.'[6] Volcker's successor, Alan Greenspan, has also expressed concern over the debt build-up: a 'leveraging of the

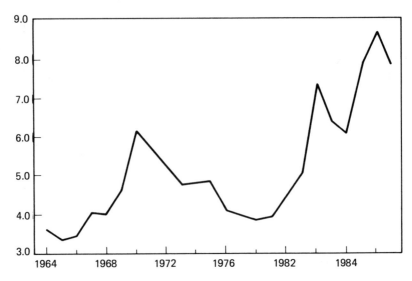

Figure 11.5   Nonfinancial corporate debt/profit ratio

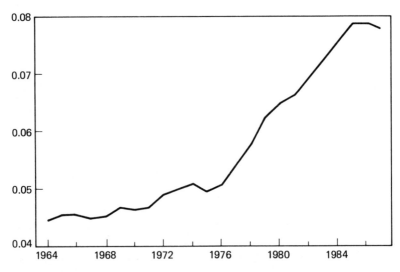

Figure 11.6   Household interest/disposable income ratio

household sector is emerging which is almost as worrisome as that in the corporate sector'.[7]

Academic economists have also expressed worries about rising private sector indebtedness, although concern seems less widespread in academia. Benjamin Friedman (1986, p. 47), for example, concluded that 'the historically high levels of individual and business indebtedness outstanding

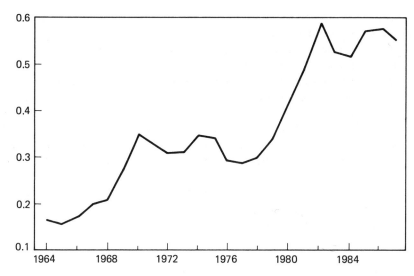

Figure 11.7   Nonfinancial corporate interest/profit plus interest ratio

as of the midpoint of the 1980s suggest that the onset of a major new business recession under these circumstances could easily lead to debt service problems of a kind that would, in turn, further magnify the initial contractionary movement in nonfinancial economic activity.' Ben Bernanke and John Campbell (1988) argue that recent increases in firm indebtedness will require strong profit growth to maintain the financial health of the corporate sector. 'Should this earnings growth fail to materialize, measures of corporate financial stress could reach unprecedented levels.'[8]

In light of the widespread concern over the build-up of private sector debt, it is somewhat surprising that these issues receive little emphasis in mainstream macroeconomic models. In the traditional textbook *IS/LM* model, the financial side of the economy is linked to the real side only through the money market determination of the interest rate. The monetarist framework allows for short-run effects of monetary policy (or unanticipated monetary 'shocks' in the case of new classical approaches) on real activity, but debt seems to have little to do with the 'transmission mechanism'. In most real business cycle models, financial markets are ignored or merely mirror real disturbances.

The inattention to financial structures in these approaches can be attributed to two lines of thought. First, most theoretical macroeconomic models are based on the assumption, implicitly or explicitly, that centralised capital markets efficiently allocate finance to real activities with full information and negligible transaction costs.[9] Therefore, no desirable consumption or investment expenditure will be constrained by the lack of finance. Second, economists often assume that the extent of internal indebtedness has no *aggregate* effects because one agent's debt is another's asset. In this environment, bankruptcy simply reshuffles asset ownership and has no important impact on aggregate demand or supply.

These observations raise several questions. Do those analysts who believe that increased indebtedness would magnify the severity of a future recession ignore the potential for capital markets to overcome financial constraints? Are they overlooking the basic fact that the vast majority of private sector liabilities are also private sector assets? Or, is there a solid basis for thinking that widespread debt service problems can have an important influence on the course of the business cycle? If the answer to the latter question is yes, how can macroeconomic models capture this idea? In what follows, we explore some answers to these questions.

11.3 DEBT AND INSTABILITY IN A MACROECONOMIC MODEL

In this section, we argue that there is sound justification for the view that widespread debt service problems will affect both the demand and supply sides of real aggregate economic activity.[10] Two ideas are key to our analysis. First, when lenders do not have complete information about the quality of borrowers, changes in debt, internal net worth, and financial structure can have an important impact on the effectiveness of financial intermediation.[11] The resulting financial constraints can cause disruptions to real aggregate demand and supply, affecting the course of the business cycle. A second, related point is that bankruptcy and even near-bankruptcy are costly processes, involving more than just a redistribution of ownership claims. The more debt carried by economic agents, the greater the chances that financial distress during an economic downturn will magnify the severity of a recession.

Recent research on the functioning of credit markets when borrowers and lenders have different (asymmetric) information about the quality of the financed activity demonstrate that real expenditure may depend on internal net worth. The crux of the argument is that when providers of external funds cannot distinguish high quality borrowers from those more likely to default, the cost of external finance rises relative to the opportunity cost of internal funds.[12] Therefore, aggregate demand can be 'excessively sensitive' to fluctuations in firm profits or household income. This effect magnifies the real consequences of a downturn because aggregate demand declines by more during a recession than it would in the absence of the financial constraints. The effect of financial constraints on real demand is likely to be more severe when agents are heavily indebted because cash flow 'margins of safety' for new debt will be lower and agents will have fewer readily marketable assets to pledge as collateral for new loans.

These results are reinforced by the fact that bankruptcy is a costly process; it is not simply a neutral redistribution of ownership claims. Borrowers who become insolvent send a signal to credit markets and, in the face of imperfect information, will find future credit impossible or very costly to obtain. Even borrowers with negative net worth face bankruptcy costs, because they lose legal ownership rights that may again be valuable if future events affecting their asset values are favourable. Moreover, in a highly indebted economy that is subject to aggregate fluctuations, generalised financial distress may force the sale of assets at times when other agents must also sell and prices are unfavourable.

Borrowers cannot control the macroeconomic conditions that lead to financial distress, but they can cut back expenditure, especially on investment and consumer durables (Mishkin, 1976; Fazzari, Hubbard and Petersen, 1988b). While creditors' gains may sometimes offset the losses of debtors, the gain is unlikely to symmetric to the loss. Bankruptcy and foreclosure proceedings consume legal resources. Agency and moral hazard problems can also reduce the value of the assets involved in bankruptcy proceedings.[13] Therefore, widespread bankruptcy or an increased threat of bankruptcy in a recession is likely to cause further demand contractions and exacerbate the downturn.

High levels of indebtedness also have the potential to disrupt aggregate supply. Credit intermediation is a central aspect of production in modern, financially sophisticated economies. As agents become more heavily indebted, the probability of bankruptcy and the costs of intermediation rise. As Bernanke (1983) argues, credit intermediaries may not be able to pass these higher costs on to their customers, however, if asymmetric information prevents them from distinguishing good risks from bad risks. Therefore, intermediaries may cut back on the real quantity of credit intermediation services they provide to support production, reducing supply throughout the economy.[14]

These theoretical links between financial distress and aggregate demand and supply modify some central conclusions arising from traditional macroeconomic analysis. According to standard theory, a recession initiated by a reduction in aggregate spending is self-correcting over time. Widespread excess capacity and reduced demand for labour and commodity inputs eventually cause the aggregate price level or the inflation rate to decline. This reduction in prices relative to the path they would have followed had the economy remained at potential output is generally assumed to stimulate aggregate demand for two reasons. First, lower prices increase the real supply of liquidity in the economy, reduce the premium agents will pay to hold money, and cause the interest rate to fall (the 'Keynes effect'). Lower interest rates stimulate consumption and investment, increasing aggregate demand. Second, deflation or slowing of inflation relative to nominal money growth increases the real value of outside nominal assets. This expansion in private wealth stimulates an increase in consumption (the 'Pigou effect'). Both of these effects offset the negative demand shock that started the recession and return the economy to its 'natural' rate of output. In view of the stabilising role of prices, the short-run real effects of the demand shock arise because the price level does not adjust instantaneously to its new long-run equilibrium value. Mainstream theory concludes that increased price flexibility would reduce the real output losses experienced by the economy.

This analysis and the conclusions regarding the long-run stability of macroeconomic systems can change radically when we incorporate the kinds of bankruptcy and financial distress effects discussed previously. First, the initial real effects of a demand shock will be magnified by financial constraints. When aggregate income falls, cash flows fall to firms and households reducing the margins of safety for debt payments and increasing the threat of bankruptcy. As discussed above, asymmetric information in capital markets under these circumstances can lead to reductions in the availability of external finance, further reducing aggregate demand. The quantitative significance of these problems is likely to rise as agents in the economy become more heavily indebted. This observation has important implications for the conduct of macroeconomic policy. For example, if the Federal Reserve chooses to fight inflation by tightening monetary policy, the initial negative effect on output and employment will be larger in an economy with high debt, the circumstances the US faces today.

Incorporating debt into mainstream macro analysis thus implies that contractionary demand shocks are likely to have more severe real effects when financial margins of safety are narrow, but there are also more fundamental changes that must be made to conventional theory. Recall that in standard models, declining prices or inflation rates increase aggregate demand through the Keynes and Pigou effects. This result is crucial in establishing the widely held belief that greater price flexibility will speed the economy's return to its long-run potential output level. But when one accounts for the effects of debt on aggregate demand, these conclusions can change dramatically.

Most debt contracts in the US have nominal repayment terms that are not fully indexed to changes in the price level. Therefore, an unanticipated deflation or disinflation will reduce nominal cash flows relative to what agents expected at the time they set up their nominal debt contract. This process will push households and firms closer to insolvency and may lead to costs of financial distress. These problems could reduce aggregate demand. Thus, in an economy with high debt levels, *a fall in prices or the inflation rate can reduce aggregate demand*, if the demand-constraining effects of financial distress empirically dominate the Keynes and Pigou effects.

This change in an otherwise standard model can cause a fundamental change in its predictions. When the effects of financial distress are incorporated into aggregate demand, greater aggregate price flexibility might *not* speed the return of the economy to full employment and potential output during a recession. In the conventional interpretation of Keynesian results, sticky wages or prices are blamed for the real effects of aggregate demand shocks. It seems to follow as a corollary that greater price flexibility, therefore would ameliorate these real effects. Our analysis is consistent with the first proposition; some kind of nominal stickiness may be responsible for Keynesian effects of aggregate demand on real macroeconomic performance. When we recognise the influence of lower prices on nominal debt contracts, however, the standard corollary does not necessarily hold. A faster fall in wages and prices during a recession need not stabilise the real economy. In fact, greater nominal flexibility can *magnify* the severity of the output and employment losses following a negative demand shock. Nominal rigidity may be the source of the Keynesian 'problem', but greater nominal flexibility may not be the 'solution'.[15]

The actual impact of debt on aggregate demand and the associated implications for macroeconomic research and policy analysis must be determined empirically. It may be that the demand-constraining effects of financial distress are not strong enough to offset the endogenous stabilising tendencies of the Keynes and Pigou effects. Certainly, financial distress effects will not be constant over time; they will be greatest when debt payment commitments are large relative to income flows, that is, when financial margins of safety are low. We turn to these empirical issues in the next section.

11.4 THE IMPACT OF DEBT AND FINANCIAL DISTRESS IN THE NEXT US RECESSION

The relation between debt and macroeconomic fluctuations has not received much attention in empirical research, probably because it has not received much emphasis in most theoretical models. This lack of research makes it difficult to predict the impact of recent increases in debt levels on the course of the next recession. It also leaves a potentially important gap in the economic analysis necessary to design effective policy for responding to debt problems and financial instability. In this section we summarise the findings of some new empirical work that sheds light on these important issues.

Ben Bernanke and John Campbell (1988) recently examined a fifteen-year time series of debt-to-asset and debt service-to-cash flow ratios for about 650 publicly traded nonfinancial firms.[16] They ask how many of these firms would have become insolvent or experienced debt service problems with their higher leverage in 1987–8 if the economy would have experienced recessions similar to those in 1974–5 or 1981–2. Bernanke and Campbell's simulations showed that a recession with 1974–5 severity would have driven 10 per cent of their sample to insolvency in 1987. If the US economy experienced the high interest rates of 1981–2 in 1987, fewer firms would have become insolvent (largely because of the stability of equity values in 1981–2 relative to 1974–5). But perhaps more important, 10 per cent of the firms would have been unable to service their debt out of their cash flows.[17]

In view of the reasons given in the previous section for thinking that widespread bankruptcy or financial distress can depress aggregate demand and lead to less stable dynamics in the aggregate economy, the Bernanke and Campbell findings clearly are cause for concern about rising private sector debt burdens. Further evidence of the potential empirical significance of financial distress effects in a future US recession is provided in a recent study of our own (Caskey and Fazzari, 1989). We construct a small dynamic macroeconomic model that includes the effects of financial distress on consumption and investment spending. We estimate the parameters of the model using US data from 1975 through 1986, and simulate the dynamic response of the model economy to a recessionary shock for a range of parameters around the estimated values.

The results from this study support the view that debt and financial constraints can be important factors in determining the path of the business cycle. The consumption and investment functions each have two terms that estimate the impact of financial constraints on aggregate demand: a variable that measures the 'excess sensitivity' of expenditure to variations in cash flow or income, and variables that measure the sensitivity of consumption and investment to fluctuations in real debt service burdens.[18] These financial variables have a significant effect on the simulation results. Using our estimated parameter values, we simulated the output loss over a ten-quarter horizon following a reduction in autonomous spending equal to 1 per cent of potential GNP. Including the estimated effects of the financial variables in the dynamic simulation increased the output lost over 10 quarters by 15.8 per cent.[19] The initial output loss in the quarter following the shock rose by 18.2 per cent when the financial effects were included in the simulation. These results support the theoretical conclusions reached earlier that incorporating financial constraints in a macro model will increase the magnitude of output fluctuations in the business cycle.

Our simulations also show that including the financial constraint variables in the equations that determine aggregate demand can cause a significant change in the qualitative behaviour of the system. The table below shows the cumulative output loss in the simulations as a percentage of potential GNP for varying degrees of price flexibility. The initial shock is a reduction in autonomous expenditure equal to 1 per cent of real GNP.

The price flexibility parameter is the quarterly reduction in the annualised inflation rate for each percentage point deviation of actual output from its potential level. Our estimated value of the price flexibility parameter is 0.16.

Price flexibility parameter	Output loss with financial effects set to zero	Output loss with financial effects at estimated values
0.00	0.944	1.055
0.16	0.923	1.069
0.32	0.901	1.086

The second column of the table shows that, in the absence of destabilising financial effects, increased price flexibility reduces the simulated output loss after a negative demand shock, as the standard analysis predicts. When we include the financial distress effects, however, greater price flexibility *increases* output losses. Therefore, the financial distress effects are sufficiently strong (given our estimates) to overcome the economy's endogenous stabilising mechanism.[20]

These results have important implications for analysing the practical relevance of recent increases in US indebtedness. As agents in the economy have become more indebted, the problems that our simulations identify have likely become more severe as well. For example, our simulations are based on actual values of the variables for 1985. If we cut the debt service burdens of firms and households by 50 per cent, to a level roughly consistent with the actual data in the late 1960s, price flexibility becomes stabilising.

11.5 CONCLUSION

Almost any measure of private sector indebtedness indicates that the debt burdens of US households and firms have grown very quickly to unprecedented levels over the past decade. This development has created serious concerns among some economic analysts and policy-makers. In spite of this fundamental change in financial structure, however, surprisingly little economic research has examined the implications of high debt burdens on macroeconomic performance.

This chapter offers some perspective on the theoretical channels through which high debt levels may destabilise the economy and on the possible quantitative consequences of high debt for the severity of a future downturn in business activity. Because this topic has not been thoroughly studied, and also because the current indebtedness of the private sector is without precedent in the post-war period, the analysis presented here must be viewed as preliminary. Nevertheless, several conclusions emerge that may provide insight into the potential dangers of high indebtedness and the associated public policy responses that may help contain the threat these dangers pose to macroeconomic stability.

The recent substantial increase in debt can make the economy more fragile, increasing the likely severity of a future recession and weakening the economy's endogenous stabilisers. In the short run, this result implies that policy-makers must be cautious in their use of fiscal and monetary measures. The Federal Reserve has tried to show resolve and credibility by using tight money to fight inflation. But in the context of high debt and debt service burdens, this policy is especially risky. The high interest rates caused by restrictive monetary policy will squeeze cash flow margins of safety and reduce the market value of assets, bringing private sector debtors closer to insolvency. Should this policy lead to widespread financial distress, the research presented here suggests that the real costs of fighting inflation could be exceedingly high. As a result of the tax cuts of the 1980s, there is also little flexibility left for fiscal policy. High budget deficits, even as the economy enjoys its longest peacetime expansion, may not allow the federal government to engage in expansionary fiscal measures to sustain private cash flows for households and business in the next recession. Coupled with the high indebtedness documented here, this problem increases the risk of widespread financial distress that will magnify the severity of the next recession. We conclude that short-run inflation fighting as well as deficit reduction must be executed carefully and conservatively. In particular, the Federal Reserve must not worship 'credibility' in the fight against inflation if tight money threatens to send the economy into a financial tailspin.

Over a longer horizon, the structure of policy can be better informed by research on the implications of high debt levels for macroeconomic stability. To the extent that further research supports the findings reported in this chapter, high indebtedness creates a 'negative externality'. That is, agents' privately rational decisions to take on heavy debt burdens lead to negative macroeconomic consequences by reducing aggregate stability. In these circumstances, the appropriate policy response may well include tax incentives to reduce the use of debt. One change that would clearly have such an effect is to limit the deductibility of interest expense. Some steps in this direction were taken by the Tax Reform Act of 1986, but the complete deductibility of interest at the corporate level and the generous mortgage interest deductions at the personal level still represent a substantial subsidy to debt at a time when our analysis suggests that debt use should be discouraged. Along similar lines, a consumption tax or value-added tax would discourage consumption and reduce households' use of debt.

To encourage greater internal finance of investment and limit the need for business debt, especially in fast-growing industries that are most likely to face the asymmetric information problems discussed previously, the current corporate profits tax could be replace by a 'cash flow' tax. This reform would allow firms to fully deduct investment expenses, regardless of whether the investment was financed with internal funds or debt. Dynamic firms with high investment spending that exhausts their internal funds would pay no tax under this scheme, helping them to maintain their investment even in the face of economic downturns. This change would strengthen the economy's automatic stabilisers. Furthermore, under a cash flow tax, the tax system would no longer encourage mature firms to pay out their internal funds at the same time they take on more debt.[21]

In conclusion, we believe that the dramatic increases in private debt level observed over the last decade are indeed a cause for concern. The impact of debt burdens on the economy is complex and multi-faceted with the potential to become a significant destabilising influence in the next economic downturn. The dangers created by high debt, therefore, should be a central aspect of business cycle research and an important consideration of macroeconomic policymaking.

DATA APPENDIX

Figure 11.1:   Ratio of household total credit market liabilities to household total financial and nonfinancial assets (Federal Reserve Flow of Funds).

Figure 11.2:   Ratio of nonfinancial corporate business total credit market liabilities to nonfinancial corporate business total financial and nonfinancial assets (Federal Reserve Flow of Funds).

Figure 11.3:   Ratio of total private domestic nonfinancial debt (Federal Reserve Flow of Funds) to nominal GNP (Business Conditions Digest).

Figure 11.4:   Ratio of household total credit market liabilities (Federal Reserve Flow of Funds) to nominal annual disposable personal income (Business Conditions Digest).

Figure 11.5:   Ratio of nonfinancial corporate business total credit market liabilities (Federal Reserve Flow of Funds) to nonfinancial corporate profits before taxes, capital consumption and inventory valuation adjustments (National Income and Production Accounts (NIPA), table 1.16).

Figure 11.6:   Ratio of household interest payments to nominal annual personal disposable income (Business Conditions Digest). Household interest payments are defined to be the sum of interest paid by individuals in their capacity as consumers (NIPA, table 8.8) and imputed net interest on owner occupied nonfarm housing (NIPA, table 8.9).

Figure 11.7:   Ratio of interest payments of nonfinancial corporate business (NIPA, table 8.8) to the sum of business interest payments and nonfinancial corporate profits before taxes, capital consumption and inventory valuation adjustments (National Income and Production Accounts (NIPA), table 1.16).

Notes

* The views expressed in this chapter are solely those of the authors and do not necessarily reflect the views of the Federal Reserve Bank of Kansas City or the Federal Reserve System.

1. See the data appendix for sources and explanations of the data used in the figures.
2. Consider, for example, the immediate effects of the October 1987 crash in stock prices.
3. Bernanke (1981) emphasises the importance of flow measures of insolvency because it is costly in practice to convert non-liquid assets into cash to meet current consumption and debt payment needs, particularly over a short horizon. The emphasis on financial flows is also evident in the financial theory of investment presented by Minsky (1975).
4. See the discussion in Levy and Levy (1983).
5. Quoted in the *Wall Street Journal*, 5 March 1988, p. 1.
6. From the *Federal Reserve Bulletin*, June 1986, pp. 398–9.
7. Quoted in the *Wall Street Journal*, 2 February 1987, p. 10. More recently, Greenspan warned of the dangers of debt created by leveraged buy-outs. See the *Wall Street Journal*, 27 October 1988, p. A8.
8. Bernanke and Campbell (1988, p. 125). We will consider the basis for this conclusion in more detail later in this chapter.
9. This view has been challenged by recent theoretical and empirical work. See the survey by Gertler (1988).
10. These ideas are part of a long tradition in macroeconomic analysis going back at least to Fisher (1933) and Keynes (1936), and carried on in the work of Minsky (1975, 1986), and Tobin (1975, 1980), among many others.
11. See Bernanke (1981) and (1983), and Blinder and Stiglitz (1983).
12. See, for example, the papers by Bernanke and Gertler (1987) and Fazzari, Hubbard and Petersen (1988b). The latter reference provides empirical support for the hypothesis that investment depends on internal funds.
13. Caskey and Fazzari (1987) and Bernanke and Campbell (1988) provide a more detailed discussion of the impact of bankruptcy and the threat of bankruptcy as well as further references.
14. Bernanke and Gertler (1985) present a formal model exhibiting these features. Stiglitz and Weiss (1981) present a model in which external credit is rationed due to adverse selection problems created by asymmetric information.
15. These results are derived formally in Caskey and Fazzari (1987) DeLong and Summers (1986b) reach similar conclusions about the potentially destabilising role of price flexibility, although the key aspect of their analysis is the increase in real interest rates caused by expected future deflation or disinflation rather than the increase in real debt burdens caused by lower current prices.
16. It is interesting to note that these ratios for Bernanke and Campbell's sample of mostly large corporations exhibit the same patterns as the aggregate measures derived from the Federal Reserve flow of funds presented earlier in this chapter.
17. This point suggests that a recession comparable to 1981–2 with 1987 leverage may have been accompanied by a bigger decline in equity prices and, therefore, the incidence of insolvency may well have been greater than Bernanke and Campbell's simulations suggest.
18. The consumption specification is based on the liquidity-constrained consumption equation presented in Hall and Mishkin (1982) modified to include

innovations in consumer debt service and interest rates. The investment equation comes from Fazzari and Athey (1987). See Caskey and Fazzari (1989) for further details.

19. See Caskey and Fazzari (1989) for extensive discussions about the robustness of the simulations. The results reported here do not include the destabilising effect of rising real interest rates caused by disinflation emphasised by Delong and Summers (1986b). This issue is also analysed in our 1989 paper.

20. In spite of the importance in standard analysis of the stabilising role of price flexibility, it has not been subjected to much empirical research. Notable exceptions are the studies by Calomiris and Hubbard (1985) of historical price flexibility in a vector autoregression model, the historical study of DeLong and Summers (1986a), and the comparison between Japan and the US by Taylor (1987).

21. See Fazzari, Hubbard and Petersen (1988a) for further discussion of taxes and investment when firms face asymmetric information problems in capital markets.

References

Bernanke, Ben S., 'Nonmonetary Effects of the Financial Crisis in the Propagation of the Great Depression'. *American Economic Review*, vol. 73 (June 1983) pp. 257–76.

Bernanke, Ben S. and John Y. Campbell, 'Is There a Corporate Debt Crisis?', *Brookings Papers on Economic Activity*, (1988) pp. 83–139.

Bernanke, Ben S. and Mark Gertler, 'Banking in General Equilibrium', NBER Working Paper no. 1647 (June 1985).

Bernanke, Ben S. and Mark Gertler, 'Agency Costs, Net Worth and Business Fluctuations', Princeton University (December 1987).

Blinder, Alan and Joseph Stiglitz, 'Money, Credit Constraints, and Economic Activity', *American Economic Review*, vol. 73 (May 1983) pp. 297–302.

Calomiris, Charles and R. Glenn Hubbard, 'Price Flexibility, Credit Rationing and Economic Fluctuations: Evidence for the US 1879–1914', NBER Working Paper, no. 1767 (November 1985).

Caskey, John P. and Steven M. Fazzari, 'Aggregate Demand Contractions with Nominal Debt Commitments: Is Wage Flexibility Stabilizing?' *Economic Inquiry*, vol. 25 (October 1987) pp. 583–97.

Caskey, John P. and Steven M. Fazzari, 'Price Flexibility and Macroeconomic Stability: An Empirical Simulation Analysis', Federal Reserve Bank of Kansas City, Research Working Paper Number 89-02 (March 1989).

DeLong, J. Bradford and Lawrence Summers, 'The Changing Cyclical Variability of Economic Activity in the United States', in Robert Gordon (ed.), *The American Business Cycle: Continuity and Change* (Chicago: University of Chicago Press, 1986a).

DeLong, J. Bradford and Lawrence Summers, 'Is Increased Price Flexibility Stabilizing?', *American Economic Review*, vol. 76 (December 1986b) pp. 1031–44.

Fazzari, Steven M. and Michael J. Athey, 'Asymmetric Information, Financial Constraints and Investment', *Review of Economics and Statistics*, vol. 69 (August 1987) pp. 481–7.

Fazzari, Steven M., R. Glenn Hubbard and Bruce C. Petersen, 'Investment,

Financial Decisions and Tax Policies', *American Economic Review*, vol. 78 (May 1988a) pp. 200–5.

Fazzari, Steven M., G. Glenn Hubbard and Bruce C. Petersen, 'Financing Constraints and Corporate Investment', *Brookings Papers on Economic Activity*, 1 (1988b) pp. 141–206.

Fisher, Irving, 'The Debt-Deflation Theory of Great Depressions', *Econometrica*, vol. 1 (October 1933) pp. 337–57.

Friedman, Benjamin, 'Increasing Indebtedness and Financial Stability in the United States', *Debt, Financial Stability, and Public Policy*, Federal Reserve Bank of Kansas City (1986).

Gertler, Mark, 'Financial Structure and Aggregate Economic Activity: An Overview', *Journal of Money Credit and Banking* (August 1988) pp. 559–88.

Hall, Robert E. and Fredric Mishkin, 'The Sensitivity of Consumption to Transitory Income: Estimates from Panel Data on Households', *Econometrica*, vol. 50 (March 1982) pp. 461–81.

Kaufman, Henry, 'Debt: The Threat to Economic and Financial Stability', *Debt, Financial Stability, and Public Policy*, Federal Reserve Bank of Kansas City (1986).

Keynes, John M., *The General Theory of Employment, Interest and Money* (London: Macmillan, 1936).

Levy, S. Jay and David Levy, *Profits and the Future of American Society* (New York: Harper & Row, 1983).

Minsky, Hyman P., *John Maynard Keynes* (New York: Columbia University Press, 1975).

Minsky, Hyman P., *Stabilizing an Unstable Economy* (New Haven: Yale University Press, 1986).

Mishkin, Fredric, 'Illiquidity, Consumer Durable Expenditure, and Monetary Policy', *American Economic Review*, vol. 66 (September 1976) pp. 642–53.

Taylor, John B., 'Differences in Economic Fluctuations in Japan and the U.S.: The Role of Nominal Rigidities', mimeo (Stanford University, October 1987).

Tobin, James, 'Keynesian Models of Recession and Depression', *American Economic Review*, vol. 65 (May 1975) pp. 195–202.

Tobin, James, *Asset Accumulation and Economic Activity* (Chicago: Chicago University Press, 1980).

12 Pricing, Profits and Corporate Investment

Edward J. Nell

Economists dissatisfied with the conventional theory of the firm have recently begun to examine the connections between a corporation's pricing and investment decisions. Prices are seen as linked to potential output, rather than to current output, as in conventional theory. Perfectly competitive firms, according to the latter, take prices as given and choose the optimal output, while in imperfect markets firms take the demand curve as given and choose the optimal combination of price and current output. In both cases productive capacity and the cost structure are taken as given. This may be reasonable for a small family firm, which at the outset makes a once-for-all choice of its optimal size, thereafter adjusting its current activity to changing conditions. But modern industrial corporations do not choose an optimal size; they invest regularly and grow. The conventional picture is not so much wrong as out of place – it is as though someone had painted a scene from the Middle West and tried to pass it off as a portrait of the Rockies. There are similarities, to be sure. The sky is blue and the grass is green, in both cases, and the sky lies above the land. Granted, but prairies are not mountains; it is not even 'as if' they were mountains. Corporate firms grow, and their pricing policies must be understood in relation to their growth if we are to accurately picture how the modern economy works.[1]

Three studies of pricing and investment particularly stand out – those of Alfred Eichner (1980), Geoff Harcourt and Peter Kenyon (1976), and Adrian Wood (1976). All three try to determine not only prices and quantity of investment, but also the choice of the optimal method of production and the division between internal and external finance. At the same time, however, these three models also exhibit a basic defect in this approach, as it has developed thus far. For all three fail to give adequate attention to the relationship between investment, pricing and the growth of demand, and as a result, ignore significant relationships while relying on unacceptable *ad hoc* principles. Eichner employs the Keynesian marginal efficiency schedule, in spite of having assumed market conditions in which it would not be valid, while Harcourt and Kenyon, and in a different way, Wood, treat the growth of demand as exogenous, and rely upon an implicit accelerator, and so wholly fail to connect prices with the growth of demand.

12.1   INVESTMENT, PRICING AND DEMAND: CRITICAL NOTES

12.1.1   Eichner and the Marginal Efficiency Curve

Eichner sets out to determine, not the mark-up itself, but the change in the mark-up from some given initial situation. His strategy is to consider the demand for and supply of funds for investment in relation to a rate of interest. In the case of the demand for investment the traditional marginal efficiency schedule relates the quantity of investment that will be demanded to the market rate of interest. Individual investment projects can be ranked according to their marginal efficiencies, which are determined by finding the discount rate that equates the net earnings of a project over its lifetime to its supply price or cost of construction. The schedule is then created by aggregating, for each level of the marginal efficiency, all the projects earning that level or above. Thus it will be rational to invest in all projects whose marginal efficiency is equal to or greater than the supply price of funds; when the supply price falls, investment will increase, since more projects will become viable. The supply of funds, on the other hand, depends on the mark-up, which generates profits which can be retained, but a high mark-up will also lead to entry by competitors and substitution by customers, thus reducing the flow of funds, especially in the longer term. For each mark-up there will be a stream of internally generated funds, such that higher mark-ups are associated with higher profits, but also with more substitution and entry. The loss due to substitution and entry, appropriately discounted and summed over the lifetime of the project, divided by the lifetime gains (also appropriately discounted), due to the higher mark-up provided an implicit rate of interest on internally generated funds, which can be compared to the going rate of interest on external funds. This defines a rising supply curve. For each level of the mark-up an increasing amount of external funds can be raised at a proportionately higher implicit interest rate. Thus with the demand curve for investible funds sloping down and the supply curve rising the amount of funds, and the mark-up will be determined as shown in Figure 12.1. Then by comparing the implicit interest rate (equal to the marginal efficiency of the investment) to the going rate of interest, the proposition (if any) of external finance can also be settled. If the demand curve for investment cuts the supply curve at an implicit interest rate above the going market rate, then internal funds will be supplied up to the point where the implicit interest rate equals the market rate, and external funds thereafter, until the marginal efficiency of capital has fallen to the level of the market interest rate.

Eichner emphasises the important connection between pricing and investment which he treats as expansion, rather than adjustment, in contrast

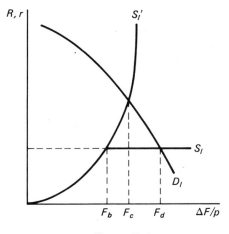

Figure 12.1

to the mainstream approach.[2] His analysis of pricing is therefore consistent with modern growth theory.[3] Moreover, he develops an interesting discussion of internal and external funds, but the demand side is seriously inadequate. First, the marginal efficiency schedule poses problems under the best of conditions. If it is a disequilibrium construction we need an explanation for the long-term stability of the prices according to which we value output and inputs over the lifetime of the projects. If it is an equilibrium concept, however, when the rate of interest changes, equilibrium will not be re-established until the rate of profit has realigned itself. But changes in the rate of profit imply changes in prices and capital values. As the re-switching controversy showed, the order of projects may change, and the capital values involved may change sharply. For example, a fall in the rate of interest could lead to a decrease in the amount of investment, if the consequent decline in the rate of profit engendered a sufficient drop in the prices and (due to switches of technique) qualities of inputs in the viable projects.

If this were the only problem Eichner would be in no worse a position than traditional Keynesians. A suitable, if necessarily *ad hoc*, explanation would be required for the disequilibrium stability of the prices of inputs and outputs over the lifetime of projects. The foundations might be weak, but the construction could be defended as useful or illuminating.

Unfortunately, there also appears to be an internal inconsistency in the argument. The implicit cost of funds, R, on the supply curve is positively related to the margin above costs. But as this margin is increased, substitution and entry of competitors cut into the expected market, reducing expected revenue. For that very reason, as we move up the supply curve, required capacity will be less with each successive step. In other words, the demand curve also depends on the margin above costs, by Eichner's own reasoning, which shows that the higher the margin above costs, the lower must be the demand for investment. This implies that there will be a family of investment-interest demand curves, one for each choice of profit margin. Spelling this out: in Eichner's notation, a higher R must imply a higher n, so will imply substitution and entry cutting into the cash flow. But this reduction comes about by reducing physical volume, while price increases. Hence less capacity will be needed, since fewer items will be sold. Thus as the mark-up rises the need for new capacity falls. In short, the supply curve for funds and the demand for investment are not independent. So Eichner's model is over-determined and is thus not acceptable.

12.1.2 Harcourt and Kenyon and 'Vintages'

Harcourt and Kenyon (1976) also have a problem with demand. They draw two curves, plotting expected price or cost against the level of output to be catered for by new investment. As shown in Figure 12.2, the P_1P_1 curve is downward sloping at each end, but has a long horizontal stretch in the middle. It shows the price that will have to be charged to cover costs for providing capacity to cater for different levels of output. The negative slope, surprisingly, is explained from the supply side. The firm is assumed to operate plants of varying vintages, older vintages having higher running costs. The higher the price, therefore, the older the vintage that can be currently operated, so the less new investment will be needed to provide the capacity to meet expected future demand. Conversely, the lower the price the fewer the vintage plants that will be operable, so the more investment will be needed. The horizontal stretch indicates that while a new plant can be run at varying levels of output, the price that will be charged this period to generate the internal funds to build up the plant, will depend only on the fact that the plant has to be built. Any expected output within that range will require construction of a new plant, and will require the same corresponding price this period. Harcourt and Kenyon then draw their P_2P_2 curve, rising from left to right and intersecting P_1P_1.

This second curve shows the output that will be producible by the plants that can be built with the funds generated by a certain price, assuming a given best-practice technique. So we have an intersection of a supply of funds curve from retained earnings and a demand for funds for investment.

This intersection is supposed to show the unique point at which expectations regarding the supply and the demand for funds are consistent. Yet Harcourt and Kenyon's own interpretation of these curves suggests other possibilities. For example, suppose prices were set higher than the intersection, and, in particular, above the horizontal pattern of p_1p_1.

Then only a small amount of new capacity will be required, since vintage plants will provide most of the required output, but a large amount could

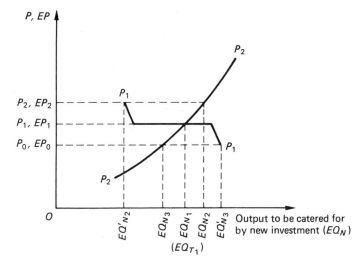

Figure 12.2

be afforded; so, after meeting demand funds would be left over. Then why not construct a large capacity plant, replacing some of the older vintage equipment, and use any extra funds in a selling or marketing campaign? To be sure, this might be a gamble, but in the world of the large corporation, high mark-ups and heavy marketing often win out over low mark-ups and reliance on normal demand.

On the other hand, suppose little or no older vintage capacity is available? (For example, older vintages can only produce goods of uncompetitive quality, or the market has expanded so much that vintage plants make up only a tiny proportion of total capacity.) What will replace the $p_1 p_1$ curve under these conditions?

But the main problem is that the expected future demand, that is, the growth of demand from its current or immediately past level, has been taken as independent of the mark-up chosen. The authors argue, correctly, that the evidence shows that oligopolistic producers adapt output to variations in short-run demand, leaving price unchanged, since price has been set to provide internal finance. But the reason for trying to maintain the flow of finance is that it is needed to build capacity; and they assume that decisions to build capacity will be taken whenever long-period expectations of demand change. Clearly these latter are of prime importance, yet no account whatsoever is provided of the determinants of long-period demand. It is simply taken as given, exogenous to the representative firm, presumably determined by macroeconomic forces. Yet by their own admission (when discussing Eichner's work) if the mark-up is above normal, substitution and entry can be expected, which of course, reduces the future level of demand. Surely this must be taken into account in planning the construction of capacity? If so, however, firms must be admitted to have some ability to influence their own future levels of demand. Since the approach deals with oligopolies, this can hardly be distressing, but somehow it never made it into the formal analysis. What of expenditures on selling, or investment in establishing distribution networks? The authors are silent. Perhaps they can be forgiven for overlooking this topic; but not for making their firms schizophrenic: they have them invest in long-lived plant on the basis of given expectations of demand, and choose a mark-up to finance this investment, even though they also hold expectations about the effect of changes in the mark-up on the physical volume of demand in the periods ahead.

Harcourt and Kenyon basically accept Eichner's theory of the supply of investible funds, but have replaced his use of the marginal efficiency of capital schedule by a demand construct based on given expectations and the notion of vintages of plant and equipment.[4] The main problem has been left untouched: A given mark-up, by providing the finance for investment, is associated with a certain growth of capacity; but it affects demand by encouraging or discouraging substitution and entry, and, unmentioned so far, the ability of the firm to develop new markets. Hence it should also be linked theoretically with the growth of demand.

12.1.3 Wood, Exogenous Demand Growth and the Accelerator

Adrian Wood (1976) tries to do this but he bases his analysis on a problematical relationship of the investment coefficient to the accelerator principle, which creates difficulties not unlike those of Harcourt and Kenyon. The theory is simple and elegant. He defines an 'opportunity frontier', showing the highest profit margin attainable for each rate of growth of sales, given the capital/output ratio, and a 'finance frontier', showing the profit margin required to finance each rate of growth, also depending on a capital/output ratio. On the opportunity frontier, the relation between the profit margin and the rate of growth is negative, as shown in Figure 12.3, for the given capital coefficient. On the finance frontier, it is positive. For a given profit margin, the relation between the capital coefficient and the growth rate will be positive on the opportunity frontier (more capital per unit output means lower labour and current costs per unit output, so a higher profit margin) and negative on the finance frontier. The object of the corporation is to maximise its growth rate of sales. The model determines the growth rate, the profit margin and capital/output ratio together.

Attractive as this theory is, there are nevertheless serious difficulties.[5] To define the finance frontier Wood argues that given the capital coefficient, the growth rate of demand will determine the amount of investment

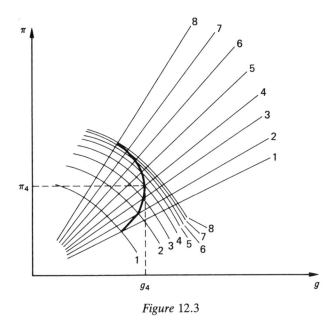

Figure 12.3

needed to provide the required capacity. Then given the external finance ratio and the payment rate, the profit margin necessary to generate the required internal finance follows. The capital coefficient thus functions as a one-period accelerator.

However, this creates a considerable difficulty for the interpretation of the opportunity frontier. Wood clearly wants to present a theory in which the corporation can exercise some control over the growth of its market, as in fact corporations obviously do. But if capital investment takes place exclusively in response to growth of demand, as the accelerator requires, then the only variable left by means of which the corporation could influence the growth of demand is the profit margin. But the relation shown in the opportunity frontier between the profit margin and the growth rate of sales is repeatedly described as 'the maximum profit margin attainable given any particular growth rate of sales' (Wood, 1976, pp. 66–9). That is, the growth rate of demand is the independent variable, and the profit margin the dependent one. At first glance this may seem a matter of convention, but the economic interpretation is significant. For if the firm takes the growth rate of sales as given and reacts by setting the best profit margin it can get in the light of what its competitors are doing, then Wood is not entitled to say, as he does on p. 84, that when the investment coefficient is given, a firm 'can increase the growth of demand for its products only by reducing its best attainable profit margin'. To say this, implies that by reducing its profit margin a firm can raise its growth rate of sales, quite a different matter from saying that faced with a rise in the growth rate of its sales the firm will find that the best profit margin it can get will decline because of the pressure of its competitors.

Nor is that all. Wood's analysis determines three variables: the rate of growth, the profit margin, and the investment coefficient. The latter is supposed to influence both the opportunity frontier and the finance frontier. The effect on finance is obvious; a higher capital coefficient implies a greater need for finance per unit output. But the alleged effect on the opportunity frontier is easily understood only if the rate of growth of demand is exogenous to the firm; given such a growth rate a higher capital coefficient, by reducing unit operating costs, will increase the maximum attainable profit margin. This is straightforward. By constrast, it is more difficult to argue that, given a profit margin, a higher capital coefficient will make it possible for the firm to increase the growth rate of its sales. To maintain a given profit margin with lower operating costs, price would have to be cut proportionately; but why will a lower price raise the *rate of growth* of demand, as opposed to the level? Further, if price and the rate of growth of demand are related in the appropriate way, then price should replace the profit margin as the variable to be determined.[6]

The point underlying Wood's approach is certainly reasonable; he claims on the one hand that by reducing prices demand will be stimulated, and on the other, that when unit selling costs have been increased (for good reasons, of course) sales will be stimulated – that is, the demand curves facing firms will be shifted as a consequence of the increased sales effort. So the growth rate of demand, this period's demand minus last period's, divided by last period's, will be increased – at least this appears to be the argument (pp. 65–6). Taken literally, however, the implication is that an unchange profit margin will be associated with a *ZERO* growth rate of sales; only changes in the profit margin will be associated with changes in demand, and levels with levels, as in traditional theory. Why a lower profit margin will raise the rate of growth of demand, as opposed to its level, is left unexplained.

Another aspect of the argument leads to an additional problem. An increase in selling costs means adding more sales personnel, more office equipment, perhaps more office space. Capital costs as well as current costs will be involved. Within limits, selling effort, as measured by unit selling costs, sales personnel, etc., could no doubt be increased temporarily by using existing office equipment and space more intensively. But in the long run changes in the capital invested in office space and equipment will be required. In the light of this consider the interpretation of the capital coefficient. Some increases in capital – increases in sales capital – will tend to cause changes in demand, while other changes in capital – production capital – will come in response to changes in demand. The simple and valid point that corporations can affect their demand by incurring selling costs sits uneasily in the company of the accelerator principle.[7]

These problems are compounded by the fact that Wood explicitly takes the growth rate of aggregate demand as given exogenously (p. 64) and describes companies as competing 'for a limited total amount of demand' in any period (p. 66). So any given company or sector can deviate from the general growth rate in a given period only if other companies of sectors deviate in exactly offsetting ways. One party's growth boom requires another's growth slump.

In short, either Wood means for the growth of demand to be exogenous, or he assumes that firms can influence it. But if demand growth is exogenous, the value of the analysis is more limited than appears, and the reason that higher growth rates lead firms to lower their margins is unclear. If firms are supposed to influence the growth of demand, then the relationship intended is clear enough, but the price, rather than the margin, is the appropriate variable, and it still needs to be explained why lowering price or margin raises the growth rate rather than the level of sales.

12.1.4 Conclusions

All three approaches to pricing and investment make the point that the mark-up on the output of normal capacity must be set so as to provide the funds which will finance the construction of the capacity needed to supply the expected future demand. All make the further point that the choice of the mark-up will influence and be influenced by the division of finance between internal and external funds, and two of the three also relate the mark-up decision to the choice of the best method of production. But none of them succesfully connect the mark-up to the growth of demand; indeed, all three fail to provide an adequate treatment of the relation of pricing and investment to demand. That is the task to which we must turn now.

12.2 CORPORATE PRICING AND INVESTMENT DECISIONS

When firms are small and the market is new, no one firm will have any control over the growth of demand, nor will any one have a body of established and closely attached customers. But with maturity a few large firms producing somewhat differentiated products will acquire a sufficiently dominant position that they will possess a well-defined and indentifiable body of established customers and be able to influence, at a price, the growth of their sales. The analysis which follows concerns a representative firm of such a kind.

12.2.1 Established and New Markets

A firm's established market is where it is well recognised and can count on a loyal and reliable set of customers, either households or businesses, who have incorporated its products into their lifestyles or production processes, so that to switch to an alternative product would entail at least some costs. Switching products thus becomes an investment decision – the stream of gains from the new product, properly discounted, must more than cover the cost of making the switch. Substituting products will therefore not be lightly done, so sales will be predictable, and, within some reasonable range of prices, customers will continue to prefer the firm's products. An established market thus carries itself; the current selling effort is negligible and for all practical purposes capital selling costs are sunk.[8]

Established markets can exist for intangibles – services – as well as for tangible goods, and, in both cases, we can distinguish between durable and non-durable purchases. Durable goods last, removing the customer from the market; non-durable require continuous re-entry into the market. Durable services produce results that last – the surgeon as opposed to the general practitioner, the architect as opposed to the gardener. As established market for a non-durable (an operating input into a household or business) means that there is a regular clientele that repeatedly purchases the good or service for use in its established operating procedures. So it plans for the use of the good, budgets for it, and would have to change its routine to substitute another good or service. In the case of durable, new purchasers similar to those of the past, coming from the same neighbourhood, social class or industry, regularly enter along with replacement purchasers, drawn by the product's reputation and suitability, including the ready availability of ancillary services.

Consider a representative firm, or a representative division of a conglomerate corporation, producing a well-defined product with an established clientele. The firm or division has to earn the profits necessary to finance its own growth, either directly by spending internally generated funds, or by showing earnings that will justify the required level of borrowing. In a moment we will see that, given the various costs, the level at which the firm sets the price will determines the growth rate that it can finance. First, however, we must explore the relationships between the level at which price is set and the rate at which the market can be expected to grow. Over a wide range the large established market will be comparatively insensitive to price, but, by contrast, the smaller new markets which the firm wishes to develop or penetrate will react quite strongly to prices. This can be shown in a pair of diagrams as in Figure 12.4. The left-hand diagram represents the established market, the broken line indicating that it is much larger. The steepness of the demand line indicates that the good is strongly complementary with other goods in the household's normal lifestyle, or in business's production systems. The high and low breaks mark the points where substitution will take place, and customers leave and enter. In the smaller new market, shown on the right hand, demand is quite sensitive to changes in price. (The price does not actually have to be the same in the two markets, but if they are different, they must be strictly related and move together.) The current sales drive can be assumed to be

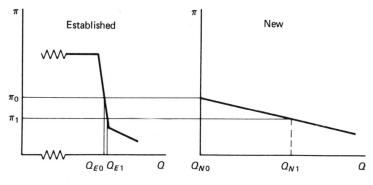

Figure 12.4

concentrated in the new market, and the level of investment in sales and distribution will determine the position and slope of the demand curve confronting the firm in this market. Other things being equal, the higher this level of investment the higher the intercept and the flatter the slope of this demand curve. (Similarly, the position of the demand curve in the established market depends, among other things, on past investments in sales and distribution.) The implication, then, is that a change in price, say from high to lower, will not affect the established market much, but will have a strong impact on the new. At the lower price, the ratio of the new market to the old will be higher. But this ratio represents the growth of sales.

In the notation of Figure 12.4, at the price π_0, the rate of growth of sales will be $\dfrac{Q_{N0}}{Q_{E0}}$;

at $\pi_1 < \pi_0$, it will be $\dfrac{Q_{N1}}{Q_{E1}} > \dfrac{Q_{N0}}{Q_{E0}}$

So as the price falls, the rate of growth of sales increases, for a given investment in sales and distribution. The maximum price for the price-rate of growth function will be the price at which the new market vanishes. The maximum rate of growth, corresponding to the minimum price, will be given by the horizontal intercept of the new market's demand curve as shown in Figure 12.5.

The slope of the growth of demand function, then, will be

$$\frac{(\pi_0 - \pi_1)}{Q_{E0} + \dfrac{Q_{N0}}{Q_{E0}} - Q_{E1} + \dfrac{Q_{N1}}{Q_{E1}}}$$

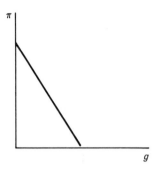

Figure 12.5

which can be rewritten

$$Q_E \frac{(\pi_0 - \pi_1)}{Q_{N0} - Q_{N1}} = Q_E \frac{\Delta\pi}{\Delta Q_N}.$$

In the special case where $Q_{E0} = Q_{E1} = Q_E$ we have

$$\frac{Q_{E0} Q_{E1} (\pi_0 - \pi_1)}{Q_{E1} Q_{N0} - Q_{E0} Q_{N1}}.$$

If the demand curve in the established market is quite steep this will be a good approximation to the slope of the price-growth of demand function.

To fix the position of the new market demand function, it is necessary to know the investment in sales effort. This should be explained. There are current costs, both fixed and variable, involved in selling, but the larger part of selling costs constitute an investment. The aim is to capture the loyalty of a set of customers. The time, effort and expense in selling are to be applied not only to the immediate sale, which may only be a trial order, but to all future sales in that market. A sales campaign requires training and equipping a sales force, providing warehouses, showrooms, office space, personnel, dealers, distributions, delivery systems, servicing arrangements, warranties, and insurance. Independent distributors may be used, but then contracts must be drawn up covering all of the above, and franchises issued. This will involve commitments over various lengths of time. The firm's object is not merely to expand its market, but to develop one that is reliable. It is committing resources to building plant and equipment; it must develop a market corresponding to this new productive capacity that will last as long as the new factories, or at least as long as it takes to write them off. So the expenses in developing the market should be considered investment; they entail the commitment of capital in construction, training and the assumption of contractual obligations. These are long-term arrangements and they are expected to yield long-term benefits.

Investment in market development will shift the growth of demand frontier, but successive investments will not necessarily shift it the same amount. There are good reasons for believing that there will be diminishing returns to investment in sales and marketing. The 'pool' of potential customers can be defined geographically and socially. Near the centre of the pool it will be comparatively easy and inexpensive to convert potential customers into actual ones, but the further from this centre the more expensive and problematical the process will become. Transport and transactions costs will rise, and the 'fit' between the potential customer and the product will be poorer. This will be important later on.

To summarise the assumed circumstances: The product is well-defined and the established market is given. The productive capacity supplying it has been built, the sales investment has been made and customer loyalties established. The new market has been targeted and projections drawn. It is expected that sales will follow a certain course, depending on the prices charged and the sales investment made. Other things being equal, firms will pursue the most rapid possible course of expansion. Their long-term expectations will be assumed to be correct, though allowance will be made at times for unexpected short-term fluctuations in demand. The analysis, then, will hold for the time it takes to carry the project through – that is, to develop the market and build the capacity to service it. After that, the new market becomes part of the established market and attention can be turned to the next investment project. The length of this planning-and-execution period will be longer than the conventional short run, because the new capacity has not only to be built, it has to be operated and the new market consolidated. But the time this takes will itself depend on market conditions and may vary from sector to sector and even from firm to firm.

12.2.2 The Supply of Finance for Growth

Given the foregoing relationships between the corporation's projected growth in sales, its prices, and sales investment, the company's next problem must be to ensure adequate financing to underwrite the investment in sales and to build and equip the new plant to supply the expected new markets. The calculation it must make is relatively straightforward. The company will have a policy, to be explored in a moment, with respect to the burden of debt it wishes to assume relative to its equity. This will depend on the balance between the advantages of leverage and the costs and risk of default. Given this policy the total funds available over the development period will consist of profits plus borrowing, while these funds will be used to cover expenditure on construction of new plant, building up sales and distribution networks, and, of course, meeting existing fixed costs. Thus,

$$P + B = I_F + I_S + F$$

where the symbols stand, respectively, for profit, borrowing, investment in factories, investment in sales development and fixed expenses. So, remembering the earlier symbol for price, and introducing Y for capacity, W for the capacity wage bill plus materials costs, and g for the growth rate of capacity output, we have

$$\pi Y + W = I_F + I_S + F - B$$

and rearranging,

$$\frac{\pi Y}{K} = g + \frac{(I_S + F + W - B)}{K}$$

or

$$\pi = gv + \frac{(I_S + F + W - B)}{Y}$$

where $v = \dfrac{I_F}{Y}$.

The rate of growth, g, is defined as $\dfrac{I_F}{K} = \dfrac{Q_N}{Q_E}$

so that productive investment is proportioned to the expected size of the new market. The ratio of productive investment to capacity output, v, is the fraction of normal capacity income or output devoted to increasing productive capacity, and it appears as the slope of the finance relation between price and the rate of growth. This ratio is based on the firm's judgement of its competitive situation, its need for investment spending to keep up with advances in technology, and on its expectations of the long-term development of its markets. The intercept will normally be positive, since we can reasonable expect that $(I_S + F + W) > B$.

An increase (decrease) in sales investment will cause the finance relation to shift up (down), just as sales investment causes the price-growth of demand to shift out or in. In addition, the function will shift up with rises in the wage rate, increases in fixed costs, or restrictive monetary policies which reduce borrowing. Figure 12.6 illustrates these relationships.

Underlying the definition of g, the rate of growth, is the assumption that the firm's marginal capital–output ratio equals its average. That is, g can be defined as above because $I_F = \alpha Q_N$ and $K = \alpha Q_E$.

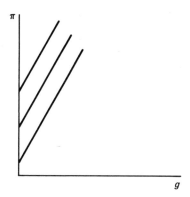

Figure 12.6

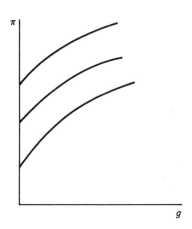

Figure 12.7

Dividing the second equation into the first, the alphas cancel, and the result is g. If the marginal is not equal to the average, but is constant, little is changed. The growth of capacity will simply be proportionate to the growth of demand rather than equal to it. But if there are economies of scale in investment – as there often are – then the relationship between the two rates of growth will vary. As the size of the new market increases, the investment required to service a unit of it declines; hence the finance required per unit of the new market also declines. This can be illustrated readily in a modified version of the preceding diagram, as in Figure 12.7. Instead of lines of constant slope, we have curves, starting from the same intercepts and rising, but falling in slope as g rises.

The finance function is defined for capacity output, since the planning period comprises a number of short periods and the relevant concept is the expected norm for the whole period. Nevertheless the model must be capable of analysing short-period fluctuations, since these are real problems which businesses face. When actual income falls short of the normal operating rate, the finance intercept is increased – the firm will need a higher price to generate the required finance. But the slope of the finance function will remain unaffected, for the firm will not change its judgment of the fraction of its capacity output that it should invest with every shift in the short-run winds.

12.2.3　External Finance

The level of the firm's demand for B will be set by increasing risk. Higher levels of B imply higher levels of F in the future; but F/K is set by a balance between the advantages of additional leverage, and the costs of insuring against default, where the risk and the cost of default increase as F/K rises. The risk arises from the probability that a downswing will cut into revenue deeply enough to make it impossible to meet F; clearly the larger F/K, for a given normal rate of profit, the smaller the downswing needed to cause trouble. Given a normal size distribution of fluctuations in sales, risk will increase at a rising rate as F/K rises. The costs of default are the resulting penalties, legal fees, loss of credit rating, and/or reorganisation, and these clearly increase additively with the severity of the default. But after a point they also interact; when the default is serious, for example, legal fees will be incurred not only to defend the initial default, but also to postpone the penalties, hold off the loss of other credit, defend against reorganisation and so on; in other words, the interaction will be multiplicative. So the costs will tend to rise exponentially, once they begin to interact.[9]

For a given capital–output ratio, a given rate of interest, and a given normal rate of profit, then the firm's desired level of $B/I = F/K$ will be set at the point where the gain from additional borrowing (a constant) is just offset by the (increasing) cost of the insurance premium to offset the (rising) risk and cost of default as it can be seen in Figure 12.8. If there were economies of scale the marginal gain from borrowing would increase, as indicated by the dotted line, and a larger ratio B/I would be justified.

12.2.4　Growth and Sales Investment

The growth of demand frontier and the finance function can now be put together on the same diagram, remembering that each relationship is also a function of the amount invested in sales and marketing.[10] Increases in sales investment require the finance function to shift up in a constant proportion, but they shift the growth of demand frontier outward in a diminishing proportion. These shifts can be graphed as in Figure 12.9; the intersections trace out the curve indicated. The solution will therefore be to choose the unique price and level of investment in sales that will maximise the rate of growth, g.

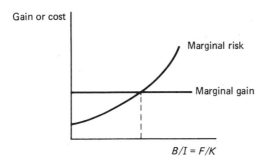

Figure 12.8

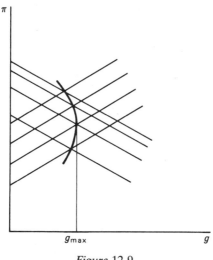

Figure 12.9

Nothing much is changed by the presence of economies of scale in productive investment. As shown earlier, the finance lines will then rise in a progressively shallower curve, but the intersections with the demand lines will still trace out a curve of the same shape, so that there will still be a unique maximising solution, as in Figure 12.10.

These solutions are predicated on given levels of F, W, B and Y. If either F or W rise, or if B or Y decrease, then the set of finance lines must shift up, and the equilibrium planned price will be higher. The effects on g, however, require a closer look in at least one case. A rise in F or a decline in B, *ceteris paribus*, will simply shift the set of finance lines, having no effect on the growth of sales frontier[11] as in Figure 12.11. Hence g will fall. But changes in W are more complicated. A rise in W if it is general and known to be general, implies a general increase in household incomes and so new growth in consumer spending.[12] If the firm's products are consumer

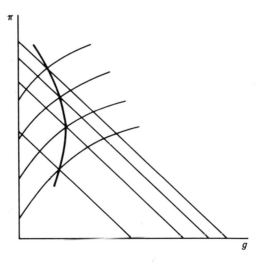

Figure 12.10

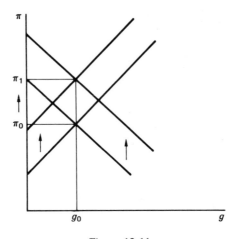

Figure 12.11

goods, the growth of sales lines will shift up, too. Price will increase, but g will be unaffected. In the diagram, Figure 12.11, the rise in W raises the finance line, and it also shifts up the growth of sales line. If the two are affected in the same proportion, the growth rate will be unchanged, and the entire effect of the rise in wages will be to increase prices. But there is another possibility. The increase in wages could increase spending (at every price) in the established markets in the same proportion that spend-

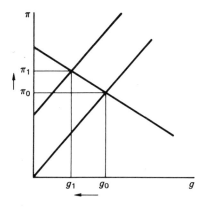

Figure 12.12

ing is increased in the new markets. If, at every price, spending in the old and new markets has increased in the same proportion, spending in the old and new markets will stand in the same ratio as before the wage increase, so there will be no effect at all on the growth of sales. The rise in W will have shifted up the finance line but will have left the growth of sales line unaffected, resulting in an equilibrium with a higher price and a lower rate of growth as in Figure 12.12.

12.2.5 Choice of Technique

Modern industrial processes can frequently be computerised and automated, substantially reducing labour costs, raising fixed costs, and increasing the capital–output ratio. We will assume, however, that fixed costs will be set by the calculation of risk above, and that no technique will be considered which implies a rise in F. Alternative techniques therefore change the finance frontier; they cause it to differ in slope and intercept; the technique with the lower intercept – lower W – has the higher capital–output ratio, so is steeper, rising from left to right. Consider two techniques as drawn in Figure 12.13: at some point they will cross. If the demand-growth line is steep, cutting the techniques below their intersection, the relatively capital-intensive technique, since it has the lower intercept, will yield the higher rate of growth. But if the demand-growth line is relatively flat and cuts the finance lines above their intersection, then the less capital-intensive technique will give rise to the higher growth rate.

The choice of technique is normally treated entirely in terms of supply side considerations. By contrast, the analysis here implies that the possibilities for growth of demand play a significant role in determining technique.[13]

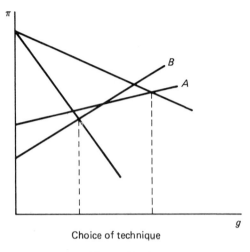

Choice of technique

Figure 12.13

12.2.6 Impact of Exchange Rate Changes

Foreign goods may be imported and sold for domestic currency, either with or without further processing; or foreign capital equipment, energy or intermediate goods may be used in production. In either case a change in the exchange rate changes the costs which must be covered by the supply of finance; but in the first case, the change increases the cost of sales inventory, in the second it affects the cost of productive capacity. Hence a change in the exchange rate alters the intercept of the finance frontier of a firm importing foreign goods for sale, while it alters the slope in the case of a firm importing foreign capital equipment.

Consider a firm making candy that imports its chocolate and syrup from Europe, processing it with domestic equipment, and compare it to another firm, making scientific instruments, that imports high-grade equipment from Europe, but uses domestic materials. For the sake of the argument, suppose that the finance frontiers of both initially have the same intercepts and the same slopes, and further suppose that imported materials are the same percentage of the 'intercept' costs that imported equipment is of total capital. The exchange rate change will therefore have the same percentage impact in both cases.

In Figure 12.14 both the intercept and the slope are shown to double (a very large change, representing a 50 per cent decline in the value of the domestic currency, if all the relevant costs are incurred in foreign currency.) The two new finance frontiers will intersect at a certain point. If the price–demand lines are similar and both steep enough to lie below the intersection we can see that the capital-importing industry will raise its

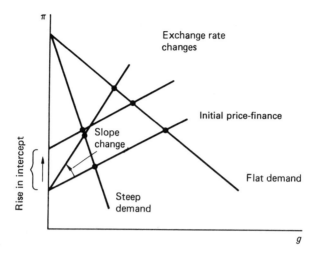

Figure 12.14

price less and suffer less growth slowdown than the materials importing industry. If the price–demand lines are similar and both flat enough to lie beyond the intersection, just the reverse will be true. In general, the flatter the price–demand lines, the less the impact on price, and the greater the impact on growth. But in neither case will the full impact of the exchange rate change be passed along as a price increase.

The usual explanations for variations in exchange-rate pass-along, bottleneck and beachhead effects, are based exclusively on suppy-side concerns; by contrast, once again the account here depended crucially on demand, but not on the level of demand – it is the relationship between price and the rate of growth of demand that matters.[14]

12.2.7 Temporary or Cyclical Variations in Demand

The argument so far has been concerned exclusively with expected long-term normal costs and sales, and the variables determined have been planned on 'benchmark' prices and the target rate of growth of sales. But this same framework can be used to determine the appropriate responses to short-run or cyclical variations in aggregate demand, affecting the firm's current and immediately future rate of sales. To make the adaptation, we assume that the underlying parameters remain unchanged, and that the firm wishes to maintain its long-run position as well as possible.

Notice, however, that there is an asymmetry between short-term increases and declines in demand. When demand falls, the firm will not necessarily want to cut investment spending, since the long-term pattern of growth is unchanged. But the recession will probably mean that new markets will temporarily dry up. Hence it will be able to exploit its

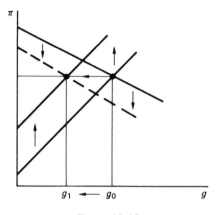

Figure 12.15

established market by increasing prices enough to maintain the flow of funds required for growth. When demand rises, however, the new rate of growth indicated by the new intersection could not be sustained (since the increase is temporary). So there is no point in moving to it by cutting price and setting up a sales campaign – which could be rudely upset if demand fell back to normal and prices had to be raised. So a rise in demand will not lead to a fall in price; indeed, if the rise is large enough (and regarded as temporary enough) firms might well react by adding surcharges or service fees to ration the demand.

In Figure 12.15, the price–demand growth line is unaffected, since the demand change is only temporary. A fall in demand raises the finance line, a rise lowers it. To maintain normal growth when the demand falls firms will have to raise price to the point on the new finance line. When demand rises, since cutting price will not be a desirable strategy, maintaining price permits a buildup of reserves sufficient, if invested at a later date (to make up for a recession), to raise the growth rate by the amount indicated.

Cyclical downturns, however, can become depressions, and last long enough to affect plans. The effects of such a decline can be analysed in the same way. Consider first the case of a recession, in which (only) new markets will tend to dry up; the sales growth lines will shift down, offsetting the rise in finance requirements. If the shifts are equi-proportional, price would remain unchanged, while the growth rate would fall. If the shifts are not perfect offsets, the major effect will still be on g, while the change in price would be relatively minor. Recessions do not tend to lower corporate prices.

There is another possibility. A decline in incomes, perhaps due to layoffs, may reduce demand in the established markets as well as in the new markets. If demand is reduced in both in the same proportion, then, as in the case of a rise in W, the ratio of spending in new markets to spending

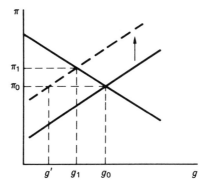

Figure 12.16

in old, for each level of price, will be the same after the change as before. Hence the sales-growth line will not shift, and the entire impact of the decline is brought about by the upward shift of the finance line, resulting in a higher price and a lower rate of growth (Figure 12.16).

If corporations adjust prices in these ways, trying to maintain cash flow, and reserves, in the face of variations in demand, what will be the effects on employment and output in the aggregate?[15]

12.3   CORPORATE PRICING AND AGGREGATE DEMAND

In the modern economy the largest part of output is produced by giant firms with substantial market power, operating large-scale industrial processes with significant indivisibilities. Let us assume that we can neglect the behaviour of small businesses, so that the aggregate relations between prices and investment are dominated by what corporations do.

To examine this the economy can be subdivided into two sectors, producing capital goods and consumer goods respectively. In each case the output will be a composite commodity, and the sector will consist of the capital and labour required, directly and indirectly to produce the normal capacity output. Each capital coefficient thus consists not only of the various capital goods directly required, but also of those required to make the direct inputs, and those further required to manufacture the inputs of the inputs, and so on. Similarly, the labour inputs are those directly required, plus those required for the indirect inputs, and so on. Thus an increase in demand for investment will require an increase not only in the direct inputs of labour and capital goods, but also in the inputs of suppliers of these direct inputs, and suppliers of these suppliers. This impact runs through all the input–output relationships of the economy, and is summed up in the sectoral coefficients; but it consists purely of inter-industry

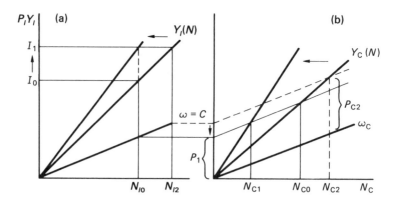

Figure 12.17

Source: Nell (1988, p. 125)

relationships; the spending by households of the additional wages paid when investment output rises, is not included. That effect, showing up in additional demand for consumer goods, is a relationship between the sectors. It is the subject of what follows.

Each sector's coefficients can be re-interpreted as a utilisation function, showing, for given capacity, output as depending on the level of employment in that sector (Nell, 1988, ch. 5 appendix). The real wage can be taken initially as given, so the wage bill in each sector will also be a direct function of employment. Wages will be assumed to be wholly consumed, investment will be taken as exogenous. For simplicity, and because it is reasonable, all the functions will be assumed to be linear in the relevant ranges. All quantities are shown in money values: that is, 'output' is the money price of output times the amount; the wage bill is the money wage times the amount of labour. The wage rate is shown in each sector by the angle of the wage line, indicating the fraction of the money value of that sector's output that the money wage commands. The price ratio of the two composite outputs must be such that the real wage per unit of labour is the same in the two sectors.

Now consider Figure 12.17, showing the demand relationship between the two sectors. The spending of the wage bill in the capital goods sector generates the realised profit in the consumer goods sector. When businesses keep prices steady and adjust output, an increase in investment demand will therefore raise employment and output in both sectors. But now consider a rise in investment demand in conditions of corporate markets. Faced with increased demand which they may fear to be temporary, while training and start-up costs may be large, such firms could reasonably choose to raise prices to ration demand. (Faced with a decline in sales, and the drying up of new markets, they might also raise prices, to try to maintain their cash flow, in view of their financial commitments.) Suppose that prices are raised in the capital goods sector just enough to absorb the increased demand. Employment, output and the wage bill will be unchanged, but profit will be higher.[16]

But since the relative price of capital goods has increased, to restore the terms of trade between sectors, firms in consumer goods industries must raise their prices also – not, however, in exactly the same proportion, but more or less than in proportion, according to the ratio of their capital/labour ratio to that in the capital goods sector. For example, if the consumer sector is relatively labour-intensive, as drawn here, their price will rise less than in proportion. But the equality between the full capacity profit rates of the two sectors must be restored; if it is not, credit ratings in the less profitable sector will decline, and borrowing there will become more expensive – bringing an upward shift of the finance frontiers of consumer firms. In anticipation of this, to protect their credit rating, consumer sector firms must raise prices. But such price increases will have unfortunate short-term consequences for the sector as a whole: both employment and output must fall, although the level of profit will remain unchanged.[17]

The strategy of raising prices rather than output in the face of increased demand works in the short run to the benefit of firms in the capital goods sector at the expense of consumer goods firms and workers. This applies even when the new demand is directed at the consumer goods sector itself, so long as both sectors raise prices in order to maintain the relation between their profit rates. For the price rise in the capital goods sector lowers its wage bill and thus correspondingly reduces the profits of the consumer sector, transferring to the former a portion of the profit arising from the additional demand for consumer goods. If consumer goods firms had increased output, they would have captured the entire additional profit from the increased demand. But, of course, it might seem that the increased demand could turn out to be temporary, so that raising prices would be more sensible than going to the trouble of hiring more workers. Nor can any individual firm know for certain that firms in another sector will follow suit.

As we saw earlier, a decline in demand will normally shift the finance function up, but in some cases may leave the sales-growth frontier unaffected, resulting in a rise in price. If this behaviour becomes dominant in the capital goods sector, the new lower level of money demand will be accompanied by a still lower level of output and employment – lowered in proportion to the price rise. Consequently, with a lower wage bill, consumer profits, output and employment will be reduced, and the need to raise prices in consumer industries to maintain credit ratings will reduce output and employment still further. But although total profits remain the same, the realisation of profits is shifted from the consumer goods sector to capital goods.

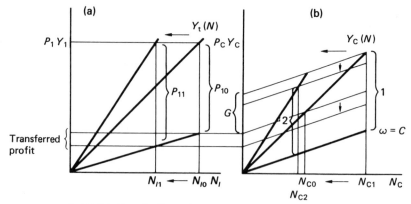

1 possible P_C, adjusting output
2 actual P_C after both sectors raise prices

Figure 12.18

Source: Nell (1988, p. 127)

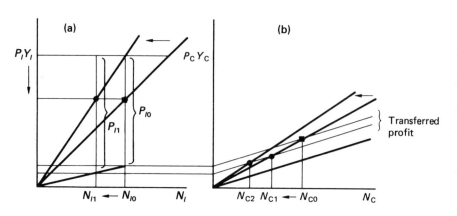

■ after drop in demand, before price increase
● after price increase, in capital goods

Figure 12.19

Source: Nell (1988, p. 128)

So, in the short run, with a given money wage, a policy of raising prices in response to demand changes tends to benefit the capital goods sector at the expense of workers and the firm in the consumer goods sector, regardless of the direction of the initial change in demand.[18] Nor surprisingly, a symmetrical result can be established for price declines. If demand falls and prices are lowered, say, in the capital goods sector, more items will be sold, so if the drop is equi-proportional to the decline in demand, employment will be maintained unchanged, and consequently the wage bill will be the same, though profits will be less. Competitive pressures may tend to lower prices in the consumer goods sector. If they do, then output and employment will be higher than otherwise there, too. Since the wage bill of the capital goods sector generates the profit of the consumer goods sector, the effect will be to raise the proportion of profit realised in the consumer goods sector.

A policy of raising prices in response to variations in effective demand tends to lead not only to inflation, but to sluggishness or even recession in output and employment, while a policy of price-cutting in response to demand declines can tend to help to prevent slumps from worsening. This corresponds to empirical finds: in the era of pre-corporate capitalism, before the rise of the great oligopolies and conglomerates, downturns showed up primarily in falling prices, with relatively minor fluctuations in output. Since the 1920s, however, prices have fallen very little or not at all during downswings, in recent years even rising, while the fluctuations in output and employment have been considerable (Nell, 1988, ch. 4; Sylos-Labini, 1984, part III; Semmler, 1984, ch.3).

Notes

1. The relation between pricing and growth has received official recognition. During the late 1960s and the 1970s the British National Board of Prices and Incomes used 'the effect which a particular level of profit has on the firm's ability to finance future investment' as one of the criteria for approving a higher price (Pickering, 1971, p. 232).
2. In the traditional theory, growth is understood to mean movement toward the optimal size. For example, in his classic *Structure of Competitive Industry*, E. A. G. Robinson (1931) devotes chapters to discussing optimal technical size and managerial size, the optimum financial unit and the optimal marketing unit, thus necessitating a separate chapter on the 'Reconciliation of Differing Optima'.
3. Eichner (1987) presents a simple algebraic model, starting from the expression for the required investment in an industry,

$$z_i = g_i b_i (p_i q_i) = p_i q_i - c_i q_i,$$

where p is price, q quantity, b the capital–output ratio, and g the growth rate of demand, all for the ith product. Then,

$$(p_i - c_i)/p_i = m_i = g_i b_i,$$

or

$$g_i = \frac{m_i}{b_i},$$

which Eichner contends is the Harrod-Domar relationship, since m is the profit margin, or corporate saving ratio. Further

$$p_i = \frac{c_i}{(1 - g_i b_i)}$$

a positive relationship between the growth rate of demand for the ith product and its price. Eichner argues that this enables us to connect pricing and growth in an input-output formulation since costs can be broken down. But what stands out here is that the rate of growth of demand is taken as given. The ith industry's price has no influence on the rate of growth of its demand, nor does its investment, which implies either that it does not invest in sales and distribution, or that such investment has no impact.

4. Harcourt and Kenyon (1976) accept Eichner's idea that the division of finance between internal and external is a matter of cost. When the implicit interest rate on internal funds lies below the market rate, retained earnings will be used; when investment requirements rise to where the implicit rate exceeds the market rate, the firm will turn to external sources. The firm can raise money by raising prices, or by borrowing, and it will do whatever is cheaper. This implies that in times of low real interest rates firms will turn extensively, even exclusively, to external financing; the historical record does not support this. Nor does this approach mention the problem of increasing risk – the larger the proportion of borrowing, the greater the risk of default in the event of a cyclical downturn. Yet such risk is surely a major factor limiting the use of external funds.

5. Wood (1976) and Harcourt and Kenyon (1976) both analyse the firm's problems in choosing methods of production. Whatever the other merits of their discussions, both contend that the choice of technique will influence and be influenced by the optimal price policy; since both analyses run into difficulties over the price–demand relationships, both solutions to the problem of selecting the best technique must be set aside.

6. The traditional approach has focused on the possibility of the firm using price to exercise some control over its current level of demand. In a growing economy with technical progress, prices will have to be related to investment; moreover, macroeconomics suggests that firms cannot reliably control current demand. But in the long run, there is an important distinction between conditions in which they can and those in which they cannot reasonably expect to influence the growth of their markets (Nell, 1980). Elsewhere I have tried to set out an analytical treatment of the case where firms adopt prices that will finance the capacity to serve a growing market over which they have no control (Nell, 1988). This will normally be a kind of competitive market; certainly it need not be an oligopoly. But prices will tend to be inflexible in the face of short-run variations in demand.

7. Inelastic-steep-demand curves are characteristic of markets for manufactures, both consumer and capital goods, because there tend to be strongly complementarities in their use. Consumer goods have to fit together into a coherent lifestyle; capital goods into a manufacturing process. Only rarely can a single element be changed, the others remaining the same. However, at very high prices purchases will be cut back and other less appropriate goods substituted, or perhaps that part of the lifestyle or process will be adjusted, so that many goods will be affected.

8. New markets may be markets of the same social class or group, but located in a

different geographical region; or they may be in the same region, but involve an appeal to a new social grouping. In the former case new distributional outlets will be needed; in the latter, a new advertising and promotional campaign will have to be devised. So the implications for sales investment will be different in the two cases, but in each sales investment will be called for.

9. The calculation here concerns borrower's risk. Lender's risk may also exist, in which case the costs of borrowing would rise, rather than being flat as shown in the diagram. Cf. Minsky (1986), Kalecki (1971), Harcourt and Kenyon (1976).

10. In the theory of monopolistic competition selling costs are considered, but they are treated exclusively as current costs; the capital costs incurred by developing new markets are never examined (Chamberlin, 1962; Taylor and Weiserbs, 1972; Eichner, 1976; Kaldor, 1950-1). As early as 1931 E. A. G. Robinson referred to the 'whole expenditure on wages, buildings, equipment and organization necessary to bring the goods to market' (p. 65), and later noting the long-term effects of a selling effort, he points out that 'once the market has been won, it can be retained at a lower selling cost than necessary to secure it initially' (p. 68). Clearly long-term costs are incurred for long-term gains.

11. A restrictive monetary policy, causing i to rise, will after a time raise F; by the same token, as credit is both more expensive and more difficult to obtain, it will reduce B. Thus restrictive monetary policy both tends to raise prices and lower the growth of sales – it exacerbates inflation and tends to bring recession.

12. The rise in W is due to a rise in the wage rate; hence the new spending will come out of the additional wage income, which might require some adjustment lag, unless some form of consumer finance is available to bridge the gap.

13. The pre-existing 'book of blueprints' is a neo-Classical fiction, and has no role in a realistic theory. There may be, and often is, more than one way to produce a particular item; there are seldom many ways, and in general different methods of production will result in products with different characteristics (Hollis and Nell, 1975). These differences may appear unimportant at first, but later turn to have considerable significance in marketing. Process innovations tend to arise from learning by doing, and learning by using (Rosenberg, 1980) and product innovation from learning by selling.

14. 'Beachhead' and 'bottleneck' models undoubtedly contain a certain amount of good sense (Baldwin, 1988; Dornbusch, 1987; Dixit and Stiglitz, 1987). Entry and exit conditions are asymmetrical; if an exchange rate change induces entry, and equivalent change back will not cause all entrants to exit, an exchange rate change is assumed to increase capacity; when it changes back, however, capacity does not decrease. The result will be a discontinuity in marginal costs, and therefore in the movement of prices. But all such models rely on the framework of monopolistic competition, in which current output and prices are adjusted together. Exchange rate changes, however, take place in the context of a growing economy, and their effects have to be examined in the context of corporate planning for the financing of growth.

15. Marshall referred to the danger of "spoiling the market' by reckless price-cutting; many business leaders have bemoaned cut-throat competition (Brown, 1924).

16. Mainstream attempts to explain the comparative stickiness of prices in the face of demand fluctuations have centred on the role of money wages, assuming that if wages hold steady prices will too. But if prices are not governed by marginal costs, this assumption may well be unjustified. Their explanations of money wage rigidity are likewise unconvincing. Rigidity has been attributed to 'implicit contracts', to 'efficiency wage' considerations, and to 'imperfections' such as

inadequate flows of information and the absence of an auctioneer. But the important implicit contract for labour, one US unions long tried to make explicit, would concern *incomes* – a Guaranteed Annual Income – not wage rates. It is simply not clear why and how an implicit contract on wage rates would benefit both sides sufficiently to ensure voluntary compliance over the cycle. Why should either side continue to comply during a long period of boom/slump in which the maintenance of the contract is to their disadvantage? As for efficiency wage explanations, they rely on *ad hoc* assumptions about asymmetry of information, set in the context of a wholly implausible account of labour supply. Imperfectionist arguments can be used to justify 'rationed' supply and demand functions, but the foundations are therefore once again *ad hoc*. A further strain on credibility comes with the requirement that the current spending of firms is to be constrained by their current income. If this were so we would not have the kind of credit markets that we do have.

17. The output of each sector consist of heterogeneous goods that must be aggregated, and the diagram cannot be drawn unless we know the amount of consumer goods that a unit of capital goods commands. These value relationships are derived from the long-term 'normal' prices in the established markets, for these are the prices on the basis of which contracts have been drawn, fixed capital constructed, and employment relationships established. These prices, of course, are not strictly fixed, but they will tend to move slowly. Such prices correspond to Classical 'natural' prices or prices of production; they are associated in each industry with a normal rate of profit. The rates vary between industries according to special conditions. The chief of these, we have argued, are variations in the growth possibilities of new markets, in conjunction with technological requirements expressed in the capital–output ratio. Together with the conditions for external finance, these explain the deviations from the norm in the profits of particular firms.

18. Such a price increase cannot be distinguished from a productivity increase on the diagrams here. Both are represented by an upward swing of the productivity line, since every level of employment will produce a higher money value of output. If the diagrams were in real terms, then the distinction is easily made; but we are taking investment demand to be set in monetary terms.

References

Andrews, H. W. S., *Manufacturing Business* (London: Macmillan, 1949).
Andrews, H. W. S., *On Competition in Economic Theory* (London: Macmillan, 1954).
Asimakopulos, A., *Microeconomics: An Introduction to Economic Theory* (Oxford: Oxford University Press, 1979).
Bain, Joe S., *Barriers to New Competition* (Cambridge, Mass: Harvard University Press, 1956).
Baldwin, R., 'Hysteresis in Import Prices: The Beachhead Effect', *American Economic Review* (September 1988).
Baran, P., and P. Sweezy, *Monopoly Capital*, rev. edn (New York: Harcourt Brace and World, 1967).
Baron, D., 'Limit Pricing, Potential Entry and Barriers to Entry', *American Economic Review*, 63(4), (1973) pp. 666–74.

Baumol, W., *Business Behavior, Value and Growth*, rev. edn (New York: Harcourt Brace and World, 1967).

Berle, A. and G. Means, *The Modern Corporation and Private Property* (New York: Macmillan, 1933).

Bhagwati, J., 'Oligopoly Theory, Entry-Prevention and Growth', *Oxford Economic Papers*, 22 (1970) pp. 297–310.

Blair, J., *Economic Concentration: Structure, Behavior and Policy* (New York: Harcourt Brace Jovanovich, 1972).

Brown, Donaldson, 'Pricing Policy in Relation to Financial Control', *Management and Administration*, articles 2–4, vol. 7 (1924) pp. 195–8, 283–6, 417–22.

Chamberlin, Edward H., *The Theory of Monopolistic Competition: A Reorientation of the Theory of Value* (Cambridge, Mass.: Harvard University Press, 1962).

Chandler, A. D., *The Visible Hand: The Managerial Revolution in American Business* (Cambridge, Mass.: Harvard University Press, 1977).

Clifton, J., 'Competition and the Evolution of the Capitalist Mode of Production', *Cambridge Journal of Economics*, vol. 1 (June 1977) pp. 137–51.

Clifton, J., 'Administered Prices in the Context of Capitalist Development', *Contributions to Political Economy*, 2 (1983) pp. 23–38.

Comanor, W. and T. Wilson, 'Advertising Market Structure and Performance', *Review of Economics and Statistics*, 49 (November 1967) pp. 423–40.

Cornwall, J., *Modern Capitalism* (New York: M. E. Sharpe, 1977).

Coutts, K., W. Godley and W. Nordhaus, *Industrial Prices in the United Kingdom* (Cambridge: Cambridge University Press, 1978).

Dalton, J. A., 'Administered Inflation and Business Pricing: Another Look', *Review of Economic and Statistics*, 55 (November 1973) pp. 516–19.

Dixit, Avinash and Joseph Stiglitz, 'Entry and Exit Decisions of Firms Under Fluctuating Real Exchange Rates', mimeo (September 1987).

Dornbusch, R., 'Exchange Rates and Prices', *American Economic Review*, vol. 77, no. 1 (March 1987).

Eatwell, J., 'Growth, Profitability and Size – The Empirical Evidence', in R. Marris and A. Wood (eds), *The Corporate Economy* (Cambridge, Mass.: Harvard University Press, 1971) pp. 379–422.

Eatwell, J., 'Competition', in Bradley and Howard (eds), *Classical and Marxian Political Economy: Essays in Memory of Ronald Meek* (London: Macmillan, 1982) pp. 23–46.

Eckstein, D. and G. Fromm, 'The Price Equation', *American Economic Review* (December 1958) pp. 1159–83.

Eichner, A., *The Megacorp and Oligopoly* (Cambridge: Cambridge University Press, 1976).

Eichner, A., 'A General Model of Investment and Pricing', in E. Nell (ed.), *Growth, Profits and Property* (Cambridge: Cambridge University Press, 1980) pp. 118–33.

Eichner, A., *The Macrodynamics of Advanced Market Economies* (New York: M. E. Sharpe, 1987).

Godley, W., 'Cost Prices and Demand in the Short Run', in Surrey (ed.), *Macroeconomic Themes* (Oxford: Oxford University Press, 1959).

Grossman, J. and D. Hart, 'Implicity Contracts Under Asymmetrical Information', *Quarterly Journal of Economics*, 98 (1983) pp. 123–56.

Hall, R. and C. Hitch, 'Price Theory and Business Behavior', *Oxford Economic Papers*, no. 2 (1936).

Harcourt, G. and P. Kenyon, 'Pricing and the Investment Decision', *Kyklos*, 29 (1976) pp. 449–77.

Hazledine, I., 'Determination of the Mark-up Under Oligopoly: A Comment', *Economic Journal*, 84 (December 1984) pp. 967–70.

Herman, S., *Corporate Control, Corporate Power* (Cambridge: Cambridge University Press, 1981).

Hodgson, G., *Economics and Institutions* (Cambridge: Cambridge University Press, 1988).

Hollis, M. and E. Nell, *Rational Economic Man* (Cambridge: Cambridge University Press, 1975).

Hymer, S., *The Multinational Corporation: A Radical Approach* (Cambridge: Cambridge University Press, 1979).

Kaldor, N., 'The Economic Aspects of Advertising', *Review of Economic Studies*, 18 (1950-1) pp. 1–27.

Kalecki, M., 'Costs and Prices', in *Selected Essays on the Dynamics of the Capitalist Economy, 1933–1970* (Cambridge: Cambridge University Press, 1971) pp. 43–62.

Kaplan, A., J. Dirlam and R. Lanzilotti, *Pricing in Big Business* (Washington, D.C.: The Brookings Institution, 1958).

Lagan, P., 'Changes in the Recession Behavior of Wholesale Prices in the 1920's and Post World War II', *Explorations of Economic Research*, winter, vol. 2 (1975) pp. 54–104.

Lanzilotti, R., 'Pricing Objectives in Larger Companies', *American Economic Review*, 48 (December 1958) pp. 921–40.

Lee, F., 'The Marginalist Controversy and the Demise of Full Cost Pricing', *Journal of Economic Issues*, vol. 18, no. 4 (1984).

Leijonhufvud, A., 'Capitalism and the Factory System', mimeo University of California-Los Angeles (1985).

Levine, D., 'Aspects of the Classical Theory of Markets', *Australian Economic Papers* (June 1980) pp. 1–15.

Marris, R. and A. Wood, *The Corporate Economy* (Cambridge, Mass.: Harvard University Press, 1971).

Marshall, A., *Principles of Economics*, 8th edn (London: Macmillan, 1920).

Means, G., *Industrial Prices and Their Relative Inflexibility*, 74th Cong. 1st, sess. Doc. 13 (1935).

Means, G., *Hearings on Administered Prices*, part 9. Senate Subcommittee on Antitrust and Monopoly, 86th Cong. 2nd sess. (1959) pp. 4745–60.

Means, G., 'The Administered Price Thesis Reconfirmed', *American Economic Review*, 61 (June 1972) pp. 292–306.

Meilo, R., *Pricing and Employment in the Trade Cycle* (Cambridge: Cambridge University Press, 1963).

Milberg, W., 'Exchange Rate Pass-Through Under Full Cost Pricing', mimeo (University of Michigan-Dearborn, 1988).

Modigliani, F., 'New Developments on the Oligopoly Front, *Journal of Political Economy*, 64 (1958) pp. 215–33.

Morris, D., P. Sinclair, M. Slater and S. Vickers, *Strategic Behavior and Industrial Competition*, (Oxford: Clarendon Press, 1986).

Mueller, D., 'The Persistence of Profits Above the Norm', *Economica*, 44 (1977) pp. 371–80.

Munkirs, J., *The Transformation of American Capitalism* (New York: M. E. Sharpe, 1985).

Nell, E., 'Competition and Price-Taking Behavior', in E. Nell (ed.), *Growth, Profits and Property* (Cambridge: Cambridge University Press, 1980) pp. 99–117.

Nell, E., *Prosperity and Public Spending* (London and Boston: Unwin Hyman, 1988).

Nell, E., *Transformational Growth and Effective Demand: Economics After the Capital Critique* (London: Macmillan, 1990).

Nordhaus, W. and W. Godley, 'Pricing in the Trade Cycle', *Economic Journal*, 82 (September 1972) pp. 853–82.

Okun, A., *Prices and Quantities* (Oxford: Basil Blackwell, 1981).

Penrose, E., *The Theory of the Growth of the Firm* (New York: John Wiley, 1959).

Pickering, J. F., 'The Price and Incomes Board and Price Sector Prices: A Survey', *Economic Journal*, 81 (June 1971) pp. 225–41.

Robinson, E. A. G., *The Structure of Competitive Industry* (Cambridge: Economic Handbooks, 1931).

Robinson, J., 'The Basic Theory of Normal Prices', *Quarterly Journal of Economics*, 76 (1962) pp. 1–19.

Roncaglia, A., *Sraffa and the Theory of Price* (New York: John Wiley, 1978).

Rosenberg, Nathan, 'Learning by Using', unpublished manuscript (1980).

Semmler. W., *Competition, Monopoly and Differential Profit Rates* (New York: Columbia University Press, 1984).

Solow, R., 'On Theories of Unemployment', *American Economic Review*, 70 (1980).

Steindl, J., *Maturity and Stagnation in American Capitalism* (New York: Monthly Review Press, 1976).

Stiglitz, J. and C. Shapiro, 'Equilibrium Unemployment as a Worker Discipline Device', *American Economic Review*, 74 (1984).

Sylos-Labini, P., *Oligopoly and Technical Progress* (Cambridge, Mass.: Harvard University Press, 1969).

Sylos-Labini, P., *The Forces of Economic Growth and Decline* (Cambridge, Mass.: MIT Press, 1984).

Taylor, Lester D. and Daniel Weiserbs, 'Advertising and the Aggregate Consumption Function', *American Economic Review*, vol. 62 (September 1972) pp. 642–55.

Tobin, J., *Macroeconomics, Prices and Quantities* (Oxford: Basil Blackwell, 1983).

Wenders, J., 'Entry and Monopolistic Pricing', *Journal of Political Economy*, 75 (1967) pp. 755–62.

Weston, J., 'Pricing Behavior of Large Firms', in J. Weston and Ormstein (eds), *The Impact of Large Firms* (Lexington, Mass.: Lexington Books, 1973).

Wood, A., *A Theory of Profits* (Cambridge: Cambridge University Press, 1976).

COMMENT

Richard Kopcke

Edward Nell's chapter certainly is ambitious and wide-ranging in discussing the principles behind a corporation's choice of output, prices, investment, leverage, and technology. However strongly we might accept with his theory of the firm, his story is stimulating and provocative. We have become too accustomed to regarding the theories of production, investment, and corporate finance as reasonably distinct topics, which frequently are published in different circles. Nell reminds us that all these theories can become much richer and more interesting once we transcend these artificial distinctions. Though I admire his ambition and vision, the problems he encounters also remind me why I generally stick to more limited theories of business behavior.

At the heart of Nell's chapter is an old issue: why do corporations pay dividends? Textbook theories, resting on assumptions of free competition, constant returns to scale, supply equalling demand, and often steady states, imply that dividends are either arbitrary or dictated by institutional details such as the incidence of income taxes, bankruptcy costs, agency costs, or the need to send signals to potential stockholders. Nell takes another approach that I find very promising: if corporations are oligopolistic competitors, if their return on assets falls as they expand their scale of operation, and if the number of profitable investment opportunities grows over time, then optimal dividends are dictated by the basic theory of the firm. If corporations distribute too little of their earnings to shareholders, they will grow too fast, their return on assets will dwindle, and their share prices will be depressed enough to invite a 'takeover'. If they distribute too much of their earnings as dividends, they risk being displaced by other firms, or their reliance on debt financing will become too great. The corporation's pricing policy, investment strategy, financial structure, and dividend payments are fundamentally coupled together in models such as Nell's.

Though I very much endorse this feature of the model, I have reservations about the way Nell's model put this feature to work. Other things equal, as a firm elects to grow more rapidly, the price of its products must fall in order to attract sufficient demand – the demand curve, expressing price as a function of the rate expansion, is downward-sloping. In contrast, with more rapid growth a firm must receive a greater price in order to finance the additional investment while maintaining its capital structure – the supply curve is upward-sloping. In essence, the model assumes that the firm's rate of growth is dictated by the intersection of these demand and supply curves. This may be true if the corporation is attempting to maximise its rate of growth, but this intersection may not describe a stable solution. We know that a profit-maximising monopolist chooses a rate of output and a price that lies neither on its demand curve nor on its average cost curve. By allowing the intersection of Nell's demand and supply curves to dictate the corporation's rate of growth, the firm is maximising neither its rate of profit nor its stock price; the firm also is not investing at the rate required to equate Tobin's q with one on marginal investments. Consequently, if the corporation invests at the rate dictated by the intersection of the demand and supply curves, it is vulnerable to 'raiders' who could profit by changing the firm's investment strategy.

The chapter's description of the corporation's choice of debt financing also invites second thoughts. As borrowing increases, the firm's fixed costs increase. If we admit that the sales are variable, the risk of default increases with leverage. The chapter proposes that the optimal leverage is described by that point where the constant gain from additional borrowing equals the implicit insurance premium required to offset the rising cost of default. But, increasing leverage tends to increase the rates of discount that both bond-holders and stock-holders use to value their investment income. Consequently, the value of the firm on the stock exchange potentially depends on the corporation's choice of leverage. The choice of leverage that maximises stock prices, for example, ordinarily does not coincide with the leverage that equates the gain from borrowing with the implicit insurance premium.

The chapter also examines how the firm might respond to unexpected shifts of the demand schedule for its output. Part of the analysis describes how the corporation might cope with a temporary drop in demand by raising the price of its product in order to sustain cash flow and to continue financing its long-run investment in the customary fashion. My reading of industries such as automobiles, steel, aluminum, etc. in the United States suggests that the effective price of output ordinarily falls, instead of rises, under these circumstances. My relationship with banking also compels me to mention that most corporations cultivate relationships with financial institutions (financial 'shock absorbers') to help them insulate their total sources of funds and their business planning from the vagaries of short-term business conditions. Often the maintenance of market share or of operations is of paramount importance during temporary slumps. Nell alludes to the firm's building of financial reserves in order to cope during recessions. I simply wish to stress that these reserves may take the form of prearranged calls on funds as well as cash balances. Some also contend that the finance capitalism which emerged earlier this century, that the conglomerates which may be considered diversified investment trusts, and that the emergence of 'banks' within modern industrial corporations, are other ways firms can 'hedge' their sources of funds. Corporations may value expansion for reasons other than merely earning a profit.

With the recent emphasis on asset-based financing and collateralisation by many lenders, firms that choose techniques of production that require greater capital-labour ratios may have relatively little difficulty in establishing lines of credit with financial intermediaries. This credit may not only supply a financial reserve or 'working capital', it also may allow the firm to increase its leverage as collateral encourages lenders to regard low coverage ratios with more patience. For this reason, as well as others related to fixed costs and the volume of cash flow, the consequences of the choosing a capital-intensive technology rather than a labour-intensive technology may be more complex than the chapter suggests.

The final section of the chapter provides an interesting analysis of the economy's response to a demand shock. Through examples, this section illustrates the conclusion that business pricing behaviour can amplify or dampen business cycles, both for industries producing consumer goods and industries producing investment goods. But, in these examples, pricing behaviour depends only on the market power of corporations, not their access to capital, which depends on the characteristics of financial institutions.

Nell observes that business cycles before the 1920s influenced prices more than output. Before the rise of oligopolies, firms were less able to protect their cash flow by raising prices during slumps. After the 1920s, however, business cycles have influenced output more than prices, presumably due to the rise of oligopolies. I have four principle reservations about this conclusion. First, my reading of the literature on oligopoly pricing suggests that it is not at all clear that oligopolists' prices ought to be less procyclical than those of competitive firms. Second, except for the 1930s, prices may have varied less after the Second World War than they did before the First World War (depending on the measure of prices and the intervals compared), but also business cycles generally have been less severe since the Second World War. Third, monetary policy, corporations' access to financing, and savers' faith in financial institutions seem to have become more stable after the Second World War for many reasons. This financial stability might diminish the influence of short-term business conditions on corporations' sources and uses of funds and on their pricing strategy. Last, taking into account both foreign and domestic competition, it is not clear that his is the age of the great oligopolies when we consider the market power exercised by many firms from the 1880s to the 1930s.

In summary, Nell's chapter is stimulating because it encourages us to consider a richer theory of the firm by linking descriptions of production, prices, investment, and corporate finance. Despite the considerable scope and ambition of the theory, I would suggest that it still wants development in two fundamental respects. First, I would like to see more analysis of the objectives of the corporation. Can or should its single goal be the maximisation of growth? Second, in order for the theory to describe the behaviour of prices and investment during business cycles, I would like to see a more explicitly dynamic, rather than static, model of the firm, wherein corporations weigh their objectives over more than one year in order to make this year's decisions.

13 The Twin Deficits

Robert Eisner

My message in this chapter is that deficits can be good for you. In fact, deficits can be too large, and they can be too small. But we cannot tell which until we know how to measure them. And most people talking about deficits really have no notion how they are measured. The fact is that the way we do measure them has very uncertain economic relevance, and, in particular, the US federal budget and the deficit are calculated in a way which would send chills up the spines of almost any sensible private business accountant.

First, let me point out that deficit adds to debt. As everyone knows, a deficit is the difference between what one is spending and what one is taking in. If we spend more than we take in as income, we have a deficit. This is true for an individual, a business or government. Thus we need to borrow as we do. The alternative, of course, is to sell off assets. Then we run up a debt, and if we have a debt at one point of, say, $10 000 and we spend $1000 more than we take in, our debt goes up to $11 000; and so it is for the federal government. However, we must remember that one person's debt is another person's asset. Indeed, I often wonder how many people stop to think when they worry about federal government debt and want to reduce it or even convert it into some kind of a surplus, that if the federal government had a surplus, it means the private sector would have a deficit. The government debt is your asset. Let me suggest that if, for example, the government had decided to give a number of people each $100 000 in new Treasury bills this, of course, would raise the federal debt by $100 000 times the number of people to whom the new bills were given. Now it seems quite natural that each of the beneficiaries of the give-away bills would feel richer and probably therefore decide that they need not save as much, but can go out and spend more. And that is precisely what economic theorists would correctly argue, a few exceptions notwithstanding. So the general notion is that if the US federal debt is bigger, the private sector is richer and it will spend more. By including more spending, a federal debt is not necessarily bad. Obviously, if people try to spend more than can be produced then there will be inflation. And at some point, I concede, when we get close to the maximum of what can be produced and people are still trying to spend more because everybody is giving out these $100 000 in Treasury bills, which is what the federal government does when it runs a deficit, then we would have to worry about how costly inflation would be and what to do about it.

Table 13.1   Inflation tax and real debt
(all figures in US billions)

1979	Debt	$800
1980	Inflation tax	− 80
1980	Old real debt	720
1980	Deficit	+ 60
1980	Real debt	$780
	$800 to $780 =	$20 Real surplus

On the other hand, while recognising that the deficit adds to debt, we have to discern that what would affect private spending is not just the money value of the debt, but what it is worth in real terms, which so many people tend to forget. That fact led, I would say, to some grievous mistakes of public policy by the previous administration in the US. It was thought the US had deficits, when, as it will be shown below, it did not then have a *real* deficit, real in the sense that economists would mean, adjusted for inflation.

At the end of 1979, as is shown in Table 13.1, we had a debt of approximately $800 billion in round numbers. It had, however, an inflation rate such that the value of the dollar was falling by about 10 per cent, which meant it had what can be called an inflation tax on the holders of the government debt, so that by the end of 1980 the old $800 billion was worth only $720 billion when adjusted for inflation. The deficit in the national income accounts showed as $60 billion for 1979; thus, the total debt, the £720 billion left from the previous year adjusted for inflation and the new $60 billion, was in real terms $780 billion. Did the country really have a deficit then? A deficit adds to debt, but in *real* terms; the debt in this instance had gone down and the deficit therefore was not a real deficit, but a real surplus.

The Carter administration did not recognise that, but thought that since the country had a terrible inflation it must cut the deficit by tightening the money supply. Paul Volcker, the then Federal Reserve Board Chairman, was encouraged to do this despite the objections by some members of the administration. And what was the result? In fact even in 1981 the Reagan administration, partly because Congress resisted immediate tax cuts, was following the Carter policy and the US found itself in the worst recession since the Great Depression, with unemployment reaching 10.7 per cent. I blame that on a combination of real budget surplus which was drawing purchasing power away from the public, and the tight money.

As shown in Table 13.2 the federal US unified budget for 1988 had an official deficit of $155 billion. You will recall I indicated earlier that federal accounting would put chills down the spine of any private business such as General Motors and IBM the biggest and most profitable companies,

Table 13.2   Adjusted and unadjusted deficit, FY 1988
(all figures in US billions)

Federal unified budget deficit	− $155
Net investment (estimated)	+ 70
Federal budget, current account deficit	− 85
State and local budgets surplus	+ 55
Total government budget deficit	− 30
Inflation tax: 3.6% of 2050	+ 74
Total government, adjusted surplus	+ $ 44

which by federal government accounting would have been showing almost every year a deficit. What I mean by 'a deficit' is that these corporate giants are spending more than their revenues. 'How is it possible?' one might ask. 'There is borrowing,' it would be the answer. Even when their debt would go up year after year, it would never occur to anyone to say that since these companies are running deficits, are in danger of bankruptcy, because as business accounting would have it , IBM and General Motors do not count capital spending in the profit and loss statements, but only the depreciation; that is, the using up of capital assets, not the cost of acquisition. If the same accounting scheme was used for the federal government, on the basis of the official OMB estimates for federal government investment spending which is over $200 billion a year, calculating a reasonable depreciation allowance and substituting that depreciation allowance for the capital investment spending, which means subtracting net investment by the federal government from the budget, these accounting modifications would have resulted in a decrease of $70 billion in the federal budget. This immediately would have reduced the $155 billion deficit – shown for 1988 – down to $85 billion.

Next, since we are interested not just in the federal government, but the total impact of government on the economy, we have to recognise that the state and local governments are in many ways much larger, receive a big income from the public, and the federal government gives them over $100 billion dollars a year in grants. It does not make much sense to say, look at this big federal deficit, and forget that the federal government is running a deficit in part because it gives money to state and local governments which in turn have a surplus. If we then combine the two and take the state and local budget surpluses which totalled $55 billion over the last fiscal year and subtract it from the federal deficit, we shall further reduce it down to $30 billion.

Finally and with reference to Table 13.2, what is relevant to the economy is the real debt. We have to say, therefore, that the real debt did not go up

Table 13.3   Deficit with constant debt-to-GNP ratio
(all figures in US billions except ratios)

	Debt	GNP	Ratio
1988	$2050	$4900	.418
7.465% growth	153	366	.418
1989	$2203	$5266	.418
Deficit – increase in debt – $153			

by $30 billion in 1988 because the inflation rate had been in the last fiscal year about 3.6 per cent; its effect on $2050 billion, the gross debt held by the public at the end of the year, was approximately $74 billion. We need to take that $74 billion of inflation tax away from the $30 billion which in turn yields a surplus of $44 billion.

There is obviously a particular scheme of accounting which ignores economic theory and economic relevance and which private business practises. Table 13.3 indicates what I would suggest is an appropriate notion of balance. If we were to ask ourselves what the United States' debt is now and what it was ten years ago, we may recognise that as a result of a purchase, for example, of a real asset our debt perhaps is higher now than then. But now perhaps our income is twice what it was ten years ago. If our debt is a smaller portion of our income, we might determine that it is not as much of a problem.

Similarly, let me suggest that a good notion of balance for the government, like for a business or an individual, is to keep debt in line with income. The relevant measure of income for the government would be national income or gross national product which is growing; it grew in 1989 at precisely 7.465 per cent. This means that for the debt to stay in the same ratio to GNP, which in 1988 was 41.8 per cent, it can grow for the year 1989, by 7.465 per cent, if GNP continues to grow at that rate. As shown in Table 13.3, 7.465 per cent of $2050 billion – the total accumulated debt as of 1988 – yields $153 billion. This limit would maintain the same ratio of debt to GNP for 1989, which means it would be just about in balance, as indeed the numbers in the Economic Report of the President will indicate; that is the debt/GNP ratio is now stabilised.

It can be argued that perhaps it should be lower or higher. But the first thing to ask is, what is so out of line now? Unlike in previous years, in fact, the deficit even conventionally measured in 1989 was only about 3 per cent of GNP as opposed to 1983 when it was 5.4 per cent of GNP. In 1989, it was almost half of what it was. Of course, it may be asked why should it not be zero?

Why have a special rule for the government that it cannot borrow. We do not tell individuals or businesses they cannot borrow, particularly if their incomes or revenues are increasing.

Table 13.4 Federal government consolidated balance sheet*, liabilities and tangible and financial assets

Item	Year and amount (billions of dollars)			
	1945	1960	1980	1984
Tangible assets	186.2	205.8	822.5	1118.0
Reproducible assets	179.3	187.4	648.1	915.2
Land	6.8	18.4	174.4	202.8
Financial assets	102.8	124.7	720.9	887.4
Total assets	289.0	330.4	1543.4	2005.4
Total liabilities	332.6	331.8	1161.6	2063.3
Net debt (total liabilities) minus financial assets)	229.8	207.1	440.7	1175.9
Net worth	−43.7	−1.3	381.3	−57.9

*Including Federal Reserve and credit agencies, based on market or replacement values.
Source: Robert Eisner, *How Real Is the Federal Deficit?* (1986), table 3.3, p. 29.

Let me move to some other dramatic points I want to make. First, one might have been troubled by my argument about IBM and General Motors borrowing. One may say, that they have assets to show for it. In the case of federal borrowing, the assets we should be concerned with are the wealth of the American people, the whole wealth of the country; ultimately, we can say the government can borrow against that wealth.

But even looking at the federal government balance sheet narrowly, Table 13.4 shows that while in 1945 we had by reasonably conventional measures a negative net worth, despite year after year of deficits – almost all the years were deficits, even before President Reagan, I assure you – we, by 1980, had a net worth which was substantially positive because the value of our assets kept growing. The government and affiliated agencies, credit agencies, were acquiring many financial assets. It is true that by 1984 our net worth was again a negative number, but Michael Boskin, who is now the current chairman of the Council of Economic Advisors, has done work parallel to mine and in it he includes assets of the government such as the natural resources on federal lands which when added will yield a substantially positive number.

In Table 13.5, you will notice that the ratio of debt to GNP, which I have mentioned earlier, would have been thought of as troublesome, if not a disaster (113.9 per cent), in 1946. However, despite years of deficits, by 1980 the same ratio was down to 26 per cent. It is true that the Reagan Administration deficits brought it up over 40 per cent, but it is pretty much stabilised, as I pointed out earlier. In 1988, it was precisely 41.8 per cent. In any event, how can we be so certain that 42 per cent is a disaster, that we have to say the education president cannot spend more on education or the

Table 13.5   Measures of the federal debt*

| Year | Gross federal debt held by public | | Net debt per capita |
	Billions of dollars	% of GNP	1982 dollars
1945	232.2	110.2	8639
1946	241.9	113.9	7227
1960	237.2	46.0	3576
1970	284.9	28.1	2815
1980	715.1	26.2**	2219
1984	1312.6	34.5	4496
1986	1746.1	40.9	5963
1987	1888.1	41.3	
1988	2050.0	41.8	
Change,			
1945–80	+479.9	−84.0	−6420
Change,			
1980–84	+597.5	+8.3	+2277
Change,			
1984–86	+433.5	+6.4	+1467
Change,			
1986–88	+303.0	+0.9	

*Adapted and updated from Eisner, *How Real Is the Federal Deficit?* (1986) tables 2.3 and 2.5, pp. 18–19, 21.
**Percent of 3rd quarter GNP for this and subsequent years. For years up to 1970, where fiscal years ended 30 June, percents were of corresponding calendar year GNP.

drug czar has no more money to put into fighting drugs because the ratio is 42 per cent? Even when John F. Kennedy took office, the same ratio was 46 per cent.

Figure 13.1 taken out of a previous work (Eisner, 1986) shows the relation of deficits to the economy – an old Keynesian notion with which everyone is familiar. The relation incidentally is also confirmed by least squares regressions and first-order autoregressive corrections. The relationship is between the deficit which is now adjusted for inflation – what can be otherwise called as the structural, high employment deficit – and the subsequent growth in real GNP, over the years 1959 to 1984. Notice that when the deficit was lower, the growth in real GNP was less the next year. Conversely, when the deficit was bigger, the growth in real GNP was bigger as well. The few years when the US experienced a real surplus, the GNP went down.

It can be argued that the relation is spurious or a simplistic way of looking at it, that there may have been other factors at work; perhaps the economy normally somehow rebounds every other year. But I am persuaded that it is not, because there is good theory behind it which relates to just what I mentioned earlier. If one gets an extra $100 000 in Treasury

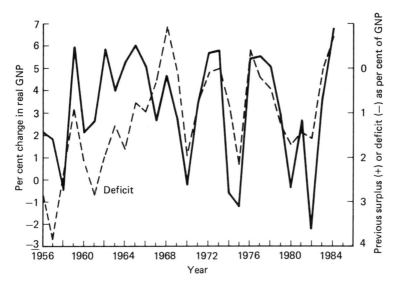

Figure 13.1   Adjusted deficit and change in GNP

Note: The greater the price-adjusted high-employment deficit (broken line), the greater the subsequent growth in gross national product (solid line).
Source: R. Eisner, *How Real is the Federal Deficit* (1986) figure 8.2, p. 91.

bills, one is likely to spend more. And that is what the effect of a deficit is. It makes people spend more. Of course, one might tell us that we cannot spend more and raise GNP if we are at full employment and cannot produce more. The sad and most fundamental part of my story, at least over these years, is that we were hardly ever at full employment. Therefore, wherever people were able to spend more, the effect was not to bid up prices, but to give us more real GNP. If GNP goes up in real terms, employment goes up too and unemployment goes down. Figure 13.2 tells us exactly that; it shows that the bigger the surplus or the less the deficit, the bigger the growth in unemployment the following year.

The next figure, 13.3, illustrates an interesting relation. You will recall that in 1987 we were told that the market crashed because of the budget deficit; it must have caused it. I would like to point out that if that were the case, it is curious that just before the crash the deficit had gone down. To the extent we believe in rational expectations and efficient markets, it was the new news that counted. The new news in October was that the budget deficit for that fiscal year would be less than expected. Figure 13.3 depicts the change in the deficit against the change in the Dow Jones industrials average – the same results confirmed by least squares regressions as well. Notice the bigger the increase in the deficit, the more the Dow went up. What has happened with all these years of deficits? Have they ruined the stock market or has the market been soaring? I do not really want to insist

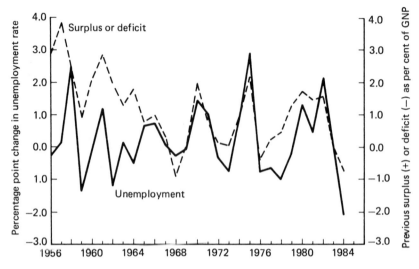

Figure 13.2   Adjusted surplus and change in unemployment

Note: Lesser surpluses or greater deficits (broken line) go with reduced unemployment (solid line).
Source: R. Eisner, *How Real is the Federal Deficit* (1986) figure 8.3, p. 93.

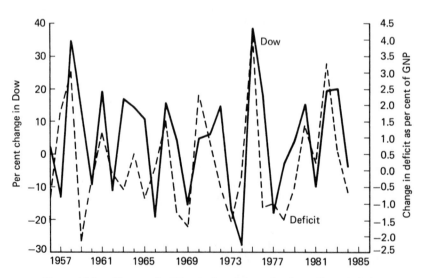

Figure 13.3   Changes in Dow industrials and price-adjusted deficit
Source: R. Eisner, *How Real is the Federal Deficit* (1986) figure 11.1, p. 138.

on this relationship since I believe that matters are undoubtedly much more complicated and remote.

On the other hand, it has been argued that the problem with deficits is associated with borrowing against the future; that is, a burden is being imposed on a future generation. This has been expressed, I believe, rather naively in that each newborn child inherits many thousands of dollars of debt. Debt to whom? To whom does he owe it? He owes it to every child being born today. So at this level of abstraction the issue does not make very much sense. You will recall, one person's debt is another person's asset. So the fact that there is a lot of debt does not make anyone poorer. It is not a debt owed to foreign countries, and I shall come back to this issue later.

Another issue is that somehow the deficit hurts investment. Investment, you will recall, is the acquisition of something which will be productive in the future. Suppose I convinced you that deficits are creating current prosperity – that, you would acknowledge – but at the expense of the future because they are leading us to invest less in the future. This means we are living it up now at the expense of our children and our grand-children. Then the question is, what is happening to investment? Part of the problem here is that too much of the public and most of the economics profession are mesmerised by, not the investment of economic theory which is the acquisition of any kind of good or capital that will be productive in the future, but by a very narrow measure of investment that we call gross private domestic investment.

Table 13.6 includes the least squares regressions not just of GNP, but of its components, of consumption, investment, government expenditures and net exports, and the change in the monetary base (ΔMB). Money does matter and the relationship indicates that increases in the monetary base are associated with growth in real GNP. Let me now concentrate on several of these results.

Notice in the GNP line in the table that the coefficient under the column marked PAHES, which is price-adjusted, high-employment surplus, is minus 1.568. This simply bears out the relation depicted in Figure 13.1 indicating that each percentage point of deficit as a percent of GNP was associated on average with an increase in real GNP of 1.568 per cent the next year. The explanation might be that it was all from a consumption binge. In fact, it was not. If we look at the consumption line of Table 13.6, we will notice that there is a significant coefficient for consumption, minus .642, indicating that consumption tended to grow by .642 of 1 per cent of GNP for each percentage point of deficit. But looking at the next line we notice that investment was even more. We had a 1.383 per cent growth in investment as a percent of GNP for each percentage point of deficit.

There is also the argument that deficits crowd out investment. That is, the amount that people save that would otherwise go to finance investment

Table 13.6 Real high-employment budgets, changes in monetary base, and changes in components of GNP*

$$\Delta COM_t = b_{01}X_1 + b_{02}X_2 + b_1PAHES_{t-1} + b_2\Delta MB_{t-1}$$

$$X_1 = 1, X_2 = 0 \quad \text{for } t = 1962,...,1966$$

$$X_1 = 0, X_2 = 1 \quad \text{for } t = 1967,...,1984$$

Regression coefficients**

Constants

Component (COM)	1962–66 (b_{01})	1967–84 (b_{02})	$PAHES_{t-1}$ (b_1)	ΔMB_{t-1} (b_2)	$\bar{R}$	D–W
Consumption	3.401 (0.675)	2.339 (0.303)	–0.642 (0.263)	2.393 (1.592)	.580	1.91
Investment	2.613 (1.176)	1.135 (0.541)	–1.383 (0.414)	3.587 (2.411)	.570	1.99
Government	1.195 (0.558)	0.483 (0.270)	–1.113 (0.172)	–0.660 (0.981)	.354	1.52
Net exports	–1.615 (1.273)	–0.766 (1.012)	0.399 (0.137)	1.625 (0.811)	.512	1.45
GNP	6.208 (1.296)	3.371 (0.585)	–1.568 (0.479)	7.172 (2.830)	.735	2.03
Domestic	7.405 (1.506)	3.934 (0.675)	–2.141 (0.560)	5.149 (3.295)	.767	1.93

*From Eisner (1986) table 9.8, p. 110.
**Least squares with Cochrane-Orcutt, first-order autoregressive corrections; standard errors in parentheses.
ΔCOM = change in component as per cent of GNP.
$PAHES$ = price-adjusted high-employment surplus as per cent of GNP.
ΔMB = real change in monetary base as per cent of GNP

instead goes to buy government securities. Again the fact is, if we look at the gross private domestic investment, we did not have crowding out. We had what I shall call crowding in. The reason is not far to seek, since if we go out and buy another car, the car manufacturer will invest more not less. Thus, if consumption goes up, investment tends to go up as well, as long as there is capacity to produce more investment goods.

Finally, another matter we might note here is that of the line on net exports – and there I have a concession to make. Budget deficits have contributed to trade deficits. Why do budget deficits cause trade deficits? Because if the budget deficit makes us spend more, we are not only going to buy Chryslers, we might buy Toyotas and Sonys as well. As long as we are not a closed economy some of our increased prosperity is manifested as increased demand, spills into foreign purchases causing imports to go up

Table 13.7   Capital stocks, 1981*

Component of capital	Billions of current dollars
Business	6 085.9
Tangible	5 528.9
Intangible (R & D)	557.0
Nonprofit	248.2
Government	2 220.4
Government enterprise	476.3
Household	14 626.0
Tangible	3 949.7
Intangible (human)	10 676.3
Total	23 746.4

*From Eisner, 'The Total Incomes System of Accounts', *Survey of Current Business* (January 1985) tables 13 and 14, p. 47.

which create a trade deficit. But if we look at it that way, that is, the budget deficit created a trade deficit, then to eliminate both the budget and the trade deficits, it will mean preventing us from spending as much. So should we say that we are so poor we cannot buy Toyotas any more or Chryslers either, and as a result let the Chrysler workers be laid off in the state of Michigan? I think this would not be the solution for the trade deficit. But I shall come back to this.

I discussed earlier the matter of investment and that investment creates capital which is productive and helps the economy to produce goods and services in the future. If we look at the statistics of capital stocks in 1981 as illustrated in Table 13.7 taken from an earlier article of mine (Eisner, 1985), we shall notice that business tangible capital, that is, plant and equipment, was $5528 billion while total capital was $23 000 billion. The business tangible investment which is included in the gross private domestic investment is approximately 25 per cent of the total. I have analysed and estimated various measures of income, output and capital elsewhere (Eisner, 1989), but let me mention briefly that there are, of course, many other sorts of capital, such as government tangible capital, government enterprise, non profit, household tangible, and close to half of the total is perhaps the most important: the human capital of education, knowledge, health, research, etc., which contributes to future growth.

It must be evident by now that I am neither alarmed about the deficit nor am I alarmed about the reported low measure of saving as we measure it. But I am alarmed when I read, for example, that our 13-year-olds, when stacked up against the Japanese, the South Koreans, some Western Europeans and some British Columbians in Canada, come out last in tests of

Table 13.8 Official and adjusted US net international investment position, 1970–87 (billions of dollars)

(1)	(2)	(3)	(4)	(5)	(6)	(7)
					Adjusted US	
		Revaluations on			intl. investment	
	Official	direct investment			position, based on	
	International		Replace-	Revalua-		Replace-
	Investment		ment	tions	Market	ment
Year	position	Market value	cost	on gold	value	cost
1970	58.5	20.0	24.5	.9	79.3	83.8
1971	45.5	29.6	35.1	2.6	77.8	83.3
1972	37.0	47.2	46.4	7.6	91.8	91.0
1973	47.9	50.5	78.1	19.5	117.9	145.5
1974	58.7	34.8	107.8	42.1	135.7	208.6
1975	74.2	69.9	117.1	27.1	171.2	218.4
1976	83.6	49.8	126.6	25.6	158.9	235.7
1977	72.7	64.4	153.9	34.2	171.4	260.8
1978	76.1	91.1	191.7	50.9	218.1	318.7
1979	94.5	121.0	233.4	124.4	339.8	452.3
1980	106.3	139.0	275.9	144.7	390.0	526.9
1981	141.1	90.8	253.1	93.8	325.8	488.1
1982	136.9	70.7	240.6	110.4	318.0	488.0
1983	89.4	103.6	216.2	88.4	281.5	394.1
1984	3.5	90.2	182.2	69.2	162.9	254.9
1985	−110.7	170.1	222.9	74.8	134.2	187.0
1986	−269.2	292.9	273.9	91.5	115.1	96.1
1987	−368.2	310.8	368.2	116.5	59.1	116.5

mathematics and science literacy. How then is cutting the deficit going to help that? An answer might be that if we cut the deficit by decreasing federal aid to education, we will make the local school boards learn how to educate their kids. Maybe some believe that the local school boards are not doing the right job, but reducing aid is not going to make them do it better.

Lastly, look at Table 13.8; it shows the twin deficits. I have already suggested that we perhaps do not have a real budget deficit at all; but what about the trade deficit? We have heard people say that the trade deficit has necessitated foreign investment into the US and has therefore made it the world's greatest debtor nation.

We have heard this statement over and over again as a mark of disaster, but I do not think many know how the trade deficit is calculated. The US is not a debtor nation at all, literally. The trade deficit measure published by the Bureau of Economic Analysis does not mean debt and they caution us as such, but no one pays any attention to it. It is simply the difference, by their measure, between the Americans' investments abroad and foreign investments here. At the end of 1987, this measure reached by their calculation the tremendous figure of $368 billion. US investments abroad were worth $368 billion less than foreign investments here. But this does not reflect debt. These are motels that foreigners own – most of it is not what we owe. To be sure, some of it is debt we owe, but it is a diverse portfolio of assets. The point is, however, as the Bureau of Economic Analysis will confirm, these measurements are calculated at original cost. Thus, the value of our foreign investments abroad, most of which were initiated years ago, are valued at cost, unlike the Japanese who have been investing in the US at current times. If we take the market value of US investments abroad and the market value of foreign investments here, and in addition we adjust for the fact that we are measuring our gold reserves at $42 an ounce when we all know it is close to $400 an ounce, we shall find that the US is not the world's greatest debtor nation. As it can be seen from Table 13.8, the value of US assets abroad is worth more than foreign assets are worth in the US contrary to conventional wisdom. The issue then might be that if the United States keeps running a trade deficit, foreigners will continue to acquire its assets and it shall eventually become a 'debtor' nation. This issue, we have to remember, is complex and it also depends on the actions of the Federal Reserve. If the Federal Reserve would stop trying to either lower or prop up the dollar or allow foreign central banks to do so, and if, furthermore, foreigners decide not to hold all their foreign claims in dollars and the US continues to have a trade deficit, then the dollar will likely go down in value; this means that the value of US assets abroad will increase further. So there will even be a self-correcting mechanism in this instance too.

References

Eisner, R., 'The Total Incomes System of Accounts', *Survey of Current Business*, vol. 65 (i) (1985) pp. 24–48.
Eisner, R., *How Real is the Federal Deficit?* (New York: The Free Press, 1986).
Eisner, R., 'Extended Accounts for National Income and Product', *Journal of Economic Literature*, vol. 26 (2) (1988) pp. 1611–84.
Eisner, R., *The Total Incomes System of Accounts* (Chicago: The University of Chicago Press, 1989).

Part III
Instability

14 A Dynamic Approach to the Theory of Effective Demand

Anwar Shaikh

14.1 INTRODUCTION

This chapter attempts to re-situate the theory of effective demand within a dynamic non-equilibrium context. Existing theories of effective demand, which derive from the works of Keynes and Kalecki, are generally posed in static equilibrium terms. That is to say, they serve to define a given level of output which corresponds to the equilibrium point between aggregate demand and supply. We propose to generalise this analysis in three ways. First, we shall extend the analysis to encompass a dynamic, that is, moving short-run path of output, rather than a merely static level. Second, we shall show that this dynamic short-run path need not imply an equilibrium analysis, since it can arise from either stochastically sustained cycles or deterministic limit cycles.[1] And third, we will provide generalisation of the theory of effective demand and a possible solution in the instability of warranted growth.

The issue of warranted growth has long been problematic. On the Keynesian side the question was originally taken up by Harrod and Domar, and on the Kaleckian side by Kalecki himself. All of them ended up concluding that the warranted path was highly unstable (Harrod, 1939; Domar, 1946; Kalecki, 1962). This conclusion has yet to be overthrown. We shall show that the secret to this puzzle lies in the contradiction between the static short-run level of output which results from the conventional formulation of effective demand theories, and the dynamic path of output which is the point of departure for considerations of warranted growth. This will allow us to show that the actual path of the economy does indeed gravitate around the warranted path in a cyclical sense.

We shall also show that it is possible to derive two distinct types of growth cycles which follow quite naturally from the short-run and long-run dynamics considered above: a fast growth cycle arising from the oscillations of growing aggregate supply around growing aggregate demand; and a slower growth cycle arising from the oscillations of the average supply path generated by the fast process around the corresponding growth path of capacity. These two intrinsic growth cycles appear to provide a natural foundation for the observed 3–5 year inventory cycle (since imbalances in aggregate demand and supply will show up as inventory fluctuations), and for the observed 7–11 year fixed capital cycle (van Duijn, 1983).

14.2 FAST AND SLOW MACRODYNAMICS

Modern macrodynamics have traditionally focused on two quite different adjustment processes, each operating at its own characteristic range of speeds (Kaldor, 1960, pp. 31–3): so-called short-run adjustments in aggregate demand and supply in the face of excess demand or supply; and so-called long-run adjustments in aggregate supply (output) and capacity in response to under- or overutilisation of existing capacity.

The fairly fast adjustments in aggregate demand and supply are the most familiar ones. If these processes are stable, in the sense that demand and supply end up gravitating around some balance point, one may assume that the two are roughly equal over some appropriate period of time. Such an assumption is implicit in the basic Keynesian and Kaleckian notions that aggregate demand and supply are equated by some 'short run', that is, relatively fast process. But this does not imply that aggregate demand and supply need ever be in some state of 'equilibrium', because their average equality achieved over some interval of time is perfectly consistent with a process of perpetual oscillation (limit cycling) around a balance point.[2] Nor does it exclude the general possibility that this average equality defines a dynamic, that is, growth path rather than a mere static level of output and employment (Hicks, 1965 pp. 105–6). Both of these points will play an important role in what follows.

The relatively fast process described above creates a rough equality between average aggregate demand and average supply, and hence between average aggregate investment and savings. But that portion of aggregate investment which is made up of fixed investment serves to expand the stock of fixed capital and hence to augment the (normal economic) capacity to produce.[3] It is natural, therefore, to ask how fixed investment responds to discrepancies between the average aggregate demand/supply generated over the fast process and the corresponding average level of aggregate capacity. Notice that this new adjustment process is implicitly slower, because it operates on the average result of the fast process. Moreover, the issue itself is intrinsically dynamic because capacity is continually being expanded by ongoing net investment. This is the second major adjustment process which has traditionally occupied macroeconomic theory.

The relatively slow adjustment process between the path of average output and the path of average capacity was the principal focus of the seminal contributions by Harrod and Domar. But their analysis of this second adjustment process produced one of the most enduring puzzles of modern macrodynamics. In effect, they came to the 'rather astonishing' conclusion (Baumol, 1959, p. 44) that the normal feedback of the market would cause the actual growth rate to fly away from the particular growth rate needed to maintain a balance between capacity and actual production. What Harrod calls the 'warranted' path and Domar the 'required' path will in general be knife-edge unstable (Kregel, 1987, vol. 3, pp. 601–2). This unsettling result has continued to fascinate and frustrate economists to the present day (Sen, 1970, pp. 23, 227–30; Goodwin, 1986).

The central issue at hand is whether or not a long-run disequilibrium adjustment process will either converge to the warranted path or oscillate around it, so that average aggregate output will roughly equal average aggregate capacity.

If such an average equality does hold, capacity utilisation will fluctuate around its normal level, the actual profit rate will fluctuate around the normal (potential) profit rate, and the associated growth will be internally driven, in the sense that it arises from the reinvestment of profits even when there is no technical change (or population growth, since normal capacity growth does not imply the full employment of labour). Moreover, since the normal rate of profit and the wage share are inversely related for a given state of technology, the understanding of this latter relation becomes crucial to the analysis of the long-term growth patterns of capitalist growth.[4] This is precisely why the inverse relation between wages and profits has always played such a crucial role in growth theory, in neoclassical and neoricardian economics, and in their classical and marxian antecedents.[5] It should be noted, however, that an average equality between output and production capacity does not imply that labour is fully employed, since the normal capacity of capital need not be adequate to the full employment of labour. Indeed, Goodwin (1967) has most elegantly shown that capitalist long-run dynamics are perfectly consistent with a persistent unemployment.[6]

On the other hand, if normal capacity utilisation is not attainable, then it seems reasonable to displace the regulating role of profitability by the influence of other factors such as expectations, government intervention, population growth and technical change. This is exactly the direction taken by the bulk of growth theory, in the face of the apparently impossibility of normal capacity growth.

By far the most prevalent response to the Harrod–Domar problem of knife-edge instability has been to try and spirit it away by simply assuming that the actual growth rate equals the warranted rate. Attention is then either shifted to the properties of this assumed path, or to the relation between this path and the natural rate of growth defined by population growth and the rate of growth of productivity. The Solow–Swan models are of this class (Sen, 1970, Introduction, ch. 10). So too is the famous ceiling/floor growth-cycle model of Hicks (1950) and the elegant nonlinear growth-cycle model by Goodwin (1967).[7]

The second most common response to the Harrod–Domar paradox has been to treat growth as an 'exogenous trend' and concentrate instead on cyclical fluctuations around this given trend. The basic Lucas Rational Expectation models and Nordhaus Political Business Cycle models fall into this category (Mullineaux, 1984, ch. 3), as do the nonlinear cycle models from Kaldor (1940), Hicks (1950), and Goodwin (1951) (Mullineaux, 1984, ch. 2).[8] The various versions of Kalecki's model also fall into this camp, though he does indicate that his provisional recourse to an exogenously given growth trend awaits a more satisfactory solution to the problem of growth (Kalecki, 1971, pp. 165–6; Steindl, 1981).

Multiplier–accelerator models form the third major branch of macro-economic modelling since Harrod. Here, over certain parameter ranges one can get damped oscillations around a stationary path, and over other ranges one can get growth asymptotic to some non-warranted rate (still other plausible ranges yield explosive oscillations). But warranted growth is generally not possible in either the basic models or in more complex ones in which price, wage, money supply, and technology effects are added onto the multiplier–accelerator relation.[9]

To sum up. Warranted growth is implicit in many approaches to macro-dynamics. Yet such growth appears difficult to justify because of the apparently intractable instability of the warranted path. This difficulty has had a major effect on the growth and cycle literature, and has even convinced many theorists 'that the warranted growth path is one place the economy will never be' (Goodwin, 1986, p. 209). The aim of this chapter is to show that such a conclusion is, so to speak, quite unwarranted. The problem of warranted growth arises from the attempt to move beyond the short-run considerations of the theory of effective demand to the long-run considerations of output and capacity growth. We shall try and show that the difficulty in explaining warranted growth has its roots in a contradiction between the static focus of conventional theories of effective demand and the dynamic focus inherent in the question of warranted growth. Harrod had hoped to create a 'new branch of economics' which would replace the static approach of Keynesian theory with a new approach formulated from the start in 'dynamic terms' (Harrod, cited in Kregel, 1980, pp. 101–2). Yet this famous instability result actually ended up inhibiting the study of dynamics. It is our contention that this ironic result came to pass because Harrod did not take his dynamic approach far enough. That is to say, that he did not begin from a dynamic analysis of the short run.

14.3   A DYNAMIC APPROACH TO THE THEORY OF EFFECTIVE DEMAND

The theory of effective demand centres around the (relatively fast) reactions of aggregate demand and supply to any imbalances between the two. If we define excess demand E as the (positive or negative) difference between aggregate demand and supply, then we may express this as the corresponding difference between aggregate investment demand I and aggregate savings S. Following Kalecki and Kaldor, we adopt a classical savings function (though this is not critical to the results), so that $S = sP$ where s = the propensity to save out of profits and P = aggregate profit on produced output. As defined here, produced profit P is profit net of interest-equivalent on capital advanced – that is, what Marx calls profit-of-enterprise.[10] This means that we must include the interest-equivalent as part of costs. Next, we write total investment as $I = Ic + Iv + If$, where Ic = investment in working capital, that is, in raw materials and goods-in-progress, Iv = the change in the desired level of finished goods inventories (not to be confused with actual change in finished goods inventory levels), and If = investment in fixed capital. This division of total investment into several components is standard, although not all authors interpret it in the same way.[11] Iv represents the portion of final goods which would be desired as additions to final goods inventories even when demand and supply are balanced ($E=0$). When $E=0$, actual inventory levels will equal desired levels (the latter depending on the particular specification of Iv). On the other hand, when demand and supply are *not* balanced, actual final goods inventory levels will depart from the desired levels, production plans will be revised in response to the discrepancy, and input levels will therefore also adjust. It is this latter reaction in the use of circulating capital that is captured in Ic. Taken together, Ic and Iv represent the 'inventory adjustment' portion of total investment.

$$E = I - S = Ic + Iv + If - sP \qquad (1)$$

We now turn to the effects of Ic, Iv, and If on other variables. The determinants of these same investment components will be treated later.

Investment in fixed capital results in a change in aggregate capacity, since changing the stock of fixed capital also serves to change the capacity to produce, that is, to potential output. This link was at the heart of the issues addressed by Harrod and Domar. In the same way, investment in circulating capital leads to a change in the level of production, because any planned change in the level of production will require a corresponding change in the use of raw materials and labour power required. If purchases of these additional circulating inputs are strongly connected to their use, then investment in circulating capital will be linked up to the change in the level of production. This is an empirically sound assumption, and is in fact the basis of Leontief's input–output analysis (since the observed input–output coefficients are the ratios of purchased inputs to outputs).

Notice that there is an exact parallel here between the Harrodian assumption that fixed investment purchases lead to an increase in the capacity to produce and the Ricardo–Marx–Leontief assumption that circulating investment purchases lead to an increase in the level of production. Moreover, just as the former does not imply that the capacity will actually be utilised, so too the latter does not imply that the output will be actually sold. Indeed, equation (1) above tells us that aggregate output and demand generally do not balance. Finally, it should be noted that whereas the link between circulating capital and output is algebraically similar to some formulations of an 'accelerator relation', it is conceptually quite different. This is because our input-to-output relation implies that the change in output depends on the level of circulating investment, whereas an accelerator relation implies that the level of investment depends on the (past or future) change in output.[12] We will turn to the question of investment functions in the next section.

Investment in final goods inventories is different from the above two, because it represents a virtual (benchmark) flow rather than a real one. As we noted earlier, some allowance has to be made for changes in the desired inventory level even when demand and supply balance. For example, if the ratio of desired inventories is proportional to sales, then in a growing economy some portion of output corresponds merely to this desired additions to stocks, and this must be allowed for either as a nominal 'investment demand', or as a deduction from total product so as to arrive at the effectively available supply. Either way, it will show up as one of the determinants of excess demand E.

Let us now formalise the effects of fixed and circulating capital investments. Let the notation P' stand for the change in P, etc. We can then express the effect of circulating capital investment Ic on aggregate output Q and (through the profit margin) on aggregate produced profit-of-enterprise P. Let C = total circulating capital, Q = aggregate output, $Ic = C'$

$$Q' = (1/k)C' = (1/k)Ic \tag{2'}$$

$$P' = m \cdot C' = m \cdot Ic, \ 1 + m = 1/k \tag{2}$$

where m = the profit margin on prime costs (circulating capital, including the interest-equivalent of capital advanced), and k = prime costs per unit output (average variable cost). m and k are provisionally constant in the short-run. The case of variable margins is taken up at a later point.

Next, consider the effect of fixed capital investment on capacity. Let Kf = stock of fixed capital, N = aggregate capacity, $If = Kf'$.

$$N' = q \cdot Kf' = q \cdot If \tag{3}$$

where q = the capacity–capital ratio.[13]

Lastly, we define capacity utilisation u as the ratio of output Q to capacity N, so that $u = 1$ corresponds to normal capacity utilisation. Then over- or under-utilisation of capacity corresponds to positive or negative levels, respectively, of excess utilisation X.

$$X \equiv u-1 \equiv (Q-N)/N \tag{4}$$

where $u = Q/N$ = capacity utilisation rate.

Equations (1–2) above represent the core of the fast adjustment ('short-run') process centering around on the interactions of aggregate demand and supply. Equations (3–4) in turn represent the core of the slow adjustment ('long-run') process centering around the interactions of aggregate supply and capacity. In order to proceed any further, we need to now consider the determinants (as opposed to the effects) of each of the three investment components, first in the short run and then in the long run.

14.3.1 The Fast Adjustment Process

$$E = I - S = Ic + Iv + If - sP \tag{1}$$

$$P' = m \cdot Kc' = m \cdot Ic \tag{2}$$

To fill out the picture of the fast adjustment process, we must supplement the core equations (1–2) with specifications of the 'short-run' determinants of Ic, Iv, and If. It is here that the question of a dynamic versus a static specification becomes crucial. A dynamic specification is one in which allowance is made for the possibility that variables may be moving over time, so that all adjustments take place relative to any trends in these variables. Such relative adjustments must therefore either be in terms of changes in ratios of variables, or in terms of changes in growth rates.

By contrast, static specifications tend to focus on the level, rather than the path, of the main variable, so that adjustments are posed in terms of changes in absolute levels rather that relative ones.[14] Not surprisingly, static specifications tend to yield static results.

Conventional formulations of the theory of effective demand yield static results because they are implicitly specified in static terms. To show this, we will derive the standard Kaleckian/Keynesian short-run equilibrium by closing our core equations in a static way. Fixed investment will be assumed to be constant in the short run, on the usual grounds. Desired final goods inventory levels will be assumed constant in the short run, so that *ex ante* inventory investment (which represents the change in the desired levels) will be zero.

$$If = \text{constant} \tag{5}$$

$$Iv = 0 \tag{6}$$

Now consider possible reactions of the system to a positive or negative level of excess demand. The basic Kaleckian and Keynesian approach is to assume that production levels will adjust whenever aggregate demand and supply do not balance. This is because realised profits $P+E$ will differ from produced profits when $E \neq 0$, and if the margin of produced profit on costs (the degree of 'mark-up')[15] does not vary with excess demand (because the relation of costs to prices does not change), produced profit will equal the normal profit, so that positive or negative excess demand will be a measure of positive or negative excess profits. On this basis, $Q' = F(E)$. But from equation 2' above, $Q' = (1/k)Ic$, since any change in production requires a prior (positive or negative) investment in circulating capital. Therefore, $Ic = f(E)$. We shall assume $f(E)$ to be linear.

$$Ic = h \cdot E, \ 0 < h < 1 \tag{7}$$

Substituting equations (5–7) into equation (1), and then substituting P' for Ic from equation (2), we get

$$Ic/h = Ic + If - sP$$

$$P'/mh = P'/m + If - sP$$

$$P' = [smh/(1-h)] \cdot [If/s - P] \tag{8}$$

The first term in brackets is positive because s, m, and h are all positive, and $h < 1$. The term If/s is constant in the short run, which means that whenever P is greater than this term, P' will be negative and P will fall back, while whenever P is smaller than this term P' will be positive and P will rise toward it. This is a monotonic process which converges to the familiar short-run equilibrium level of profit in the Kaleckian and Keynesian model (with the usual 'multiplier' $= 1/s$).

$$P^* = If/s \tag{9}$$

Since P^* is constant in the short run, $P^{*\prime} = 0$, which from equation (2) implies that $Ic^* = 0$, which in turn from equation (7) implies $E^* = 0$. Actual inventory levels will also be constant in equilibrium, since $E^* = 0$.

$$E^* = 0 \text{ and } Ic^* = 0 \tag{10}$$

We see therefore that the familiar static results of Kaleckian/Keynesian economics are merely the consequences of having implicitly specified the adjustment process in static terms. *Growth then appears as something external to the 'short run'.*[16]

It was Harrod's intention to supplant this traditional static approach with a new one formulated from the start in 'dynamic terms'. In order to do so, he begins by translating the short-run condition that investment = savings into a long-run statement about the relation between the actual rate of growth and the warranted rate, only to find that the apparently stable short-run equilibrium implies an apparently unstable long-run equilibrium.

A central contention of this chapter is that Harrod did not take his dynamic approach far enough. Or, more precisely, he did not move to a dynamic framework early enough in his analysis. Harrod begins from the short-run equilibrium of Keynesian economics. But as we have seen, this short-run equilibrium is inherently static. Thus his 'new' dynamic formulation is in fact an inconsistent mixture of short-run statics and long-run dynamics. This suggests that in order to formulate a consistent dynamic approach, we must reformulate the theory of effective demand itself. Hicks has pointed out, for instance, that the general solution to the equations of short-run balance involves a time path in output, employment, and profits (Hicks, 1965, ch. 10, pp. 105–6). This can be seen by noting that when $E=0$ in equation (1), total investment $I = Ic + Iv + If$ = total savings S, so that if $Ic>0$ then from equation (2), $P' = m \cdot Ic > 0$, which means that produced profit and hence output is growing over time. Conversely, only if $Ic = 0$ do we get a static solution.

Kalecki and Keynes implicitly select the static solution to the general time path defined by short-run equilibrium. But if, in the spirit of Harrod, we are to dynamise the short-run theory of effective demand, then like Harrod we must do *two things*: show that a short-run dynamic path exists; and show that it is stable.

The first step in this proposed reformulation is to recall that a dynamic specification requires that adjustments be posed in trend-relative terms, that is, as changes in either ratios of variables or in their growth rates. Let us therefore begin by first expressing all variables relative to the level of produced profit P.

Let $e \equiv E/P$, $ac \equiv Ic/P$, $av \equiv Iv/P$, and $af \equiv If/P$, where the latter three terms can be interpreted as the average aggregate 'propensities to invest' in, or 'accumulation ratios' of, the corresponding three types of *ex ante* investments. Our fast adjustment core equations (1–2) then become

$$e = ac + av + af - s \tag{11}$$

$$P'/P = m \cdot ac \tag{12}$$

The next step is to write dynamic analogues to the previously derived static investment functions. Where static theory takes the level of fixed investment, *If*, as constant in the short run, we will take the corresponding accumulation ratio *af* to be approximately fixed, on the grounds that it is a slowly changing variable in the short-run. Where static theory takes the desired level of final goods inventories to be fixed, we will take the corresponding ratio *v* of desired inventories to circulating capital *C* to be fixed. Since inventory investment is the change in desired inventories, $Iv = v \cdot C' = v \cdot Ic$, so that $av \equiv Iv/P = v \cdot Ic/P = v \cdot ac$.

$$af = \text{constant} \tag{13}$$

$$av = v \cdot ac \tag{14}$$

The dynamic specification of our circulating capital reaction function requires a bit more work. Recall that in the static model it was assumed that the level of circulating capital investment changes in response to the level of excess profit, and that the level of the latter is measured by the level of excess demand *E* if the margin of produced profit over costs (the 'mark-up') does not vary with *E*. A dynamic equivalent of these connections would be to assume that the accumulation ratio of (the propensity to invest in) circulating capital changes in response to *the excess profit margin* μ (the excess of the realised profit margin on prime costs *C* over the normal margin). This amounts to assuming that the trend of planned production changes when demand and supply do not balance. Thus $ac' = f(\mu)$.

$$ac' = h \cdot \mu, \; h > 0 \tag{15}$$

Equations (12–15) form a dynamic analogue to the static model of effective demand. The properties of the resulting system will then depend on how we specify the determinants of the excess profit margin μ.

Suppose we retain our earlier assumption that the ratio of costs to prices does not vary with excess demand, so that the profit margin does not vary over the cycle (see equation 7 above). Then excess profit is the same as excess demand, and the excess profit margin $\mu = E/C = (E/P) \cdot (P/C) = e \cdot m$.

$\mu = m \cdot e$ when the mark-up m is constant   (16)

Equation (16) completes our short-run dynamic system. Substituting equations (13–14) into equation (11), we get $e = ac(1+v) + af - s$, and since af and s are constant in the short-run, $e' = ac'(1+v)$. Substituting equation (15) into this gives

$e' = H \cdot \mu$, where $H = h(1+v)$ (17)

and combining equations (16–17) gives

$e' = Hm \cdot e$, $H > 0$.   (18)

Equation (18) is a linear first order differential equation which describes a system with a short-run positive feedback loop between the level of relative excess demand e and its rate of change e'. It is exactly analogous to the Harrod–Domar long-run positive feedback loop between the level of capacity utilisation and its rate of change. *And like the latter, the former is also knife-edge unstable around its corresponding short-run dynamic balance path.* A rise of e above zero (excess demand) will make $e' > 0$, so that e will rise still further, and so on. Similarly, a fall in e below zero (excess supply) will reduce it still further, and so on.

In the light of the apparent instability of short-run equilibrium growth, it is natural to ask whether other factors might alter this result. In an earlier paper, I began from the premise that the basic accumulation reaction function in equation (15) should be modified to allow for the negative effects of debt service commitments. On this basis I was able to show that while an excess of investment over savings showed up in the commodity market as a growth accelerating excess demand, the corresponding debt service on the borrowing which fuelled this excess demand showed up as a growth decelerating decline in the liquidity of firms. The net result was to stabilise accumulation around a dynamic short-run path defined by $e = 0$ and characterised by a constant rate of growth of output. When subject to random perturbations, this model yielded a stochastically sustained cycle in which the system perpetually cycled around the balance path (Shaikh, 1989).

In this chapter I show that there exists an alternate mechanism by which the apparent instability of short-run equilibrium growth may be contained. This apparent instability was derived on the assumption of a cyclically constant profit margin. But it is a well-established empirical fact the profit margin varies systematically over the business cycle. In the early stages of a boom, prices rise faster than costs and the profit margin rises. However, as the boom proceeds, costs begin to accelerate and eventually overtake prices, thus reducing profit margins. The opposite pattern holds in the bust (Klein and Moore, 1981). To quote Wesley Clair Mitchell:

The very conditions that make business profitable gradually evolve conditions that threaten a reduction of profits. When the increase in business . . . taxes the productive capacity of the existing industrial equipment, the early decline of supplementary costs per unit of output comes gradually to a standstill. Meanwhile, . . . active bidding among business enterprises for materials, labour, and loans funds . . . sends up their prices. At the same time the poorer parts of the industrial equipment are brought back into use, the efficiency of labour declines, and the incidental wastes of management rise. Thus the prime costs of doing business become heavier. After these processes have been running cumulatively for a while, it becomes difficult to advance selling prices fast enough to avoid a reduction of profits by the encroachment of costs, (Mitchell, 1913, cited in Klein and Moore, 1981, p. 56)

To capture the idea of changing cost/price ratios, we must replace equation (16) (which was predicated on a constant cost/price ratio) with a more general formulation. Equations (1–15) will not be affected, since they were in any cases defined in terms of constant prices and profit margins. But their meaning is slightly changed, since now P is normal aggregate profits, s in equations (1) and (11) is the propensity to save out of normal profits, and m in equations (2) and (12) is the normal profit margin.

With the price level of output as numeraire, all quantities are in real terms, aggregate excess demand is $E = D - Q$ and realised aggregate profit $PR = D - pC$, where D, Q, C, p are real demand, output, inputs, and input costs, respectively. Let $pn = $ some normal level of relative input costs (corresponding to $E = 0$), and write realised profits PR in the form

$$PR \equiv D - pC = (D - Q) + (Q - pn \cdot C) + (pn - p)C$$
$$PR = E + P + (pn - p)C, \text{ where } P \equiv Q - pn \cdot C = normal$$
$$\text{produced profit}$$

$$\text{Excess Profits} \equiv PR - P = E + (pn - p)C$$
$$\mu = \text{excess profit margin} \equiv (PR - P)/C = (E/P)(P/C) + (pn - p)$$

$$\mu = e \cdot m + (pn - p), \text{ where } m \equiv P/C = normal \text{ profit margin (19)}$$

It now remains to model the behaviour of relative input costs p over the various phases of the fast cycle. According to our formulation, these phases will consist of alternating episodes of positive and negative excess demand. At the beginning of an upturn, costs will still be falling relative to prices. But as the recovery turns into a boom, costs will overtake prices so that relative costs will begin to rise. Consider the upturn phase of the stylised cycle in Figure 14.1 below: point A marks the beginning of the recovery, at a point which the cycle has bottomed out ($e' = 0$) but there is

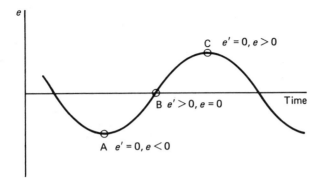

Figure 14.1

still excess supply ($e < 0$). Relative costs are falling here, so that $p' < 0$ at this point. Point B marks the point at which the cycle passes through the transitory point at which aggregate demand and supply balance ($e = 0$) and hence $p' = 0$. And point C marks the top of the boom, at which the cycle has peaked ($e' = 0$) but there is still excess demand ($e > 0$). Here, relative costs are rising so that $p' > 0$. A similar partition can obviously be constructed for the downturn phase.

It is evident that the phases of the stylised cycle are characterised by varying levels of e and e'. Accordingly, we may generally consider a relative cost reaction function of the form $p' = f(e, e')$, subject to the requirements delineated above.

One simple function which satisfies the above conditions is

$$p' = ae + b(e) \cdot e', \tag{20}$$

where $b(e) \cdot b \cdot e^2$.

The coefficient $b(e)$ is made an increasing function of the *size* of excess demand[17] to capture the idea that the influence of the rate of change of excess demand itself depends on the tightness of the market: when e is small, the rate of change of e is of no great consequence; but when e is large, then the impact of the rate of change of e is correspondingly more serious. It is easily shown that equation (21) satisfies the requirements for p' at the various phases of the cycle.

Equations (12–15) from our previous system, and equations (19–20) (which replace the previous equation 16) form a new dynamical system. As we noted previously, equations (11), (13–15) can be combined to derive $e' = H\mu$ (equation 17 above), so that

$$e'' = H\mu' = H(m \cdot e' - p') \text{ (from equation 19)} \tag{21}$$
$$= Hme' - Hae - H(be^2) \cdot e' \text{ (from equation 20)}$$

$$e'' + H(be^2 - m) \cdot e' + Hae = 0 \tag{22}$$

Equation (22) is the reduced form of our new dynamical system. It can be shown that it is also a particular expression of a general second order nonlinear differential equation known as the Lienard Equation (see the Appendix for the proof), so that it *has a unique stable limit cycle around the critical point e = 0* (Lakin and Sanchez, 1970, section 4.4). That is to say, the system perpetually cycles around the point at which aggregate demand and supply balance, alternately overshooting and undershooting it. The system never settles into a 'short-run equilibrium'. And yet, aggregate demand and supply balance on average, precisely because they are subject to mutually offsetting errors. The order in the system is expressed in-and-through its disorder.

The fact that the system cycles around $e = 0$ implies investment approximately equals savings, over an average cycle.

$$I \approx S \dashrightarrow ac(1 + v) + af \approx s \text{ (from equations 11, 13, 14)} \tag{23}$$

Secondly, $e \approx 0$ implies $\mu \approx 0$, so that the actual profit margin $m + \mu$ fluctuates around the normal profit margin m, rising in the boom and falling in the bust. And thirdly, since $ac \approx (s - af)/(1 + v)$ from equation (23), and $P'/P = mac$ from equation (12), we get the result that the gravitational path around which realised and produced profit perpetually oscillate is an *endogenously generated growth path*, provided the propensity to invest in fixed capital $af < $ average aggregate propensity to save s (because then $ac > 0$). Lastly, $e \approx 0$ implies that the actual inventory/sales ratio will fluctuate the desired ratio v.

Figures 14.2 and 14.3 show the simulation results of the model for the indicated values of the parameters. Figure 14.2 depicts the pure limit cycle in e, while Figure 14.3 shows the corresponding path of realised and produced profits.

The above approach opens up a new dynamical perspective on the theory of effective demand. Its properties provide an interesting contrast to those of the Kaleckian and Keynesian theories of effective demand. For instance, these latter theories predict that a rise in the propensity to consume (a fall in the propensity to save) is beneficial in the short run because it stimulates aggregate demand and hence output and employment. Yet within our new dynamic model, a rise in the propensity to consume has two contradictory effects which operate at different speeds. It initially raises excess demand by raising consumption demand, which at first raises the average level of output and employment above its trend level. This is the 'Keynesian' effect. But since a rise in the propensity to consume is a drop in the propensity to save s, it lowers the short-run trend rate of growth $P^*/P^* = m \cdot ac^* = (af - s)/(1 + v)$. This is the Classical

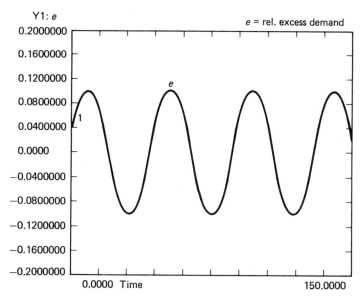

Figure 14.2 Limit cycle in *e*

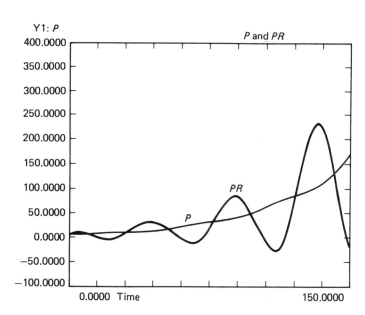

Figure 14.3 Realised and produced profit

effect. Since the system ends up gravitating around a new lower rate of growth, the eventual effect is to lower the level of output below what it would otherwise have been. *A rise in the proportion of government deficit spending has the same effect*, other things being equal, because it is equivalent to a rise in the average propensity to consume.[18]

14.3.2   The Slow Adjustment Process

Perhaps the most remarkable thing about a dynamic solution to the fast adjustment process is that it opens up a host of natural solutions to the famous puzzle of the Harrod–Domar knife-edge. To see how this works, let us first reproduce some of our previously derived equations.

$$N' = q \cdot Kf' = q \cdot If \tag{3}$$

where Q = aggregate output, C = prime costs, $Ic = C'$ = investment in circulating capital, N = aggregate capacity, Kf = stock of fixed capital, $If = Kf'$ = investment in fixed capital, and $q = N/Kf$ = the (constant) capacity–capital ratio.

$$X \equiv u - 1 \equiv (Q - N)/N \tag{4}$$

where $u = Q/N$ = the actual capacity utilisation rate, and the normal rate is defined as 1. Thus X is the positive or negative degree of overutilisation of capacity.

$$P'/P = m \cdot ac \tag{12}$$

Finally, since over the average result of the fast adjustment process is $e \approx 0$, we can write from equations (11) and (14)

$$ac(1 + v) + af \approx s \text{ (average result in the short run)} \tag{23}$$

Combining equations (3–4),

$$N'/N = (q/N) \cdot If = If/Kf = (If/P) \cdot (P/Kf) = af \cdot r = af \cdot rn \cdot u \tag{24}$$

where $r = P/Kf$ = the actual rate of profit on fixed capital, $rn = r/u$ = the normal capacity rate of profit on fixed capital (which we will take as constant over the long run, since we are not considering technical change and long run distributional variations here).

We have already noted that over an average fast adjustment cycle the excess profit margin $\mu \approx 0$, so that the actual profit margin $m + \mu \approx m =$ the short-run normal profit margin, which we took to be given in the short run. Then since $m \equiv P/C$ and $Q \equiv P + C$, a constant m implies a constant profit share P/Q so that $P'/P = Q'/Q$. Thus equation (12) becomes

$$Q'/Q = m \cdot ac \tag{25}$$

In the fast adjustment process, the average propensity to invest in fixed capital *af* was taken to be approximately constant, on the grounds that it was a slow variable. Now, over the slow adjustment process, *af* is a variable, and it seems plausible that it would react to $X \equiv u - 1$, the positive or negative degree of overutilisation of capacity. With this, we can show that the secret to the apparent dynamic instability of the long-run warranted path actually lies hidden in the analysis of the short run. Harrod began from the static solution to the short-run problem, and found that the long-run dynamic path is then knife-edge unstable. We can show, on the other hand, that if we begin from a *dynamic* solution to short-run balance, then the long-run path is stable.

Equations (23–25) enable us to see why a dynamic solution to the short-run adjustment process unlocks the secret of the warranted path puzzle. In effect, any dynamic short-run path in which $e \approx 0$ implies that total investment = total savings, which in turn implies that the propensities to invest in circulating capital, inventories, and fixed capital must all sum to the given propensity to save. But $av = v \cdot ac$, so that the short-run restriction on the sum of investment propensities really implies the circulating and fixed investment propensities are *inversely* related, as is indicated by equation (23) above. But equation (24) tells us that the growth rate of capacity is positively related to fixed capital propensity, while equation (25) tells us that the growth rate of output is proportional and positively related to circulating capital propensity. This means that any long-run adjustment process which raises the fixed capital propensity *af* (say because capacity utilisation is above normal) will also lower the circulating capital propensity *ac*. The former effect will raise the growth rate of capacity, while the latter will lower the growth rate of output, and these two acting in concert will serve to lower the level of capacity utilisation back toward normal. The opposite movement would occur if the capacity utilisation was initially below normal. *The end result is a process which is stable around the warranted path.*

Let us now formalise the above argument. The fixed investment propensity *af* is assumed to react to the degree of over- or under-utilisation of capacity.

$$af' = k \cdot X = k \cdot (u - 1) \tag{26}$$

To complete the picture, we need to supplement the above fixed capital accumulation reaction function with an expression for X'. From $u \equiv Q/N$,

$u'/u = Q'/Q - N'/N = Q'/Q - af \cdot rn \cdot u$, from equation (24).

$u'/u = Q'/Q - af \cdot rn \cdot u = P'/P - af \cdot rn \cdot u = mac - af \cdot rn \cdot u$

since $P'/P = mac$ from equation (2). Substituting for ac from equation (23), and recalling that $X \equiv u - 1$

$$u'/u = X'/(1 + X) = (s - af)/(1 + v) - af \cdot rn \cdot u$$

$$X' = [(s - af)/(1 + v)] \cdot (1 + X) - af \cdot rn \cdot (1 + X)^2 \qquad (27)$$

Equations (25–26) form a nonlinear dynamical system which is stable around $u = 1$. *In other words, it is stable around the Harrodian warranted path.* It can be shown that for all plausible values of the reaction coefficient k, the stability is oscillatory as long as the system is at all profitable. Moreover, when subject to random shocks, actual capacity utilisation u oscillates endlessly around the point $u = 1$, alternately overshooting and undershooting this point but never settling down to it. Finally, the corresponding critical value of the fixed capital investment propensity af is $af^* = ms/(m + rn) > 0$, which along with the fact that $u \approx 1$, implies from equation (24) that the system follows a growth path (as we already know from fact that it is stable around the warranted path). *The end result is a slow fixed capital cycle which complements the fast inventory cycle previously derived in section 14.3.*[19]

Figure 14.4 shows the simulation results for the path of capacity utilisation u, and Figure 14.5 shows the corresponding paths of actual produced profit and normal produced profit, both with random noise added to the system.

14.3.3   Summary and Conclusions

This chapter is an attempt to wed Kalecki's analysis of the business cycle to Harrod's analysis of dynamic paths. Kalecki argued that growth had 'no independent entity' from cycles, and that the proper way to proceed was to formulate the problem 'in such a way as to yield the trend cum business-cycle'. Yet in spite of his repeated attempts to extend his cycle analysis to the issue of growth, he never quite found a formulation which he considered satisfactory (Kalecki, 1968, p. 78). From the other side, Harrod tried to extend his analysis of growth to encompass the theory of cycles, but he too remained frustrated (Kregel, 1980, pp. 99–102). In the end, a satisfactory synthesis of the theories of growth and cycles seemed to elude them both.

It has been the aim of this chapter to show that the above synthesis is possible, and that it can be achieved precisely by integrating Kalecki's

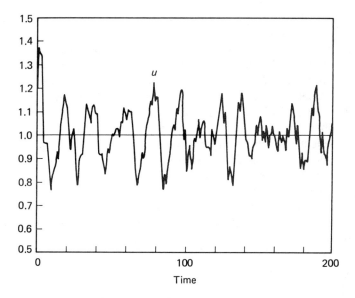

Figure 14.4   Capacity utilisation

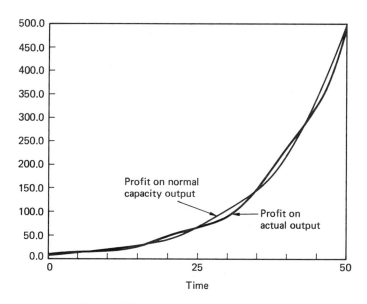

Figure 14.5   Produced and normal profit

treatment of endogenous cycles with Harrod's treatment of endogenous growth. To this end, we have shown that one can formulate a non-equilibrium theory of effective demand in which aggregate demand and supply trace out a dynamic 'short-run' growth path as they perpetually cycle around each other, and in which the resulting average output and capacity themselves trace out a dynamic 'warranted' as they cycle around each other. The combined dynamic consists of a fast cycle marked by mutually offsetting imbalances of demand and supply (which will be therefore reflected in corresponding inventory fluctuations), and a slower medium cycle consisting of mutually offsetting imbalances of output and capacity (reflected in corresponding fluctuations in capacity utilisation). Most interestingly, a rise in a factor such as the proportion of government deficit spending can be shown to have an *initial* Keynesian 'pumping' effect on the *level* of output and employment, attended by a corresponding Classical 'drag' effect on the *rate of growth* of output and employment, so that the *eventual* effect is to lower the level of output and employment below what it would otherwise have been.

APPENDIX

The nonlinear dynamical system in equation (22) can be written in the form

$$e'' + f(e)e' + g(e) = 0 \qquad (22')$$

where $g(e) = Hae$, with constants $H, a > 0$
$\quad f(e) = H(be^2 - m)$, with constants $b, m > 0$
Lakin and Sanchez (1970) list six conditions which ensure a unique limit cycle for such a (Lienard) equation.
(i) $g(e) = - g(e)$
(ii) $eg(e) > 0$ for $x \neq 0$
(iii) $f(e) = f(-e)$
(iv) $f(0) < 0$
(v) $f(u)du = F(u) \dashrightarrow \infty$ as $e \dashrightarrow \infty$
(vi) $F(e) = 0$ has a unique positive root $e = n$
Conditions (i) to (iv) are easily verified. Condition (vi) is also easily verified, since $f(e)$ has roots $\pm (m/b)^2$, so that it has a unique positive root $n = (m/b)^2$. This leaves condition (v) which is also satisfied since

$$H(bu^2 - m)du = H(b^u3/3 - mu) \mid = H(be^3/3 - me)$$
$$= He(e^2/3 - m) = F(e) \dashrightarrow \infty \text{ as } e \dashrightarrow \infty$$

It follows that the equation system 22' has a *unique stable limit cycle* (Lakin and Sanchez, 1970, pp. 92–3).

Notes

1. Deterministic limit cycles arise from local instability which is reversed by bounding forces. Stochastically sustained cycles can arise from (generally nonlinear) stable oscillatory solutions which are kept alive by random pertubations representing the turbulence inherent in an uncertain and fluctuating economic environment.

2. Goodwin's famous Lotka-Volterra limit cycle model of the relation between the wage share and the unemployment rate yields constant *average* values for these variables even though their *actual* levels perpetually fluctuate around these average levels (Goodwin, 1986, p. 207).

3. Production capacity as defined here refers to economic, not engineering, capacity.

4. The investment–savings equality brought about in the fast process may be expressed as a relation between the rate of growth of fixed capital, the capacity utilisation, and the normal rate of profit. Let $I = S = s \cdot P$, where $s =$ the propensity to save out of profits, and $P =$ aggregate profits. Since actual profits $P = u \cdot Pn$, where $u =$ the rate of capacity utilisation and $Pn =$ the normal capacity level of profit, then by dividing through by the aggregate capital stock K, we get $g \equiv I/K = s \cdot u \cdot (Pn/K) = s \cdot u \cdot rn$, where $g =$ the rate of growth of capital and $rn =$ the normal rate of profit. It is evident then that if some process results in an average $u = 1$, then the resulting long-run rate of accumulation $g^* = s \cdot rn$ is regulated by the wage share and technology which lie behind the normal rate of profit rn.

5. Smith, Ricardo and Marx typically abstract from supply/demand and supply/capacity variations in order to focus on the long-term patterns produced by the effects of factors such as technical change, population growth, and fertility of land, on the relation between real wages and the normal rate of profit. Sraffa's inverse relation between the wage share and the uniform rate of profit is a direct extension of Ricardo's problematic, and is predicated on the implicit assumption that the so-called uniform rate of profit expressed a normal rate of capacity utilisation (if it did not, then the increased effective demand consequent to a rise in the wage share might conceivably raise the rate of capacity utilisation u more than the increased wage costs served to lower the normal rate of profit rn, so that the actual rate of profit $r = rn \cdot u$ would actually rise). See Garegnani (1978) p. 183.

6. Goodwin (1967) has shown that the interaction between the growth of real wages and the level of unemployment is perfectly capable of producing perpetual oscillations around a stable level of unemployment. Thus the notion that supply and demand balance over a fast process, and that supply and capacity balance over a slow process, need not carry with it any notion that labour is ever fully employed, even in the longest of runs.

7. Goodwin (1967) assumes a constant capital–'output' ratio because of Harrod-Neutral technical change. But such technical change only yields a constant ratio of capital to potential output (capacity), since it tells us nothing about the use of this capacity. Thus Goodwin implicitly assumes that output is equal to capacity, which is equivalent to assuming that the actual growth rate is equal to the warranted rate. This warranted rate is made flexible linking it to a tradeoff between the unemployment rate and the growth rate of real wages (Gandolfo, 1985, pp. 474–81). The end result is that the warranted rate ends up fluctuating around the exogeneously given natural growth rate in such a way that the two are equal over any one complete cycle. To derive this last result, note that

Goodwin assumes that all profits P are invested, so that the actual (and warranted) rate of growth of capital $\equiv g =$ the rate of profit $\equiv r = P/K$. The natural growth rate, on the other hand, is $gn \equiv \alpha + \beta$, where $\alpha =$ the growth rate of productivity, and $\beta =$ the growth rate of labour supply. But $r \equiv P/K = (P/Y) \cdot (K/Y) = (1 - W/Y) \cdot (K/Y) = (1 - u)k$, where $u \equiv W/Y =$ the wage share and $k =$ the given capital–output ratio. Substituting the average value of u over one complete cycle (Gandolfo, 1985, pp. 481, 478) yields $r = \alpha + \beta$, which is the same thing as $g = gn$.

8. Hicks (1950) bounds the unstable parameter range of a multiplier–accelerator model with exogenously given ceilings and floors which grow at some exogeneously given growth rate. The model then fluctuates around this externally given growth trend (which seems to be the Harrodian natural rate of growth gn since Hicks abstracts from productivity growth and suggests that the ceiling is a full employment ceiling) (Mullineaux, 1984, pp. 16–8).

9. R. G. D Allen exhaustively analyses the structure of multiplier–accelerator models (Allen, 1968, ch. 17). Stable growth itself requires a particular range of parameters, and even this limited possibility does not yield normal capacity utilisation because the warranted growth rate s/v is generally inconsistent with the characteristic equation of the system. This result is not altered by models such as those by Phillips or Bergstorm, which embed the multiplier–accelerator relation in a more general set involving prices, wages and the rate of interest (Allen, 1968, ch. 20).

10. If $r =$ the rate of profit, $i =$ the interest rate, and $K =$ the money value of capital advanced, then $re = r - i =$ the rate of profit-of-enterprise and $P = re$ $K = (r - i)K =$ the mass of profit-of-enterprise.

11. For instance, Keynes says that total investment 'consists of fixed, working capital or liquid capital' investment, where by liquid capital he means inventories of finished goods (Keynes, 1964, ch. 7, p. 75). Kalecki distinguishes between 'fixed capital investment' and 'investment in inventories', whereby in the latter categories he apparently lumps investment in both working capital and final goods (Kalecki, 1971, ch. 10, pp. 121–3). Harrod divides investment into 'circulating and fixed capital' (Harrod, 1948, pp. 17–8); Hicks divides it into fixed and 'working capital' (Hicks, 1965, ch. 10, p. 105), and Joan Robinson divides it into investment in 'capital goods, including equipment, work-in-progress, technically necessary stocks of materials, etc.' (Robinson, 1966, p. 65). Similar distinctions play a vital role in the classical and marxian traditions, as well as in input–output analysis and Sraffian economics.

12. For instance, Kalecki has circulating investment depending on past changes in output, 'with a certain time lag' (Kalecki, 1971, ch. 10, p. 122), while Hicks has circulating capital investment depending on the expected change in (future) output (Hicks, 1965, ch. 10, pp. 105–6).

13. The capital–capacity ratio q is also taken to be given for any one production period (see the previous note), but can be variable across periods.

14. Keynes was so used to thinking in static terms, in which output change appears as a '*once over*' change in the level, that he initially found it difficult to grasp Harrod's notion of a steady advance inherent in a dynamic path (Kregel, 1980, p. 99, footnote 5).

15. The fact that the profit margin *measures* the 'markup' over costs does not imply that this profit margin is a reflection of monopoly power. A given normal competitive rate of return will also imply a particular 'markup'.

16. Keynes writes to Harrod that 'growth [is] a long-period conception' (cited in Kregel, 1980, p. 100).

17. An alternate formulation would be $b(e) = b \cdot |e|$.
18. With government taxes T and spending G, equation (1) becomes $I + G = S + T$, which can be written as $I = S - GD$, where $GD \equiv G - T$ is the government deficit. A rise in the ratio of the government deficit to profits would then be equivalent to a drop in the combined savings rate $s^* \equiv s - gd = S/P - GD/P$.
19. The proofs of the properties of our slow adjustment process are presented in Shaikh (1989).

References

Allen, R. G. D., *Macroeconomic Theory: A Mathematical Treatment* (London: Macmillan, 1968).

Baumol, W. J., *Economic Dynamics* (New York: Macmillan, 1959).

Domar, E. D., 'Capital Expansion, Rate of Growth, and Employment', *Econometrica*, 14 (April 1946) pp. 137–47.

van Duijn, J. J. (1983), *The Long Wave in Economic Life* (London: George Allen & Unwin, 1983).

Gandolfo, G., *Economic Dynamics: Methods and Models* (Amsterdam: North Holland, 1985).

Garegnani, P., 'Notes on Consumption, Investment, and Effective Demand: A Reply to Joan Robinson', *Cambridge Journal of Economics*, 3 (1978) pp. 181–7.

Goodwin, R. M., 'The Nonlinear Accelerator and the Persistence of Business Cycles', *Econometrica*, 19:1 (January 1951) pp. 1–17

Goodwin, R. M., 'A Growth Cycle', in *Socialism, Capitalism, and Economic Growth (Essays Presented to Maurice Dobb)* (Cambridge: Cambridge University Press, 1967) pp. 54–8.

Goodwin, R. M., 'Swinging Along the Turnpike With von Neumann and Sraffa', *Cambridge Journal of Economics*, 3 (1986) pp. 203–10.

Harrod, R. F., 'An Essay in Dynamic Theory', *Economic Journal*, 49 (March 1939) pp. 14–33.

Harrod, R. F., *Towards a Dynamic Economics* (London: Macmillan, 1948).

Hicks, J. R., *A Contribution to the Theory of the Trade Cycle* (Oxford: Oxford University Press, 1950).

Hicks, J. R., *Capital and Growth* (London: Oxford University Press, 1965).

Kaldor, N., 'A Model of the Trade Cycle', *Economic Journal*, 50 (March 1940) pp. 78–92.

Kaldor, N., *Essays on Value and Distribution* (London: Duckworth, 1960).

Kalecki, M., *Essays in the Theory of Economic Fluctuations* (London: Allen & Unwin, 1938).

Kalecki, M., 'Observations on the Theory of Growth', *Economic Journal* (March 1962) pp. 135–53.

Kalecki, M., *The Theory of Economic Dynamics* (New York: Monthly Review Press, 1965).

Kalecki, M., 'The Marxian Equations of Reproduction and Modern Economics', *Social Sciences Information*, no. 6 (1968) pp. 73–9.

Kalecki, M., *Selected Essays on the Dynamics of the Capitalist Economy: 1933–1970* (Cambridge: Cambridge University Press, 1971).

Keynes, J. M., *The General Theory of Employment, Interest, and Money* (New York: Harcourt, Brace, and World, 1964).

Klein, P. and G. H. Moore, 'Monitoring Profits During Business Cycles', in H. Laumer and M. Zeigler (eds), *International Research on Business Cycle Surveys* (Athens: 15th CIRET Conference Proceedings, 1981).

Kregel, J. A., 'Economic Dynamics and the Theory of Steady Growth: An Historical Essay on Harrod's 'Knife-Edge', *History of Political Economy*, 12:1 (1980) pp. 97–123.

Kregel, J. A., 'Natural and Warranted Rates of Growth', in J. Eatwell, M. Milgate and P. Newman (eds), *The New Palgrave: A Dictionary of Economics* (London: Macmillan, 1987).

Lakin, W. D. and D. A. Sanchez, *Topics in Ordinary Differential Equations* (New York: Dover Publications, 1970).

Mullineaux, A. W., *The Business Cycle after Keynes: A Contemporary Analysis* (New Jersey: Barnes & Noble Books, 1984).

Robinson, J., *The Accumulation of Capital* (London: Macmillan, 1966).

Sen, A., *Growth Economics* (Harmondsworth: Penguin, 1970).

Shaikh, A., 'Accumulation, Finance and Effective Demand in Marx, Keynes, and Kalecki', in W. Semmler (ed.), *Financial Dynamics and Business Cycles: New Perspectives* (New York: M. E. Sharpe, 1989).

Steindl, J., 'Some Comments on the Three Versions of Kalecki's Theory of the Trade Cycle', in J. Los, *et al.* (eds), *Studies in Economic Theory and Practise* (Amsterdam: North-Holland Publishing Co., 1981).

15 Profitability and Stability

Gerard Duménil and Dominique Lévy

The purpose of this chapter is to discuss the importance of profitability. This issue has been at the centre of our research programme for several years[1] and the present essay is a synthesis of several earlier aspects of our work. Our organising theme concerning the importance of profitability is that *Profitability matters because it is one important determinant of stability*.

By stability we mean the ability of the economic system to maintain a balanced growth path, without being subjected to constant cycles, overheating or stagnating.

The logic of our hypothesis can be summarised in five propositions:

1. In the short run, a lower rate of return modifies the pattern of costs that firms must carry when they confront disequilibria – for example, an increase in the cost of holding excess inventories.
2. When low returns endure, firms respond to declining profitability by improving their management, economising on the capital invested.
3. These two related consequences of a decline in the profit rate induce tighter management policies, in the specific sense of quicker and more intense adjustments to disequilibria – for example, larger values of what we shall call reaction coefficients.
4. This alteration of adjustment behaviour increases the macro instability of the economy. The link in the chain which relates profitability to stability is therefore paradoxical, since it appears that more efficient individual management is, in fact, detrimental to macro stability.
5. Profitability is not the unique determinant of stability. The problem of stability must be analysed in relation to the institutional framework of regulatory agencies and government policies which also condition stability. However, the transformation of this framework, which must periodically adapt to new situations, can be lengthy, and before this adaptation is carried out successfully, instability may dramatically ensue.

Our analysis seeks to provide a theoretical framework in which the new instability which was observed in the US economy since the 1970s can be analysed. The contrast between the 1960s and 1970s is striking in this respect. Ten years of steady activity ushered in a new period of instability let alone the acceleration of inflation which is beyond the scope of this chapter. It is well known that profitability declined in the US in the transition between the 1960s and 1970s. We would argue that these two developments are not coincidental, but related. The low levels of profitability are an important determinant of the instability.

The chapter is divided into four parts. In part 1, we show that adjustment to disequilibrium is a rational behaviour for a firm facing a demand function subject to random shocks. This demonstration relies heavily on Blinder's previous work (Blinder, 1982). Part 2 presents a dynamic model based on the same adjustment principle as that analysed in part 1. The market structure assumption adopted is that of monopolistic competition. We show how intense reactions to disequilibrium can be responsible for macro instability. In part 3 we discuss the relationship between the rate of return, management and stability. Part 4 is devoted to an empirical analysis of US manufacturing industries after The Second World War, focusing on the relationship between the recent trends in profitability and the new instability, since 1970, which we explain by the transformation of the reaction of firms in relation to these returns.

15.1   RATIONAL ADJUSTMENT BEHAVIOUR

In this part we draw from a previous study of ours (Duménil and Lévy, 1989b) in which we show that rational behaviour can take the form of adjustment. By 'rational behaviour' we mean the maximising of an objective function on the basis of the expectation of future magnitudes, while by 'adjustment' we mean the reaction to past disequilibria. In this study we limit the investigation to *output* and *price* decisions of firms resulting from the behaviour of a firm facing a demand function which is subject to random shocks. We shall first determine the equation modelling adjustment, and then – under the assumption that firms respond quickly to disequilibrium between supply and demand in comparison to the variations of demand – we shall derive the form of the decisions used in part 2 below (equations 15 and 16). In our previous work (1989b) we have analysed the same model in considerable detail.

The model is described in section 1, while in section 2 the derivation of the behaviour of the firm is summarised, and the equations for determining rational price and output adjustments are stated.

15.1.1   The Model

Considered below is the simple case of a price and quantity maker (a monopoly) confronted with a demand function known up to a stochastic additive disturbance. When this firm makes its decision concerning the level of production and price, it ignores the demand shock of the period, although we assume that it forms a set of rational expectations. The firm incurs two types of costs: production costs and inventory costs. (We shall sometimes refer, parenthetically, to the cost of changing the level of production.)

The model is a sequential model. With the notation Y_t, for the output of period t, D_t, for demand or firm's sales, p_t, for price on market t, and S_t, inventories at the end of market t (held during production $t + 1$), the sequence of operations can be represented as follows:

$$
\begin{array}{ccccc}
 & Y_t & p_t & Y_{t+1} & \\
—| & \!\!\!\!\!\!—————— & —————— & —————— & |— \quad t \\
 & S_{t-1} & D_t & S_t & \\
 & \underbrace{} & \underbrace{} & \underbrace{} & \\
 & \text{Production } t & \text{Market } t & \text{Production } t + 1 &
\end{array}
$$

We determine below the decisions of the firm on Y_t and p_t, at the end of market 0, since S_o is known. Inventories, outputs, and demand are related by the following accounting relation:

$$S_t = S_{t-1} + Y_t - D_t \tag{1}$$

Demand is modelled as

$$D_t = d_o - d_1 p_t + \eta_t \tag{2}$$

where d_o and d_1, are two constant parameters and η_t, the stochastic disturbance. This disturbance follows an $AR(1)$ process. With v_t denoting an independently and identically distributed disturbance, we have

$$\eta_t = \varrho \eta_{t-1} + v_t \text{ with } 0 \leqslant \varrho \leqslant 1 \tag{3}$$

If $\varrho = 0$, η_t is itself an independently and identically distributed disturbance. If $\varrho = 1$ then we have the case of random walk.

Production costs are quadratic and equal to $\frac{c}{2} Y_t^2$

Inventory costs can be analysed as the sum of the cost of holding inventories and the cost of lost sales as shown in Figure 15.1. Given the analytical forms of these two components, inventory costs are also quadratic in the form

$$\frac{c_s}{2} (S_t - \bar{S})^2 + c_s' \tag{4}$$

Parameter c_s' does not play any role in our demonstration, and can therefore be eliminated. $\bar{S}$ corresponds to the minimum cost, and is not the target value for inventories computed below.

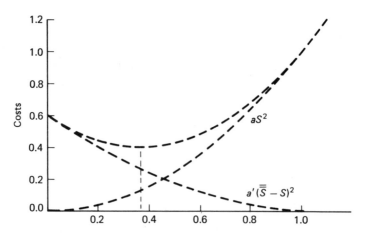

Figure 15.1   The two components of inventory costs

Notes: Inventory costs are the sum of aS^2, the cost of holding inventories and the cost of lost sales. For $S \geqslant \bar{\bar{S}}$ the likelihood of losing sales is negligible and this cost can be considered as nil. Below that, this cost is equal to $a'\,(\bar{\bar{S}} = S)^2$. The sum of the two costs can be written as $c_s/2\,(S - \bar{S})^2 - c_s'$, with $\bar{S} < \bar{\bar{S}}$ and $c_s/2 = a + a'$. We do not consider the case of unfilled orders ($S < 0$), since we limit our investigation to the vicinity of equilibrium.

The firm *maximises its expected profits* represented by

$$\pi = E_0 \sum_{t=1}^{\infty} \delta^t \left(p_t(d_0 - d_1 p_t + \eta_t) - \frac{c}{2}\,Y_t^2 - \frac{c_s}{2}\,(S_t - \bar{S})^2 \right) \tag{5}$$

subject the constraint of equation (1). δ is a discount factor and the expectation (E_0) is established as of time zero.

Inventory costs are the sum of, aS^2, the cost of holding inventories and the cost of lost sales. For $S \geqslant \bar{\bar{S}}$ the likelihood of losing sales is negligible and this cost can be considered as nil. Below that, this cost is equal to $a'\,(\bar{\bar{S}} - S)^2$.

The sum of the two costs can be written as $\frac{c_s}{2}(S - \bar{S})^2 + c_s'$, with $\bar{S} < \bar{\bar{S}}$ and $\frac{c_s}{2} = a + a'$. We do not consider the case of unfilled orders ($S < 0$), since we limit our investigation to the vicinity of equilibrium.

15.1.2   Price and Output Rational Adjustments

In this section we summarise the demonstration presented in our previous study (1989b).

First, we construct the Lagrangian and determine the first order conditions. Then, we determine the targets around which variables p, Y, and S gravitate

$$\tilde{Y} = \frac{d_0}{2 + d_1 c} \tag{6}$$

$$\tilde{p} = \frac{d_0}{d_1} \frac{1 + cd_1}{2 + cd_1} \tag{7}$$

$$\tilde{S} = \bar{S} - (1 - \delta) \frac{d_0 c}{c_s(2 + d_1 c)} \tag{8}$$

After elimination of p and S from the first order conditions, one obtains a second order non-homogeneous difference equation in Y such as

$$\delta Y_{t+1} - \alpha Y_t + Y_{t-1} = \beta_t \text{ for } t = 2, 3, \ldots \tag{9}$$

with $a = 1 + \delta + \dfrac{c_s}{c}\left(1 + \dfrac{d_i c}{2}\right)$ and $\beta_t = -\dfrac{c_s}{2c}(d_0 + \eta_t)$ (10)

The resolution of equation (9) yields two behavioural equations

$$Y_1 = \tilde{Y} - \varepsilon(S_0 - \tilde{S}) + \phi\eta O \tag{11}$$

$$p_1 = \tilde{p} - \varepsilon'(S_0 - \bar{S}) + \phi' \eta O \tag{12}$$

with $\varepsilon = \dfrac{c_s}{c(a - \delta - \mu_1)}$ and $\phi = \dfrac{\varepsilon}{2}\dfrac{\varrho}{1 - \mu_1\varrho}$ (13)

$$\varepsilon' = \frac{c\varepsilon}{2} \text{ and } \phi' = \frac{c\phi}{2} + \frac{\varrho}{2d_1} \tag{14}$$

In these equations

1. μ_1 is the zero of equation of $\mu^2 - \alpha\mu + \delta = 0$ which is smaller than 1.
2. η_0 measures the difference (recorded after the previous market) between actual demand and the model of demand in the absence of shocks: $\eta_0 = D_0 - (d_0 - d_1 p_0)$.
3. S_0 denotes initial inventories.
4. ε, ε', ϕ, and ϕ' are *reaction coefficients*. They measure the intensity of the reaction of the firm to disequilibria.

In part 3, we shall comment on the fact that reaction coefficients reflect the structure of costs as is, for example, the use of ε in equation (13).

Notice that ε is a function of the two costs c and c_s, directly and indirectly through α and μ_1.

The structural form of the behavioural equations actually depends to a larger extent than stated above, on the pattern of the disequilibrium costs. Following Holt, Modigliani, Muth and Simon (1960), it is possible to include the cost of varying production levels, for example, the costs of hiring and firing workers as

$$c_d(Y_t - Y_{t-1})^2$$

In this case, the resolution is more difficult. Equation (9) is transformed into a fourth order difference equation. In the absence of shocks, one obtains

$$Y_1 = \widetilde{Y} + \sigma(Y_0 - \widetilde{Y}) - \varepsilon\,(S_0 - \widetilde{S}) \tag{15}$$

$$p_1 = \widetilde{p} + \sigma'(Y_0 - \widetilde{Y}) - \varepsilon'\,(S_0 - \widetilde{S}) \tag{16}$$

In Duménil and Lévy (1989b), we show that, independently of the cost of varying the production level, the assumption that the firm's adjustment of supply to demand is quicker than the movements of demand themselves, yields the same result as above. The two terms $\sigma(Y_0 - \widetilde{Y})$ and $\sigma'\,(Y_0 - \widetilde{Y})$ can be substituted for $\phi\eta_0$ and $\phi'\eta_0$ in equations (11) and (12). Thus, two distinct reasons justify equations (15) and (16). Equation (15) is reminiscent of early works on stability based on adjustment (Samuelson, 1939; Metzler, 1941; Lovell, 1961 and 1962; Tobin, 1975).

15.2 STABILITY AND INSTABILITY IN A DYNAMIC MODEL

In this part, we use the adjustment principle derived in part 1 to construct a dynamic model in which the macro stability of the economy can be analysed. In the demonstration below, equations (15) and (16) play a crucial role.

In part 1, we used a partial equilibrium perspective for a monopoly. We now turn to the case of a general equilibrium in which, for example, demand is endogenous. Section 1 is devoted to this transition. The model is then introduced in section 2 with the simplest possible assumptions concerning the institutional environment, particularly with relation to monetary phenomena. We derive the macro stability condition in section 3 while in section 4 we briefly analyse what occurs when the stability condition is not met.

15.2.1 General Equilibrium

The transformation of the partial equilibrium perspective of part 1 into the simple general equilibrium model of this section requires three types of revisions:

1. Instead of a single monopoly, the economy must be conceived of consisting of n identical competing firms with same technology and same costs.
2. In part 1, it was possible to assume that parameters d_0 and d_1 in the demand function were given. Demand is now endogenous.
3. The values of the two costs c and c_s were given. We assume now that they vary proportionally with, p_t, the general level of prices, such that $c = \bar{c}p_t$ and $c_s = \bar{c}p_t$, in which $\bar{c}$ and $\bar{c}_s$ are given real costs.

In the rest of this section we consider successively (i) aggregate demand and its distribution among firms, (ii) firms' targets, and (iii) firms' behaviours.

1. Demand

Aggregate demand is a function of aggregate income. However, in order to account for the impact of monetary phenomena affecting the formation of demand and the ensuing consequences concerning stability, we also include the real balance of money, $m_t = M_t/p_t$. Let us assume a linear function of the form

$$D_t = dY_t + e\,\frac{M_t}{p_t} + f \tag{17}$$

The n firms must share this aggregate demand on the basis of their relative prices. The individual demand function for firm i in period t is modelled as

$$D_t^i = \frac{D_t}{n}\left(1 - \Psi\left(\frac{p_t^i}{p_t} - 1\right)\right) \tag{18}$$

in which p_t is the average price, $p_t = \frac{1}{n}\sum_{i=1}^{n} p_t^i$ and Ψ is a parameter which accounts for the intensity of competition. It is also possible to include random shocks η_t^i.

The following can be made relating to this equation:

(a) For any set of prices p_t^i, one has: $\sum_{i=1}^{n} D_t^i = D_t$. Equation 18 actually expresses the distribution of aggregate demand among the n enterprises.

(b) This equation can be derived from a utility function (Duménil and Lévy, 1989b).

(c) If $\Psi = 0$, there is no price competition and $D_t^i = \dfrac{D_t}{n}$. The same uniform distribution is obtained if all prices are equal.

Finally, equation (18) can be written as $d_0 - d_1 p_t^i$ with:

$$d_0 = \frac{D_t}{n}\,(1 + \Psi) \tag{19}$$

$$d_1 = \frac{D_t}{n}\,\frac{\Psi}{p_t} \tag{20}$$

2. Equilibrium and Firms' Targets

Equilibrium can be characterised by two conditions. The first traditional condition for equilibrium is that supply equals demand, $Y^* = D^*$. The second condition is specific to the existence of price-makers. Firms' individual targets must coincide with the average values of the variables.

Beginning with Y, M, and p, at the aggregate level, equations (17), (19), and (20) allow for the determination of the individual demand functions. Equations (6) and (7) provide the values of the two individual targets $\widetilde{Y}$ and $\widetilde{p}$. The second equilibrium condition concerning prices, $\widetilde{p}(p) = p$, allows for the determination of Y^*, the equilibrium total demand, Y^* $= n\,\dfrac{\Psi - 1}{\Psi}\dfrac{1}{c}$. Notice that there is no equilibrium value of prices, but when equilibrium prevails, prices are constant. The real balance at equilibrium can be obtained from equation (17)

$$m^* = (Y^*(1 - d) - f)/e$$

Aggregate inventories at equilibrium, S^*, are determined as well as individual inventories S^*/n.

$$S^* = n\,\overline{S} - (1 - \delta)\,\frac{\overline{c}}{\overline{c}_s}\,Y^*,$$

Using these equilibrium values, equation (17) for aggregate demand, can be rewritten as

$$D_t = Y^* + d(Y_t - Y^*) + e\,\frac{M_t}{p_t} - m^* \tag{21}$$

3. Firms' Behaviour

In order to derive the equations modelling the behaviour of firms, it is not possible to directly use the results obtained in part 1, since the parameters which define the demand function and the costs vary over time.

In what follows, we shall render the model manageable subject to the following two restrictions:

1. Our investigation will be limited to the vicinity of equilibrium, that is, the gravitation of the economy around equilibrium. Under such conditions, the demand parameters and costs also gravitate in the vicinity of their equilibrium values.
2. The equilibrium values of these parameters will be substituted for their actual values.

With the above two restrictions, the results derived in part 1 will hold while the equations for rational individual behaviour are:

$$Y_{t+1}^i = \frac{Y^*}{n} + \sigma \left(Y_t^i - \frac{Y^*}{n} \right) - \varepsilon \left(S_t^i - \frac{S^*}{n} \right) \tag{22}$$

$$p_t^{i+1} = p_t \left(1 + \sigma'' \left(Y_t^i - \frac{Y^*}{n} \right) - \varepsilon'' \left(S_t^i - \frac{S^*}{n} \right) \right) \tag{23}$$

15.2.2 The Model

In this section, we first aggregate individual behaviours (subsection 1) and then proceed in subsection 2 to the modelling of monetary phenomena. Last, the equations of the model are defined in subsection 3.

1. The Aggregation of Individual Behaviours

We are concerned in this study with the overall stability of the economy and so we shall need to aggregate individual behaviours. Thus, the aggregation of equations (22) and (23) yields

$$Y_{t+1} = Y^* + \sigma(Y_t - Y^*) - \varepsilon (S_t - S^*) \tag{24}$$

$$p_{t+1} = p_t \left(1 + \frac{\sigma''}{n} (Y_t - Y^*) - \frac{\varepsilon''}{n} (S_t - S^*) \right) \tag{25}$$

2. Monetary Phenomena

The issuance of money is a complex phenomenon; we shall model it as follows:

$$\Delta M_{t+1} = M_{t+1} - M_t = M_t(a(Y_t - Y^*) + b(S_t - S^*)) \tag{26}$$

This equation synthetically accounts for a complicated set of phenomena. A high level of activity, for example a large $(Y_{t+1} - Y^*)$, stimulates the demand of the firm for loans. Large inventories, for example a large $(S_{t+1} - S^*)$, are an inducement for firms to extend credit to their customers. Although this mechanism is not included in the above equation, the variation of the general price level could be added as a new argument. This new term in the equation would account for monetary authority attempts to control the general level of price.

3. The Equations

Equations (24), (25), (26), (1), and (21), define a relation of recursion with five variables Y, p, M, S, and D. It is possible to eliminate D and to substitute m for M and p. Thus a relation of recursion with three variables, Y, S, and m, is obtained and the three resulting equations are

$$Y_{t+1} = Y^* + \sigma(Y_t - Y^*) - \varepsilon(S_t - S^*)$$

$$S_{t+1} = S_t + (Y_{t+1} - Y^*)(1 - d) - e(m_{t+1} - m^*)$$

$$m_{t+1} = m_t + m^* a - \frac{\sigma''}{n}(Y_t - Y^*) + m^* b + \frac{\varepsilon''}{n}(S_t - S^*)$$

The third equation has been given a linear from which does not affect the study of stability.

15.2.3 The Macro Stability Condition

The model described above has an equilibrium for $Y = Y^*$, $S = S^*$, and $m = m^*$ which we call 'normal equilibrium'. We now turn to the issue of the local stability of this equilibrium.

The polynomial characteristic of the Jacobian matrix of the recursion is

$$P(\lambda) = \begin{vmatrix} \lambda - \sigma & \varepsilon & 0 \\ (d-1)\lambda & \lambda - 1 & e\lambda \\ \dfrac{\sigma''}{n} - a\,m^* & (\varepsilon''_n + b)m^* & \lambda - 1 \end{vmatrix}$$

Equation $P(\lambda) = 0$ has three roots λ_i for $i = 1, 2, 3$, three eigenvalues of the Jacobian matrix. Local stability is insured if the modulus of these three eigenvalues is smaller than 1: $\lambda_i < 1 \; \forall \, i$.

It is possible to empirically verify in a straightforward manner that the dominant eigenvalue is real and close to 1, investigating the relationship

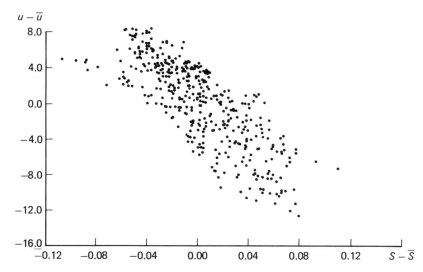

Figure 15.2   Plot of *u* against *s* (residual around the trends) manufacturing industries, 1950–85.

between the variables when the economy moves out of equilibrium. This relation is determined by the eigenvector associated with this dominant eigenvalue. Figure 15.2 displays the relationship between production levels and inventories for the period 1950–85, using monthly data. Because of the effect of growth between 1950 and 1985, it is necessary to normalize Y and S, using the capacity utilisation rate u, and the ratio of inventories to sales s. Moreover, the trends of these two variables have been subtracted. It is evident from this figure that a trade-off exists. This trade-off in the plane (u, s) represents the eigenvector associated with the eigenvalue 1 (Duménil and Lévy, 1989a). This observation proves that (i) the economy is constantly maintained in a vicinity of the stability limit $\lambda = 1$, (ii) equation (22) is a good model of the decision to produce.

As a result of this maintenance near $\lambda = 1$, the general level of activity is very unstable. This is reflected in the constant oscillation of the capacity utilisation rate as shown in Figure 15.3 for manufacturing industries in the US after the Second World War.

A priori, the stability condition can be violated in three distinct ways: (i) a real eigenvalue becomes larger than 1; (ii) a real eigenvalue becomes smaller than –1; (iii) two complex conjugate eigenvalues have moduli larger than 1. Another consequence of this proximity to 1 of the dominant eigenvalue is that the analytical study of stability can be simplified, since only the first condition must be studied.

The condition $P(1)>0$, a necessary condition for $\lambda<1$, for example, the stability of the economy, can be easily expressed as

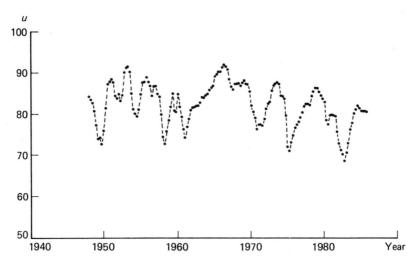

Figure 15.3   Capacity utilisation rate manufacturing industries, quarterly data
(1948–85)

$$\theta = \sigma + \varepsilon \; \frac{a - \sigma''}{\varepsilon'' + b} < 1 \tag{27}$$

In this condition, the reaction coefficients σ'' and e'' account for the real balance effect. This action is obviously very limited in comparison to that of the issuance of money. Thus, equation (27) can be written in an even simpler manner as

$$\theta = \sigma + \varepsilon \; \frac{a}{b} < 1 \tag{28}$$

One can observe in this expression the role played by ε. Large values of this reaction coefficient jeopardise the stability of the system. We shall elaborate on this property in part 3, but before turning to this discussion, we shall briefly comment on what happens when condition (28) is not met.

15.2.4   Beyond the Stability Limit[2]

All behavioural equations described so far are linear equations. This is appropriate as long as the investigation is limited to the vicinity of normal equilibrium. Away from equilibrium, or when normal equilibrium is unstable, this representation of behaviour cannot be maintained. For example, in the short run for a given stock of fixed capital, a maximum feasible output sets a frontier to the expansion of production. The consideration of

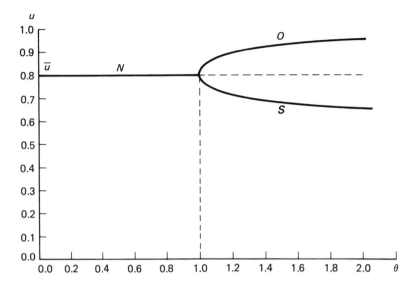

Figure 15.4   The pitchfork. The configuration of equilibria

Note: This figure represents the configuration of the equilibria with respect to the value of the capacity utilisation rates obtained, as functions of θ. Stable equilibria are represented by a dark line and the unstable normal equilibrium for θ > 1, by a doted line. *N*, *O*, and *S* respectively denote 'normal equilibrium', 'overheating', and 'stagnation'. The gap between overheating and stagnation increases with θ.

such nonlinearities is important in the investigation of what occurs at a distance from equilibrium.

Nonlinearities do not alter the results obtained about the existence of normal equilibrium and its stability which is insured under condition (28). The consideration of nonlinearities affects what occurs beyond the stability limit. There is a bifurcation and two new stable equilibria exist, one with a lower than normal capacity utilisation rate, which we designate 'stagnation', and the other with a capacity utilisation rate larger than normal, which we call 'overheating'. As θ in equation (28) increases beyond 1, the gap between the two stable equilibria and the unstable normal equilibrium also increases. As shown in Figure 15.4, the pattern obtained is that of a pitchfork, with two prongs, one corresponding to stagnation (*s*) and the other to overheating (*o*).

We interpret business cycles as recurrent but non-repetitive successions of switches from one of these equilibria to the other in different configurations. The traditional nineteenth-century-style business cycle can be analysed as a specific chain of events: six of seven years of normal equilibrium, a switch to overheating for a few months, a sudden collapse into stagnation (a recession), and finally a progressive restoration of normal equilibrium. The stop-and-go characteristic of the 1950s can be viewed as a successful of flips from overheating to stagnation and back to overheating.

The pitchfork provides an interpretation of what occurs when condition (28) is violated. This is not a rare event but instead, as was shown previously in Figures 15.2 and 15.3, a habitual feature of our economies.

15.3 THE RATE OF RETURN, MANAGEMENT AND STABILITY

In section 1 of this part, we analyse the impact of the pattern of disequilibrium costs on the target values of the variables and reaction coefficients. Section 2 is devoted to a brief discussion of the notion of progress in management, while the impact of the rate of return on the pattern of disequilibrium costs and the transformation of management is considered in section 3. Finally, we conclude with a consideration of the relationship between management and stability.

15.3.1 The Pattern of Disequilibrium Costs

In disequilibrium, firms incur additional production and inventory costs. The rational management of the firm confronted with a positive demand shock requires, for example, some degree of arbitration between the additional production costs and a diminished risk of lost sales. The characteristics of the shocks determine those of rational management for given disequilibrium costs.

Disequilibrium costs determine both the target values of the variables and the reaction parameters. The targets for output, price and the stock of inventories have been defined in equations (6) to (8), and the optimal values of the reaction parameters ε, ϕ, ε', and ϕ' have been given in equations (13) and (14).

As analysed in Figure 15.1, inventory costs are the sum of two components: the stock of holding inventories and that of lost sales. With this distinction, the effect of disequilibrium costs on management is as follows:

1. If a (which determines the cost of holding inventories) increases, c_s is raised, and $\bar{S}$ and $\tilde{S}$, the target values of inventories, are diminished. The values of the reaction coefficients, ε, ε'', σ and σ'' become larger. The firm maintains less inventories and reacts more intensely to disequilibrium.
2. If a' (which determines the cost of lost sales) increases, c_s, $\bar{S}$ and $\tilde{S}$ are increased. The value of the reaction coefficients, ε, ε'', σ and σ'' become

larger. The firm maintains more inventories and reacts more intensely to disequilibrium.

In sum, the increasing costs of holding inventories and lost sales have an ambiguous effect on the target value of inventories, but they always contribute to the more increase reactions to disequilibrium. (Recall that Y and $\tilde{Y}$ are independent from inventory costs.)

15.3.2 Progress in Management

In the previous section, the point of view was that of rational management. It was taken for granted that firms optimise with given costs, demand and shocks within a particular managerial environment. The notion of progress in management is excluded from this approach, just as in the paradigm of the rational behaviour of a firm, the state of technology is assumed as given.

The history of capitalism reveals, however, that management is the object of constant transformations, in the direction toward increased efficiency. The industrial revolution was accompanied and followed by a managerial revolution.

It is important to notice here that management itself has a cost which must be compared to its efficiency benefits. For example, the control of inventories requires the gathering and transmission of information. A prominent aspect of the progress in management is the reduction of disequilibrium costs. In order to maximise the rate of return, it is necessary to maintain as little inventory as possible, to reduce inactive cash to a minimum without being forced to face shortages; an inability to produce when demand suddenly grows due to a lack of productive capacity or liquidity, or an inability to respond to increased demand as a result of insufficient buffer inventories. Better management, for example, allows for a lower *inventories/sales* ratio but maintains a high degree of capability to avoid shortages. This is equivalent to a smaller $\tilde{S}$ and larger reaction parameters.

15.3.3 The Rate of Return and Management

The effects of progress in management – implying a reduction in the cost of management – are very similar to those of increased disequilibrium costs. The combined requirements of saving on each fraction of capital and minimising the negative consequences of disequilibrium have specific effects on the target values of the variables and reaction coefficients.

In both cases, *management* is related to the levels of *profitability*.

1. Considering management as given, a diminished rate of return alters the pattern of disequilibrium costs. The cost of holding inventories is not

only that of storage, but also includes a financial component since the expansion of inventories results in expensive short-term indebtedness. This cost cannot be considered in isolation, but must be related to the profit rate of the firm. A low profit rate results in a comparatively lower cash flow and requires an increased dependence on short-term borrowing.

2. Progress in management as well as technological change must not be viewed as a smooth and autonomous processes. Innovation is required and develops in a reactive manner under the pressure of events. The recurrent *profitability squeezes*[3] that have been observed along the history of capitalism were the primary stimulative factors in the progress in management and oftentimes transformations were undertaken under crisis circumstances.

15.3.4 Management and Stability

The next link in the chain that relates profitability to stability follows in a straightforward manner from the models presented in parts 1 and 2. It is clear from condition (equation) (28) that a tighter management in the sense of a larger reaction parameter ε, jeopardises stability.

As was stated in the introduction, this relationship between management and stability is paradoxical since individual efficiency is related to overall instability. This questions the widely held view that individual and general interests necessarily coincide.

The answer to the question 'why does profitability matter?', stresses the impact of profitability on stability. The understanding of the nature of the relation is not common in conventional economic theory which assumes:

1. a mechanistic application of general equilibrium analysis implying that profitability does not matter as long as there is a positive price for capital.
2. that in a growth model, profitability matters for a given propensity to consume of capitalists, since it conditions the rate of growth in the long run (as in the so-called 'Cambridge relation' $\varrho = sr$, with obvious notation) and
3. that within a Keynesian perspective, expected profitability – the marginal efficiency of capital – determines the inducement to invest and thus, directly affects the production level in the economy.

15.4 RECENT TRENDS IN PROFITABILITY AND INSTABILITY

In this part, we provide an empirical test of our hypotheses that:

1. The variation of the rate of return impacts on the stability of the economy; when the rate of return falls and before what we called the

'institutional framework' is adapted to the new situation, instability is manifested in a specific pattern.
2. The link between profitability and stability is the value of the reaction coefficients (ε and σ, in particular).

Our empirical analysis is based on the US manufacturing industry since the Second World War for which appropriate data are available. Our test demonstration is made in three steps: in section 1, we review the changing pattern of the business cycle after the Second World War. In section 2, we provide an estimate of the reaction coefficients ε and σ, and in section 3, we present the profile of the profit rate since the war and its lower levels since 1970.

15.4.1 Instability Since the Second World War

The careful examination of Figure 15.3 suggests a periodisation of three sub-periods which, quite conveniently, correspond to the 1950s, the 1960s, and after 1970. Each sub-period possesses its own characteristics which can be outlined briefly as follows:

1. In the 1950s, the economy displays constant short oscillations.
2. In the 1960s, the economy stabilises and is slowly and steadily pulled upward. After the fall in 1967, the activity is still very high and a new plateau is maintained until the end of 1969.
3. After 1970, a new instability is manifested. The economy displays ample oscillations without stabilising, but with plateaux of very short duration. Another striking feature of this period is that the capacity utilisation rate reveals a downward trend.

From these observations, we derive the general view that the economy during this period remained in a vicinity of its stability conditions, but in three distinct ways. In the 1950s, the stability condition is violated consistently, but to rather limited proportions. In the 1960s, stability is restored, while, since 1970, the stability limit has been violated in larger proportions.

15.4.2 Measuring σ and ε

In order to verify our interpretation of the pattern of stability and instability since the war, we shall focus on reaction coefficients σ and ε. Parameter θ in condition (28) is an increasing function of σ and ε. A large σ or ε is consequently a factor of instability. These reaction coefficients are volatile since they are subject to many short-term determinants such as, for example, the rate of interest – which is a component of inventory costs – which renders their estimation difficult over a short period of time. It is possible, however, to at least attempt to estimate trend values of σ and ε over the period.

We use the model of determination of the production level as described in equation (15), but normalise all variables to correct for the effect of growth in the economy. Thus, we substitute the capacity utilisation rate, u, for Y, and s, the inventories/sales ratio for S; then, the model is determined as

$$u_{t+1} = \bar{u} = \sigma(u_t - \bar{u}) - \varepsilon (s_{t+1} - \bar{s}) + e_t \tag{29}$$

in which e_t denotes the error term. In this equation we use s_{t+1}, instead of s_t, since the periodicity of the available series is longer than the lag in the actual decision process.

The trend value of ε is represented by a polynomial in time t. The more significant results are obtained for a polynomial of the fourth degree: $\varepsilon(t) = \sum_{n=0}^{4} \varepsilon_n t^n$. The use of a polynomial in time for σ does not give significant results. We estimated σ and the parameters of the polynomial in ε by a least square method, with the following equation:

$$u_{t+1} = a + \sigma u_t + \sum_{n=0}^{4} \varepsilon_n (t^n s_{t+1}) + e_t$$

This procedure yields the following result:

$$
\begin{array}{llllll}
u_{t+1} = & 23.5 & + \; 0.850 \, u_t + & 803 - & 5\,108 \, t + & 11.693 \, t^2 \\
& (t = 11.7) & (t = 60.9) & (t = 3.8) & (t = 4.0) & (t = 4.0) \\[6pt]
& -\,11\,671 \, t^3 & +\;4\,280 \, t^4 & s_{t+1} + e_t & R^2 = 0.97 \\
& (t = 4.1) & (t = 4.1)
\end{array}
$$

in which $t = (\text{Year} - 1900)/100$.

The trend of ε, represented by the polynomial in t, is displayed in Figure 15.5. Notice that reaction coefficient ε reveals a minimum in the mid-1960s and, what we consider as the main result of this computation, it has been soaring since 1970. These observations are consistent with those made in section 1 above, that is restoration of stability in the 1960s and the new instability since 1970.

15.4.3 Diminished Returns

It has been shown that the levels of profitability in the US since 1970 have been reduced in comparison to those achieved in the 1950s as well as those obtained in the 1960s. The overall trend of the profit rate for manufacturing corporations, after indirect business and profits taxes, over the net stock of capital is displayed in Figure 15.6. The doted lines show the average levels for each sub-period; 16.9 per cent in the 1950s, 19.0 per cent in the 1960s, and 11.0 per cent since 1970. The ratio of the average rate obtained in the later period to that characteristic of the 1950s is 0.654

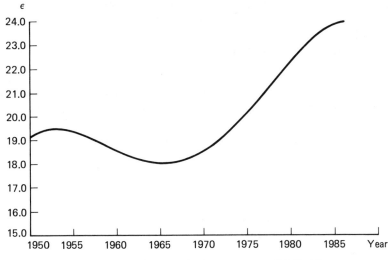

Figure 15.5   The trend of parameter ε (1950–85)

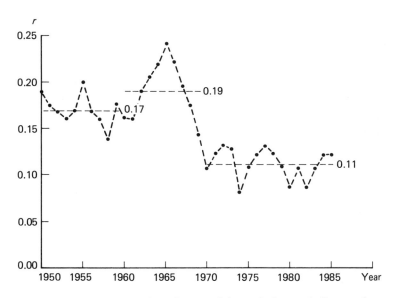

Figure 15.6   The rate of profit, net of depreciation and all taxes for
manufacturing corporations (1950–85)

(11.0/16.9). The relationship between the trends observed in Figures 15.5 and 15.6 is striking. Coefficient ε is large when profitability is low, and conversely.

These observations show that there are some grounds to the assertions of this study, that

1. The specific features of the stability problem in each period are related to the movements of the rate of return (Figures 15.3 and 15.6)
2. The 'missing' link between the two variables must be located in the behaviour of firms – their reaction to disequilibrium

low →	large →	increased
profit rate	reaction coefficients	instability

The relationship between the rate of return and ε, is evident by the comparison between Figures 15.5 and 15.6, while the relationship between ε and instability is evident from the stability condition (28) and the comparison between Figures 15.3 and 15.5.

APPENDIX

15.A List of Figures

15.1 The Two Components of Inventory Costs.
15.2 Plot of u Against s (Residual Around the Trends) Manufacturing Industries, 1950–85. u=CU and s=CFINISS/CSHIPM. u and s are detrended using a polynomial of the second degree in time. The variables used are the residuals.
15.3 Capacity Utilization Rate Manufacturing Industries, Quarterly Data (1948–85). CU.
15.4 The Pitchfork: The Configuration of Equilibria.
15.5 The Trend of Parameter ε (1950–85). u=CU and s=CFINISS/CSHIPM. $e(t) = \Sigma_{n=0}^{4} \varepsilon_n t^n$.
15.6 The Rate of Profit, Net of Depreciation and All Taxes Manufacturing Corporations (1950–85). r=1/K, with = NCPM + (NCCAM-KDEPCM) + NIVACM (the term within parenthesis is the Capital Consumption adjustment) and K=KM+KGOPOM.

15.B Sources

1. Labels of the Variables

The first letter in the label of a variable indicates the origin of this variable:
C   Citibase Tape, CITICORP 1086
K   BEA Wealth Data Tape, B.E.A. (1986b)
N   NIPA, B.E.A. (1986a)
The first label (or number) in the tables below is that of the variable in its original source. The second label, in bold face, is that given to the variable in the present study.

2. Variables from the Citibase Tape: C

Capacity Utilisation Rate (Manuf.)	1948–85	IPXMCA	CU
Invent. of Finished Goods (Manuf.)	1946–85	IVM3	CFINISS
Shipments (Manuf.)	1947–85	MFGS	CSHIPM

3. Variables from BEA Wealth Tape: K

The Government Owned Privately Operated (GOPO) stock of capital is considered. There is no residential capital in manufacturing industries.

In the table below, we give the numbers of the section and of the series:

Stocks of Capital:			
Net, Corp, Manuf.	Cur. Cost	(1246)	KM
Net, GOPO, Manuf., All Agencies	Cur. Cost	(1621)	KGOPOM
Depreciation:			
Corporate, Manufacturing	Cur. Cost	(1246)	KDEPCM

4. Variables from NIPA: N

Corporate Profits After Tax by Industry:			
Manufacturing	1929–85	6.21A(13), B(12)	NCPM
Corporate Capital Consumption Allowances by Industry			
Manufacturing	1929–85	6.24A(12), B(11)	NCCCAM
Inventory Valuation Adjustment to Nonfarm Income by Legal Form:			
Corporate Bus.,			
Manufacturing	1929–85	6.6A(5)	NIVACM

Notes

1. For example, Duménil and Lévy, (1988a, 1988b).
2. This section summarises the demonstrations presented in our previous studies (Duménil and Lévy, 1985, 1986a, 1987).
3. In Duménil, Glick and Lévy (1988) we present an estimate of the profit rate from 1869 to 1985, which illustrates this notion of recurrent declines and restorations. The main observation is that, in spite of major fluctuations, the profit rate before all taxes tends to decline from the late nineteenth century to the 1920s, and from the Second World War to the present, but that the depression and the Second World War resulted in the most dramatic restoration of profitability over this period of more than a century. It is important to notice, however, that this recovery benefited the state through taxation, and conferred to the post-Second World War years its specific profile of prosperity with considerable state intervention.

References

B.E.A., The National Income and Product Accounts of the United States, 1929–85, Data Tape, Department of Commerce, Bureau of Economic Analysis (1986a).

B.E.A., Wealth Data Tape, Department of Commerce, Bureau of Economic Analysis (1986b).

Blinder, A. S., 'Inventories and Sticky Prices: More on the Microfoundations of Macroeconomics', *American Economic Review*, vol. 72, no. 3 (1982) pp. 334–48.

Citicorp, Economic Data Base, Global Investment Banking, New York (1986).

Duménil, G., M. Glick and D. Lévy, *Long-term Trends in Profitability: The World War II Leap Forward* (Paris: CEPREMAP, 1988).

Duménil, G. and D. Lévy, *Stability and Instability in a Dynamic Model of Capitalist Production* (Paris: CEPREMAP, 1985).

Duménil, G. and D. Lévy, 'Stability and Instability in a Dynamic Model of Capitalist Production' (abridged version), in W. Semmler (ed.), (1986d).

Duménil, G. and D. Lévy, 'La concurrence classique à la croisée des chemins', in *La formation des crandeurs économiques, PUF* (Paris, CEPREMAP, 1986b).

Duménil, G. and D. Lévy, 'The Macroeconomics of Disequilibrium', *Journal of Economic Behaviour and Organization*, vol. 8 (1987) pp. 377–95.

Duménil, G. and D. Lévy, 'Real and Financial Stability in Capitalism: The Law of the Tendency toward Increasing Instability', in W. Semmler (ed.), (1988a).

Duménil, G. and D. Lévy, *Why Does Profitability Matter?* (Paris: CEPREMAP, LAREA-CEDRA, 1988b).

Duménil, G. and D. Lévy, *The Classical Legacy and Beyond* (Paris: CEPREMAP, LAREA-CEDRA, 1988c).

Duménil, G. and D. Lévy, *Micro Adjustment Behaviour and Macro Stability* (Paris: CEPREMAP, LAREA-CEDRA, 1989a).

Duménil, G. and D. Lévy, *The Rationality of Adjustment Behaviour in a Model of Monopolistic Competition* (Paris: CEPREMAP, LAREA-CEDRA, 1989b).

Holt, C. C., F. Modigliani, J. F. Muth and H. A. Simon, *Planning Production, Inventories, and Work Force* (Englewood Cliffs, New Jersey: Prentice-Hall, 1960).

Lovell, M., 'Manufacturers' Inventories, Sales Expectations, and the Acceleration Principle', *Econometrica*, vol. 29, no. 3 (1961) pp. 293–314.

Lovell, M., 'Buffer Stocks, Sales Expectations, and Stability: A Multi-Sector Analysis of the Inventory Cycle', *Econometrica*, vol. 30, no. 2 (1962) pp. 267–96.

Metzler, L. A., 'The Nature and Stability of Inventory Cycles', *Review of Economic Statistics*, vol. 3 (August 1941) pp. 113–29.

Samuelson, P. A., 'Interactions between the Multiplier Analysis and the Principle of Acceleration', *Review of Economic Statistics* (May 1939).

Semmler, W., 'Competition, Instability, and Nonlinear Cycles', in W. Semmler (ed.), *Lecture Notes in Economics and Mathematical Systems*, no. 275 (Berlin: Springer-Verlag, 1986).

Semmler, W. (ed.), *Proceedings of the Conference on 'Economic Dynamics and Financial Instability'* (New York: M. E. Sharpe, 1988).

Tobin, J., 'Keynesian Models of Recession and Depression', *American Economic Review* (Papers and Proceedings of the A.E.A., 1975).

16 Debt and Macro Stability

Marc Jarsulic*

16.1 INTRODUCTION

There has been much recent interest in the problem of financial instability in the macro economy. Some researchers have looked for cyclical and secular co-movements between debt accumulation, financial crises, and problems in the real economy. Others have tried to rationalise, in formal models, the apparent connections between finance, changes in expectations, and macro instability. Two different points of view are embodied in this work. One, deriving from the work of Minsky, emphasises the importance of ignorance and psychology. Firms are seen as financing accumulation on the basis of unverifiable expectations, accumulating debt burdens in the process. When the debt burdens are large enough, the economy becomes vulnerable to downward revisions of expectations. Such revisions reduce effective demand and stimulate financial crises. A second view emphasises a structural determinant of instability – declining profitability. Problems with profits are viewed as a major cause of debt burdens, and the source of potential financial crisis.

What follows is an attempt to synthesise these two viewpoints into a manageable analytical framework. To set the stage, we begin with a brief review of Minsky's ideas, which have to this point received the greater attention. This is followed by a discussion of the structuralist view and some of the key supporting empirical evidence. Next a Keynes–Kalecki model of growth with debt is constructed. It suggests that in economies where debt finances accumulation, stable and unstable configurations of economic variables coexist simultaneously. The proximity of these regions is shown to depend on expectational and distributional factors. The model therefore introduces a way to characterise financial fragility in terms of stability theory, and shows how structuralist and Minskian ideas complement each other.

16.2 RECENT WORK ON FINANCE AND MACRO STABILITY

Minsky (1982) has long worked to develop a theoretical connection between debt and economic fluctuations which is basically Keynesian in spirit. He begins by looking at an economy at the end of a large-scale depression. As a consequence of widely experienced economic disaster, existing firms will accept little debt, will prize liquidity, and will make cautious estimates of the potential profits from investment projects. Their rates of accumulation will therefore be low, they will easily meet their debt commitments, and gradually their confidence in the future will rise. Hence they subsequently will raise estimates of future profitability, accept lower liquidity and higher debt burdens, and increase rates of accumulation. This becomes a self-reinforcing process which proceeds happily until some event disrupts the financial system. Minsky suggests that an increase in interest rates is the usual culprit. In an economy in which the demand for credit is interest inelastic, because of high debt burdens, and credit supply is also inelastic, because of policy or endogenous restrictions, increased interest rates spark a crisis. The difficulty firms have in making debt payments causes them to revalue the wisdom of investments. As investment demand declines, so do profits, which amplifies the problem. The depth of the decline will depend on how indebted firms are and how the government reacts. If the ultimate downturn is not too severe, it sets the stage for further expansion of debt and larger problems in the future.

Minsky's account is clearly driven by changes in expectations. Those expectations are presumed to be formed in a Keynesian world, in which the future is truly unknown; in which there are no contingent claim markets for all enumerable eventualities; and in which actors have enough experience to know that the future may generate events for which there is no current vocabulary. A neat, partial formulation of the Minsky view has been provided by Taylor and O'Connell (1985). Using a linear dynamic model, and making expected future profitability dependent on the deviation of interest rates from some normal value, they are able to show that changes household liquidity preference – a proxy for confidence in the economy – can switch the model from a stable to an unstable state.

In the Minsky-inspired strand of analysis, variability of income shares is not considered an important part of the story. Recent empirical work suggests this may be a significant omission. There is a long tradition of neo-Marxian research on the cyclical and trend profit squeeze in the US economy (Boddy and Crotty, 1975; Weisskopf, 1979; Hahnel and Sherman, 1982; Bowles, Gordon and Weisskopf, 1989; Bowles, 1983; Michl, 1987). Recently Wolfson (1986) made a very detailed study of financial crises in the post-war US economy, using NBER business cycle dating techniques. He observed (pp. 145–6) a regular relationship between changes in the profit share and financial crisis:

> In every crisis period, a particular timing relationship has – with only one exception – occurred. Peaks have been reached in profit and investment variables for the nonfinancial corporate sector, in relation to the financial crisis, in the following order: (1) the profit [share], (2) new contracts and orders for plant and equipment (in constant dollars), (3)

investment and plant and equipment (in constant dollars), (4) the
financial crisis and (5) the financing gap [that is, the difference between
capital expenditures and internal funds]. (materials in brackets added)

He concludes:

the financing gap increased in periods immediately preceding financial
crises not only because investment spending increased, but also because
internal funds declined. The failure of internal funds to maintain their
rate of growth, in fact their tendency to decline, resulted in an increasing
financing gap . . . a decline in profits occurring near the peak of the
expansion generally has been responsible for this decrease in internal
funds . . . it was the decline in profits that resulted in the corporations
having difficulty in meeting their fixed payment commitments – due to
involuntary plant and equipment investment as well as debt.

Robert Pollin has looked at competing hypotheses which explain the
rising corporate debt in the post-war period. He concludes (1986, p. 227)
that the increase is a function of declining profitability and competitive
pressure:

The overall results of the econometric test and other statistical evidence
point to one central conclusion: the trend decline in the corporate profit
level and rate over phase two, 1967–80, provides the primary explanation for the rise of corporate debt dependency over that period . . . With
internal funds down, corporations were forced to borrow to an increasing extent in order to maintain a competitive level of spending and
support their markets through trade credit extensions.

The model developed in the subsequent section incorporates ideas from
Minsky and from those who emphasise profitability. It will be used to show
why an economy with debt can have stable and unstable regions, and how
changes in expectational and structural factors may affect the proximity of
those regions.

16.3 A MODEL OF ACCUMULATION WITH DEBT

We begin with a closed economy in which aggregate demand, composed of
investment and consumption, determines the rate of output. Goods markets will be assumed to clear immediately, and money prices will be
assumed fixed. To determine flows of output we need an investment
function. This is always a difficulty for anyone constructing a Keynesian–
Kaleckian macro model. If the world is really characterised by ungrounded

expectations, how does one represent accumulation as a function? Perhaps the best we can do is suggest that long-term expectations are given, but within the constraint of those expectations some functional relationships obtain. One commonsense relationship might be that capacity utilisation below a minimally acceptable level will exert downward pressure on accumulation. On the other hand, in a world of genuine uncertainty, it may make sense to grow with the market, even if capacity utilisation is not total. Another sensible step is to carry over some of the insights of Kalecki, which have reappeared in the so-called 'New Keynesian' literature on finance constraints and accumulation (Fazzari *et al.*, 1988). One begins with the not too startling assumption that capital markets are not perfect. Lenders have difficulty evaluating investment projects, and have agent problems in monitoring and assessing outcomes. Hence firms may be forced to wait for self-finance to support viable projects, and lenders may use cash-flow or indebtedness measures to evaluate suitability of borrowers. Also, as Kalecki suggests, firms may have definite aversion to bankruptcy risk, and thus restrict their use of finance as cash-flow declines or debt rises. Hence, even when the cheshire-cat smile of capitalists' expectations is hanging firmly in place, variations in debt or cash-flow will alter the rate of accumulation. This view will be represented by writing the desired rate of capital accumulation, gd, as

$$g^d = \alpha(Y/K - \varepsilon) + \beta\pi - \gamma rd \qquad \alpha, \varepsilon, \beta, \gamma > 0, \gamma > \beta \qquad (1)$$

where Y is real output, K is real capital stock, π is the flow of profits divided by the capital stock, r is the rate of interest, and d is the ratio of firm debt to capital stock. This functional form is self-explanatory, with the exception of the differing parameters β and γ. This allows positive cash flows to have a negative effect on desired accumulation, which makes sense if dividends are to be paid to stockholders and principal is to be retired. A larger relative value of γ would indicate a more cautious mood on the part of capitalists.

Since there are acknowledged lags between order and construction in the capital goods sector we will assume that the rate of accumulation, $g = \dot{K}/K$, moves according to

$$\dot{g} = \lambda(g^d - g - \eta g^2), \lambda > 0, \eta > 0 \qquad (2)$$

This is a standard partial adjustment model with one innovation.[1] The value of η reflects the capacity limits of the economy. If $g^d - g > 0$ and g is not so large that capacity is strained, then $\dot{g} > 0$. However, upward movements in g will be self-limiting,[2] since large enough values of g will produce negative values for $\dot{g}$. Given this relationship, we next turn our attention to the determination of the debt burden in this economy. It will be assumed that borrowing takes place only to finance capital accumulation or make interest payments which cannot be covered by retained earnings. Thus we have the relationship

$$\dot{D} = rD + I - \theta\Pi \tag{3}$$

where D is the real value of debt, I is investment, $1 \geqslant \theta \geqslant 0$ is the corporate retention ratio, and Π is the real value of profits. If corporate retained earnings always exceed investment expenditures, there will be no debt. Defining $d = D/K$, we have the identity

$$\dot{d} = \dot{D}/K - dg \tag{4}$$

and substitution of (3) into (4) gives

$$\dot{d} = rd - \theta\pi + g - dg \tag{5}$$

The dynamical system given by (2) and (5) is the one which will be used to analyse the ideas on finance and stability which were discussed in the previous section. This will be done in a series of cases, which make different assumptions about income distribution, aggregate demand, and the determination of the interest rate.

16.3.1 Case 1: Keynesian Savings, Interest Rate and Income Shares Fixed

As a first case consider an economy in which savings is proportional to income, and in which labour's share of income is taken to be determined exogenously by the relative power of workers and capitalists. Then capacity utilisation is given by

$$Y/K = g/s, \ 1 > s > 0 \tag{6}$$

where s is the constant savings propensity. The rate of profit is

$$\pi = (1 - \omega)g/s \tag{7}$$

where ω is labour's share. The rate of interest will be taken as fixed. Now this assumption may not be as strong as it seems. Unless one believes that the central bank can drive the long-term rate of interest to zero, which would imply unlimited funds for every borrower and a very lenient capitalist system indeed, then it is likely that there is minimum rate of interest on debt used to finance accumulation. So long as there is, the following argument will go through. Expressions (6) and (7) can be substituted into

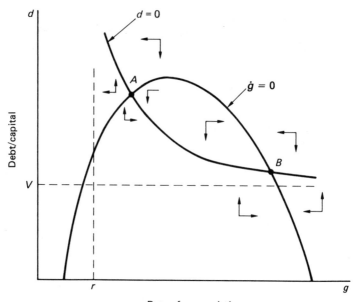

Rate of accumulation

Figure 16.1

$\dot{d} = 0$ isocline : $d = \dfrac{vg}{g - r}$

$\dot{g} = 0$ isocline : $d = (\phi g - \eta g^2 - \alpha\varepsilon)/\gamma r$

(2) and (5) to obtain the corresponding dynamical system. Assuming $\phi = [(\alpha + \beta(1 - \omega))/s] - 1 > 0$, which is necessary for g ever to be positive, and $v = 1 - [\theta(1 - \omega)/s] > 0$, which is necessary to explain the existence of debt, we can write the dynamical system as

$$\dot{g} = \phi g - \gamma rd - \eta g^2 - \alpha\varepsilon$$

$$\dot{d} = rd + vg - dg \qquad\qquad (8)$$

where coefficients are implicitly redefined to account for the value of λ. The dynamics of (8) can be represented by the phase diagram given in Figure 16.1. Assuming that (8) has two solutions, they will correspond to critical points *A* and *B* in the diagram.

The motion around these points is indicated in Figure 16.2 which can be derived from consideration of the vectors of motion given in Figure 16.1. Clearly point *A*, with a lower rate of growth and higher debt capital ratio, is locally a saddle point; while *B* is locally stable.[3] Their juxtaposition suggests the following intuitions about this model economy: Near point *B*,

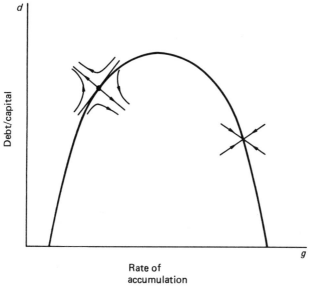

Rate of
accumulation

Figure 16.2

the economy will respond to small enough shocks by converging to point *B*. This might be taken to represent non-explosive business cycle behaviour. Larger shocks, however, might move the economy so far to the northwest that it would begin to experience self-amplifying difficulties. Growth rates would decline and debt burdens would increase. That is, a financial crisis would develop.

Consider now the effects of a change in the distribution of income. An increase in labour's share would decrease profitability at every rate of accumulation, thus shifting the $\dot{g} = 0$ isocline downward. Similarly, the decline in profitability would shift the $\dot{d} = 0$ isocline upward, reflecting the fact that for any rate of accumulation, more external finance would be required. The net effect of these changes, illustrated in Figure 16.3 is to move the stable point and the equilibrium points closer together. A shock which previously generated local oscillations around the stable point is now capable of causing a financial crisis. Thus declining profitability makes the economy, in a measurable way, more fragile.[4]

It is also possible to examine how changes in the attitudes of capitalists and in financial market conditions affect the fragility of this economy. A deterioration in long-period expectations might be represented by an increase in the coefficient γ. This would shift the $\dot{g} = 0$ locus downward, moving the equilibria closer together and increasing fragility. An increase in the interest rate would shift the $\dot{g} = 0$ locus upward, while shifting the $\dot{d} = 0$ locus downward. This would also increase fragility. Shifts of these sorts would

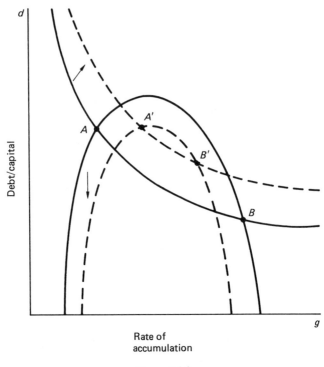

Figure 16.3

represent the kind of changes suggested by Minsky. However, the model indicates that fragility can exist without the shifts, and that changes in profitability can induce greater fragility without changes in expectations or changes in financial market conditions.

16.3.2 Case 2: Keynesian Savings, Income Shares Fixed, Interest Rate Variable

It is reasonable to consider in more detail whether the coexistence of stable and unstable regimes depends on the fixed interest rate assumption or on ignoring the ability of government expenditure to keep capacity utilisation at some non-negative level. Clearly the ability of government to maintain aggregate demand is not, by itself, sufficient to eliminate instability. To see this, let us assume that the government tax-finances an expenditure proportional to the capital stock of t. Then $Y/K = t + g/s$ and the d intercept of $\dot{g} = 0$ isocline is a positive value. However, this does not change the qualitative dynamics of the economy. Then what about a variable interest rate, together with aggregate demand help from the government? To make the rate of interest responsive to levels of demand, write a Keynesian market clearing function for an exogenously given stock of money, M, as

$$r = \zeta(Y/M), \; \zeta > 0 \tag{9}$$

This assumes an interest sensitive transactions demand for money only. If central bank policy is represented by $M = mK$, $m > 0$, the bank can drive the interest rate up or down depending on how m changes. Then (9) can be rewritten as

$$r = \sigma(g/s + t), \; \sigma = \zeta/m > 0 \tag{10}$$

In this case, unless m is infinite, a somewhat unlikely bank policy, the rate of interest is not zero. Substitution of (10) into (8) will leave the dynamics unchanged.

16.3.3 Case 3: Kaldorian Savings, Income Shares Variable, Interest Rate Fixed

As a final exercise, let us consider a case in which profitability is related to utilisation in a more complex manner. The profit rate will be assumed to vary according to

$$\pi = F(Y/K), \quad \begin{array}{l} F' > 0, \, (Y/K)^* > Y/K \\ F' = 0, \, (Y/K)^* = Y/K \\ F' < 0, \, (Y/K)^* < Y/K \end{array} \tag{11}$$

That is, profit rates are a one-humped function of capacity utilisation, with the slope changing from positive to negative at some value of the utilisation rate $(Y/K)^*$. A relationship such as this is derived and investigated empirically in the work of Bowles *et al.* (1989), and is consistent with the empirical work on profitability over the business cycle. Assuming a Kaldorian consumption function, utilisation will be given by

$$Y/K = Cg - D\pi \quad C, D > 0 \tag{12}$$

where c_ω is the fraction of wages consumed, c_π is the fraction of profits consumed, $1 > c_\omega > c_\pi \geq 0$, $C = 1/(1-c_\omega)$, $D = (c_\omega - c_\pi)/(1-c_\omega)$. These two relationships are represented in Figure 16.4.[5] It is clear from this figure that capacity utilisation will increase with accumulation, but the profit rate will increase and then decrease. Hence the solution to (11) and (12) will be represented for expository purposes as

$$\pi = \mu_1 g - \mu_2 g^2, \quad \mu_1, \mu_2 > 0 \tag{13}$$

where $(C - D\mu_1) > 0$. Substitution of (12) and (13) into (2) and (5) gives a dynamical system of the form

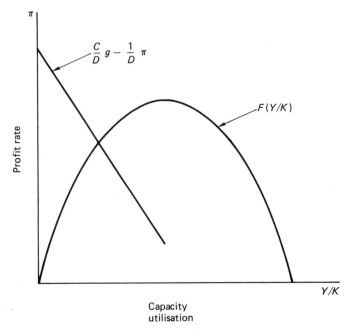

Figure 16.4

$$\dot{g} = -\alpha\varepsilon + \psi g - \gamma rd - \tau g^2$$

$$\dot{d} = rd + (1-\theta\mu_1)g + \theta\mu_2 g^2 - dg \qquad (14)$$

where $\psi = \alpha C + (\beta-\alpha D)\mu_1$ and $\tau = (\beta-\alpha D)\mu_2$. The sign of τ will turn on the sign of $(\beta-\alpha D)$. A positive value for $(\beta-\alpha D)$ can be read to indicate that, in the determination of desired rates of capital accumulation, the negative effects of increased profitability on utilisation are outweighed by the positive effects of increased cash flow. Since this fits the view of investment behind (1), it will be assumed that $(\beta-\alpha D)$ is positive in what follows. In (14) the capacity constraint is ignored and the coefficient η, from equation (5), has been set to zero. Thus the dynamics of (14), unlike those of (8) examined in the previous cases, do not depend on a capacity constraint.

System (14) is represented in the phase diagram of Figure 16.5 under the assumption that $(1 - \theta\mu_1) \geq 0$. In this case, there are now stable and unstable points. (If the term $(1 - \theta\mu_1)$ is less than zero there will be only an unstable point.) In this system, changes in expectational factors have the same effects on the proximity of the stable and unstable points as in (8). And a decrease in the potential profits at any rate of capacity utilisation, which would be represented by a decrease in the parameter μ_1 or an

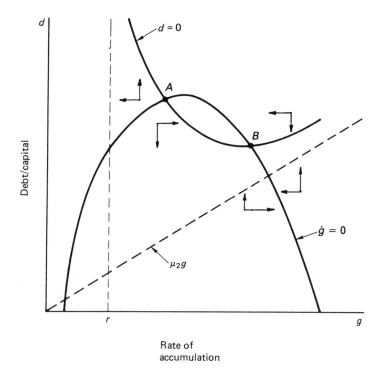

Rate of
accumulation

Figure 16.5

$\dot{d} = 0$ isocline : $d = ((1 - \theta\mu_1)g + \mu_2 g^2)/(g - r)$

$\dot{g} = 0$ isocline : $d = (\psi g - \tau g^2 - \alpha\varepsilon)/\gamma r$

increase in the parameter μ_2, will shift the $\dot{g} = 0$ locus down and the $\dot{d} = 0$ locus up, thereby making this system more fragile. Thus changes in potential profits can have, under certain conditions, the same effects in all three systems.

16.4 CONCLUSION

The model developed in the previous section provides a tractable framework for examining the connection of debt to macroeconomic stability. It shows that, under a variety of assumptions common to the Keynes–Kalecki tradition, an economy will have both stable and unstable regions. For some combinations of growth rate and debt burden, an economy will be stable. Shocks of a reasonable size may cause oscillations, but the economy will tend toward acceptable values. For other growth rate and debt burden combinations – generally for lower growth rates and higher debt burdens –

the system will be unstable. The closer these regions, the more vulnerable is the system to shocks which move it away from the locally stable region.

The model therefore has the virtue of providing a definition of financial fragility in terms of stability theory. The closer the stable and unstable basins, the more financially fragile is the system. Moreover, since proximity is determined by expectational, distributional, and interest rate factors, the model argues for a multivariate analysis of the causes of any financial crisis. Finally, since some of the implications of the model are quite unambiguous, it gives potentially falsifiable form to some of the ideas in the financial stability literature.

Notes

* The research on which this paper is based has been supported in part by the Jerome Levy Economics Institute of Bard College. The paper was previously published in the *Eastern Economic Journal* (April–June 1990).
1. Partial adjustment models are discussed in many places, for example Gandolfo (1980, pp. 235, 258).
2. In this case the maximum value for g is determined by setting $\dot{g}=r=0$ and the rate of profit at its global maximum, and solving what will turn out to be – once functional values for Y/K and π are introduced – a quadratic in g. Note that while the upper limit to the growth rate is set here by capacity, accumulation may reach a limit before any capacity constraint is reached. An example is discussed below as case 3.
3. While the stability properties can be deduced from the phase diagram, they can be easily established algebraically in a particular case. Note that for the dynamical system (8), which has a $\dot{g} = 0$ isocline given by $d = (\phi - \eta g^2 - \varepsilon)/\beta r$, the slope of the $\dot{g} = 0$ isocline is given by $\phi - 2\eta g$. To the left of $g^* = \phi/2\eta$ the slope is positive, and to the right it is negative. Note also that $d > v$ when $\dot{d} = 0$. Now the stability of a fixed point like A or B can be derived from the Jacobian matrix

$$J = \begin{bmatrix} \partial\dot{g}/\partial g & \partial\dot{g}/\partial d \\ \partial\dot{d}/\partial g & \partial\dot{d}/\partial d \end{bmatrix}$$

evaluated at the fixed point (Arrowsmith and Place, 1982, pp. 85–6). When $Det(J) > 0$ and $Tr(J) < 0$, the point is stable. When $Det(J) < 0$, it is a saddle. Taking the derivatives of (8) gives the Jacobian

$$J = \begin{bmatrix} \phi - 2\eta g^* & -\gamma r \\ v - d^* & r - g^* \end{bmatrix}$$

where d^* and g^* are the equilibrium values of d and g.

Now $Det(J) = (\phi - 2\eta g)(r - g) + \gamma r(v - d)$. Substituting and rearranging gives $Det(J) = g(2\eta g - \eta r - \phi) + r\varepsilon$. Hence $Det(J) > 0$ if $g > ((\phi + \eta r)/2\eta)$. In the case where $\varepsilon = 0$, (8) can be solved for g to give an equilibrium $g^* = \{ -(\phi + \eta r) + [(\phi + \eta r)^2 - 4\eta r(\phi + v\gamma)]^{1/2}\}/(-2\eta)$. If g^* is to have two positive solutions, then it will be the case that the larger value of g^* will be greater than $(\phi + \eta r)/2\eta$. The smaller value of g^* will be less than this value. Hence A will be a saddle point, while B will be a stable point. For cases in which $\varepsilon \neq 0$, direct solutions for g require solving a cubic equation. Hence we are content with the qualitative analysis of the phase diagrams. Note that in Figure 16.2 there are no oscillations in the convergence to B. However, for the isoclines of Figure 16.5, it may be possible that trajectories oscillate while converging.

4. Of course this is a *ceteris paribus* analysis, and decreasing profitability might, for example, cause firms to raise their retention rate, thereby generating offsetting tendencies. This may not always be possible, of course, if firm owners need to consume from profits. Moreover, the retention ratio cannot exceed 1, while if the wage share is large enough, borrowing will be necessary.

5. This graphical framework was suggested in an informal presentation by David Gordon of the theory underlying his recent econometric work. However, the inclusion of debt, the analysis of dynamics and the conclusions are things for which he cannot be implicated.

References

Arrowsmith, D. and C. Place, *Ordinary Differential Equations* (New York: Chapman & Hall, 1982).

Boddy, J. and R. Crotty, 'Class Conflict and Macro Policy: The Political Business Cycle', *Review of Radical Political Economics* (Spring 1975).

Bowles, S., D. Gordon and T. Weisskoft, 'Business Ascendancy and Economic Impasse', *Journal of Economic Perspectives* (Winter 1989).

Fazzari, S., R. Hubbard and B. Petersen, 'Financing Constraints and Corporate Investment', *Brookings Papers on Economic Activity*, no. 1 (1988).

Gandolfo, G., *Economic Dynamics: Methods and Models* (New York: Elsevier, 1980).

Hahnel, R. and H. Sherman, 'The Rate of Profit Over the Business Cycle', *Cambridge Journal of Economics* (June 1982).

Michl, T., 'An Anatomy of the Reagan Recovery', in R. Cherry *et al.* (eds), *The Imperiled Economy, Book I* (New York: Union for Radical Political Economics, 1987).

Minsky, H.; *Can 'It' Happen Again?* (Armonk, NY: M. E. Sharpe, 1982).

Pollin, R., 'Alternative Perspectives on the Rise of Corporate Debt Dependency: The U.S. Postwar Experience', *Review of Radical Political Economics*, no. 2 (1986).

Taylor, L. and S. O' Connell, 'A Minsky Crisis', *Quarterly Journal of Economics*, supplement (1985).

Weisskopf, T. E., 'Marxian Crisis Theory and the Rate of Profit in the Postwar US Economy', *Cambridge Journal of Economics* (December 1979).

Wolfson, M., *Financial Crises* (Armonk, NY: M. E. Sharpe, 1986).

17 Expectation Dynamics, Financing of Investment and Business Cycles

Reiner Franke and Willi Semmler

17.1 INTRODUCTION

Recently, there have been several papers originating from Keynesian macroeconomic theory and Kalecki's work on the business cycle that have attempted to integrate monetary and financial variables in macrodynamic models.[1] This development seems to overcome the unfortunate separation of financial and real aggregate magnitudes present in macrodynamic modelling. Moreover, due to the emphasis given to the role of financial markets for macro fluctuations, the formation of expectations has again been stressed as an important aspect in determining asset holding and investment decisions that generate macroeconomic fluctuations.[2] This chapter also seeks to make a contribution to this line of research. However, expectations or as we prefer to call them, a general state of confidence, will not be taken as given as in the Keynesian sense of 'animal spirits', but will be assumed as endogenous instead.

Before presenting the model in detail it is worth emphasising some general features and their grounding in the economic literature. The first feature concerns the role of expectations and confidence in business cycle theories. In the *General Theory*, Keynes stressed that macroeconomic instability and business cycles are mainly caused by the volatility of investment which, in its turn, responded to the marginal efficiency of capital. In it (Keynes, 1967, ch. 22), he also argued that the varying market evaluation of the marginal efficiency of capital is mainly due to unsteady beliefs about an uncertain future.[3] Other writing on the trade cycle in the 1930s have emphasised the role of beliefs, confidence and profit expectations for aggregate economic instability.[4] Even Kalecki, who in his early writings saw the role of objective factors such as the time delay of the gestation period for investment goods as the main cause for macroeconomic fluctuations, published a version of his business cycle theory (after Keynes's *General Theory* had appeared) where he stressed prospective profits as an important determinant of investment expenditures (Kalecki, 1937a, p. 86). He, too, pointed out the strong variations in prospective profits over the business cycle and their significance for (firms')

330

investment decisions and the resulting aggregate fluctuations.[5]

Many schools of economic analysis seem to consider these notions of expectations as old-fashioned since they are not grounded in the methodological assumptions of optimising agents and efficient forecasts which are based on available information. Yet, in view of what has been mentioned above, expectations and beliefs about an uncertain future as, for example, put forward by Keynes, the current theory of expectation formation should more appropriately be termed 'extrapolative expectation', as has been already suggested (Nerlove, 1984), by which future values are obtained as proxies for anticipations. Keynes expressed strong scepticism when expectations are formed solely on the basis of the most 'probable forecast'. To what extent the forecast will be made an important decision variable depends, as he put it, 'on the confidence with which we make the forecast' (Keynes, 1967, p. 148). In addition, with respect to more distant future events, he maintained that 'there is no scientific basis on which to form any capable probability whatsoever' (Keynes, 1937, p. 215).[6]

The simple macroeconomic model developed in this chapter incorporates these verbal statements. The central decision variable to which these motions are applied is investment which surely requires no further justification. Formally, we introduce an expectation variable representing the general 'state of confidence' and make the desired growth rate of the capital stock directly an increasing function of it. This determinant of investment may be supplemented by other more objective economic variables, such as the present degree of capacity utilisation, the accelerator principle or the level of profitability. Our purpose, however, in developing our macro dynamical model was to concentrate fully and strictly on the role of expectation.

The state of confidence will have an impact on other economic decision variables as well, most especially on the side of finance. Our approach takes account of that, but in a more indirect way. Roughly speaking, in studying the effects of a change in expectations we are not primarily postulating a volatility of confidence in financial markets, the disturbance of which may or may not be transmitted to the real sector, since, should that have been the case, the economy might be seen as being too much dependent on the psychology of financial speculators. Rather, financial and real variables are affected simultaneously, where the impact on investment demand is most direct. The change in investment will then alter finance conditions and trigger additional mechanisms which will encompass the whole economy. The interplay of the real and financial sector is hence essential, but not as expectational bubbles.

What are then the forces governing the motions of the state of confidence? We introduce a form of expectation dynamics that is partly based on comparatively objective factors and partly on subjective ones, the latter to a great extent reflecting the discussion in the 1930s. The subjective or conventional factors, of which we shall say more later, can be briefly characterised as optimism feeding optimism and pessimism feeding pessimism. To anticipate a main result, as one would expect, the subjective factors will be destabilising, whereas conversely the objective ones would contribute to stability. In particular, depending on their relative strength, persistent cyclical behaviour may be obtained. Moreover, the features of the oscillations such as, for example, the amplitudes or the length of cycles may change if there is a shift in the weights of the objective and conventional factors on the state of confidence.

Lastly, it is appropriate to indicate how financial and real sectors are integrated. The connecting link is the financing of the firms' investment expenditures. Generally, there are three sources available to them: internal finance through retained earnings, external finance through equity issuance, and loans from commercial banks. The proportion of equity financing is considered to be determined by a conventional rule. Likewise internal finance is obtained from profits net of tax and interest payments – and after dividend pay-outs. Once the level of investment has been determined, debt financing becomes the closure of the gap between predetermined levels of investment on one side and equity financing and retained earnings on the other of the investment–finance identity of firms; that is, it represents a residual.[7] This hierarchy in the financial structure of firms has been suggested recently in many works of the literature on credit and financial constraints (cf. Stiglitz and Weiss, 1981; Greenwald *et al.*, 1984; Fazzari *et al.*, 1988), which stress that, compared to debt financing, equity financing is more difficult to obtain and more costly as well.

The rest of the chapter is organised as follows. In the next section, all essential elements are introduced to formulate transactions on financial and goods markets, and temporary equilibrium is characterised by the all too familiar *IS* and *LM* equations. In the third section, the existence and uniqueness properties are ensured, and the most important comparative static properties are also derived. The fourth section is devoted to the study of the long-run dynamics of the model, while the formal proofs of the model's statements are collected in the appendix.[8] The chapter ends with our concluding remarks.

17.2   THE *IS-LM* CONFIGURATION

The model is basically made up of two constituent parts: an *IS-LM* configuration and a dynamic system. The *IS-LM* part is always in temporary equilibrium whereas the dynamic part determines the motion of the entire system over time.

Let us first begin with the financial relationships. They can be best described by looking at the balance sheets represented in Table 17.1. Four groups of agents are distinguished: the central bank, commercial banks,

Table 17.1 Balance sheet statement

Assets			Liabilities
		Central Bank	
High-powered money	F	$: D^c$	Deposits of commercial banks (interest-free bank reserves)
		Commercial Banks	
Bank reserves	D^c	$: D^0$	interest-free deposits from the public
Loans to firms	L	$: D^i$	interest-bearing deposits from the public
		Firms	
Capital stock (valued at the demand price)	$P_k K$	$: L$	Loans from commercial banks
		$: P_e E$	Equity
		Public	
Deposits with commercial banks	D^0	$: W$	Wealth
	D^i	$:$	
Equity	$P_e E$	$:$	

firms, and wealth holders or rentiers, denoted here as the public which excludes workers who play a passive role in that they spend their wages instantaneously and do not own assets.

Firms are the main actors on the real and financial side of the economy, K being the physical capital stock, P the price level and i the (uniform) interest rate on bank loans and deposits. Let $r^g = $ (gross profits)/PK and $r = $ (gross profits $- iL$) / PK stand for the gross and net rate of profit respectively.[9] These are connected by the relation

$$r^g = r + i\lambda \tag{1}$$

where $\lambda = L/PK$, is the degree of indebtedness of firms. On the other hand, the overall 'state of confidence', the basic role of which has already been discussed in the introductory part, is denoted by ϱ which is defined here as the difference between expected and actual rates of profit. That is, $r^g + \varrho$ is the expected gross profit rate, $r + \varrho$ the expected net profit rate on the assumption that expectations with respect to the interest rate are negligible. The capitalised value of expected earnings per unit of investment, P_k, or the demand price of capital, can then be defined as

$$P_k = \frac{r^g + \varrho}{i} P \tag{2}$$

P_k gives the market value of the capital stock, as opposed to its replacement costs, PK. P_k/P thus resembles Tobin's q. Notice, however, that even in a long-run equilibrium position P_k/P may exceed unity. Thus, the difference $P_k/P - 1$ could consequently be interpreted as the risk premium on non-financial investment.

As for share prices P_e, we shall assume that their formation is exclusively determined by the variables determining $P_k K$. Excess volatility or bubbles in the stock market are excluded since they do not seem to be central for the basic model developed here. If E represents the number of shares, we can obtain the following equation

$$P_e E = P_k K - L \qquad (3)$$

which is identical to the firms' balance sheet position.

Shares are bought by rentiers who plan to have their wealth split up into

$$P_e E = eW , \quad D^0 = d^0 W , \quad D^i = (1 - d^0 - e)W \qquad (0 < e < 1) ,$$

where e is a continuously differentiable function of the two relevant prospective rates of return, $e = e(r + \varrho , i)$. Thus,

$$e_r = \partial e / \partial (r + \varrho) > 0, \; e_i = \partial e / \partial i < 0.$$

Given the above relations, we are sufficiently equipped to derive an equation that characterises the clearing of financial markets. Aggregating the balance sheets for the whole economy results in $W = F + P_k K$; substituting $P_e E = eW$, we can write equation (3) as $W = (P_k K - L)/e$. If we employ a number of algebraic manipulations, for example defining $\varnothing = F/PK$, dividing the two equations by PK, equating them and utilising equations (1) and (2) above, we can obtain the equilibrium (LM) condition

$$(LM) \quad e(r + \varrho, i) - (r + \varrho) / [r + \varrho + i(\lambda + \varnothing)] = 0$$

Notice that this is a stock market equilibrium where market clearing is brought about by variations of the rate of interest; thus, we have labelled it a LM-equation. λ and ϱ are given in every instance of time, whereas r is determined in the real goods markets. On the other hand, $\varnothing$ is taken as a constant ratio implying that the central bank, via D^c, imposes no restriction on the credit volume of commercial banks (Franke and Semmler, 1989, section I.2).

Turning now to the real goods side of the economy, we first introduce the investment function of firms. We postulate again that the planned rate of growth of the capital stock is a continuously differentiable function of the 'state of confidence'. Denoting it by h, we have $h = h(\varrho)$, with $h' = dh/d\varrho > 0$.[10] We further make the assumption that h can always be financed as well as realised when appearing as demand on the real goods markets.

Secondly, rentiers' households have to be considered. Their current flow of income consists of dividend payments from firms, plus interest payments iD^i, plus profits of commercial banks, $i(L - D^i)$, plus capital gains, P_eE. To keep the analysis sample, we suppose that the latter are not consumed and thus completely added to the stock of wealth. The public's propensity to save out of this income is denoted by s_h. This is also assumed to be a constant magnitude $(0 < s_h < 1)$.[11]

Thirdly, we assume that the excess of government expenditure or the budget deficit, PG, is solely financed by the creation of base money (Tobin, 1982, p. 178), for example, $PG = F$. As our fourth conceptual assumption we hold the price level constant.[12] In conjunction with $\phi = F/PK = $ constant, we can then deduce $PG = \phi PK$ (for $PG/F = F/F = K/K$).

Clearing of the real goods markets is tantamount to equality between government expenditures, rentiers' consumption, and net investment on the one hand, gross profits on the other. Dividing through by PK, it reduces to the *IS*-equation

$$(IS) \qquad (1 + \phi) \ h(\varrho) - s_0 r - s_h \lambda = 0$$

where $s_0 := s_f + s_h - s_f s_h$

Notice that with $s_f = 0$ and $\phi = 0$ the *IS*-equation would reduce to $h = s_h(r + i\lambda) = s_h r^g$, which is the familiar Cambridge equation.

The equilibrating variable is the level of production or, in relative terms, utilisation of capital, for example the ratio of output to capital. Technology and the wage share being fixed, utilisation stands in a definite relation to the gross rate of profit and thus, to the net profit rate. To simplify notation we leave these relationships (together with distribution) under the surface and take directly r as the variable responsible for equilibrium which is chosen for simply a matter of convenience.

In this way we are dealing with four key variables: λ, ϱ, r, and i while ϕ is treated as a constant. Predetermined values of λ and ϱ induce a temporary equilibrium which is characterised by the *IS-LM* equations and brought about by simultaneous adjustments of r and i. Changes in λ and ϱ cause changes in the corresponding values of r and i. The motions of the debt–asset ratio λ and the state of confidence ϱ, on the other hand, are governed by dynamic equations to be introduced later, after we turn to an analysis of the temporary equilibria.

17.3 ANALYSIS OF TEMPORARY EQUILIBRIA

Our aim in this section is to obtain the rate of interest i and the net profit r as functions of λ and ϱ, express them by $r = R (\lambda, \varrho)$ and $i = J (\lambda, \varrho)$, such that the two market clearing conditions (*IS*) and (*LM*) are simultaneously fulfilled. The procedure is very similar to that in our previous work (Franke and Semmler, 1989) where also a discussion of its economic meaning can be found. Here, we confine ourselves to stating the assumptions employed and the propositions derived from them.

The analysis is pursued in two steps. First, besides λ and ϱ, r is also considered as given and we look for an interest rate that establishes the *LM*-equation. We shall designate it as $i = j\,(\lambda,\,\varrho,\,r)$. In the second step with respect to a given pair $(\lambda,\,\varrho)$, a net profit rate r is sought such that putting $i = j\,(\lambda,\,\varrho,\,r)$ the *IS*-condition is satisfied. If this r is designated $R\,(\lambda,\,\varrho)$ and $r = R\,(\lambda,\,\varrho)$, $i = J\,(\lambda,\,\varrho)$: $= j\,(\lambda,\,\varrho,\,R\,(\lambda,\,\varrho))$ are inserted in (*IS*) and (*LM*) then, by construction, both equations will be simultaneously fulfilled.

Assumptions 1 and 2 ensure existence and uniqueness of the *LM*-equilibrium, with respect to λ, ϱ, and r given. These refer to a functional expression

$$\varepsilon(\lambda,\,r + \varrho,\,i) := (r + \varrho) / [r + \varrho + i(\lambda + \emptyset)]$$

Assumption 1

For all values r, ϱ with $r + \varrho > 0$ the following holds.

(i) $0 < e(r + \varrho,\,0) \leqslant 1$ and there is a point i such that $e(r + \varrho,\,i) > \varepsilon(0,\,r - \varrho,\,i)$;

(ii) $i \geqslant r + \varrho$ implies that $e(r + \varrho,\,i) < \varepsilon(1,\,r + \varrho,\,i)$;

Lemma 1

Let λ, and r be given, $0 \leqslant \lambda \leqslant 1$, $r + \varrho > 0$, and suppose that Assumption 1 holds true, then there exists a rate of interest i such that (*LM*) is satisfied. Furthermore, $r + \varrho > i$ for all these i.

Assumption 2

For all values λ, ϱ and r with $0 \leqslant \lambda \leqslant 1$, $r + \varrho > 0$, and with respect to $i = j(\lambda,\,p,\,r)$, defined as the greatest number that brings about $e(r + \varrho,\,i) = \varepsilon(\lambda,\,r + \varrho,\,i)$, the following strict inequality holds,

$$e_i := \partial e(r + \varrho,\,j(\lambda,\,\varrho,\,r)) / \partial i < \partial \varepsilon(\lambda,\,r + \varrho,\,j(\lambda,\,\varrho,\,r)) / \partial i$$

In addition,

$$-e_i = -\partial e(r + \varrho,\,j(\lambda,\,\varrho,\,r)) / \partial i = \partial e(r + \varrho,\,j\,(\lambda,\,\varrho\,r)) / \partial(r + \varrho) =: e_r$$

The latter part of Assumption 2 says that locally around $i = j(\lambda,\,\varrho,\,r)$ the function e is of the form $e = e(r + \varrho - i)$.

Lemma 2

Let Assumption 1 and 2 apply. Then the function $j(\lambda,\,\varrho,\,r)$ defined in Assumption 2 is continuously differentiable and

$\partial j/\partial r = \partial j/\partial \varrho > 0$, $\partial j/\partial \lambda > 0$, and
$r + \varrho \rightarrow 0$ implies $j(\lambda, \varrho, r) \rightarrow 0$.

With respect to a given pair (λ, ϱ), $0 \leqslant \lambda \leqslant 1$, we are now prepared to look for a point r_0 making the function $r \rightarrow F(\lambda, \varrho, r)$ vanish, where

$$F(\lambda, \varrho, r) := (1 + \emptyset)h(\varrho) - s_0 r - s_h j (\lambda, \varrho, r)\lambda.$$

From Lemma 1 it is immediately seen that F is strictly decreasing in r. Hence $F(\lambda, \varrho, r) < 0$ if only r is sufficiently large[13] and the desired r_0 exists if $F > 0$ for a small enough r. We ensure this by

Assumption 3
The analysis is restricted to a non-degenerate interval D of the state of confidence, where $\varrho \varepsilon D_\varrho$. In this domain the investment function satisfies
$$h(\varrho) \quad > \quad s_0 \varrho / (1 + \emptyset)$$

Lemma 3
Let Assumptions 1–3 apply. Then for every pair (λ, ϱ), $0 < \lambda < 1$, $\varrho \varepsilon D_\varrho$, there exists a uniquely determined net rate of profit $r_0 > -\varrho$ bringing about $F(\lambda, \varrho, r_0) = 0$.

As stated above, it now suffices to set $R(\lambda, \varrho) = r_0$ with respect to the r_0 of Lemma 3 and define $J(\lambda, \varrho) = j(\lambda, \varrho, R(\lambda,))$. In this way the temporary equilibrium functions of r and i are obtained. It is furthermore only a short step to determine their partial derivatives. Fortunately, in most cases the signs are unambiguous. The results, which shall prove useful in the next section, are collected in the following statement.

Theorem 1
Under Assumptions 1–3, there are two continuously differentiable real functions J and R, defined on the set $[0, 1] \times D_\varrho$, such that (IS) and (LM) are satisfied with $r = R(\lambda, \varrho)$ and $i = J(\lambda, \varrho)$. Both are uniquely determined and $0 < J(\lambda, \varrho) < R(\lambda, \varrho) + \varrho$ on the whole domain. The following partial derivatives have definite sign as follows:

$$\partial R/\partial \lambda < 0, \; \partial J/\partial \varrho > 0, \; \partial R/\partial \varrho - \partial J/\partial \varrho < 0.$$

Moreover, $\partial R/\partial \lambda - \partial J/\partial \lambda < 0$ (at least) if $\emptyset < 1$,

$\partial J/\partial \lambda > 0$ if and only if

$$\eta_{e,\,r} < [s_h i(\lambda + \emptyset) + s_0(r + \varrho)]/(S_h + A_0 e),$$

$\partial R/\partial \varrho > 0$ if and only if $h' > s_h \lambda A_i / [(1 + \emptyset)A_r]$

where (at the corresponding temporary equilibrium values)

$$A_0 := [r + \varrho + i(\lambda + \phi)]^2$$
$$A_r := A_0 e_r - (r + \varrho)(\lambda + \phi) > 0$$
$$A_i := A_0 e_r - i(\lambda + \phi) > 0, \text{ and}$$

$\eta_{e, r} := (r + \varrho)e_r / e$ is the elasticity of the equity holding function with respect to changes in $r + \varrho$.

It will be expected that an increase in the demand of firms for credit leads to a rise in the rate of interest. Translated into the present framework, one would expect a higher degree of indebtedness to bring about a higher interest rate, for example, $\partial J/\partial \lambda > 0$. The condition given in the theorem is indeed not too restrictive. To demonstrate this let us adopt the following numerical parameters, which have been derived from statistical sources in Franke and Semmler (1990). Notice, however, that because of the fixed price level the interest rate should rather correspond to the real rate of interest

$$\phi = 0.140, \lambda = 0.260, r = 15.22\%, i = 2.50\%.$$
$$s_f = 0.177, s_h = 0.228.$$

Then $\partial J/\partial \lambda > 0$ results if the elasticity of the equity holding function, $\eta_{e, r}$, falls short of 10.2. Hence, the (possibly) counterintuitive case $\partial J/\partial \lambda < 0$ requires a comparatively high reaction intensity of equity holders – a detailed discussion of the mechanism considered here can be found in our previous work (1989, section II).

Also the condition for the net profit rate to increase with the state of confidence can be seen as normally being satisfied. It turns out that the expression $\sigma := s_h \lambda A_i / [(1 + \phi)]$ is a decreasing function of the elasticity $\eta_{e, r}$. One obtains $\sigma = 0.183$ for $\eta_{e, r} = 0.50$, $\sigma = 0.125$ for $\eta_{e, r} = 0.60$, values which the derivative h' should certainly exceed in order to bring about sufficient fluctuations in the growth rate of capital. It can be observed that $h = h(\varrho)$ and ϱ have the same dimension, for example, they are both measured in percentage points. The elasticity $\eta_{e, r}$, on the other hand, must not be much smaller if it is not to violate Assumption 2.

17.4 LONG-RUN DYNAMICS

To describe the evolution of the debt–asset ratio λ over time, we have to consider how investment is financed. We assume that firms have access to three sources for funds: retained earnings, issuance of new shares (at the prevailing price P_e), and (net) borrowing from commercial banks. Retained earnings have already been introduced to be given by $s_f rPK$, where the retention ratio s_f is supposed to be constant. New shares are issued up to a fraction γ of total net investment. For lack of systematic information on the reaction to variations in the other variables we take γ as a constant, too. Thus, with $I = K$ = investment, the finance equation of firms reads,

$$PI = s_f rPK + \gamma PI + oc\dot{L} ,$$

where, as discussed in the introductory part of this essay, $\dot{L}$ is determined as a residual.[14]

In relative terms, after dividing through by PK, and taking account of the desired growth rate of the capital stock $h = h(\varrho)$, the identity becomes

$$h(\varrho) = (s_f r = \gamma h(\varrho) + (\dot{L}/L) \lambda.$$

Solving for the growth rate of loans and substituting i from the equations $\hat{\lambda}/\lambda = \dot{L}/L - \dot{K}/K = \dot{L}/L - h$, leads to

$$\hat{\lambda} = (1 - \gamma - \lambda) h(\varrho) - s_f r. \tag{4}$$

Turning to the motions of the other dynamic variable, ϱ, we take up the discussion initiated in the introductory section. We recall that ϱ represents long-term expectations. In forming expectations, it would be foolish to attach great weight to matters which are very uncertain.

> It is reasonable, therefore, to be guided to a considerable degree by the facts about which we feel somewhat confident, even though they may be less decisively relevant to the issue than other facts about which our knowledge is vague and scanty. . . . The state of long-term expectation . . . does not solely depend, therefore, on the most probable forecast we can make. It also depends on the *confidence* with which we make this forecast – on how highly we rate the likelihood of our best forecast turning out quite wrong. (Keynes, 1967, p. 148; italics in the original)

It is within this context that ϱ is called the 'state of confidence' and where for simplicity, differences between heterogenous groups of agents have been abstracted.

In practice, the state of confidence depends on a myriad of factors. Considering the question how its change over time is determined, more 'objective' and more 'psychological' factors are to be included. In chapter 12 of the *General Theory*, Keynes maintains that even professional investors are less concerned with what an investment is really worth. They are rather largely concerned with what the market will value its worth to be, under the influence of mass psychology, three months or a year hence. They devote their intelligences to anticipating what average opinion expects the average opinion to be a judgement of the 'third degree' (Keynes, 1936, p. 156). Thus, they fall back 'on what is, in truth, a *convention*' (p. 152; emphasis in the original). Moreover, foreseeing changes on the conventional basis of valuation of the general public, is by no means the outcome of a wrong-headed propensity.[15]

The usual practice of conventional valuation is to 'take the existing situation and to project it into the future, modified only to the extent that we have more or less definite reasons for expecting a change' (p. 148). For the present model this simply means that if ϱ, the state of confidence, is high then further improvements will be expected, so that the time derivative of ϱ is positive. Conversely, in a bad state of confidence things will be expected to worsen. This may be reinforced by some other 'more or less definite reasons', or they may be counteracting. So, an objective factor such as a high debt–asset ratio, signalling possible future financing problems of firms, may keep a curb on the positive evolution of γ, or even reverse it. Another variable, also indicating risk, is the difference between the net rate of profit and the interest rate, $r - i$ (Kalecki, 1937a). If the present optimistic opinion of the general public is not accompanied by a sufficiently high gap between the two rates of return, the positive evolution of ϱ may likewise come to a halt. We summarise these considerations in the behavioural function

$$\varrho = v(\lambda,\, r - i,\, \varrho) \tag{5}$$

where $v_\lambda = \partial v/\partial \lambda \leq 0$

$$v_{r-i} = \partial v/\partial(r - i) \geq 0$$

$$v_\varrho = \partial v/\partial \varrho \geq 0$$

Our macrodynamic model thus consists of the four equations (LM), (IS), (4), (5) in the four variables r, i, λ, ϱ. By virtue of Theorem 1 it can be reduced to two differentiable equations in the two variables λ and ϱ which for that reason have been conferred the short-hand expression 'dynamic variables',

$$\dot\lambda = (1 - \gamma - \lambda)\, h(\varrho) - s_f R(\lambda,\, \varrho) =: U(\lambda,\, \varrho) \tag{D1}$$

$$\dot\varrho = v(\lambda, R(\lambda,\varrho) - J(\lambda,\varrho),\varrho) \qquad =: V(\lambda,\, \varrho) \tag{D2}$$

The adjustment processes of the temporary equilibria in the real goods and financial markets have a direct impact on the state of confidence through the argument $r - i$ in the adjustment function $v(.,.,.)$. In equation (D1) only the profit rate shows up explicitly. However, since it is determined simultaneously with the rate of interest, the evolution of the debt–asset ratio is directly influenced by current transactions on both sets of markets as well. In addition, both variables λ and ϱ feed upon themselves, but also cross-effects can be recognised, directly and mediated through the temporary equilibrium functions $R(\lambda, \varrho)$ and $J(\lambda, \varrho)$. Aggravated by various non-linearities this makes the differential equations (D1) and (D2) a fairly complex dynamical system (at least potentially dependent, as will be stressed below, on the shape of the adjustment function v). We shall nevertheless be able to point out the most important long-run tendencies.

The first question of our analysis concerns the stationary points of system (D1), (D2), which will constitute steady state solutions for the economy under consideration. The existence and uniqueness properties can be derived from further assumptions that have been shown in Franke and Semmler (1989), but which in this chapter are taken for granted.

Assumption 4

There exists a unique pair (λ^*, ϱ^*), $0<\lambda^*<1$, $p^* = 0$, such that $U(\lambda^*, \varrho^*) = V(\lambda^*, \varrho^*) = 0$

$\varrho^* = 0$ is required for reasons of consistency, since ϱ has been interpreted as the difference between expected and current rates of profit. For further analysis, the following statements on the partial derivatives of $U(\lambda, \varrho)$ are useful.

Theorem 2

Suppose that Assumptions 1–4 hold, denoting the steady state values by an asterisk, and letting $g^* = h(\varrho^*) = 0$ be the steady state growth rate, then

$\partial U(\lambda^*, \varrho^*)/\partial\varrho > 0$, and

$i^* < g^* r^*(\lambda^* + \emptyset)/[g^*(\lambda + \emptyset) + s_f r^*]$ together with $i^* < g^*/s_h$ imply

$\partial U(\lambda^*, \varrho^*)/\partial\lambda < 0$.

The condition that $\partial U/\partial\lambda$ must be negative is not necessary. It can, however, safely be regarded as being satisfied. Using the numerical parameters of the previous section one computes

$$g^* r^*(\lambda^* + \varrho)/[g^*(\lambda + \emptyset + s_f r^*] = 0.065, \; g^*/s_h = 0.220.$$

Thus, $\partial U(\lambda^*, \varrho^*)/\partial\lambda < 0$ is ensured if the steady state (real) interest rate $i = i^*$ falls short of 6%.

In this way a first stability tendency can be identified. Fix $\varrho = \varrho^*$ and consider the partial dynamical process in the debt–asset ratio as

$$\dot{\lambda} = U(\lambda, \varrho^*)$$

It follows from Theorem 2 and the ensuing discussion that it is stable, at least in the local sense. λ would rise if $\lambda^* < 0$, and fall if $\lambda > \lambda^*$ – provided that the state of confidence remained unaltered.

Stability of the partial dynamical process in the state of confidence is less definite. Fix $\lambda = \lambda^*$ and consider

$$\dot{\varrho} = V(\lambda^*, \varrho),$$

its stability is determined by the sign of the expression

$$\partial V / \partial \varrho = v_{r-i} [\partial R / \partial \varrho - \partial J / \partial \varrho] + v_\varrho$$

The first term is non-positive by virtue of Theorem 1 while the second non-negative. Stability thus depends on the relative strength of the two reaction coefficients v_{r-i} and v_ϱ. The negative feedback effect brought about by v_{r-i} and the 'objective' factor $r - i$ is stabilising, the positive feedback effect of v_ϱ further increases deviations of ϱ from its steady state value ϱ^*.

In general, stability of each partial process does not necessarily imply stability of the integrated system since it adds interaction effects between the two variables. But here it is the case, at least locally. Denote the Jacobian matrix of (D1), (D2), evaluated at (λ^*, ϱ^*), by the letter Q – it is made up of the entries $\partial U / \partial \lambda$, $\partial U / \partial \varrho$ in the first row and $\partial V / \partial \lambda$, $\partial V / \partial \varrho$ in the second. Stability of the partial processes gives trace $Q < 0$. On the other hand, from Theorem 1

$$\partial V / \partial \lambda = v_\lambda + v_{r-i} [\partial R / \partial \lambda - \partial J / \partial \lambda] \leqslant 0$$

can be inferred, and $\partial U / \partial \varrho > 0$ is stated in Theorem 2, so that the determinant of Q is positive. Hence both eigenvalues of Q have negative real parts and the long-run equilibrium (λ^*, ϱ^*) of process (D1), (D2) is locally and asymptotically stable.

The argument also shows that this result is preserved if the partial process in ϱ is slightly unstable, which means that the positivity of $\partial V(\lambda^*, \varrho^*) / \partial \varrho$ is so moderate that both trace Q and det Q do not change sign. The integrated process (D1), (D2) will, however, become unstable if $\partial V / \partial \varrho$ is sufficiently large or, in other words, if conventional forces in the variations of the state of confidence (sufficiently) dominate the more objective influences. If the reaction coefficient v_ϱ is very large, then saddle-point instability arises (since det $Q < 0$)); if it is not too large, the steady state position will be repelling, if, besides trace $Q > 0$, det Q is still positive.

As a contribution to business cycle theory, instability is more remunerative because it creates the possibility of cyclical behaviour. This presupposes that, in some distance from the steady state, the divergent forces in the conventional adjustments, for example in the function $v(.,.,.,.)$, are checked by considerations on the unfavourable evolution of $r - i$ and, possibly, the degree of indebtedness λ. In fact, the state of confidence may be continuously rising for some time (and with it economic activity, particularly the growth rate of the capital stock $h = h(\varrho)$). Because of $\partial U/\partial \varrho$ >0 (as an extension of the corresponding statement in Theorem 2), λ may be rising too, but, for the sake of the argument, let us suppose that it is less dramatically. Common sense and experience tell us, however, that ϱ is not to increase indefinitely. The higher ϱ, the more the public opinion has to be prepared for a reversal. Conventional valuation may still exhibit a positive influence on ϱ. The agents, however, will be more and more on the alert not to miss the beginning of the downswing (which would do more harm than misjudging the speed at which ϱ increases). This means that the weight of the third coefficient v_ϱ in the function $v(.,.,..)$ diminishes.

In the meantime both rates of return, r and i, have risen too, but the profit rate less rapidly than the rate of interest (cf. Theorem 1). It follows that in the adjustment function v now the influence of $r - i$ takes the lead. The rise of the state of confidence slows down, until finally its motion is reversed. In this region of the (λ, ϱ) -plane the function $U(\lambda, \varrho)$ is still positive,[16] signifying that the debt–asset ratio is further increasing. Depending on the size (the absolute value) of V_λ, ϱ may obtain an additional push. Moreover, during the contraction of ϱ that is now beginning, the conventional forces in its adjustments gain ground again, so that the downfall of the state of confidence soon accelerates and, due to $h = h(\varrho)$, the economy steers for a recession. The only comfort is that the debt–asset ratio λ no longer increases; it eventually declines. From then on we have a (more or less distorted) mirror image of the expansion phase with its final downturn. On the whole, however, the contracting forces generated further away from the equilibrium keep the fluctuations in a bounded interval, whereas the repelling forces about the long-run equilibrium keep the economy from converging toward its steady state values. Thus persistent cyclical behaviour will produce (mathematically speaking) a limit cycle.

It may finally be added that for v_r sufficiently small in the vicinity of λ^*, ϱ^* the model exhibits, as Leijonhufvud (1973) has coined it, corridor stability. Small perturbations of the equilibrium values do not prevent the economy from converging back to its steady state position, whereas stronger shocks lead to divergent behaviour. Also in the latter case, however, stabilising forces are not completely absent – they only take effect further away from the steady state. Moreover, when they come into being, their impulse is so strong such as to reverse the motions of the variables one by one. On the whole this interplay of stabilising and destabilising forces generates persistent fluctuations around the long-run equilibrium.[17]

17.5 SOME CONCLUSIONS

This chapter refers to a long tradition of economic theory in which the shift in expectations or the state of confidence were assigned a central role for the explanation of recurrent cyclical fluctuations of business activities. In our model, however, the shift in expectations or confidence is not considered an autonomous causal factor for macrofluctuations but are integrated in the modelling framework as endogenously determined. Moreover, the turning points of business activities are not seen as a by-product of financial speculations or speculative bubbles as such, possibly transmitting instability to the real sector, but rather brought about by an interplay of investment decisions and asset holding decisions and their dependence on an expectational variable. The effect of the expectational variable works itself out dynamically through the interdependence of different markets. The shifting weights for the factors determining the expectational variable can give rise, as has been shown, to different scenarios and different types of cyclical behaviour. Among them, for economically realistic parameters, the interesting case is the one that generates limit cycles. As was also demonstrated for our model there exists a dynamics with limit cycles which has, in terms of Leijonhufvud, the property of corridor stability.

The model advanced in this chapter employs a simplified investment function by referring to the expectational variable as its only argument. It can, however, be shown that other variables especially the utilisation of capacity can be included as an argument without altering the qualitative results of the model. In the literature of late, the role of financial constraints is assigned an important role in business fluctuations. Preliminary explorations have revealed that with slight modifications those considerations can be further studied in the context of our model. Lastly, another important problem concerns a dynamics for the price level which may be a significant further destabilising factor, as has been suggested since Fisher's work in the 1930s but not considered here. We still have abstained from including it at the current stage will pursue it in a future project.

Notes

 1. See Taylor and O'Connell (1985), Foley (1986, 1987), Day and Shafer (1985), Woodford (1986a, 1986b, 1989), Asada (1989), Duménil and Lévy (1989), Franke and Semmler (1989).

2. Cf. in particular the work of Taylor and O'Connell (1985) and Woodford (1986a, 1986b, 1989).
3. He writes: 'Thus with markets organised and influenced as they are at present, the market estimation of the marginal efficiency of capital may suffer such enormously wide fluctuations that cannot be sufficiently offset by corresponding fluctuations in the interest rate' (Keynes, 1967, p. 320).
4. An excellent survey on the role of expectation and confidence in business cycle theories is given in Boyd and Blatt (1988). As usually stated by economic theorists, the asymmetry in the upturn and downturn of the business cycle, for example the sharp and sudden drop first in financial and then in real economic variables, seemed to be caused by the inherent instability of business confidence and sudden changes in the expectations about the future. This is an observation made much earlier by others in the nineteenth century (Marx, Mill, and Marshall) and can be seen in the writings of Lavington (1921), Hawtrey (1950), Keynes (1967, chs. 5, 12, and 22), and Minsky (1975, ch. 3).
5. Kalecki also draws attention to nonlinearities in the movement of prospective profits over the cycle (cf. Kalecki, 1937a, pp. 86–9).
6. In this context we want to mention again the work of Woodford who has attempted to develop a theory of expectations formation and its influence on investment decisions resembling the statements made by Keynes and his contemporaries in the 1930s. Woodford refers to self-fulfilling revisions of expectations. It turns out that they, independently of shocks to fundamental variables – taste, endowment and technology – are destabilising and generate persistent macroeconomic fluctuations (Woodford, 1986a, 1986b).
7. The above considerations would still apply even if equity finance and retained earnings were more complicated functions of some economic key variables.
8. Proofs for Theorems 1 and 2 are not provided but the interested reader can obtain these directly from the authors.
9. Even though taxes are not considered their inclusion would not alter the analysis.
10. As mentioned before, we want to restrict ourselves to a simple investment function by referring to the expectational variable only. Preliminary explorations have shown that including, for example, the utilisation of capacity in the investment function will not substantially alter the stability properties of our model.
11. The flow of savings increases the stocks of D^0, D^i, and P_eE. In what proportion is captured by the function d^0 and e introduced above. Since d^0 has been eliminated in the course of deriving the LM-equation, its role will be only implicit.
12. This leaves aside the (possibly) destabilising effects of debt deflation. These would be considered at a later stage.
13. More precisely, this follows from the fact that the negative $\partial F/\partial r$ is bounded away from zero.
14. There are of course other versions of financing regimes possible. One might, for example, assume that in a wider distance from the steady state investment that expenditures are constrained, if firms (have to) maintain their dividend payments and equity financing policy and banks set an upper limit to the growth rate of loans. Such a possibility is not considered in this chapter.
15. At least not at the stock exchange, 'For it is not sensible to pay 25 for an investment of which you believe the prospective yield to justify a value of 30, if you also believe that the market will value it at 20 three months hence' (Keynes, 1967, p. 155).

16. This statement, strictly speaking, does not follow from Theorem 2 but has been observed in all our preliminary simulation experiments.
17. Similar dynamic properties have been obtained in a different model by Semmler and Sieveking (1990).

References

Asada, T., 'Monetary Stabilization Policy in a Keynes–Goodwin Model of Growth Cycle', in W. Semmler (ed.), *Financial Dynamics and Business Cycles: New Perspectives* (New York: M. E. Sharpe, Inc., 1989).

Boyd, I. and J. M. Blatt, *Investment, Confidence and Business Cycles* Heidelberg/ New York: Springer-Verlag, 1988).

Brealey, R. and S. Myers, *Principles of Corporate Finance* (New York: McGraw-Hill, 1984).

Clark, P. K., 'Investment in the 1970s: Theory, Performance, and Predictions', *Brooking Papers on Economic Activities*, no. 1 (1979) pp. 73–124.

Clower, R. W., 'A Reconsideration of Microfoundations of Monetary Theory', *Western Economic Journal*, 6 (1967) pp. 1–9.

Coddington, E. A. and N. Levinson, *Theory of Ordinary Differential Equations* (New York: McGraw-Hill, 1955).

Day, R. H. and W. Shafer, 'Keynesian Chaos', *Journal of Macroeconomics*, 7 (3) (1985) pp. 277–95.

Duménil, G. and D. Lévy, 'The Real and Financial Determinants of Stability: The Law of the Increasing Tendency Toward Increasing Instability', in W. Semmler (ed.), *Financial Dynamics and Business Cycles: New Perspectives* (New York: M. E. Sharpe, Inc., 1989).

Economic Report of the President (Washington D.C.: United States Government Printing Office, 1984, 1988).

Eisner, R., 'A Permanent Income Theory for Investment: Some Empirical Explorations', *American Economic Review*, vol. 57, no. 3, (June 1967) pp. 363–89.

Fazzari, S., R. G. Hubbard and B. C. Petersen, 'Financing Constraints and Corporate Investment', *Brooking Papers of Economic Activity*, no. 1 (Washington D.C., 1988) pp. 141–95.

Foley, D., 'Stabilization Policy in a Nonlinear Business Cycle Model', in W. Semmler (ed.), *Competition, Instability, and Nonlinear Cycles, Lecture Notes in Economics and Mathematical Systems* (New York/Heidelberg: Springer-Verlag, 1986) pp. 200–11.

Foley, D., 'Liquidity-Profit Rate Cycles in a Capitalist Economy', *Journal of Economic Behaviour and Organization*, no. 8 (1987) pp. 363–77.

Franke, R. and W. Semmler, 'Debt Financing of Firms, Stability, and Cycles in a Macroeconomic Growth Model', in W. Semmler (ed.), *Financial Dynamics and Business Cycles: New Perspectives* (New York: M. E. Sharpe, Inc., 1989).

Franke, R. and W. Semmler, 'A Dynamical Macroeconomic Growth Model with External Financing of Firms: A Numerical Stability Analysis', in E. Nell and W. Semmler (eds), *Nicholas Kaldor and Mainstream Economics: Growth, Distribution and Cycles* (London/New York: Macmillan, 1990).

Goodwin, R. M., 'Secular and Cyclical Aspect of the Multiplier and Accelerator', *Employment, Income and Public Policy, Essays in Honor of A. H. Hansen* (New York: W. W. Norton, 1948) pp. 108–32.

Goodwin, R. M., 'The Nonlinear Accelerator and the Persistence of Business Cycles', *Econometrica*, 19, no. 1 (1951) pp. 1–17.

Greenwald, B. C., J. E. Stiglitz and A. Weiss, 'Informational Imperfections in the Capital Market and Macroeconomic Fluctuations', *American Economic Review* (May 1984) pp. 194–200.

Greenwald, B. C. and J. E. Stiglitz, 'Imperfect Information, Finance Constraints, and Business Fluctuations', in M. Kohn and S. C. Tsiang (eds), *Finance Constraints, Expectations, and Macroeconomics* (Oxford: Clarendon Press, 1986) pp. 103–40.

Greenwald, B. C. and J. E. Stiglitz, 'Money, Imperfect Information, and Economic Fluctuations', in M. Kohn and S. C. Tsiang (eds), *Finance Constraints, Expectations, and Macroeconomics* (Oxford: Clarendon Press, 1986b) pp. 141–65.

Guttentag, J. and R. Herring, 'Credit Rationing and Financial Disorder', *Journal of Finance*, (December 1984) pp. 1359–82.

Hawtrey, R. G., 'The Trade Cycle', in American Economic Association's *Readings in Business Cycle Theories* (first published 1926) (London: Allen & Unwin, 1950).

Hicks, J. R., *A Contribution to the Theory of Trade Cycle* (Oxford: Oxford University Press, 1950).

Kaldor, N., 'A Model of the Trade Cycle', *Economic Journal*, 50 (March 1940) pp. 78–92.

Kaldor, N., 'Marginal Productivity and Macroeconomic Theories of Distribution', *Review of Economic Studies* (October 1966) pp. 309–19.

Kalecki, M., 'A Theory of the Business Cycle', *The Review of Economic Studies* (February 1937a) pp. 77–97.

Kalecki, M., 'The Principle of Increasing Risk', *Economica* (November 1937b) pp. 441–7.

Kalecki, M., 'A Reply', *Economica* (November 1938) pp. 459–6.

Keynes, J. M., *The General Theory of Employment, Interest, and Money* (London: Macmillan, 1967).

Keynes, J. M., 'The General Theory of Employment', *Quarterly Journal of Economics*, vol. 51 (1937) pp. 209–23.

Kopcke, R. W., 'The Determinants of Investment Spending', *New England Economic Review* (July/August 1985) pp. 19–35.

Lavington, F., *The English Capital Market* (London: Methuen, 1921).

Leijonhufvud, A., 'Effective Demand Failures', *Swedish Journal of Economics* (1973) pp. 27–48.

Minsky, H. P., *John Maynard Keynes* (New York: Columbia University Press, 1975).

Minsky, H. P., *Can 'It' Happen Again? Essays on Instability and Finance* (New York: M. E. Sharpe, 1982).

Nerlove, M., 'Expectations, Plans, and Realizations in Theory and Practise', *Econometrica*, vol. 51, no. 5 (1984) pp. 1251–81.

Semmler, W., *Financial Dynamics and Business Cycles: New Perspectives* (New York: M. E. Sharpe, Inc., 1989).

Semmler, W. and M. Sieveking, 'Nonlinear Liquidity-Growth Dynamics with Bankruptcy Risk', in P. Chen (ed.), *International Symposium on Evolutionary Dynamics and Nonlinear Economics* (Oxford: Oxford University Press, 1990).

Stiglitz, J. E. and A. Weiss, 'Credit Rationing in Markets with Imperfect Information', *American Economic Review* (June 1981) pp. 393–410.

Summers, L. H., 'Taxation and Corporate Investment: A *q*-Theory Approach', *Brookings Papers on Economic Activities*, 1 (1981) pp. 67–127.

Taylor, L., *Structuralist Macroeconomics* (New York: Basic Books, 1982).

Taylor, L., 'A Stagnationist Model of Economic Growth', *Cambridge Journal of Economics*, 9 (1985) pp. 383–403.

Taylor, L., 'Real and Money Wages, Output, and Inflation in the Semi-Industrialized World', MIT, mimeo (1988).

Taylor, L., and S. A. O'Connell, 'A Minsky Crisis', *Quarterly Journal of Economics*, vol. 100, suppl. (1985) pp. 871–86.

Tobin, J., 'Money and Economic Growth', *Econometrica*, vol. 33 (October 1965) pp. 671–84.

Tobin, J., 'A Keynesian Model of Recession and Depression', *American Economic Review*, 65 (1975) pp. 195–202.

Tobin, J., 'Money and Finance in the Macroeconomic Process', *Journal of Money, Credit, and Banking*, 14:2 (1982) pp. 171–203.

Woodford, M., 'Stationary Sunspot Equilibria in a Finance Constraint Economy', *Journal of Economic Theory*, 40 (1986a) pp. 128–37.

Woodford, M., 'Expectation, Finance and Aggregate Instability', in M. Kohn and S. C Tschiang (eds), *Imperfect Information, Finance Constraints, Expectations, and Macroeconomics*, op. cit. (1986b).

Woodford, M., 'Finance, Instability and Cycles', in W. Semmler (ed.), *Financial Dynamics and Business Cycles: New Perspectives* (New York: M. E. Sharpe, Inc., 1989).

18 A Real Growth Cycle with Adaptive Expectations

Tzong-yau Lin, Wai-man Tse and
Richard H. Day*

A real growth cycle model can be drawn up along neoclassical lines but based on adaptive expectations and temporary equilibrium instead of perfect foresight and intertemporal equilibrium as is done in most of the contemporary literature. Unlike the optimal growth version of the one sector model, which produces only monotonic growth that converges to a steady state or balanced growth path, in the adaptive case behaviour can, in addition to stable growth, exhibit periodic cycles or non-periodic, chaotic fluctuations. These various possibilities depend on the parameters of preference, productivity, expectational adjustment, the labour supply growth rate, the rate of technological advance and the rate of depreciation. When the model is viewed as a type of overlapping generations framework, cycles tend to look like 50-year Kondratieff fluctuations with one or two generations of increasing welfare followed by one or two generations that are relatively less well off.

In this chapter, we provide a detailed bifurcation analysis of model behaviour using standard functional forms. Our objective here is to explore the robustness of various types of stable, cyclic and chaotic behaviour and to see for what parameter ranges these types of behaviour occur. The basic message is (not surprisingly) expectational error can matter; growth can lead to over-investment followed by relative decline, and for some ranges of parameters, these fluctuations can have both erratic periodicity and amplitudes. These ranges may contain values that are arguably 'plausible'.

It should also be noted that for many other parameter values – also within the range of plausibility – the model is convergent. In this case fluctuations could only be propagated by shocks or perturbations and the theory is observationally equivalent to the orthodox optimal growth, random shock model.

Section 1 presents the model, section 2 a bifurcation analysis of stability and instability, section 3 numerical experiments, and section 4 compares our results to those of the usual single sector, optimal growth model.

18.1 THE MODEL

Consider the following framework for a private ownership economy. Adults of a given generation are manager-workers to whom all proceeds of production are distributed in the form of wages or salary and dividends or real interest. They determine consumption and savings for themselves and their children, who are born and survive into adulthood at a constant relative net rate n (as usually in equilibrium growth theory). The savings are invested, and the capital stock that results, allowing for depreciation in the meantime, constitutes the endowment of the next generation of adults; that is, the bequest left by the parents who have passed away.[1] As in other neoclassical growth models it is assumed that the current capital market clears. In real business cycle theories that assume intertemporal equilibrium, each generation's plan for all time is consistent with those of all its successors. In the present model each generation chooses its own consumption and endows its heirs with a sustainable level of living without considering an indefinitely long future in detail. It does so on the basis of current wages and interest alone. Succeeding generations decide for themselves what to do with the income generated by their inherited capital stock, deciding as *they* please, using modified expectations based on *their* current situations. Except in a steady state expectations are not realised. There is a tendency to save and invest too much or too little. The model is thus one of temporary equilibrium, but also one of intertemporal disequilibrium.

Supposing that capital goods are nonfungible but wear out at a constant rate δ, we have the capital accumulation identity

$$k_{t+1} = \frac{1}{1+n}[(1-\delta)k_t + y_t - c_t]. \tag{1}$$

where $s_t = (y_t - c_t)$ is savings of the tth generation, y_t per capita income c_t consumption and k_t the capital stock, all in per capita terms. If neutral technological change is taking place at a constant rate ζ, say, then the term $(1 + n)$ should be replaced by $(1 + n)(1 + \zeta)$ in equation (1) and correspondingly below. In this case labour would be measured in efficiency units relative to some base period.

Let c be current consumption, c^1 be a sustainable consumption level for the next generation. Then a given generation's preferences are assumed to be represented by

$$u(c, c^1) = v(c) + V(c^1) \tag{2}$$

where $v(\cdot)$ is the utility of current consumption and $V(c^1)$ the utility to the present generation from the bequest to its heirs. We assume that

$$v(c) := \log(c) \text{ and } V(c^1) := \gamma\log(c^1) \tag{3}$$

Note that v', $V' > 0$ and v'', $V'' < 0$. Call γ the *future weight*. If $\gamma < 1$, parents of the current generation place a higher weight on their own consumption than on the prospective stream of sustainable consumption by their descendents. If $\gamma > 1$, that situation is reversed.

The sustainable level of living to be provided by the bequest must account for the maintenance of the capital stock and the need to provide an endowment for net additions to the population so

$$c^1 = y^1 - (n + \delta)k^1 \tag{4}$$

where the income anticipated for the next generation in terms of wages w^1 and dividends $r^1 k^1$ is

$$y^1 = w^1 + r^1k^1. \tag{5}$$

The variable r^1 is the anticipated rate of return and k^1 is the planned future capital stock. The latter, of course, depends on current savings so that

$$k^1 = \frac{1}{1 + n} [y - c + (1 - \delta)k] \tag{6}$$

where y and k are current per capita income and capital stock, respectively. Define the anticipated and current *net rates of return* to be, respectively,

$$\varrho^1 := \frac{r^1 - (n + \delta)}{1 + n}, \quad \varrho^1 := \frac{r - (n + \delta)}{1 + n}. \tag{7}$$

Using (4)–(7) and collecting terms, we have the sustainable consumption level

$$c^1 = w^1 + \varrho^1 [s + (1 - \delta)k]. \tag{8}$$

Recalling that capital is nonfungible consumption must satisfy the constraint

$$0 \leqslant c \leqslant y. \tag{9}$$

The currently most preferred combination of present consumption and future sustainable consumption (c_t, c_t^1) maximises (2) subject to (8)–(9). This is equivalent to maximising

$$\mathcal{L} := v(c) + V \{w^1 + \varrho^1 [y - c + (1 - \delta)k]\} + \pi(y - c) \tag{10}$$

with respect to c and the Lagrange multiplier π. Given the properties of $v(\cdot)$ and $V(\cdot)$, it is necessary and sufficient that

$$v'(c) = \varrho^1 V'\{w^1 + \varrho^1 [y - c + (1 - \delta)k\}, \pi = 0 \quad \text{when}$$

$$c < y, \tag{11}$$

and

$$\pi = v'(c_t) - \varrho^1 V'\{w^1 + \varrho^1 [y - c + (1 - \delta)k]\} > 0 \quad \text{when}$$

$$c = y. \tag{12}$$

When $c = y$ note that, as v' is positive over its full range, equation (12) implies only that $\varrho^1 < v'/V'$ so that the net real rate of return can be positive and yet no savings occur. When this happens, increasing – or even just maintaining – the next generation's capital stock is not worth the sacrifice in current consumption. Certainly when $\varrho^1 < 0$, savings are zero and capital stock is allowed to decumulate.

As long as the anticipated rate ϱ^1 is finite, there is always a positive solution that satisfies (11) or (12). The unconstrained consumption function satisfying equation (11), is

$$c(y, k, r^1, w^1; \gamma) = \frac{1}{1 + \gamma} [w^1 / \varrho^1 + y + (1 - \delta)k]. \tag{13}$$

This function describes consumption as long as its value is less than y.

Suppose now that the income level for a given generation is given by the production function[2]

$$y = f(k) := Bk^\beta. \tag{14}$$

The current real rate of interest, which is

$$r = f'(k) = \beta y / k \tag{15}$$

and wages, which are given by

$$w = y - rk = (1 - \beta)y \tag{16}$$

are always positive for positive k. This leaves the anticipated counterparts y^1, r^1 to be specified.

In line with recognition that a given generation cannot foretell the future, suppose as a first approximation that the current income and interest levels are used as a basis for the consumption–savings–bequest tradeoff. Then we get the pure extrapolative (naive) forecast for interest and wages

$$r^1 := r; \varrho^1 := \varrho, w^1 := w = (1 - \beta)y. \tag{17}$$

Elsewhere, we consider a more general form of adaptive expectations (Day and Lin, 1990), but it greatly complicates the analysis without greatly enhancing the basic findings which are particularly transparent in the simpler, present case.

Using (14)–(17) in (13), then, we obtain the following *consumption–wealth function*

$$h(k) = \frac{1}{1 + \gamma} \cdot \frac{1 + \varrho}{\varrho} [y - (n + \delta)k]. \tag{18}$$

Of course, ϱ and y are functions of k, so after substituting $\varrho = \dfrac{r - (n + \delta)}{1 + n}$

and $r = \beta y/k$, we get

$$h(k) = \frac{1}{1 + \gamma} \left[(1 - \delta)k + Bk^\beta + \frac{(1 + n)(1 - \beta)Bk^\beta}{\beta Bk^{\beta-1} - (n + \delta)} \right]. \tag{19}$$

It can be shown that $h(\cdot)$ is a monotonically increasing function that becomes unbounded as it approaches an asymptote k^0 where $\varrho = 0$ (i.e., $f'(k^0) = n + \delta$). The production function $f(\cdot)$ is also monotonic but finite valued at k^0. Consequently, there exists a unique k^s such that $f(k^s) = h(k^s)$.
Define

$$K := [0, k^s), K^d := [k^s, \infty) \tag{20}$$

K^s is the set of per capita wealth values for which positive savings occur. K^d is the set of wealth ratios where no savings occur. Then current consumption, which is illustrated in Figure 18.1, can be written

$$c = \begin{cases} h(k), & k \in K^s \\ f(k), & k \in K^d. \end{cases} \tag{21}$$

Combining (21) and (1), we have

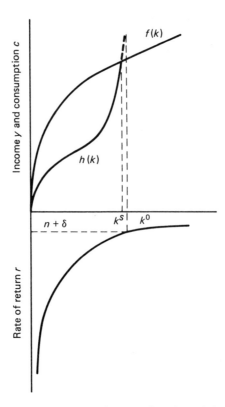

Figure 18.1   Current consumption as a function of the capital stock

$$k_{t+1} = \begin{cases} \dfrac{1}{1+n} \, [(1-\delta)k_t + f(k_t) - h(k_t)] \,, & k_t \in K^s \\[2ex] \dfrac{(1-\delta)}{1+n} \, k_t & , \quad k_t \in K^d. \end{cases} \qquad (22)$$

Substitute (19) into the top term of (22) to get

$$\theta^s(k) := \frac{1}{1+n} \cdot \frac{\gamma}{1+\gamma} \, [(1-\delta)k + Bkc^\beta] \; - \; \frac{1}{1+\gamma}$$

$$\cdot \frac{(1-\beta)Bk^\beta}{\beta Bk^{\beta-1} - (n+\delta)} \cdot \qquad (23)$$

Also, define

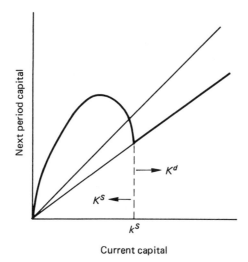

Figure 18.2   The 'phase' diagram

$$\theta^d(k) := \frac{1 - \delta}{1 + n}\ k. \tag{24}$$

Then the difference equation (22) can be re-expressed concisely by

$$k_{t+1} = \theta(k_t) = \begin{cases} \theta^s(k_t), & k_t \in K^s \\ \theta^d(k_t), & k_t \in K^d. \end{cases} \tag{25}$$

It describes the evolution of per capita wealth generation after generation. The profile of the map $\theta(\cdot)$ is shown in Figure 18.2. Using it and equations (15)–(17) the behaviour over time of all the other variables can be derived. Then, recalling that $Y_t = f(k_t)L_t = (1 + n)^t\ L_0\ f(k_t)$, where L_t is the total labour supply, the history of national income follows. Recall that if neutral technical change occurs at rate ζ, the term $(1 + n)$ must be replaced by $(1 + n)(1 + \zeta)$.

18.2   STABILITY AND INSTABILITY

Growth *may* occur in K^s, the regime in which saving is positive, but, as $\left(\dfrac{1 - \delta}{1 + n}\right) < 1$ decay *must* occur in K^d, the regime where capital depreciates at a maximum rate. We would like to know what (if any) other kinds of developments can occur in such an economy. Must trajectories converge or can fluctuations be perpetuated? If the latter, do periodic eventually emerge? Can non-periodic behaviour occur and can it be observed in the long run; that is, does it occur with positive measure? These questions can be given definitive answers using methods presented in Day and Shafer (1987) and discussed at length in Lin (1988). The answers to all questions are 'yes'; monotonic growth, dampened fluctuations, periodic cycles and chaos with zero and with positive measure are all qualitative types of fluctuations that can occur robustly. Details of the complete analysis are intricate but the bifurcations analysis demarcating parameters with stable from those with unstable behaviour is straightforward and we shall describe it briefly here. Then, we will illustrate the general theoretical possibilities with some numerical experiments.

To consider stability, we have to look at

$$\theta'(k) = \frac{1}{1+n} \left\{ \frac{\gamma}{1+\gamma} (r + 1 - \delta) - \frac{1-\beta}{(1+\delta)(1+n)\varrho^2} \right.$$

$$\left. \left[(1+n)\varrho + \frac{(1-\beta)r}{\beta} \right] r \right\}. \tag{26}$$

(Remember that $r = f'$, $\varrho = [r - (n + \delta)]/(1 + n)$ and $w = (1 - \beta)y$.) Let $\bar{r}$ and $\bar{k}$ be the steady state rate of return and capital–labour ratio, respectively. Putting $\bar{k}$ for k_{t+1} and k_t in (1) and using $c = h(k)$ from (18), we can show that $\bar{\varrho} = 1/\gamma$. From this it follows that

$$\bar{r} = f'(\bar{k}) = (1 + n)/\gamma + (n + \delta). \tag{27}$$

Using this expression and rearranging terms in (26), we find that

$$\theta'(\bar{k}) = 1 - \frac{(1-\beta)\gamma^2}{(1+n)^2(1+\gamma)} \left[\frac{1-\beta}{\beta} \bar{r}^2 + \frac{(1+n)}{\gamma} \bar{r} \right]. \tag{28}$$

For simplicity let $\varrho := \theta'(\bar{k})$. For $0 < \varrho < 1$ we get monotonic growth (or decay) converging to the steady state, $\bar{k}$; for $-1 < \varrho < 0$ two period fluctuations emerge which converge to $\bar{k}$; and when $\varrho < -1$, $\bar{k}$ is unstable and fluctuations persist. These can be periodic or non-periodic, depending on the properties of $\theta(\cdot)$. For any given value of $\varrho > 0$ we get from (28) an implicit equation in $(\gamma, \beta, \delta, n)$, which we can denote

$$H_\varrho(\beta, \gamma, \delta, n) := \frac{1-\beta}{\beta} (\bar{r})^2 + \frac{1+n}{\gamma} \bar{r} + (\varrho - 1)$$

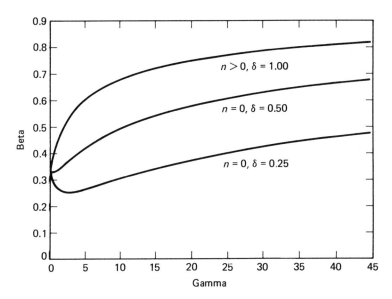

Figure 18.3   Bifurcation points between stability and instability (Points below the line are unstable; points above the line are stable)

$$\frac{(1 + n)^2(1 + \gamma)}{(1 - \beta)\gamma^2} = 0. \tag{29}$$

Let $\varrho = -1$. Using equation (27) and after a certain amount of tedious calculation, it is seen that

$$H_{-1}(\beta, \gamma, \delta, n) := 1 + \frac{\gamma(n + \delta)}{1 + n} - \frac{-1 + \sqrt{1 + 8(1 + \gamma)/\beta}}{2}$$

$$\cdot \frac{\beta}{(1 - \beta)} = 0. \tag{30}$$

In the appendix we show that for fixed values of δ and n, the loci of (β, γ) pairs that satisfy (30) are like the examples drawn in Figure 18.3. Points in the parameter space *below* a given curve give rise to *unstable* steady states; and points *above* to *stable* ones. In general, it can be seen that the smaller the capital share in output the more likely the system is to be unstable. One can also see in these examples that when n and δ are small enough so that (32) is satisfied, then changes in γ can have quite different effects on stability. *Small* enough and *big* enough values will cause fluctuations. Intermediate values will be associated with stability. The lower curve in Figure 18.3 illustrates this possibility quite clearly.

18.3 NUMERICAL EXPERIMENTS

Because we are dealing with discrete time, the qualitative properties of the model are not invariant with respect to scale. This should be borne in mind in considering the plausibility of the results. In particular, the values of n and δ that are given should vary directly with respect to the length of the period considered as well as the durability of capital. In the long-run case considered here, the value of capital depreciation and of the population growth rate should be greater than that of the short run. In general, if the long run is p units in duration, and n' and δ' are the unit period net birth and depreciation rates, then $1 + n = (1 + n')^p$ and $1 - \delta = (1 - \delta')^p$. Suppose, for example, $n' = 0.014$ and $\delta' = 0.0115$ on an annual basis. Let $p = 25$. Then on this generational time scale, $n = 0.414$ and $\delta = 0.25$. Population would double every half century and some 25 per cent of the capital stock would wear out every generation. This remark applies with equal force to the rate of return on capital. Thus, a constant annual rate return of $\bar{r} = 0.01, 0.025$ and 0.05 correspond with 'generational' rates of roughly 0.28, 0.85 and 2.4, respectively, about 28.85 and 240 per cent!

Because this is a theoretical piece and a number of important variables are held constant for analytical convenience, we don't want to be drawn into a controversy over the correct estimation method for the several parameters of the model. Nonetheless, even a theory of the simplified, essentially macroeconomic kind under consideration is of considerably more interest if its properties derive from parameter values that fall within crudely plausible ranges.

For this purpose, we note that Malthus, long ago, suggested that world population was doubling every generation ($n = 1$) while in fact it was closer to doubling every half century ($n = 0.414$). The rate speeded up after the Second World War, so the extreme figure of $n = 1$ was roughly approximated. In the meantime, the rate has fallen on a worldwide basis and in Europe has roughly achieved a *ZPG* rate of $n = 0$. Consequently, these values $n = 0, 0.414$ and 1 are all of interest.

Solow (1963, p. 87) in a classic study chose a working figure for depreciation of 4 per cent as an annual basis which yields a δ of roughly 0.64. Thus, after a generation nearly two-thirds of the capital stock available at the beginning will be worn out. Kydland and Prescott (1982, p. 1361) use an annual rate of 10 per cent which gives a value for δ of just over 0.9 so that nearly all capital stock wears out in a generation.

If one includes social capital, i.e., capital in the public sector, such as school, roads, parks, hospitals, irrigation canals, aqueducts, sewage disposal systems, railroad beds, etc., these figures may be too high. On a generational basis, it might be reasonable to consider values as low as 0.5 or even 0.25. For the illustrative purpose at hand, we include $\delta = 0.25$, 0.50 and $\delta = 1$, the latter representing an extreme in which the only capital stock available to a given generation is that constructed by its immediate predecessors. Note that when $\delta = 1$ the value of β and γ satisfying (31) are independent of n.

Turning to the production function, Solow (ibid) suggested a range of β for the US of 0.3 to 0.4 setting on a value of 0.36; while for Germany a value of 0.67 was suggested. For curiosity, we shall include values of β as low as .1 and explore the behaviour for the entire range $0.1 < \beta < 0.7$. For neutral technological change he considered a range of 0.01 to 0.05 on an annual basis a range, as we have seen, of 0.28 to 2.40 for a generation.

Finally, we come to a consideration of the subjective element in all of this; that of the 'future weight' γ. It is easily shown that, at a steady state, the net rate of return equals the reciprocal of the future weight. That is,

$$\bar{\varrho} = \frac{1}{1 + n} \; [\bar{r} - (n + \delta)] = \frac{1}{\gamma} \qquad (31)$$

Let the *subjective rate of time preference* ι be defined by $\alpha = \dfrac{1}{1 + \iota}$. Then $\iota = 1/\gamma$. If the future weight γ is large, then the subjective rate of time preference ι is small. Thus, for example, we have

ι	γ
.025	40
.100	10
2.00	.5
4.00	.25

Small values for γ are not entirely nonsensical. In a generational time frame of 25 years, a small annual discount of the future compounded through the period implies a very large discount for the future beyond 25 years. Let ι' be the annual rate of time preference, then $\iota = (1 + \iota')^{25} - 1$. We get

ι'	ι	γ
.01	.28	3.57
.05	2.39	.42
.08	5.85	.17
.10	9.83	.10

It is clear that ancient civilisations with their monumental architecture, massive roads and vast irrigation systems, all of which have still existing remnants did, *in effect*, place a very heavy weight upon the future. Modern societies have also undertaken monumental projects of great durability,

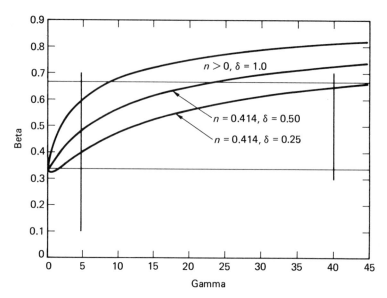

Figure 18.4   Stable–unstable parameter zones

though on balance it would seem that a much heavier weight is placed on present consumption, especially in the contemporary United States.

Rather than decide the issue, we have investigated the types of behaviour associated with a wide range of values for γ, from 0.1 to 40. A sample of these results will demonstrate the varied possibilities for stability, cycles and chaos.

Figure 18.4 gives the stability–instability bifurcation boundaries for $n = 0.414$, $\delta = 0.25$, $\delta = 0.50$ and $\delta = 1.00$. Figure 18.5 shows how the trajectories appear for a given value of β (γ) when γ (β) is varied. The four solid horizontal and vertical lines in Figure 18.4 show the ranges of parameter values to which the four bifurcation diagrams correspond. The horizontal lines are for $\beta = 0.33$ and $\beta = 0.67$, respectively. From Figure 18.4 we know that in the first case $\bar{k}$ must be unstable for all γ and that is what is shown in 18.5(a). For all γ the model appears to converge to a two-generation cycle. We can also see in Figure 18.4 that for the second case, with $\beta = 0.67$ $\bar{k}$ will be stable for values of γ up to 23 or so, after which it becomes unstable and cycles persist. This is verified in 18.5(b) which displays a typical bifurcation profile. Above roughly $\gamma = 43$ a stable four-period cycle emerges. Bifurcation diagrams for β when $\gamma = 4.95$ and $\gamma = 40$, respectively, are shown in panels(c) and (d). For values of $\beta < 0.4$ cycles emerge, and for values of β just above 0.1 and again just above 0.2 high order or chaotic fluctuations appear. Note that stable three-period cycles occur between about 1.3 and 2.0. In this range chaos 'exists' in principle but is not 'observable'.

Now suppose that population is constant so $n = 0$, but there is a constant

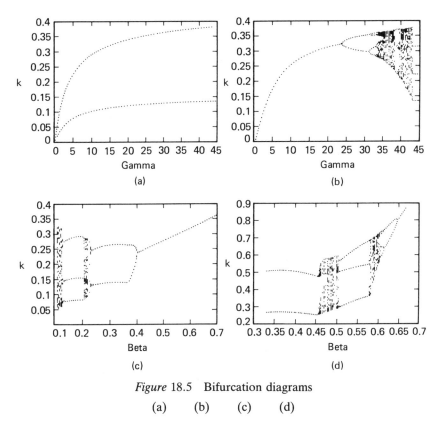

Figure 18.5   Bifurcation diagrams

(a)   (b)   (c)   (d)

rate of neutral technical progress with $\zeta = 2.4$. This is the generational rate implied by an annual rate of 0.05. Figure 18.6(a) gives the regions of stability and instability. The bifurcation diagram shown in Figure 18.6(b) is calculated for $\beta = .67$, that is, along the horizontal line in 18.6(a). These are the parameter values Solow used to represent German conditions in the 1960s. As can be seen, future weights up to 11 or 12 produce long-run, stable steady states (measured in efficiency units!). After that two-generation cycles occur followed by a full range of bifurcation results of extraordinary complexity. Clearly, extrapolative expectations combined with a high capital share and rapid technical progress has a great potential for producing generational fluctuations of a more-or-less chaotic nature when the rate of time preference is small, that is, when the future weight is large.[3]

18.4   OPTIMAL GROWTH

Before concluding, it may be of interest to compare the present results with those that follow from optimal growth. An *intertemporally optimal,*

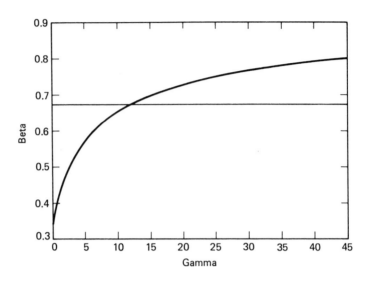

(a)

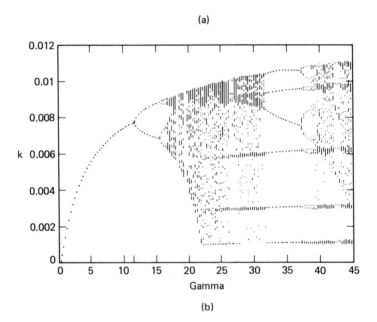

(b)

Figure 18.6   Bifurcation analysis with rapid technical change

(a) Stable–unstable parameter zones

(b) Bifurcation diagram

equilibrium growth path emanating from a fixed capital–labour ratio k_t is a consumption stream c_t^t, c_{t+1}^t . . . that satisfies

$$U(k_t) = \max \sum_{i=t}^{\infty} \alpha^{i-t} v(c_i) \tag{32}$$

subject to (1) and (14).

It is well known that the optimal trajectories are monotonic, Pareto optimal and consistent – that is, a stream beginning at generation, t will contain consumption levels for each generation that would be optimal from the perspective of that generation when its turn comes. Moreover, all trajectories converge to a unique stationary state k^* such that

$$f(k^*) - h^*(k^*) = (n + \delta)k^*$$

and

$$r^* = f'(k^*) = (1 + n)/\alpha - (1 - \delta)$$

(See Lin, 1988, pp. 8–11.) Recalling from (27) that at a steady state of our model $\bar{r} = (1 + n)/\gamma + n + \delta$ we find that $\bar{k} = k^*$ if and only if $r^* = \bar{r}$ i.e., if and only if

$$\gamma = \alpha/(1 - \alpha). \tag{33}$$

In our model, each generation only plans for its immediate heirs, but it does so in a way that allows for a sustainable level of well-being in perpetuity. Thus, instead of (32) we would write

$$W(k) = \max \left[v(c) + v(c^1)\alpha \sum_{i=t}^{\infty} \alpha^{i-t} \right]$$

$$= \max \left[v(c) + \frac{\alpha}{1 - \alpha} v(c^1) \right]. \tag{34}$$

Another way of putting it is that the present model is equivalent to suboptimal choice based on a comparison of present consumption against a constant future consumption stream. If (33) is satisfied, then $W(\bar{k}) = U(\bar{k})$.

Setting aside infinite horizon optimality, suppose agents behaved according to the recursive programming framework of the present model but they possessed perfect foresight. Then it is easy to show that capital trajectories are monotonic and converge to $\bar{k}$). If (33) holds, this value is the optimal steady state. Moreover, along such paths decisions are piecewise or temporarily optimal because expectations are fulfilled. Nonetheless, they may be suboptimal from an intertemporal point of view because the choice at any time t is based on a single postulated consumption in perpetuity $W(\cdot)$ and not on a trajectory of consumption choices for each and every future period forever $U(\cdot)$. In general, the Bellman equation derived from (1), (14) and (32) will not be satisfied, so perfect foresight eliminates intrinsic fluctuations but does not guarantee optimality. With perfect foresight, fluctuations could occur only in the presence of shocks. Imperfect foresight may – or may not – prevent convergence to optimal growth. If the economy is not stable then each generation will continue to revise the sustainable consumption stream planned for its heirs and an intrinsic real business cycle, possibly chaotic, will emerge, being driven by forecasting errors indefinitely.

18.5   CONCLUSIONS

Modelling fluctuations in the market economy using the theory of optimal growth has gradually come to dominate business cycle research. Certainly, it is a valid and interesting exercise to show, as various authors have done, that intertemporal equilibrium paths may oscillate in multi-sector models or in single-sector models if shocks are added. This does not mean, however, that such paths are good first approximations of empirical economic performance. Individuals, however intelligent, and nations, however cleverly organised and planned, never calculate for an infinite horizon, and it is unlikely that forecasting is ever perfect or that truly optimal strategies are ever learned. Moreover, considerable empirical evidence suggests that expectations are in fact adaptive. Thus, the present model represents a small step in the direction of realism. That such a small step should open up a much wider range of possible behaviours, while still converging to the optimality theory as a special case, seems to us to add much to its inherent interest and potential usefulness as a starting point for further analysis.

APPENDIX

Consider equation (30) in the text. The first term is constant for fixed γ, n, δ; the second term is a continuously increasing function of β whose value goes to zero as β goes to zero, and infinity as β goes to one. Consequently, for any given γ, $H_{-1}(\cdot)$ changes sign as β increases from 0. By the intermediate value theorem, for each γ there exists a $\beta \in (0, 1)$, say β'', (depending on γ) such that $H_{-1}(\gamma, \beta'', \delta, n) = 0$ or equivalently, such that $\theta'(\bar{k}) = -1$.
    We can therefore state

   Proposition 1: For each $\gamma > 0$ there exists $\beta'' \in (0, 1)$ (depending on γ) such that $\theta'(\bar{k}) = -1$ and such that $\bar{k}$ is unstable (stable) whenever $\beta < \beta''$ ($\beta > \beta''$).

This result means that points in the parameter space *below* the $H_{-1}(\cdot)$ curve give rise to *unstable* steady states; and points *above* to *stable* ones. Moreover, in general, the smaller the capital share in output the more likely the system is to be unstable.

The comparative dynamics for the future weight parameter γ is somewhat more complicated. To determine what the possibilities are, note that the curves satisfying (30) all intersect the β axis at $\beta = 1/3$; that is, $H_{-1}(0, 1/3, \delta, n) = 0$ for each n, $\delta > 0$. Now consider the slope of the locus of points satisfying (30), i.e.,

$$\frac{d\beta}{d\gamma} = - \frac{6H/6\gamma}{6H/6\beta}.$$

(35)

It can be seen that for $\gamma = 0$ this slope is positive, zero or negative as $\dfrac{n + \delta}{1 + n}$ is greater than, equal to or less than 3/5. But for any positive δ and any non-negative n, this slope must become positive for γ large enough. It must approach $(n + \delta)/(1 + n)$ asymptotically. Therefore, we have

Proposition 2: If

$$2n + 5\delta > 3,$$

(36)

then for each $\beta > 0$ there exists a $\gamma^u > 0$ that depends on β such that $\bar{k}$ is unstable (stable) whenever $\gamma > \gamma^u$ ($\gamma < \gamma^u$). Conversely, if

$$2n + 5\delta < 3$$

(37)

then there exist a $\beta^l < 1/3$ such that for all β satisfying $\beta^l < \beta < 1/3$ there exist γ^l, γ^u, depending on β such that $\bar{k}$ is unstable for all γ such that $0 < \gamma < \gamma^l$ and $\gamma > \gamma^u$ and stable for all γ such that $\gamma^l < \gamma < \gamma^u$. For all n, δ such that $2n + 5\delta = 3$ then $\bar{k}$ is unstable (stable) for all $\beta < 1/3(\beta > 1/3)$ regardless of γ.

The details of the proof can be left as a (tedious) exercise for the reader. (See Lin, 1988, pp. 38–42.)

Given the analysis of section 4, we can also assert

Proposition 3: For all $(\beta, \gamma, \delta, n)$ such that

$$H_{-1}(\beta, \gamma, \delta, n) > 0$$

(38)

the suboptimal temporary equilibrium path converges to the intertemporally optimal path defined by $\alpha = \gamma/(1 + \gamma)$. For all $(\beta, \gamma, \delta, n)$ such that

$$H_{-1}(\beta, \gamma, \delta, n) < 0$$

(39)

the suboptimal, temporary equilibrium path eventually fluctuates around and does not converge to the optimal, equilibrium path defined by $\alpha = \gamma/(1 + \gamma)$.

Notes

*The support of the Electric Power Research Institute is gratefully acknowledged.
1. For the importance of the bequest motive in aggregate savings behaviour, see

Ando and Kennickell (1987), Modigliani (1987) and Solow (1987).
2. The usual Inada conditions are that f is twice differentiable, that $f(0) = 0, f'(x) \to 0$ as $x \to \infty, f'(x) \to \infty$ as $x \to 0$ and $f' > 0, f'' < 0$ all $x \in (0, \infty)$. We make use of these below.
3. Actually, any of the above results can be associated with positive values of both technical progress and population growth by setting

$$(1 + n^*)(1 + \zeta) = 1 + n.$$

Any value for n^* and ζ that satisfy this equation produce the same results as for $n > 0$.

References

Ando, A. and A. B. Kennickell, 'Life Cycle in Micro Data-United States and Japan', in R. Dornbusch, S. Fischer and J. Bossons (eds), *Macroeconomics and Finance* (Cambridge, Mass.: MIT Press, 1987).

Ando, A. and F. Modigliani, 'The "Life Cycle" Hypothesis of Saving: Aggregate Implications and Tests', *American Economic Review*, 53 (1963) pp. 55–84.

Barro, R., 'The Equilibrium Approach to Business Cycles', *Money, Expectations and Business Cycles* (New York: Academic Press, 1974).

Benhabib, Jess and Richard H. Day, 'A Characterization of Erratic Dynamics in the Overlapping Generations Model', *Journal of Economic Dynamics and Control*, 4 (1982) pp. 37–55

Benhabib, Jess and K. Nishimura, 'The Hopf-bifurcation and the Existence and Stability of Closed Orbits in Multisector Models of Optimal Economic Growth', *Journal of Economic Theory*, 21 (1979) pp. 412–21.

Boldrin, M. and Luigi Montrucchio, 'Cyclic and Chaotic Behavior in Intertemporal Optimization Models', *Mathematical Modelling*, 8 (1986) pp. 627–700.

Buccola, Steven T. and Vernon Smith, 'Uncertainty and Partial Adjustment in Double Auction Markets', *Journal of Economic Behavior and Organization*, 8 (1987) pp. 587–602.

Day, Richard H., 'Flexibility Utility and Myopic Expectations in Economic Growth', *Oxford Economic Papers*, 21 (1969) pp. 299–311.

Day, Richard H., 'Irregular Growth Cycles', *American Economic Review*, 72 (1982) pp. 406–14.

Day, Richard H. and T. Y. Lin, 'A Keynesian Business Cycle', in E. Nell and W. Semmler (eds), *Nicholas Kaldor and Mainstream Economics: Growth, Distribution and Cycles* (London: Macmillan, 1990).

Day, Richard H. and Wayne Shafer, 'Ergodic Fluctuations in Deterministic Economic Models', *Journal of Economic Behavior and Organization*, 8, 3 (1987) pp. 339–61.

Dechert, W. D. and K. Nishimura, 'A Complete Characterization of Optimal Growth Paths in an Aggregated Model with a Non-Concave Production Function', *Journal of Economic Theory*, 31 (1983) pp. 322–54.

Friedman, M., 'The Role of Monetary Policy', *American Economic Review*, 58, 1 (1968) pp. 1–17.

Gabisch, Guenter and Hans-Walter Lorenz, *Business Cycle Theory* (Berlin: Springer-Verlag, 1987).

Guckenheimer, J. and P. Holmes, *Nonlinear Oscillations, Dynamical Systems and*

Bifurcation of Vector Fields (New York: Springer-Verlag, 1983).

Hartl, R. F., 'A Simple Proof of the Monotonicity of the State Trajectories in Autonomous Control Problems', *Journal of Economic Theory*, 41 (1987) pp. 211–5.

Hénon, M., 'A Two Dimensional Mapping with a Strange Attractor', *Communications in Mathematical Physics*, 50 (1976) pp. 69–77.

Koopmans, Tjalling C., 'On Flexibility of Future Preference', in M. W. Shelley II and G. L. Bryan (eds) *Human Judgements and Optimality* (New York: John Wiley, 1964) Also in *Scientific Papers of Tjalling C. Koopmans* (Berlin: Springer-Verlag, 1970a).

Koopmans, Tjalling C., 'On the Concept of Optimal Economic Growth', in *The Econometric Approach to Development Planning* (Amsterdam): North-Holland, and Chicago. Rand McNally (a reissue of *Pontifiniae Academiae Scifta Varia*, vol. 28 (1965) pp. 225–300. Also in *Scientific Papers of Tjalling C. Koopmans* (Berlin: Springer-Verlag, 1970b).

Kydland, F. E. and E. C. Prescott, 'Time to Build and Aggregate Fluctuations', *Econometrica*, 50, 6 (1982) pp. 1345–70.

Leontief, Wassily, 'Theoretical Note on Time, Preference, Productivity of Capital, Stagnation and Economic Growth', *American Economic Review*, 48 (1958) pp. 105–11.

Lin, Tzong-Yau, *Studies of Economic Instability and Irregular Fluctuations in a One-Sector Real Growth Model* (Ph.D. Dissertation, University of Southern California, Los Angeles, 1988).

Lucas, R. E., 'An Equilibrium Model of the Business Cycle', *Journal of Political Economy*, 83 (1975) pp. 1113–44.

McCallum, Bennett T., 'On "Real" and "Sticky-Price" Thunen of the Business Cycle', *Journal of Money, Credit and Banking*, 18 (1986) pp. 397–414.

McCallum, Bennett T., 'Real Business Cycle Models', in Robert J. Barro (ed.), *Handbook of Modern Business Cycle Theory* (forthcoming).

Modigliani, F., 'Life Cycle, Individual Thrift, and the Wealth of Nations', Nobel Lecture, in R. Dornbusch, S. Fischer and J. Bossons (eds), *Macroeconomics and Finance* (Cambridge, Mass.: MIT Press, 1987).

Schinasi, G. J., 'Fluctuations in a Dynamic, Intermediate-Run *IS-LM* Model: Applications of the Poincaré-Dendixson Theorem', *Journal of Economic Theory*, 28 (1982) pp. 369–75.

Smith, Vernon, Gerry Sucharek and Arlington Williams, 'Bubbles, Crashes and Endogenous Expectation in Experimental Spot Asset Markets', *Econometrica*, 56:5 (1988) pp. 1119–52.

Solow, Robert M., 'Comments', in R. Dornbusch, S. Fischer and J. Bossons (eds), *Macroeconomics and Finance* (Cambridge, Mass.: MIT Press, 1982).

Solow, Robert M., *Capital Theory and the Rate of Return*, (Amsterdam: North-Holland, 1963).

Sterman, John, 'Deterministic Chaos in an Experimental Economic System', *Journal of Economic Behavior and Organization* (forthcoming).

Stockman, Alan C., 'Real Business Cycle Theory: A Guide, and Evaluation and New Directions', *Economic Review*, 24 (1988) pp. 24–47.

Index of Authors

369

Index of Subjects